Innovation Society Today

Werner Rammert · Arnold Windeler
Hubert Knoblauch · Michael Hutter
Editors

Innovation Society Today

Perspectives, Fields, and Cases

Editors
Werner Rammert
Berlin, Germany

Arnold Windeler
Berlin, Germany

Hubert Knoblauch
Berlin, Germany

Michael Hutter
Berlin, Germany

ISBN 978-3-658-19268-6   ISBN 978-3-658-19269-3   (eBook)
https://doi.org/10.1007/978-3-658-19269-3

Library of Congress Control Number: 2017954929

Springer VS
© Springer Fachmedien Wiesbaden GmbH 2018
This work is subject to copyright. All rights are reserved by the Publisher, whether the whole or part of the material is concerned, specifically the rights of translation, reprinting, reuse of illustrations, recitation, broadcasting, reproduction on microfilms or in any other physical way, and transmission or information storage and retrieval, electronic adaptation, computer software, or by similar or dissimilar methodology now known or hereafter developed.
The use of general descriptive names, registered names, trademarks, service marks, etc. in this publication does not imply, even in the absence of a specific statement, that such names are exempt from the relevant protective laws and regulations and therefore free for general use.
The publisher, the authors and the editors are safe to assume that the advice and information in this book are believed to be true and accurate at the date of publication. Neither the publisher nor the authors or the editors give a warranty, express or implied, with respect to the material contained herein or for any errors or omissions that may have been made. The publisher remains neutral with regard to jurisdictional claims in published maps and institutional affiliations.

Lektorat: Cori Antonia Mackrodt

Printed on acid-free paper

This Springer VS imprint is published by Springer Nature
The registered company is Springer Fachmedien Wiesbaden GmbH
The registered company address is: Abraham-Lincoln-Str. 46, 65189 Wiesbaden, Germany

Foreword

To what extent and in what sense does innovation characterize our societies today?

This is the central question and common theme connecting the various contributions of this book.

This book is based on the idea that we are witnessing a shift in modern society's relationship with innovation. This is mirrored in discourse, institution-building, and innovation research. In public and academic discourse, we observe multifaceted uses of the term: 'Ubiquitous innovation,' 'disruptive innovation,' 'open innovation,' 'social innovation,' or 'responsible innovation' are but a few examples. Others involve the relabeling of institutional structures and processes as 'national innovation systems,' 'regional innovation clusters,' 'innovation policy,' or 'council of innovation'–even the European Union has declared itself to be an 'Innovation Union.' Finally, empirical studies of the practices of innovation also indicate thorough changes: an expansion of the sites of innovation, an enlargement of the drivers and actors of innovation, and a broader spectrum of types of innovation.

As a consequence, innovations are no longer limited to technology, science, and the economic sphere. Today we find them almost everywhere in society. Moreover, as the contributions to this book demonstrate, new innovation fields are emerging between economy and culture, between politics, planning, and social movements, and between science and public policy. Doing innovation is no longer restricted to inventor-entrepreneurs, start-up enterprises, or global corporations as drivers. Innovation processes are distributed between and co-produced by research universities, state agencies, and regional clusters of industry as well. The case studies in the book demonstrate that the network of innovators is augmented by crowd funders and social entrepreneurs, citizen panelists and open-source activists, user groups and creative artists.

Innovations cannot be reduced to improvements of material products and technical processes alone. Our case studies from different innovation fields indicate that the types of innovation are becoming more and more varied: deviant concepts of co-creation and valuation; different practices of caring, financing, and sharing; and new institutional forms of governance and participation are emerging, sometimes without but more often in combination with digital technologies.

This book offers new theoretical perspectives on the role of discourses, practices, and socio-material constellations in the social, institutional, and cultural change of societies. Its authors discuss theories of 'reflexive modernization' (Ulrich Beck, Anthony Giddens, Scott Lash) and the communicative or discursive construction of a 'regime of the new' based on a 'dispositif' of creativity and aesthetic sensation (Michel Foucault, Andreas Reckwitz). New concepts are developed such as 'doing innovation' by 'communicating the new,' co-producing 'fragmented fields of innovation,' or 'reflexive innovation.' The authors base their analysis on social theories of praxis and pragmatism, of communicative action, and of discourses. All studies are related to a broader concept of innovation than the economic one.

The book is a translation of an earlier publication in German: *Innovationsgesellschaft heute. Perspektiven, Felder und Fälle* (Springer 2016). More information about the authors as well as on the origins of and motivation for the book in the context of an interdisciplinary doctoral research program can be found in the introductory articles. We thank the translators David R. Antal, Nancy Chapple, Roisin Cronin, Karen Margolis, Sarah Matthews, and John Richardson, and especially the translator and chief copy editor Stephan Elkins and his colleague Eric J. Iannelli from *SocioTrans*. Last but not least, we are very grateful for the encouraging help of the editors Cori Mackrodt and Kerstin Hoffmann, both at Springer Publishers.

Berlin, the 14th of July 2017
The editors

Contents

Introduction

Expanding the Innovation Zone 3
*Werner Rammert, Arnold Windeler, Hubert Knoblauch
and Michael Hutter*

Innovation Society Today 13
The Reflexive Creation of Novelty
*Michael Hutter, Hubert Knoblauch, Werner Rammert
and Arnold Windeler*

Part I Perspectives of Social Theory and Theories of Society

Fragmental Differentiation and the Practice of Innovation............ 35
Why Is There an Ever-Increasing Number of Fields of Innovation?
Jan-Hendrik Passoth and Werner Rammert

Reflexive Innovation 65
On Innovation in Radicalized Modernity
Arnold Windeler

Communicative Action, the New, and the Innovation Society 107
Hubert Knoblauch

The Creativity *Dispositif* and the Social Regimes of the New 127
Andreas Reckwitz

Part II Between Economy and Culture

The Role of Newness in the Experience Economy 149
Michael Hutter

What Is Strategic Marketing in an Innovation Society? 165
A Frame of Reference
Franz Liebl

Innovation by the Numbers 183
Crowdsourcing in the Innovation Process
Arnold Picot and Stefan Hopf

The Berlin Innovation Panel 207
History, First Results, and Outlook
Knut Blind

Part III Between Politics, Planning, and Social Movements

'Flash Mobs' as Innovation 225
On a New Social Form of Technically Mediated Congregation
Paul Gebelein, Martina Löw and Thomas Paul

How Does Novelty Enter Spatial Planning? 247
Conceptualizing Innovations in Planning and Research Strategies
Gabriela Christmann, Oliver Ibert, Johann Jessen
and Uwe-Jens Walther

Germany's *Energiewende* 273
Path Disruption or Reinforcement of the Established Path?
Johann Köppel

Innovating Governance **295**
Epistemic and Political Reflexivities in the Remaking of Democracy
Jan-Peter Voß

Part IV Between Science and Public Policy

Epistemic Innovation **325**
How Novelty Comes About in Science
Martina Merz

Projectification of Science as an Organizational Innovation **341**
A Figurational Sociological Perspective
on Emergence, Diffusion, and Impact
Nina Baur, Cristina Besio and Maria Norkus

Social Innovation. **371**
A New Instrument for Social Change?
Cornelius Schubert

Contributors **393**

Introduction

Expanding the Innovation Zone

Werner Rammert, Arnold Windeler, Hubert Knoblauch
and Michael Hutter

Innovation as transformation of a more or less intentional nature is a timeless phenomenon. By contrast, innovation as a sustained, creative effort and the systematic generation of novelty is regarded as one of the core institutions of a modern economy. Currently, a further shift is taking place in society's relationship with innovation: innovation is transcending its traditional boundaries to become the major driving force in the society of the future.

In contrast to earlier practice, innovation has moved out of the niches of sporadic novelty in monasteries, guilds, and the arts into the observable zones of organized innovation. The preferred areas for economically defined innovation are business, markets, and enterprises. The public is most aware of technically oriented innovation, that is, the engineering of new products and processes in research and industrial laboratories. Chronologically and sequentially structured, this form of innovation fills the space between conception and invention on the one hand and diffusion on the other.

With an eye to the society of the future, for a number of decades we have observed the persistent expansion of this innovation zone to the point where innovation in society is ubiquitous, heterogeneous, and reflexive.

The first expansion to *ubiquitous innovation* is the shift beyond the economically defined, exclusively entrepreneurial zone to reach into all areas and fields of society. Concepts such as political, social, cultural, and ecological innovation reference this transformation. That said, there is still a heated debate in many fields, including climate policy, cultural reform, and scientific and university reform, over whether this is an imperial expansion of the economic criteria of innovation or a liberal expansion toward social innovation with differentiated codes of evaluation. At the same time, the innovation zone is also expanding inwardly: business and enterprises are increasingly moving beyond purely economic criteria to include other societal references, such as ecological sustainability, political fairness, and social responsibility.

The second expansion to *heterogeneous innovation* enriches the arsenal of objects and operations that usually serve to create innovations. In addition to material products and technical processes, the basis for innovation can include new symbolic artifacts and institutional forms. The spectrum of symbolic and conceptual innovation ranges from business models to computer simulation metamodels, from the aesthetic design of conventional objects to forms and formats of visualization. Examples that demonstrate the diversity of institutional and organizational innovation include the introduction of kindergarten, social security, and feed-in tariff laws that provide price incentives to supply renewable energy to the grid. Other examples are the current phenomena discussed in this book, such as flash mobs and crowdsourcing, which, although only possible thanks to the Internet and the appropriate platforms, are ultimately novel, relatively fixed forms of organizing gatherings or the technically mediated collection of many small investment contributions for risky or niche projects.

The third expansion to *reflexive innovation* extends the attention zone well beyond the gap between new prototype and mass distribution. Under the pressure of accelerating global competition, the linear chronological sequence of conception—invention—innovation—diffusion is being transformed into a reflexive, synchronized innovation process in which all steps have to simultaneously refer to each other at all times. Basic research, for example, nowadays embraces potentially 'disruptive' innovation and early-stage patenting; technical development proactively anticipates future user trends; subsequent diffusion is anticipated by open user involvement and expedited by public testing. In expectation of future distribution, the label of 'innovation' is applied to effects recently discovered in laboratories or data networks and novelties smartly packaged in future scenarios and at trade fairs, although strictly speaking they are frequently no more than potential innovations at this stage.

Such expansions of the innovation zone are changing the practice of innovation, the institutional processes that coordinate it, and the innovation regime in society as a whole. In addition to detailed empirical and comparative studies, getting a grasp on these expansions also requires efforts to develop theories for a new conceptualization of the concept of innovation, the areas of innovation, and the structures of the society of the future.

The contributions in this volume give due recognition to both concerns, though the emphasis differs. The first part highlights the theoretical work on the concepts of innovation, with constant reference to empirical studies and varying reference to theories of practice, communicative action, social differentiation, and reflexive modernization. In the other three parts, conceptual considerations and empirical case studies refer more directly to the fields of innovation within and between societal areas and are also more diverse.

This volume reflects the diversity of the fields of innovation by embracing a range of disciplines and research approaches. Besides sociologists who deal with knowledge, organizations, and discourses, with politics, spaces, and urban planning, and with economics, science, technology, and culture, the contributors include a number of economists who specialize in the production of cultural goods, creative marketing, Internet-based innovation, and the management, documentation, and promotion of innovation. Environmental and urban planning experts round out the range of perspectives.

Perspectives of Social Theory and Theory of Society

We have determined that there is a new form of social dispute in which innovations take center stage and are no longer limited to economic relationships. Today this innovation zone embraces almost all social areas. This insight is the subject of the contributions in the first part of this volume. Although from the perspective of social theory each viewpoint is somewhat different, they share one insight: innovation is no longer a process restricted to planned, long-term, largely technological improvements but has evolved into a broad, sociologically relevant social process.

A first step in the expansion of innovation is the shift in the focus of observing innovation from economic added value to the more general characteristic of communicative creation of novelty. As *Hubert Knoblauch* writes, "Innovation is ... a reciprocally reflected communicative construction of the new as something new." This construction takes place in a process of communicative action: if the *novelty* is rooted in the physical performance of acting, its mutuality forces the recognition of the novelty by others; its objectification facilitates the reflexive display of novelty as novelty, which can develop in independent discourses. On this social theoretical basis, the approach distinguishes between two competing models of handling novelty: creativity and innovation.

As *Jan-Hendrik Passoth* and *Werner Rammert* have established, the "call for innovation ... has transformed into an intensive, strategic quest for opportunities for innovation across all social domains." At the same time, the attributions to traditional functional areas such as economics, technology, science, politics, and culture are also shifting. Passoth and Rammert argue that "it is precisely the bypassing and bridging of differences specific to these social spheres that represents a key feature of innovation processes today." The result of this 'practical reflexivity' is hybrid fields of activity and discourse located in the gaps that, on account of their specific dynamics, are termed *innovation fields*. The coordination of such fields is not based on stable guiding principles clearly aligned along distinctive social spheres but "on the situational creation, practical combination, and reflexive mediation" of heterogeneous points of reference and valuation.

Arnold Windeler's focus is rooted in social theory. Taking a practice-theoretical perspective, he discusses *reflexive innovation* as a medium and result of radically modern socialization. In his view, innovation societies are characterized by the modern principle of reflexivity, ensembles of driving forces, and institutionalized positions in innovation processes. In addition, he emphasizes the importance of organizations, networks, and innovation fields as well as the skills of the participants in innovation processes.

Andreas Reckwitz takes an even wider view. Whereas the theoretical approach of the authors of the other three contributions highlights the reflexivity of the innovation orientation, Reckwitz maintains that the cultural, aesthetic switch of the *novelty regime* drives the more fundamental structural change. In his view, a dynamic disposition toward *creativity* has emerged in recent years: "As a *dispositif*, it crosses the boundaries between functionally differentiated systems, encompassing the arts as well as broad segments of the economy, the mass media, city planning, and areas of psychological counseling. Thus, late-modern society is changing direction toward a structure of expecting and producing the aesthetically new." Ubiquitous and networked, social expression is shifting to an expectation structure of creativeness. Knoblauch also emphasizes the value of creativity in addition to reflexive innovation; however, the importance that Reckwitz attributes to the aesthetic form of novelty oriented toward affective attraction succeeds in creating a different view of the 'innovation zone.'

Between Economy and Culture

In his article, *Michael Hutter* diagnoses the 'self-centered desire for experiences' as the driving force behind *innovation in the experience economy*. In this segment of the economy, novelty is not rooted in purposeful improvements. The physical experiences and mental recollections enable the participants to experience themselves as new and changeable while they search for 'familiar surprises.' Thus,

Hutter argues, experiential novelties contain their value as surprise and sensation within themselves. Participants realize the added value in the aesthetic experience, and these experience constructs are reached through the market. The experience economy thus prepares experiences and offers them either in a form for which the co-players, the spectators, or the audience are prepared to pay, or in a form, based on predetermined settings, in which they are even willing to participate as co-producers.

In his contribution, *Franz Liebl* discusses far-reaching effects of the innovation society on strategic marketing. In his view the particular entrepreneurial challenge facing business is the need to develop an innovation-oriented strategic marketing that appropriately addresses the innovative potential of both customers and society through *innovations in the business models* of enterprises. According to Liebl, companies today are faced with the task of identifying and understanding innovation activities outside their own organizations. Customer surveys are not enough. Rather, it is a question of independently developing sources of novelty, among which Liebl counts, in particular, strategic forms of embracing quality cultural products such as literature, which enable enterprises to discover elements of strategic innovation in artistic works.

In their article *Innovation with the Help of the Crowd*, *Stefan Hopf* and *Arnold Picot* analyze crowd sourcing as a new way of organizing collaborative innovation. The authors focus on forms of collective problem solving in innovation projects by—and this is crucial—integrating external actors. Their point is that, by transforming cost structures, the spread of information and communication technologies and growing dematerialization of products and services has drastically narrowed the range in which manufacturers have an advantage in creating innovations themselves. The authors think *crowd innovation* offers a solution to this problem. It also promotes the paradigm shift from manufacturer-centered to customer-oriented and collaborative innovation.

In his contribution, *Knut Blind* presents conceptual considerations and the initial results of a new global instrument to capture innovation activities in cities, the Berlin Innovation Panel. According to Blind, ongoing monitoring enables this panel to create a comprehensive analytical framework for visualizing progress and setbacks in innovation strategies in a metropolitan region. This facilitates comparisons over time between regions and industry segments. On the basis of the results, it is possible to formulate both short-term and long-term political recommendations. For instance, a representative survey of 5,000 enterprises in Berlin revealed structural differences between Berlin and Germany as a whole and between Berlin and metropolitan regions in western Germany. For instance, in terms of innovation, larger companies in Berlin are relatively weak, whereas the opposite tends to be true of micro- and small companies in Berlin: they are relatively strong innovators.

Between Politics, Planning, and Social Movement

Jan-Peter Voß, who studies hybrid innovations between politics and science, makes it clear that the fields of innovation in question lie *between* the conventional institutional areas. Significantly, hybrid innovations are also called *governance innovations*. More precisely, Voß's focus is the new institution of citizen panels; he reconstructs their emergence in recent decades. A particular characteristic of citizen panels is the role of technology and science. In his view, this reference to science and technology generates a reflexivity that passes through different stages in the course of its development. Voß talks about a veritable spiral of reflexivity that develops up to six different levels of reflexivity. He calls this reflexivity a postmodern form of regulation.

Paul Gebelein, *Martina Löw*, and *Thomas Paul* are interested in flash mobs as innovation. Flash mobs are a new social form of technologically mediated assembly. They emerged around 2003 when mobile text messaging was popularized as a means of connecting and linked with mailing lists. The result was a new form of gathering. Using ethnographic data supported by participants' informational data, Gebelein, Löw, and Paul focus on flash mobs that congregated in Dresden between 2012 and 2014. These flash mobs turned out to be a dual form of *doing innovation*. As the astonishing discontinuity of the participants shows, this is not only an innovative kind of event but also an event in which novelty in the form of surprise is itself the object.

The problem of innovation in the planning sciences is very different. When *Gabriela Christmann*, *Oliver Ibert*, *Johann Jessen*, and *Uwe-Jens Walther* inquire into the creation of novelty in spatial planning, they are interested in whether and how re-orientation in spatial planning not only optimizes tried and trusted routines but also breaks with them. Their concept of *societal innovations* indicates that the planning takes account of change not just in its environment but as part of the planning itself. Societal innovations are social constructions characterized by the production of something different in the actions of subjects and by third parties' perception of the difference as something 'novel' or 'innovative.' In their contribution they sketch their intention of applying this concept empirically to the emergence, implementation, and spread of innovations in urban development, urban restructuring, neighborhood development, and regional development.

Large-scale planning is the subject addressed by *Johann Köppel*, who looks at the energy revolution and asks whether it is a 'break in the path or a manifestation of the starting path' of an innovation. As the threat of energy crises looms, the energy sector is very open to innovation. This raises the question of whether in this regard we can observe a break with the traditional *path of renewal*. Using constellation analysis, the author breaks the issue down into the question of whether, for example, the new competition with the fossil-based energy system is a transitional phenomenon or whether, for instance, the propagation of carbon sequestration or unconventional (shale) gas extraction promotes a renaissance of the fossil energy systems—a question to which there is, admittedly, currently no final answer.

Between Science and Innovation Policy

Science is generally held to be the social area in which—freed from the need for practical action—novelty emerges as thesis, theory, or tested empirical analysis and is reflexively produced in the form of methodically verified knowledge. Science itself tends to be regarded as a source of inspiration and invention rather than as the site of technical and economic innovation. This is changing as the innovation zone expands: the types and fields of research are increasingly shaped and promoted with an eye to future exploitation and a role in shaping the future of society. Moreover, research practice and the organization of scientific activity are themselves becoming the object of reflexive innovation.

In her contribution, *Martina Merz* concentrates on *epistemic innovation*. She asks how modern science studies view the genesis of novelty in science. She reminds us of the insight of the great scholar Thomas S. Kuhn that novelties first become apparent as minor deviations and cumulative anomalies against the background of an accepted paradigm, a familiar reference system of 'normal science.' Making the dynamics of new paradigms in scientific fields and beyond comprehensible requires a microperspective viewpoint and an object-centered perspective on the practices and objects of epistemic processes such as Hans-Jörg Rheinberger and Karin Knorr-Cetina have developed. In the case of computer simulation discussed here, Merz presents a novel epistemic practice with its own specific dynamics.

The analysis by *Nina Baur, Cristina Besio*, and *Maria Norkus* looks at *organizational innovation* in science. In the early days of modern science, Jonathan Swift ironically referred to projects as 'dabbling'; today, projects in this sense have become one of the leading organizational forms in science. Their long genesis can be traced from the sporadic transfer of industrial and, later, military forms of organization of targeted research and development through to the current 'normal form' of 'projectification.' From the perspective of systems theory and figurational theory, the driving force behind this institutional innovation is attributed to the evolving interdependence between science, economics, and politics and the growth of networking between actors and authorities. Case studies from empirical university research illustrate the extent to which science's gain in the form of greater flexibility in socially defined topics and interdisciplinary cooperation goes hand in hand with the loss of autonomy and at the expense of predictable careers.

Cornelius Schubert's contribution deals critically with the concept and politics of *social innovation*. Referring to the 'sociotechnical dynamics' that apply to all social innovations, he argues against the reduction of innovation to 'purely' technical or social innovations. In his view, this is a return to positions that dematerialize the social aspect and abstract from forms of its mechanization. Regarding the growing field of European research policy, which seeks to establish social innovation as a separate funding category, he diagnoses a 'normative model' of 'good' social activities, sustained by grassroots initiatives and local actors, that have emerged in reaction to social and ecological problems that top-down policy and the markets have failed to deal with—a kind of 'caring innovation' in other words. Schubert presents this innovation policy, which has been pursued with much success by, among others, the Young Foundation, a think tank, as a notable example of reflexive innovation: the purposeful generation of knowledge about social innovations is used as a lever for selective social change, whereby the positive connotations of 'technological and economic innovation' and of 'innovation' are also used to enhance and implement change in social and ecological policy.

Reflexive innovation, one could provisionally sum up, is the key concept that defines this new principle. Increasingly, innovation processes are recursively observed and repeatedly shaped in light of information about innovations. They are becoming collaborative, spread across a growing number of heterogeneous actors and institutions, and furthered in cooperation and competition. They are also increasingly situational, evaluated, and justified in keeping with changing and hybrid references in the differentiated fields of innovation. In light of the contributions and examples collected in this volume, one might hazard the diagnosis that, as the innovation zone expands beyond the classic fields and phases of technological and economic innovation, reflexive innovation develops into the dispositive aspect in social discourses on the future, into the ubiquitous imperative of innovative activity, and into the pervasive regulative of institutional renewal. If further research in different fields can show that 'ubiquitous innovation,' 'heterogeneous innovation,' and 'reflexive innovation' in this sense are the dynamism driving contemporary society, then our thesis of the transformation into the future innovation society as well as the theoretical perspectives and case studies collected here under this title are to be taken as a contribution to the current discussion in the theory of society: they enrich the growing archive of societal diagnoses. With their variety of perspectives, they promote interdisciplinary discourse and comparisons between fields of research, and they reflect the future of modernity as mirrored in the social and historical transformation of the present.

Acknowledgements

This book is based on an interim report of the *Innovation Society Today: The Reflexive Creation of Novelty*, Research Training Group (RTG 1672) funded by the DFG (*Deutsche Forschungsgemeinschaft*—German Research Foundation), which was approved on May 13, 2011 and began its work with the first cohort on April 1, 2012. For this opportunity we thank the DFG and the group of evaluators, including the persons in the offices of the president, the dean, and the staff of the Research Promotion Section of the TU Berlin, in particular Barbara Stark, all of whom contributed to making the project possible.

Because it served many colleagues, including some of the authors in this volume, as a reference text for suggestions about and critical analysis of our core ideas and concepts (see Hutter et al. 2015), a slightly revised version of the original proposal can be found after this introduction. For us, the initiators, the proposal and the everyday program work would have been far more challenging without the enthusiastic commitment of the other 12 contributors: Nina Baur, Knut Blind, Gabriela Christmann, Christiane Funken, Hans-Georg Gemünden, Wolfgang König, Johann Köppel, Jan-Peter Voß, Harald Bodenschatz, Gesche Joost, Franz Liebl, and Uwe-Jens Walther. In recent years, the newly appointed colleagues Sybille Frank, Martina Löw, Marcus Popplow, and Jochen Gläser have joined the group. We thank all of them for their participation, creative ideas, and tutoring.

What would a research program be without doctoral students, postdocs, and visiting scholars? The doctoral students bring a constructive and critical approach to ideas and concepts. They test and correct the framework. They co-organize the summer schools and workshops. Finally, their interim reports and the eight completed dissertations provided material from which some of the contributions in this book have benefited. For their efforts we express our sincere thanks to the doctoral students of the first cohort: Dzifa Ametowobla, Anina Engelhardt, Jan-Peter Ferdinand, Miira Hill, Marco Jöstingmeier, Robert Jungmann, Henning Mohr, Anika Noack, Sören Simon Petersen, Fabian Schroth, Nona Schulte-Römer, Jessica Stock, Julian Stubbe, and Alexander Wentland; the postdoc visitors from abroad: Alexis Laurence Waller (London), Helena Webb (London), Cesare Riillo (Luxembourg), Emily York (San Diego, CA), and Cynthia Browne (Cambridge, MA); and the two postdocs of the research training group: Jan-Hendrik Passoth and Uli Meyer.

The theoretical stimuli, empirical examples, and critical comments by our international and local visitors, cooperation partners, and experts deserve special mention. These were the fruits of our summer schools on, for example, questions of 'Reflexive Innovation' or 'Doing Innovation,' and of specially tailored workshops on, for instance, 'Discourse Analysis,' 'Ethnography,' 'Grounded Theory,' and other 'Methods of Innovation Research' or on 'Novelty,' 'Expectations,' and 'Knowledge' as they relate to innovation processes. In this connection we thank, among others, Stephen R. Barley (Stanford University), Julia Black (London School of Economics), Susanne Boras (Copenhagen Business School), Paul Edwards (University of Michigan), Elena Esposito (Università degli Studi Modena e Reggio Emilia), Neil Fligstein (University of California, Berkeley), Raghu Garud (Penn State University), Giampietro Gobo (Università degli Studi di Milano), Benoît Godin (INRS Montreal), Hans Joas (HU Berlin), Candace Jones (Boston College), Reiner Keller (University of Augsburg), Karin Knorr Cetina (University of Chicago), Christine Leuenberger (Cornell University), Trevor Pinch (Cornell University), Ingo Schulz-Schaeffer (University of Duisburg-Essen), Susan S. Silbey (MIT—Massachusetts Institute of Technology), Jörg Strübing (University of Tübingen), Lucy Suchman (Lancaster University), Harro van Lente (Maastricht University), and Steven Wainwright (Brunel University).

This book would not have appeared in this form without the unfailing organizational and technical support of the coordinators Susann Schmeißer and Melanie Wenzel, the student proofreaders Philipp Graf, Hannah Kropla, and Josef Steilen, and the professionalism of the department secretary Silke Kirchhof. To them we extend our particular gratitude.

Innovation Society Today

The Reflexive Creation of Novelty

Michael Hutter, Hubert Knoblauch, Werner Rammert
and Arnold Windeler

1   A Research Framework for Reflexive Innovation[1]

Society's ability to reinvent itself is currently under debate. This discussion no longer centers solely on new technologies and economic innovations but on how novelty is currently created in all spheres of society, how it is discerned in its nascent stages, defined in different ways, and asserted in a variety of social spheres, even in the face of resistance. 'Creative districts' (Florida 2002) and 'creative capitalism' (Kinsley 2008), 'social,' 'open,' and 'public innovation' (Howaltdt and Jacobsen 2011; Chesbrough 2006) are just a few of the buzzwords being cast about in public debates in Europe and the USA. The theoretical framework presented here places the purportedly new reflexive quality of actions, orientations, and institutions, both as an overarching and crosscutting social phenomenon, at the center of its analysis. Studies that refer to this framework should help one gain a better understanding of the dynamics of creative processes in different fields of

---

[1]   This paper is an abridged and slightly revised version of the doctoral program proposal initiated by the authors of this paper at the Department of Sociology, TU Berlin and funded by the DFG *(Deutsche Forschungsgemeinschaft*—German Research Foundation). Twelve affiliated scholars contributed to the program proposal: Nina Baur, Knut Blind, Gabriela Christmann, Christiane Funken, Hans-Georg Gemünden, Wolfgang König, Johann Köppel, Jan-Peter Voß, Harald Bodenschatz, Gesche Joost, Franz Liebl, and Uwe-Jens Walther. This paper was previously published in German in 2011 (Hutter et al. 2011) and in (a former version in) English in 2015 (Hutter et al. 2015).

innovation and explain the success of specific innovations by examining social mechanisms of justification, valuation, imitation, and strategic network creation.

Our approach to analyzing the responses of different social spheres to the ubiquitous imperative of innovation differs from other agendas of innovation research and analyses of macro-level social change in various respects. First, unlike the predominant perspective with its underpinnings in economic theory, this approach does not limit itself to familiar fields of innovation such as the manufacturing and service sectors. Instead, we adopt and develop a more comprehensive concept of societal innovation rooted in the social sciences (Rammert 2010). Based on this conception, innovation is defined according to what actually counts as such in specific fields, for instance, in the arts, science, politics, or social planning. The economic concept of innovation is not abandoned in the process but rather specified in terms of its main reference points, which are increased productivity and market presence. This positioning allows us to learn from the operational success of earlier notions of innovation while adopting a critical distance toward a purely economic assessment of innovation in other social fields.

An additional defining feature of this framework lies in the crosscutting approach of examining the reflexive creation of novelty at several levels of society (micro, meso, macro). The political and economic sciences often focus on the macro level of society, politics, and economy or on specific organizations by analyzing, for instance, issues of governance or the management of innovation. With the approach under discussion, these levels remain analytically intact. The difference is that they are enriched by the specific micro level of creative and innovative action. This allows for a productive dialogue with studies that examine practices and processes of experimental inquiry, 'playful' engineering, creative and improvised planning, as well as theories of subjectivity and reflexive action.

As a third notable aspect of the framework, empirical analyses of innovation can integrate two or three observational forms. The objective is not only to capture the discourses, practices, or institutions of innovation; rather, starting from the focused analysis of a case, field, or development, scholars can identify and interrelate the semantic, pragmatic, and grammatical aspects of their chosen phenomena in order to go beyond the purely discourse-based or institutional analyses commonly found in current research. This approach should enable young researchers to differentiate between merely propagandistic (pseudo innovations), unrecognized (hidden or informal innovations), or strategic versus unintentional innovations, for example.

With this systematic perspective, individual research projects conducted across individual disciplines (e.g., new developments on the Internet; social change in various fields such as urban planning, the marketing of art, simulation in the sciences; innovations related to political instruments or financial products) can be situated in the context of a systematic theory of society, in which the contemporary signatures and regimes of an innovation society can ultimately be identified and analyzed. Further lines of inquiry in this context might include, for example, a) whether the emergence and diffusion of a new reflexive model of action can be observed across different social spheres (i.e., along the lines of Weber's rationalization thesis), b) whether the mode of institutional differentiation is shifting towards fragmented and heterogeneously networked patterns of societal coordination, and c) whether institutional innovation processes are increasingly occurring along set paths or as individualized innovation biographies.

Studies that follow this approach will therefore enrich established economic innovation research with new insights and findings and open up previously unexamined fields to a more interdisciplinary research perspective and more specific lines of questioning. This comprehensive framework will also permit researchers to touch base with relevant fields in economic sociology, the sociology of knowledge and cultural sociology, organizational institutionalism, as well as science, technology, and innovation studies and work to intensify dialogue and common points of reference among these disciplines.

2 Research Agenda

2.1 Motivation and Central Focus: Reflexive Innovation as a Pervasive Social Phenomenon

Innovation was long restricted to the labs of scientists and engineers, R&D departments in the private economy, and—though seldom acknowledged—artists' studios. Today, creative practices and innovative processes have become a ubiquitous phenomenon across all areas of society. What has changed is that the creation of novelty is no longer left to chance, ingenious inventors, and the creative habits of specialized fields. Innovations are increasingly driven with purpose, with numerous beneficiaries in mind, and in the context of broad-scale demands for strategic innovation. Innovations are managed as complex processes distributed among various entities and reflected in terms of the actions and knowledge of actors in other fields. Reflexive innovation refers to the interplay of these practices, orientations, and processes while noting that the path of an individual innovation is observed, shaped, and influenced by its specific institutional setting and ties, discursive justifications, and the forms and paths of other innovations. This new form of innovation is not confined to laboratories or R&D departments—as can be seen by cross-disciplinary and regional innovation clusters—nor does it shy away from shaping new innovation regimes. Innovation society today is characterized by a wide variety of innovative processes in all fields and by the unifying social imperative to innovate reflexively. Innovation itself has become a topic of discourse driven by a 'culture of innovation' (UNESCO 2005: 57ff.; Prahalad and Krishnan 2008) that pervades all social spheres reflexively.

The central research questions guiding the studies on the proposed reflexive innovation society today are thus these: What degree of reflexivity can be identified in contemporary innovation processes, where do these processes occur, and how are they distributed among different actors?

Hence, the main theme is the broader societal relevance of reflexive innovation. This includes practices, orientations, and processes of innovation in selected fields and how they develop and are strategically advanced within and between different areas of society. These innovative practices, orientations, and processes should not only be analyzed in the classic fields of economy (industry and services) and science (research and technology development) but also in contexts that involve culture (the arts and creative cultural production) and politics (policy-making and social-planning processes).

The objective is to analyze how specific innovative practices, discourses, and institutional arrangements have become increasingly reflexive in recent decades. We are additionally interested in whether new developments in other fields have promoted or impeded individual cases or paths of innovation. Empirical analyses in the individual fields and case comparisons will ultimately permit an assessment of the extent to which the principle of reflexive innovation has become not only a rhetorical but also a practical and institutional imperative in the current social climate of innovation.

We thus employ a more encompassing concept of innovation in society than that found in economics (Rammert 2010), which also allows us to capture new developments in the arts, social planning, and design by extending beyond the traditional economic calculations and rationalizations that surround innovation. This concept also goes further than 'social innovation' (Zapf 1989) and 'political innovation' (Polsby 1984) in addressing the links between and different constellations of technical, economic, and social innovation. As a key distinction already described by Ogburn (1922) and Schumpeter (1939), this extended concept differs from 'normal' social change in that it refers to new developments that do not just 'happen' and are then recognized and promoted. Instead, what we are interested in is the intentional, systematic creation of new material and immaterial elements, technical and organizational procedures, and socio-technical combinations of all of the above that are defined as 'new' and legitimated as an improvement compared to what came before. In contrast to Schumpeter's early writings, contemporary innovations are seldom brought forth by individual business entrepreneurs; rather, they are created by different types of collective entities (teams, communities, companies, networks) that—however influential or reflexive—are also only in partial command of the overall innovation process, which is distributed across numerous other entities.

'Doing innovation' has therefore become an explicit aspect of what social actors do with regard to knowledge, discourses, actions, social systems, and institutions. Continuous reflections on and about innovation are accompanied by elaborate discourses that justify the new developments based on the interests of specific actors and actor groups. These arguments can involve situational explanations, organizational and institutional rhetoric, and taken-for-granted ideologies. They can build on modern concepts of progress or subjectivity (Reckwitz 2008: 235ff.) or pragmatic regimes of justification (Thevenot 2001) and valuation (Stark 2009: 9), construct views that make innovation seem necessary—or even unavoidable, and promote investments in innovation. These ideas slowly crystallize into indisputable and sometimes highly authoritative 'facts' or social imperatives for all actors involved.

On the basis of the above considerations, we can specify our research focus even further: *How reflexively do actors define and organize innovation in different fields of innovation, and which justification discourses guide their practices and interpretations?*

This phrasing permits a specifically sociological approach to innovation that draws from areas such as the sociology of knowledge, organizations, economics, and science and technology studies (STS). This approach should, however, be supplemented and supported by economic, historical, political, and planning-based perspectives from other disciplines.

In contrast to the engineering sciences, the sole focus of our framework is not the production of new technologies, processes, or materials. Technical innovations in this stricter sense are a relevant point of reference; nevertheless, they are investigated in terms of their relations to non-technical social innovations as well as their reflexive ties to economic, political, cultural, or artistic innovations. In contrast to economics, the main issue is not to increase the efficiency of different factors and processes. This conceptually limited economic understanding of innovation does constitute a central reference point in terms of its practical relevance. However, it is expanded to include other areas and ultimately superseded by a more encompassing concept in which complex interrelationships count. Economic innovations can thus also increasingly draw from various other references, such as artistic (Hutter and Throsby 2008) or political innovations. Unique hybrid regimes of innovation can even emerge from incongruities or 'dissonance' between these references (Stark 2009) through the conflicts or compromises that occur as different regimes collide.

From our relatively broad social-science-based standpoint, our first concern is to develop an adequate understanding of innovation processes that are both distributed across various social fields and interconnected: How are different actors able to reflexively create and coordinate new developments on the basis of existing patterns of action and justification? Second, we are concerned with understanding practices and processes: How are new developments distinguished as 'new' by recognized institutions in different fields and deemed 'innovations'? This includes the issue of power: Why, when, and in which constellations are specific actors and institutions able to define and successfully assert specific innovations?

Ample research is available for individual fields and forms of innovation (see, among others, Rogers 2003; Braun-Thürmann 2005; Fagerberg, Mowery, and Nelson 2005; Aderhold and John 2005; Blättel-Mink 2006; Hof and Wengenroth 2007; Rammert 2008; and Howaldt and Jakobsen 2010). Innovation research, with its predominantly economic slant, has produced numerous analyses of the dynamics of technological innovations. Profit maximization, rational decision-making, and transparent price signals are built into this set of explanations. Nevertheless, these models also include insights into the boundaries of rational technology choices as well as the historic or evolutionary character of long-term technology development (see, e.g., Rosenberg 1976; Nelson and Winter 1977; Elster 1983; Utterbeck 1994). With its strong focus on management, innovation research has presented in-depth studies of relevant personnel and organizational factors at the level of the firm (cf. Gerybadze 2004; Gemünden, Hölzle, and Lettl 2006) and corporate networks (cf. Sydow 2001). This research emphasizes creativity and cooperation, trust and heterogeneous organization. More recently, however, scholarly interest in innovation has shifted from scientific and economic loci to other groups such as users, early adopters, and social movements (Hippel 1988, 2005; Chesbrough 2006) as new focal points.

In recent years, also because of technological and scientific competition and the necessity of drafting national innovation policies, research within this disciplinary tradition has further picked up on insights that innovation can include new forms of work (Barley 1990; Barley and Kunda 2004) and the creation of activity spaces (Massey 1992, 1995; Moores 2005) for individuals and collective actors. Innovation is now also viewed as a societal phenomenon, often with a transnational scope. This requires a broader conceptual framework and the integration of other social-science disciplines. Innovations have thus been increasingly investigated in the context of organizational fields (DiMaggio and Powell 1983; Hoffman 1999) as well as national innovation systems and global innovation regimes (cf. Nelson 1993; Edquist 1997; Braczyk, Cooke, and Heidenreich 1998; Blättel-Mink and Ebner 2009). Innovation paths are regarded more and more as the result of cultural constructs and institutional selection, in which non-governmental organizations (NGOs) and professions play a substantial role alongside firms (Meyer et al. 1997; Meyer 2009; Fourcade 2009). Continuity and breaks among such constellations can result in different innovation biographies (Bruns et al. 2010).

The ongoing influx of new developments in cultural fields and the new creative industries has also been analyzed by scholars in order to integrate the various interrelationships of a modern society in the grips of permanent renewal in view of changing forms of media (Castells 1996; Florida 2002). Political science and sociological governance research have broadened the economic research perspective (Powell 1990; Kern 2000; Windeler 2001; Sørensen and Williams 2002; Lutz 2006; Schuppert and Zürn 2008). The history of technology, science, and economics provide the necessary historic dimension to the phenomenon of innovation and its economy (Wengenroth 2001; Bauer 2006; David 1975; Mowery and Rosenberg 1998).

A specifically sociological view of innovation has only begun to emerge, for example, with the transfer of constructivist and evolutionary models from research on the development of new technologies to the study of innovation (Rammert 1988, 1997; Braun-Thürmann 2005; Weyer 2008), with organizational and network research focused on innovation processes (Van de Ven, Herold, and Poole 1989; Van de Ven et al. 1999; Powell, Koput, and Smith-Doerr 1996; Garud and Karnoe 2001; Windeler 2003; Hirsch-Kreinsen 2005; Heidenreich 2009), and with models of creative production and cultural innovation from the sociology of knowledge and cultural sociology (Popitz 2000; Knoblauch 2013), all of which have expanded the scope of innovation studies.

The next step towards a comprehensive sociological understanding of the innovation society is research that focuses on the practices and processes of the reflexive production of novelty. Existing approaches to sociological and social-science-based innovation research can be bundled to develop a more comprehensive perspective by drawing from various empirical studies of innovation fields in different areas of society and comparing them systematically with regard to the rules and regimes of reflexive innovation. Through this comparison, we can gain a more thorough investigation of creative practices and innovation processes. Increased attention should also be paid to more overarching topics such as the societal embeddedness and varying interrelationships of different regimes.

2.2 Analysis: Dimensions of the Research Framework

Dimension I—Observation Forms: Semantics, Pragmatics, and Grammar

Innovations are not straightforward facts. They must first be made into such through practices of perception and legitimation. Innovations are linked to justification discourses that can contain both practical ('accounts') and theoretical ('ideologies') elements. Such ascribed concepts make innovations meaningful and comprehensible to direct participants in innovation processes as well as other actors. These processes traverse several stages of development: They are labeled, imbued with meaning, linked to existing knowledge, instilled with recognition and esteem, and invested with permanence through institutionalization. They can even come to develop their own paths.

The distinction between semantics, pragmatics, and grammar—though not in the more narrow sense of linguistic analysis—has already been transferred to sociological technology studies (Rammert 2002, 2006). It furnishes us with three analytical dimensions with regard to observing society: social semantics, social pragmatics, and social grammar. Semantics refers to the significance of what is recognized in society as innovation in terms of meaning, knowledge, and discourses. However, innovation is not necessarily expressed explicitly in language; it can also be expressed primarily in actions as well as in new constellations of action and technology. We use the concept of pragmatics to refer to this dimension. Finally, grammar denotes the arrangements, regimes, and rule systems that make innovation possible in the first place, as they establish a basic framework that also places limits on innovative developments.

The three perspectives of semantics, pragmatics, and grammar allow differences in the relative importance and primacy of these elements in the creation of novelty to be captured empirically and juxtaposed for analysis and comparison. These perspectives may also diverge, such as when engaging in innovation (pragmatics) takes on a life of its own and divorces itself from that which is declared as 'new' (semantics). These aspects can override each other and assume a leading role in innovation processes in different ways. One of the research questions that follows from the proposed framework is thus to observe whether one or more of these three perspectives is absolutely critical—or perhaps even negligible—in the innovation fields analyzed as well as the significance assigned to this state in individual cases. Further, more specific lines of questioning include:

- Are there fields of innovation in which specific discourses (semantics) are strong drivers of innovation, as appears to be the case in politics and planning activities oriented toward sustainability and for artistic innovations?
- Are there fields in which systems of rules (grammar) from different areas of society either promote innovation or restrict new developments? Patent regimes could be postulated as an example of the former, the adoption of collaborative R&D forms from other countries in the USA until the mid-1980s as an example of the latter.
- Are there also fields in which innovations quietly prevail as implicit dimensions of practices or are concealed in material products (pragmatics) despite cumbersome rule systems and without explicit announcements? Social and cultural innovations that occur below the public radar could serve as examples.

In addition, as regards the interplay of different aspects of innovation processes, we are particularly interested in whether these take on a mutually reinforcing character and how this interplay might influence subsequent developments. This also lets us capture more complex social phenomena, such as those which can emerge through unintended consequences of social action and the overlapping of other social fields.

Dimension II—Aggregation Levels of Innovation: Action, Organizations, and Society

From a sociological perspective, we can observe innovations at different levels, regardless of whether we are dealing with cases of 'knowledge,' 'fiction,' or 'institutionalization.' We can distinguish between three levels of innovation: action, organizations, and society (see also Luhmann 1975; Röpke 1977). This distinction serves as a heuristic device to pinpoint the issues and areas of investigation and therefore also to coordinate project research.

At the level of conceptualizations, plans, and projections, we can consider innovation as a phenomenon rooted in action. As important as the social observation, negotiation, legitimation, and embeddedness of the innovation may be, they are usually based in action. Moreover, even though an innovative action can only be viewed as innovative (or not) in relation to other actions, our objective is to systematically account for the activity of knowledgeable subjects as the source of innovations and also to observe the creation of novelty as a micro-structural phenomenon in various research fields. One suitable point of departure for this endeavor is doubtlessly sociological theories of action, which also broach the issue of plans, imagination, and creativity (Joas 2006; Popitz 2000). Links between current forms of flexible production, the development of creative industries, and the subjectification of work (Bolte and Treutner 1983; Voß and Pongratz 1998; Moldaschl and Voß 2002) emphasize the ongoing significance of subjectivity.

If interactions are already relevant at the micro-structural level, they play an even more important role at the organizational level. Key issues at this level of analysis are the internal organization of innovations, social forms of the production of novelty, and innovation networks. Research can analyze, for example, the interactive organization of scientific work, operational production processes, and management practices geared towards innovation in firms. Further focal points can include practices and processes at the firm level, in inter-organizational networks, and in organizational fields. A central assumption is that not only the diverse relationships between different organizations—labs and patent offices, studios and museums, and architecture firms and city planning departments—but that the ways in which these organizations coordinate their interactions and relationships also hold a relevance for the creation of novelty. The arrangements and rule systems constituted by these areas form the key elements of specific innovation regimes. These areas are simultaneously the contexts in which innovations emerge in practical terms and are semantically justified.

Society is the third relevant level of observation, which increasingly calls for an analysis at the global level (i.e., as a 'world society' traversing the boundaries of individual nation states). The obvious focus in this regard falls on the distinct macro-structural features of those areas of society most likely to be gripped by the imperative of innovation (e.g., science and economy). To do justice to our concept of a more comprehensive approach, we accentuate the need to analyze fields of innovation that are most prominently situated in other areas of society (culture and politics, for example). Research at the level of society could, on the one hand, focus on sets of semantics, practices, and grammar systems with an overarching social relevance; on the other, scholars could observe the formation of transnational sets and the adoption of mechanisms and actor constellations that either drive these developments or stand in their way.

Dimension III—Social Spheres and Fields of Innovation: Technology/Science, Industry/Service, and Fields of Comparison

Innovation studies today mostly focus on technological artifacts. Novel technologies are organized primarily in the highly differentiated spheres of science and economy as well as in the increasingly dense networks between the two (cf. Bommes and Tacke 2011). Central fields of innovation in these key areas include technological disciplines in which the lines between 'pure' technology and 'pure' science are blurred (cf. 'techno science' from Latour 1987). Industrial production and the service sector are further spheres in which economic competition drives actors to demand, develop, and market 'innovative' technologies and procedures.

Besides these obvious spheres, the spectrum for investigation addressed by our framework also encompasses those fields of society which have as yet received scant attention in innovation research. This includes, for example, the production of art as well as political and planning processes. Since the Italian Renaissance, originality has been a driving ideal in the arts along with ongoing technical and institutional innovations. References to the 'creativity' in the arts have made their way into the semantics of innovation in other spheres of society: Artistic performance techniques are increasingly employed in the business world, for example (Boltanski and Chiapello 2005), and their implicit organizational structures are also transferred to processes of scientific discovery. When analyzing the arts, the objective is not to limit research to organized arts and their institutional forms in a narrow sense but to observe the broader context of the artistic creation processes (Dewey 1980) that actors themselves describe as 'creative' (Bröckling 2015). This can include, for instance, the design of human-machine interfaces, music making with software samplers, and so forth.

Starting in the mid-1970s, the field of political and social planning experienced a massive upheaval in the face of disillusionment and nation-state politics challenged by globalization. Meanwhile, the arenas of negotiation have shifted and undergone restructuring. New and in part 'high-tech' decision-making aids and policy instruments have been devised and established. The driving actors have reassured themselves and the addressees of their actions that these changes are not only new but better—in short, 'innovative'—for confronting potential problems (Djelic and Sahlin-Andersson 2006). These developments are closely aligned with innovations in other fields, particularly spatial planning. Innovations in governance have thus already emerged as a subject of research (Voß and Bauknecht 2007). Numerous social planning and policy measures are based on survey data collected along national or federal state boundaries. Yet innovation processes (e.g., in innovation clusters) do not develop in line with these geographical boundaries. New foundations and, in some cases, new instruments are therefore required for political and social planning measures in an era of reflexive innovation. This will allow them to account for heterogeneous innovation processes that transect multiple organizations by incorporating relational data.

Innovations involving technical artifacts are generally regarded as distinct from new policy instruments or innovations in other fields (Zapf 1989; Gillwald 2000; Rammert 2010). For a comprehensive perspective on innovation, we have to analyze commonalities, interrelationships, and differences with regard to innovations in individual and different fields. Possible topics could include the recombination of technical artifacts, problem-solving practices, or improved institutional processes.

Fields of innovation themselves are subject to change as the medium and result of reflexive innovation on a societal level. One basic change concerns the boundaries of the fields of innovation. We believe that the permeability of these boundaries is increasing. Research projects referring to our framework can thus be situated in both classic fields of innovation within defined areas of society and in new fields of innovation that cut across different boundaries. The research in defined areas of society permits an analysis of the extent to which reflexive innovation leads to a proliferation or perhaps even a commingling of references in relation to its justification and valuation, such as innovations in companies that increasingly apply political and ethical references in addition to economic ones (Kock et al. 2010), or scientific innovations that are subject to the dual pressures of remoralization and economic rationalization (Weingart, Carrier, and Krohn 2007; Schimank 2006). In examining heterogeneous fields, we also hope to bring up issues of co-production, co-existence, stabilization, and path creation for hybrid innovation regimes. A systematic question that links both classic and heterogeneous fields, and one that is at the heart of our research agenda, involves the comparative assessment of innovation dynamics from the 1960s to the 1980s. For example, have fundamental changes occurred in relation to innovation paths and discourses?

Examples of dissolution, transfer, and heterogeneity in innovation fields that we propose to investigate include:

- Innovations at the boundaries between science and industry (transfers, spinoffs, international networks/alliances)
- Innovations situated between science and politics (consulting, governance; urban, regional, and environmental planning)
- Innovations that cross the lines between industry and politics (regional clusters, competence networks, trend-setting technologies)
- Innovations situated between the arts and economy (design, architecture, marketing, fashion)

Research questions that cut across all fields include:

- The pragmatics and semantics of creativity in science, technology, economy, and the arts
- Comparative forms of innovative processes in organizations
- Paths of innovation, as well as discontinuities or fractures, evaluation processes, new relationships, and heterogeneous actor constellations.

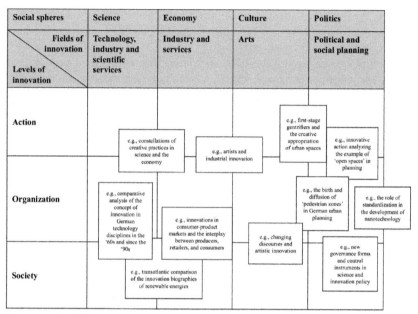

Figure 1 Possible research topics in and between innovation fields (own illustration).

3 Prospect: Pluralistic View of Theory and Research Methods

In this paper we present a research framework with which to study practices, orientations, and processes of innovation in and between various areas. Our goal is to develop a more in-depth and empirically founded understanding of the meaning of innovation in contemporary society and the social processes it involves.

The broad research concept corresponds with a pluralistic approach to methods. This pluralism should not be equated with arbitrariness. The systematic reference point of 'reflexive innovation' requires a clear formulation of initial hypotheses and a reflection on proposed methods. Certain methods are also closely associated with individual analytical perspectives. An analysis of pragmatics requires direct access to actions and objects in the field, for example, through participant observation, video analysis, technographic studies, or reconstructive interviews. Semantic analyses, on the other hand, require a stronger content-based perspective, one that employs methods such as ethnosemantics, genre or discourse analysis. A grammatical perspective can be complemented by methods such as innovation biographies, path or network analysis.

With this paper we want to open up a broad theoretical framework for analyzing the reflexive creation of novelty. A wide variety of theories can be applied in individual studies that refer to the framework. These approaches provide both competing and complementary perspectives for an examination of innovation in contemporary society. The framework's focus on reflexive innovation and the interplay of semantics, pragmatics, and grammar provides a general theoretical orientation for different research cases. Its focus is also primarily on the societal level. Given these elements, reflexive innovation can be analyzed as a central aspect of societal development using a variety of different theoretical propositions and disciplinary methods.

References

Aderhold, Jens and Rene John, eds. 2005. *Innovation. Sozialwissenschaftliche Perspektiven.* Constance: UVK.
Barley, Stephen. 1990. "The Alignment of Technology and Structure through Roles and Networks." *Administrative Science Quarterly* 35(1): 61-103.
Barley, Stephen and Gideon Kunda. 2004. *Gurus, Hired Guns, and Warm Bodies. Itinerant Experts in a Knowledge Economy.* Princeton: Princeton University Press.
Bauer, Reinhold. 2006. *Gescheiterte Innovationen. Fehlschläge und technologischer Wandel.* Frankfurt a. M.: Campus.
Blättel-Mink, Birgit. 2006. *Kompendium der Innovationsforschung.* Wiesbaden: VS Verlag für Sozialwissenschaften.
Blättel-Mink, Birgit and Alexander Ebner, eds. 2009. *Innovationssysteme. Technologie, Institutionen und die Dynamik der Wettbewerbsfähigkeit.* Wiesbaden: VS Verlag für Sozialwissenschaften.
Boltanski, Luc and Eve Chiapello. 2005. *The New Spirit of Capitalism.* London, New York: Verso.
Bolte, Karl and Erhard Treutner, eds. 1983. *Subjektorientierte Arbeits- und Berufssoziologie.* Frankfurt a. M., New York: Campus.
Bommes, Michael and Veronika Tacke, eds. 2011. *Netzwerke in der funktional differenzierten Gesellschaft.* Wiesbaden: VS Verlag für Sozialwissenschaften.
Braczyk, Hans-Joachim, Philip Cooke, and Martin Heidenreich, eds. 1998. *Regional Innovation Systems.* London: UCL Press.
Braun-Thürmann, Holger. 2005. *Innovation.* Bielefeld: transcript.
Bröckling, Ulrich. 2015. *The Entrepreneurial Self. Fabricating a New Type of Subject.* London: SAGE.
Bruns, Elke, Dörte Ohlhorst, Bernd Wenzel, and Johann Köppel. 2011. *Renewable Energies in Germany's Electricity Market. A Biography of the Innovation Process.* Dordrecht: Springer.
Castells, Manuel. 1996. *The Rise of Network Society. Vol. 1: The Information Age: Economy, Society and Culture.* Oxford: Blackwell.
Chesbrough, Henry. 2006. *Open Innovation. The New Imperative for Creating and Profiting from Technology.* Boston: Harvard Business School Press.
David, Paul. 1975. *Technical Choice, Innovation, and Economic Growth.* New York: Cambridge University Press.
Dewey, John. 1980 [1934]. *Art as Experience.* New York: Perigee Books.
DiMaggio, Paul and Walter Powell. 1983. "The Iron Cage Revisited. Institutional Isomorphism and Collective Rationality in Organizational Fields." *American Sociological Review* 48(2): 147-160.
Djelic, Marie-Laure and Kerstin Sahlin-Andersson, eds. 2006. *Transnational Governance. Institutional Dynamics of Regulation.* Cambridge: Cambridge University Press.
Edquist, Charles, ed. 1997. *Systems of Innovation. Technologies, Institutions, and Organizations.* London: Routledge.
Elster, Jon. 1983. *Explaining Technical Change. A Case Study in the Philosophy of Science.* Cambridge: Cambridge University Press.
Fagerberg, Jan, David Mowery, and Richard Nelson. 2005. *Oxford Handbook of Innovation.*

Oxford: Oxford University Press.
Fourcade, Marion. 2009. *Economists and Societies. Discipline and Profession in the United States, Britain, and France, 1890s to 1990s*. Princeton: Princeton University Press.
Florida, Richard. 2002. *The Rise of the Creative Class*. New York: Basic Books.
Garud, Raghu and Peter Karnoe, eds. 2001. *Path Dependence and Creation*. Mahwah: Erlbaum.
Gemünden, Hans Georg, Katharina Hölzle, and Christopher Lettl. 2006. "Formale und informale Determinanten des Innovationserfolges. Eine kritische Analyse des Zusammenspiels der Kräfte am Beispiel der Innovatorenrollen." *Schmalenbachs Zeitschrift für betriebswirtschaftliche Forschung* 58(54/06): 110-132.
Gerybadze, Alexander. 2004. *Technologie und Innovationsmanagement*. Munich: Vahlen.
Gillwald, Katrin. 2000. *Konzepte sozialer Innovation* (Working Papers P00-519). Berlin: Berlin Social Science Center.
Heidenreich, Martin. 2009. "Innovation in Europe in Low- and Medium-Technology Industries." *Research Policy* 38(3): 483-494.
Hippel, Eric von. 1998. *The Sources of Innovation*. New York: Oxford University Press.
Hippel, Eric von. 2005. *Democratizing Innovation*. New York: Oxford University Press.
Hirsch-Kreinsen, Hartmut. 2005. *Wirtschafts- und Industriesoziologie: Grundlagen, Fragestellungen, Themenbereiche*. Munich: Juventa.
Hof, Hagen and Ulrich Wengenroth, eds. 2007. *Innovationsforschung. Ansätze, Methoden, Grenzen und Perspektiven*. Münster: LIT Verlag.
Hoffman, Andrew. 1999. "Institutional Evolution and Change. Environmentalism and the U.S. Chemical Industry." *Academy of Management Journal* 42(4): 351-371.
Howaldt, Jürgen and Heike Jakobsen, eds. 2010. *Soziale Innovation. Auf dem Weg zu einem postindustriellen Innovationsparadigma*. Wiesbaden: Springer VS.
Hutter, Michael, Hubert Knoblauch, Werner Rammert, and Arnold Windeler. 2011. *Innovationsgesellschaft heute: Die reflexive Herstellung des Neuen* (Working Papers 4-2011). Berlin: Technische Universität Berlin.
Hutter, Michael, Hubert Knoblauch, Werner Rammert, and Arnold Windeler. 2015. "Innovation Society Today. The Reflexive Creation of Novelty." *Historical Social Research* 40(3): 30-47.
Hutter, Michael and David Throsby, eds. 2008. *Beyond Price. Value in Culture, Economics and the Arts*. New York: Cambridge University Press.
Joas, Hans. 1996. *The Creativity of Action*. Chicago: University of Chicago Press.
Kern, Kristine. 2000. *Die Diffusion von Politikinnovationen. Umweltpolitische Innovationen im Mehrebenensystem der USA*. Opladen: Leske + Budrich.
Kinsley, Michael, ed. 2008. *Creative Capitalism: A Conversation with Bill Gates, Warren Buffet, and Other Economic Leaders*. New York: Simon & Schuster.
Knoblauch, Hubert. 2013. "Projection, Imagination, and Novelty: Towards a Theory of Creative Action Based on Schutz." Pp. 31-50 in *The Interrelation of Phenomenology, Social Sciences and the Arts*, edited by M. Barber and J. Dreher. Heidelberg, New York: Springer.
Kock, Alexander, Hans Georg Gemünden, Sören Salomo, and Carsten Schultz. 2010. "The Mixed Blessings of Technological Innovativeness for the Commercial Success of New Products." *Journal of Product Innovation Management* 28(1): 28-43.
Latour, Bruno. 1987. *Science in Action. How to Follow Scientists and Engineers through*

Society. Cambridge: Harvard University Press.

Lutz, Susanne, ed. 2006. *Governance in der politischen Ökonomie. Struktur und Wandel des modernen Kapitalismus*. Wiesbaden: VS Verlag für Sozialwissenschaften.

Luhmann, Niklas. 1975. "Interaktion, Organisation, Gesellschaft." Pp. 9-20 in *Soziologische Aufklärung*, edited by N. Luhmann. 2nd ed. Opladen: Westdeutscher Verlag.

Massey, Doreen. 1992. "Politics and Space/Time." *New Left Review* 1(196): 65-84.

Massey, Doreen. 1995. "The Conceptualization of Place." Pp. 45-77 in *A place in the world? Places, Cultures and Globalization*, edited by D. Massey and P. Jess. Oxford: Oxford University Press.

Meyer, John W. 2009. *World Society: The Writings of John W. Meyer*, edited by G. S. Drori and G. Krücken. Oxford: Oxford University Press.

Meyer, John W., John Boli, George Thomas, and Francisco O. Ramirez. 1997. "World Society and the Nation State." *American Journal of Sociology* 103(1): 144-181.

Moldaschl, Manfred and Günter Voß, eds. 2002. *Subjektivierung von Arbeit*. Munich: Hampp.

Moores, Shaun. 2005. *Media/Theory. Thinking About Media and Communications*. New York: Routledge.

Mowery, David and Nathan Rosenberg. 1998. *Paths of Innovation. Technological Change in 20th Century America*. Cambridge: Cambridge University Press.

Nelson, Richard, ed. 1993. *National Innovation Systems. A Comparative Analysis*. Oxford: Oxford University Press.

Nelson, Richard and Sidney Winter. 1977. "In Search of a Useful Theory of Innovation." *Research Policy* 6(1): 36-76.

Ogburn, William Fielding. 1922. *Social Change*. New York: H. W. Huebsch.

Polsby, Nelson W. 1984. *Political Innovation in America. The Politics of Policy Initiation*. New Haven: Yale University Press.

Popitz, Heinrich. 2000. *Wege der Kreativität*. 2nd ed. Tübingen: Mohr Siebeck.

Powell, Walter W. 1990. "Neither Market nor Hierarchy. Network Forms of Organization." *Research on Organizational Behavior* 12: 295-336.

Powell, Walter W., Kenneth W. Koput, and Laurel Smith-Doerr. 1996. "Interorganizational Collaboration and the Locus of Innovation. Networks of Learning in Biotechnology." *Administrative Science Quarterly* 41(1): 116-145.

Prahalad, Coimbatore and Mayuram Krishnan. 2008. *The New Age of Innovation*. New York: McGraw Hill.

Rammert, Werner. 1988. *Das Innovationsdilemma*. Opladen: Westdeutscher Verlag.

Rammert, Werner. 1997. "Auf dem Weg zu einer post-schumpeterianischen Innovationsweise." Pp. 45-71 in *Technikentwicklung und Industriearbeit*, edited by D. Bieber. Frankfurt a. M.: Campus.

Rammert, Werner. 2002. "The Cultural Shaping of Technologies and the Politics of Technodiversity." Pp. 173-194 in *Shaping Technology, Guiding Policy*, edited by K. Sørensen and R. Williams. Cheltenham: Edward Elgar.

Rammert, Werner. 2006. "Die technische Konstruktion als Teil der gesellschaftlichen Konstruktion der Wirklichkeit." Pp. 83-100 in *Zur Kritik der Wissensgesellschaft*, edited by D. Tänzler, H. Knoblauch, and H.-G. Soeffner. Constance: UVK.

Rammert, Werner. 2008. "Technik und Innovation." Pp. 291-319 in *Handbuch der Wirtschaftssoziologie*, edited by A. Maurer. Wiesbaden: VS Verlag für Sozialwissenschaften.

Rammert, Werner. 2010. "Die Innovationen der Gesellschaft." Pp. 21-51 in *Soziale Innovation. Auf dem Weg zu einem postindustriellen Innovationsparadigma*, edited by J. Howaldt and H. Jacobsen. Wiesbaden: VS Verlag für Sozialwissenschaften.

Reckwitz, Andreas. 2008. "Die Erfindung des Kreativsubjekts. Zur kulturellen Konstruktion von Kreativität." Pp. 235-257 in *Unscharfe Grenzen. Perspektiven der Kultursoziologie*, edited by A. Reckwitz. Bielefeld: transcript.

Rogers, Everett M. 2003. *Diffusion of Innovations*. 5th ed. New York: Free Press.

Röpke, Jochen. 1977. *Die Strategie der Innovation. Eine systemtheoretische Untersuchung von Individuum, Organisation und Markt im Neuerungsprozess*. Tübingen: Mohr.

Rosenberg, Nathan. 1976. *Perspectives on Technology*. New York: Cambridge University Press.

Schimank, Uwe. 2006. "Ökonomisierung der Hochschulen: eine Makro-Meso-Mikro-Perspektive." Pp. 622-635 in *Die Natur der Gesellschaft. Verhandlungen des 33. Kongresses der Deutschen Gesellschaft für Soziologie in Kassel, 2006*, edited by K.-S. Rehberg. Frankfurt a. M.: Campus.

Schuppert, Gunnar F. and Michael Zürn. 2008. *Governance in einer sich wandelnden Welt*. Wiesbaden: VS Verlag für Sozialwissenschaften.

Schumpeter, Joseph A. 1939. *Business Cycles. A Theoretical, Historical, and Statistical Analysis of the Capitalist Process*. New York: McGraw-Hill.

Sørensen, Knut and Robin Williams, eds. 2002. *Shaping Technology, Guiding Policy. Concepts, Spaces and Tools*. Cheltenham: Edward Elgar.

Stark, David. 2009. *The Sense of Dissonance*. Princeton: Princeton University Press.

Sydow, Jörg. 2001. *Management von Netzwerkorganisationen*. Wiesbaden: Gabler.

Thevenot, Laurent. 2001. "Pragmatic Regimes Governing the Engagement with the World." Pp. 56-73 in *The Practice Turn in Contemporary Theory*, edited by T. Schatzki, K. Knorr Cetina, and E. von Savigny. London: Routledge.

Utterbeck, James M. 1994. *Mastering the Dynamics of Innovation*. Boston: Harvard Business School Press.

UNESCO World Report. 2005. *Towards Knowledge Societies*. Paris: UNESCO Publishing.

Van de Ven, Andrew H., Herold L. Angle, and Scott Poole. 1989. *Research on the Management of Innovation. The Minnesota Studies*. New York: Ballinger, Harper & Row.

Van de Ven, Andrew H., Douglas E. Polleye, Raghu Garud, and Sankaran Venktaraman. 1999. *The Innovation Journey*. New York: Oxford University Press.

Voß, Günter G. and Hans Pongratz. 1998. "Der Arbeitskraftunternehmer. Eine neue Grundform der Ware Arbeitskraft?" *Kölner Zeitschrift für Soziologie und Sozialpsychologie* 50(1): 131-158.

Voß, Jan-Peter and Dirk Bauknecht. 2007. "Netzregulierung in Infrastrukturen. Der Einfluss von Technik auf den Verlauf von Governance-Innovationen." Pp. 109-132 in *Gesellschaft und die Macht der Technik*, edited by U. Dolata and R. Werle. Frankfurt a. M., New York: Campus.

Weingart, Peter, Marie Carrier, and Walter Krohn. 2007. *Nachrichten aus der Wissensgesellschaft. Analysen zur Veränderung der Wissenschaft*. Weilerswist: Velbrück.

Wengenroth, Ulrich. 2001. "Vom Innovationssystem zur Innovationskultur. Perspektivwechsel in der Innovationsforschung." Pp. 21-32 in *Innovationskulturen und Fortschrittserwartungen im geteilten Deutschland*, edited by J. Abele, G. Barkleit, and T. Hanseroth. Cologne: Böhlau.

Weyer, Johannes. 2008. *Techniksoziologie. Genese, Gestaltung und Steuerung soziotechnischer Systeme*. Munich: Juventa.
Windeler, Arnold. 2001. *Unternehmungsnetzwerke. Konstitution und Strukturation*. Wiesbaden: Westdeutscher Verlag.
Windeler, Arnold. 2003. "Kreation technologischer Pfade: Ein strukturationstheoretischer Ansatz." *Managementforschung* 13: 295-328.
Zapf, Wolfgang. 1989. "Über soziale Innovationen." *Soziale Welt* 40(1-2): 170-183.

Part I
Perspectives of Social Theory and Theories of Society

Fragmental Differentiation and the Practice of Innovation

Why Is There an Ever-Increasing Number of Fields of Innovation?

Jan-Hendrik Passoth and Werner Rammert

1 Innovation Processes in Contemporary Society

If there is one imperative that can qualify as a hegemonic principle guiding action in contemporary society, it is the call for innovation.[1] If we look at current debates about change in society, we can see a preference for the new and a demand for innovation that is no longer confined to economic, scientific, and technological developments alone. Today, modern societies' orientation toward growth, progress, and technological innovation has spread to a wide range of different areas. Under conditions of globalization, climate change, and digitization, this orientation has transformed into an intensive, strategic quest for opportunities for innovation across all social domains. This 'new spirit'[2] of innovation has also suffused the political realm, the religious sphere, the arts, and the conduct of everyday life.

---

1   The imperative that "you must change your life" (Sloterdijk 2013) is in line with this but is less clearly defined. The "duality of the desire to be creative and the imperative to be creative: ... One *wants* to be and *is expected* to be creative" (Reckwitz 2012: 10, our translation) is a much more accurate description yet emphasizes the genealogy and aesthetic roots of the bourgeois model of creativity while failing to pay due attention to the social dynamics of innovation that emerge in the field of tension between institutionalized differences and points of reference on the one hand and the manifold referencing practices of reflexive innovation on the other.

2   As opposed to Boltanski and Chiapello (2005), whose analysis can be seen as evidence of a *broadening* of the spirit of capitalism, what we are concerned with here is

Germany's energy transition, the *Energiewende*, for instance, is of course not just about maintaining prosperity or making optimal use of available resources. It also comes with expectations that the transition of a leading industrial nation such as Germany to renewable energy sources will turn out to involve a political innovation in its modes of governance[3] and a cultural innovation in its patterns of urban mobility,[4] which together will receive recognition in the international arena, be copied in other regions and cities, and be adopted by other collective actors. Looking at the transformation of industrial manufacturing toward the digitally connected and software-based modes of production and distribution discussed under the headline of *'industry 4.0,'* we can see that the value of these innovations is not assessed on the basis of economic success alone but also on grounds of its potential to reinvigorate Germany's economic role in Europe and promote new co-production and consumption practices. The debate on the *'digitization'* of music, film, and print is ultimately not only about technical innovation and its desirable and undesirable economic consequences. The keywords that surface in this debate—such as 'cultural flat rate,' 'sharing economy,' and 'piracy'—indicate that it also revolves around the question as to whether this development also lays the groundwork for a social innovation of shared ownership and a legal innovation in regard to copyrights, property rights, and open access. In addition to this shift from manufacturer-oriented to consumer-oriented or even collaborative types of innovation, processes of cultural reorientation toward 'creative industries' or an 'experience economy' are also increasingly perceived as innovation.[5]

At least in current public debates on the future society, the focus on innovation is ubiquitous and plays a guiding role, although—and because—the concept is semantically open to a variety of different interpretations and uses.[6] That which is,

---

the *spreading* of a 'new spirit of innovation' to non-economic areas—similar to Max Weber's rationalization thesis.

3 See, for instance, Köppel's chapter (this volume) on Germany's *Energiewende* and Voß's chapter (this volume) on innovation in governance.

4 Gebelein et al. (this volume) and Christmann et al. (this volume) discuss examples of such new patterns of mobility such as 'flash mobs,' 'urban gardening,' or 'pioneers of space.'

5 On the opening up of innovation to users or creative professionals, see von Hippel (1988, 2005), Kleemann et al. (2009), Hutter et al. (2015), as well as Hutter (this volume), Liebl (this volume), and Picot and Hopf (this volume); on industry 4.0, see Hirsch-Kreinsen (2014), and on the transformation of the music industry, Dolata (2008).

6 On the semantics of innovation, see Knoblauch (this volume), and on its normative nature, see Schubert (this volume).

temporally, perceived to be 'new' (compared to something that is characterized as already existent, outdated, or at least as old); materially, viewed to be 'distinctive' (compared to something that appears to be of the same kind); and, socially, considered to be 'deviant' (compared to an implicit state of normality that is always also defined in relation to the deviant)[7] is valued, promoted, and showcased. A closer look reveals that this is not really a preference for any specific thing that is new, distinctive, or deviant but rather a general preference for newness, distinctiveness, and deviance as such. Apart from this purely discursive orientation toward the new, the practices and processes of innovation also tend to be geared more toward the principle of innovation *as such* than toward economic success or scientific and technological optimization *per se*. The principle of innovation is inherent to the paradoxical expectation that, compared to an already favorable situation in the present, 'endless renewal'[8] will pave the way for an even better future position in and beyond one's own field. This shift from an emphasis on, for instance, innovation guided by a purely economic cost-benefit rationale toward reflexive innovation that has economic but also other, very different points of reference is a characteristic feature of action among the parties involved in the distributed processes and interactive networks of innovation. Moreover, this shift also increasingly applies to the institutional forms that are utilized in the attempts to pursue these more comprehensive innovations as well as coordinate and, in conflictual processes, reconcile the various value orientations and interests involved, for instance, by means of open forums or corporative platforms, regional innovation networks, or European research clusters. In terms of the 'rules of the game'[9] underlying innovation processes, this favors a preference for types of organization, institutional structures, and regulations that are assumed to be quicker and quantitatively more productive in creating the new as a raw material for future innovations and are also thought to facilitate identifying the new early on and to be effective in establishing it. This fosters a preference for the *reflexive institutionalization* of innovation processes.[10]

In this way, the alignment of social processes along meticulously differentiated lines of unequivocal economic, scientific, or technological criteria and guiding distinctions is replaced in contemporary society by a more general, open, and un-

---

7   For a detailed account, see Rammert (2010: 29ff.).
8   Thus the title of a cultural-philosophical study in the line of Wittgenstein and Adorno on the understanding of the new and the 'paradigm of novelty' in the modern aesthetics of music (cf. 'Endlose Erneuerung,' Dierks 2015: 193).
9   Wittgenstein 1999: 47 e.
10 Cf., among others, Powell et al. (1996), Rammert (2000, 2006: 265ff.) and Windeler (this volume).

specific orientation toward innovation as such: On the one hand, the focus on whatever is new, distinctive, and deviant has supplanted the classic, clear-cut orientation toward economic productivity, technological effectiveness, and gains in scientific knowledge. On the other hand, the prerequisites and conditions of producing innovation itself have been geared toward *continuous* innovation or, in other words, toward the innovation of innovation.

The empirical study of innovation processes in and across various social spheres in light of the specific structural, semantic, and practical conditions therefore becomes a key task for social science research that seeks to understand the changes in and the nature of contemporary society (cf. Hutter et al. 2015). However, the social sciences so far are conceptually utterly ill equipped for this purpose, and this in two respects: For one, in spite of all attempts over the past few decades to expand the concept of innovation, innovation research has remained the domain of economics. For two, attempts to introduce alternative concepts in areas as different as politics and planning or art and culture mostly rely on a strategy of adding particular criteria—such as a preference for social welfare, sustainability, diversity, or aesthetic design—to economic and technological ones so as to identify and assess innovation. This procedure only rudimentarily does justice to the ubiquity and reflexivity of innovation processes in contemporary society. An adequate interpretation and diagnosis of contemporary innovation society therefore not only requires a concept of innovation that is able to overcome the narrow conception of innovation as economic innovation but also calls for a broader concept that is able to capture empirically the great variety of innovation and, by comparing processes of innovation, is capable of appropriately understanding the peculiarities of contemporary society: What accounts for the emergence of an ever-increasing number and variety of fields of innovation? The answer to this question is given below via a twofold theoretical approach that has been developed in a dialogue between the two authors and by reflecting on theories of social differentiation, reflexive modernization, and variants of a theory of practice. This theoretical approach seeks to grasp the transformation toward a *reflexive innovation regime* as a recursive relationship between fragmental differentiation and the situational practice of innovation.

This chapter addresses the consequences of such a concept of innovation[11] for a program of comparative social scientific research. It begins with the search for

---

11   A two-stage concept of innovation provides a means of distinguishing between novelty and innovation—and also between dimensions and by degree (see the chapters by Baur et al. and Christmann et al., this volume)—and of taking into account the relations between heterogeneous elements—objects, practices, concepts—as well as different

a conceptual basis for comparing processes of innovation (2). Are political innovations sufficiently different from those in the arts, and legal innovations from the ones that we are accustomed to dealing with in the domains of science and technology? Are theories of differentiation that adopt a macro-structural perspective on society capable of guiding us in distinguishing fields of innovation according to social spheres?[12] Or is it rather that the empirical study of reflexive innovation must precede making those conceptual distinctions? In its second part (3), the chapter draws on the preliminary results of some of the empirical projects conducted as part of the DFG Research Training Group *Innovation Society Today: The Reflexive Creation of Novelty* to argue that it is precisely the bypassing and bridging of differences specific to these social spheres that represents a key feature of innovation processes today.

The third part of this chapter (4) addresses this specific feature of innovation processes and zeroes in on the question of how we might get a conceptual and empirical grasp on the reflexivity of innovation. If we—in accordance with Ulrich Beck's interpretation of "the second modernity as the 'age of side effects'..." (Beck 2008: 19)—conceive of the tendency to bypass and bridge differences specific to social spheres as a characteristic feature of 'reflexive modernization' (Beck et al. 1994), then we must also understand it as an unintended side effect of increasing differentiation. If, on the basis of this initial understanding, we conceive of this tendency in a further sense—and in line with Anthony Giddens' view of 'radical modernity' (Giddens 1990)—as a consequence and driver of growing reflexivity and knowledge on the part of actors, then we must go one step further and take the increase in references seriously as an empirical macro phenomenon, while at the same time comprehending it as one way in which individual actors practically cope with the changed conditions of establishing and disseminating innovations. In a third sense, then, the reflexivity of innovation is a consequence of *practical reflexivity*: The analysis of the actual practices in innovation processes—and this

---

references, all of which account for the diversity of socially effective evaluation practices and regimes of valuation (Rammert 2010: 45f.).

12 In the following, we will conceptually distinguish between 'social spheres' *of* society and 'social fields' of innovation *in* society. We will speak of social spheres whenever we are referring to clear and unambiguous references—to the social systems of economy, politics, or the arts—that are assumed, implied, or drawn on in the emerging social fields of innovation. What we have in mind when we speak of these social fields is the realm of possibilities and potential links on the basis of which references are selected and enacted, sometimes reproducing the dominant point of reference, sometimes mixing several references, and sometimes initiating a new path of creating an innovation field. For a slightly different approach to path creation, see Garud and Karnøe (2001).

is the thesis proposed in the fourth section (5) of this chapter—is of such key importance for an understanding of contemporary society because it allows us to investigate a new form of social coordination that is simply not clearly aligned along distinctive social spheres but relies on the situational creation, practical combination, and reflexive mediation of heterogeneous fields of innovation. In our outlook (6), we therefore sketch the outlines of a research program that revolves around the emerging shift in the primary principles of differentiation at the macro level towards fragmentation, heterogeneous combination, and practical reflexivity. New fields of innovation—to answer the question posed in the title of this chapter—emerge and establish themselves in reflexive acts of doing innovation that further both the fragmentation of social spheres and the situational proliferation of points of reference and valuation.

2   Differentiation of Fields of Innovation and the Diffusion of the Reflexive Innovation Paradigm

Both the ability and the need to pose the question about what constitutes 'the new and improved' in the arts, in politics, or in law in terms of innovation are rather recent developments. For as long as the economy primarily represented the realm of innovation and—assisted by economics—provided the framework of reference for innovation discourse, innovation practice, and the institutional order of innovation processes, the differences and commonalities between innovations were not an issue. But as innovations began to mushroom in all parts of contemporary society over the past few decades, scholars started to ask whether the processes of innovation observed in various fields are comparable and in which respects it makes a difference which references and guiding orientations are employed in judging and justifying them. We can identify three different explanations for this change:

- *First*, economic innovation research—which up until three decades ago had focused on business enterprises and the core areas of industrial production—as well as management practices and innovation policy based on this research expanded their knowledge and areas of activity to an extent that transcended the immediate boundaries of the economic sphere. Step by step, the institutional environment itself, the links between non-economic actors such as researchers and sponsors, mediators and user groups, and other factors in the environment became objects of economic innovation. New developments in science, law, and politics, such as the creation of technology transfer organizations and technology parks, patenting and standardization practices,[13] or policies to promote regional networking and cluster formation, were selected and advanced depending on whether they represented infrastructural innovations that could be expected to contribute to successful economic innovation. This involved transferring the rationale and model of economic innovation to other spheres that seem to lag behind in terms of their ability for self-renewal and their contribution to innovation at the macro level (*economization and hegemonic expansion thesis*).[14]

- *Second*, the expansive push toward economic innovation has resulted in pressure to innovate that is both ubiquitous in discourse and efficacious in practice. It has grown into a general innovation imperative across all spheres of society, which not only mutually observe one another but also exchange their respective services. This has resulted not only in an inflationary use of the vocabulary of innovation, mostly for the purpose of normative justification, but also in an analytically remarkable conceptual shift that points to reflexive processes of self-renewal. Creative interventions and transgressions of boundaries are not only labeled as 'innovations' for the purpose of good publicity but, in the new light of their significance for social change, are also perceived, practically developed, and promoted as a type of non-economic innovation in their own right: Fundamental reforms of the telecommunication sector are understood as innovations in private-public partnerships. The turnaround in energy policy towards renewable energy is an innovation in international relations. Climate projects or shifts in political instruments from legislation and taxation to installing new 'mechanisms' and 'markets' for pollution rights are innovations in governance. The mixing of media and genres results in aesthetic innovations. Creative interventions in neighborhoods are innovations in urban policy. Performative transgressions of boundaries between science, art, and corporate culture are both organizational and market innovations, and the search for new forms for the presentation of knowledge in artistic practices is understood as an innovation in science. This can be grasped in terms of the theory of 'reflexive modernization' as problems resulting from functional differentiation (Beck 1992) that can no longer be solved in accordance with the logic of the respective social sphere or a dominant economic order but allow for a variety of potential references in

---

13 Cf. Blind and Gauch 2009.
14 For an overview of the thesis of the economization of other social spheres from the perspective of social theory, see Schimank and Volkmann (2012); on the continuous expansion, see, among others, von Hippel (2005) and the contributions by economists and sociologists in Fagerberg et al. (2005) and Hage and Meeus (2006).

the process of establishing fields of innovation. Compared to the extremes of reinforcing either the orientation toward the institutionalized guiding principle or a reorientation toward an alternative dominant guiding principle, a mix of various principles that serve as points of reference is becoming more common and gaining significance. What have frequently been described as phenomena of de-differentiation and de-institutionalization or even as a 'new obscurity' (Habermas: *Neue Unübersichtlichkeit*) can be analyzed positively as the formation of a 'fragmental' social order (Rammert 2006: 258ff.) in which references are recombined and reconfigured depending on the specific field in question (*fragmental differentiation and mixed, multi-referential self-renewal thesis*).[15]

- Third, a change in ways of life and types of subjectivity can be seen as the source of a new innovation culture: Growing individualization unleashes affective potentials for manifold forms of self-realization. This transformation becomes apparent in a discursive shift from an ascetic and economically calculating subject to a hedonistic one who relishes the pleasures of life and engages in creative activities. What once began as an aesthetic deviation from 'classicism' in small segments and circles of the arts—for instance, in the form of 'romanticism,' 'expressionism,' or 'surrealism'—and what was explored as new ways of living, working, and enjoying life in the niches of alternative protest cultures and lifestyles currently seems to be condensing into and establishing itself, through media, imitation, and strategic dissemination, as a new model of expressive and creative subjectivity that is in line with the social 'regime of the new as aesthetic stimulus' (Reckwitz, this volume) in late modernity (*changing discourse and dispositifs thesis*).[16]

These three attempts to explain the obvious increase in the significance of the innovation phenomenon and the effective expansion of the zones of innovation are not mutually exclusive. Rather, they can be complemented so that it is still possible to identify a common principle despite the variety of fields of innovation (cf. Rammert 2014). There is ample evidence suggesting that the emergence of a reflexive mode of social order—one which, time and again, generates new, situational fields of innovation on the boundaries of and between formerly stable social spheres—is

---

15 Cf. the critical discussion and advancement of the theory of social differentiation by Schimank (1985, 2011), Knorr-Cetina (1992), Nassehi (2004), Schützeichel (2011), and Lindemann (2011).

16 On the cultural and historical changes in the 1970s toward expressive and aesthetic orientations in the conduct of everyday life, cf. Schulze (1992) and Reichhardt (2014); on changing discourse and dispositifs, Bröckling (2004) and Reckwitz (2012).

itself the result of problems ensuing from increased social differentiation. Reflexive innovation then would not solely be a manifestation of a rhetoric of innovation or an expression of the increased dominance of economic orientations but would reflect a process of switching to a form of social coordination not based on stable and substantial orientations guiding action in the various social spheres but rather precisely on the situational creation, practical mixing, and reflexive mediation of heterogeneous points of reference in fields of innovation. The heightened attention to innovation would then have to be understood as an expression and driver of this reflexive form of social coordination.

3 Innovation Practice and the Bypassing of Field-Specific Differences

We can assume innovation to be reflexive—for one, because those involved in processes of innovation must also take the various conditions of innovative action into account, both prospectively and retrospectively; and, for another, because, in the processes of change, they refer to the familiar or assumed mechanisms of creating and disseminating the new in very different spheres in a more or less strategic manner. This renders innovation in contemporary society a paradoxical object for all involved, including those who would conduct social scientific research of innovation. This is because reflexive innovation assumes, at the practical, discursive, and institutional level, the ability to distinguish social spheres or, at the very least, specific fields of innovation. At the same time, it is precisely the reflexive reference to the familiar or assumed mechanisms that continuously relates and bridges the fields of innovation, thereby undermining the ability to distinguish between them. For those involved in innovation, this means that their innovative action is based on the assumed and habitually ingrained 'logics' associated with specific social spheres such as the economy, arts, politics, and so forth, whereas the taken-for-granted nature and reliability of these logics is gradually eroded precisely in the process of those actors taking a reflexive and strategic stance in utilizing them. For social scientific research on innovation this means that, in exploring the reasons for and consequences of reflexive innovation, it must adopt a comparative approach and ask about the different relations and references that make it possible to take a reflexive stance in different fields of innovation in the first place. At the same time, it systematically directs attention to cases that raise doubts as to whether the logic of innovation fields specific to the respective social spheres can be considered reliable and taken for granted.

When one engages in a comparative analysis of innovation processes,[17] this inevitably raises the issue of selecting a framework for comparison. Although focusing on social spheres and asking, for instance, how processes of innovation in science are different from those in the economy, in politics, or in the arts might seem to be the obvious choice, this option lulls us into a misleading sense of treading safe ground. Such a focus in fact relies on the assumption that the differences that are deemed relevant from a macro-structural perspective on society also have institutional, discursive, and practical consequences so that the expansion of the innovation imperative does indeed occur only within the confines of the social spheres that account for the important differences between innovation processes. However, this is highly unlikely because of the reflexive nature of innovation in contemporary society. Those involved in innovation must take into consideration— practically, discursively, and institutionally—the conditions and consequences of innovative action and, for this purpose, must draw on heterogeneous parameters of reference depending on the situation and in a strategic manner. It seems to lie in the logic of reflexive innovation that the differences specific to the fields in question are brought into play time and again but at the same time are virtually constantly bypassed.

For the purpose of illustrating what this means precisely, it is helpful to take a look at two of the case studies conducted over the past few years as part of the DFG Research Training Group *Innovation Society Today: The Reflexive Creation of Novelty*. What makes these cases so interesting in this context is that, in the course of systematic empirical analysis, they defied repeated attempts to get a grasp on them in terms of the research question outlined in the umbrella proposal (Hutter et al., this volume). This applies first and foremost to the studies with a focus on a specific social sphere, for instance, the one addressing the 'clean development mechanism' (CDM) as an example of specific innovation processes in the sphere of politics and regulation. Once the innovation process involved in the emergence and design of the largest-scale instrument for global climate protection was subjected to closer empirical scrutiny, this regulatory instrument turned out to be the product of a negotiation process between practitioners with different perspectives, the result of a 'sequence of experimentation and problematization' (Schroth 2014a: 10). The clean development mechanism has been "tested and developed in various experiments, in various places, and in various ways" (Schroth 2014b: 19, our translation). In the process, it has changed continuously and in relation to the specific references made by those involved:

---

17 On the expansion of the methodological toolbox for the purpose of approaching innovation empirically and from a comparative perspective, cf. Jungmann et al. (2015).

Initially it was an energy efficiency project, which was developed bilaterally and the regulation of which was the responsibility of the World Bank, the Norwegian climate fund, and a Mexican public authority. (...) With the US forest projects, compensation projects became objects of climate politics. (...) With USIJI similar de-contextualized greenhouse gas compensation projects became an object of politics, and private actors and NGOs were politically authorized to pursue climate protection activities. (...) Starting with AIJ, and increasingly so in regard to CDM, counter-factual emissions reductions became the object of climate politics (ibid.: 21, our translation).

Such instances of the empirical objects of research evading the grasp of the defined categories of differentiation is particularly striking in the projects geared toward the systematic comparison of innovation practices within or across social spheres. For instance, a comparison of innovation processes in science and the arts focused on the empirical analysis of two different objects, one of which was designed and constructed in the context of an art installation and the other in a robotics laboratory. While both, each in its own specific way, were identified and labelled as a 'novelty,' the comparison reveals that both cases involve a similar sequence of 'configurative moments' (Stubbe 2015: 120): At the point of presentation—under the aspect of 'rendering imagined objects'—both the art installation and the robotic hand are situationally created and specified through particular arrangements, body movements, and accompanying stories; at other times—under the aspect of 'material referencing'—characteristics of the objects that remain hidden in the situation or are merely of a potential nature are indicated by reference to their specific materiality: "The robotic hand, just as the media installation, not only materialises the present state of what is, but must be regarded as an agent within its own construction as novelty, as its material evokes thoughts of what could be" (ibid.: 124). Moreover, in neither of the two cases did the interviewees make any mention—neither explicitly nor as a generalizable pattern of assessment—of the configured objects in and of themselves representing a 'novelty.' Rather, the parameters of reference against which the installation and the hand qualified as new objects were situational and context-specific: they were different in the workshop and in the laboratory than at an exhibition or a conference and different again when explained to an innovation researcher from the social sciences than in a conversation with colleagues, competitors, or visitors who just so happened to pass by.

This allows us to draw two conclusions: The first conclusion is that the cases under study could be *exceptional* in that the failure to empirically correspond with the assumed differences on the basis of which they were chosen has its roots in particular features of these cases. This, however, is not very likely since the innovation processes investigated in a number of other case studies conducted as part of the Research Training Group display a similar tendency to withstand analysis along the lines of the assumed differences associated with the specific social spheres. For instance, one might look for particularities in technical innovation processes in the field of electro-mobility and discover experimental mobility cultures and an ideology of electro-mobility (Stock 2015); or one might investigate innovation processes in the field of artistic interventions in the public sphere and find that they are interwoven with heterogeneous references to urban planning, civic involvement, and cultural funding (Landau and Mohr 2015). The alternative explanation could be that the cases are *not exceptional* at all but that the research question was developed on the assumption of differentiated social spheres, and the practices, discourses, and regimes of innovation that one encounters constantly transcend these very lines of differentiation. This leads us to the second conclusion that we must assume that innovation has not simply become a general rhetorical formula. Rather, in contemporary society, innovation has become reflexive—not always explicitly and not in the speech acts of those involved but in the actual practice of what they do.

4 Reflexivization of Innovation and the Increase in References

Once such a variety of innovations in so many different areas becomes an issue of practical and theoretical concern, the traditional definitions of innovation no longer suffice. On the one hand, the precisely operationalized and strongly substantialist definition in innovation economics is too narrow and one-sided as innovation involves more than the technical efficiency of new factor combinations and their assessment in terms of strictly economic efficiency. On the other hand, a relativistic strategy of defining innovation along the lines of innovation sociology that were to fully rely on the perceptions of those involved would open the floodgates for labeling a new phenomenon of any kind as an innovation, be it a marginally improved product, a passing fashion, or some smart marketing gimmick.[18]

---

18 Of course, fashion can be the starting point of a social innovation. Only once creations take hold in new constellations—along with other references—while transcending the narrow field of fashionable apparel to acquire some long-term impact do they cease to be just seasonal novelties and gain the status of innovations in the conduct of everyday life. This hardly applies to changing dress lengths but all the more so to the practice of women wearing trousers since the 1960s all the way to today's business pantsuits with references to the emancipation of and equal opportunities for women. This corresponds with the conceptual distinction between 'fashion' and 'model' (cf. Esposito 2003). See also the shifts toward innovation-oriented marketing (Liebl, this volume).

What is called for first of all is a concept that does not define innovation a priori in terms of a physical product, a social practice, or a cultural idea, but that is open to empirically exploring all elements and their possible relations. What has hitherto frequently been perceived in a rather simplified fashion as a technical, social, or cultural innovation could then be identified as an innovative constellation, each determined in different ways, and that can involve material and technical artifacts, differently organized practices, as well as new cultural models of usage.[19] When we adopt such a perspective, artifacts, practices, or discourses can take a leading or critical role in some cases or lag behind in others. Once telephone technology— including the devices and networks for voice transmission and reception—was invented, there was a need, for instance, for concepts of usage other than telegraphy and mass reception as well as new business models such as leasing and a subscription system for it to become established as a social and cultural innovation (cf. Rammert 1990). Conversely, 'social inventions' (Ogburn 1964), scientific ideas, or artistic visions require objects that complement and specify the new constellation. For instance, organizing childcare in kindergartens requires toys, furniture, and spaces just as the practice of 'urban gardening' needs other types of gardening and cultivation techniques that can be applied to walls, roofs, boxes, and in combination with aquariums and greenhouses. Theoretical concepts such as the 'gentle grip' in robotics or an imagined arrangement that makes movements visible in new media artworks depend on a set of experimental mechanisms and materials as well (cf. Stubbe 2015).

This relational concept is not sufficient to distinguish inventions and simple novelties from innovations with long-term social effects. Innovations are novelties that, in a second step, are complemented by references that regulate the communication of a novelty as representing an innovation, the acceptance of such a claim as legitimate, the addition of this innovation to the stock of knowledge, and its institutionalization in practice. Conceptually, an innovation *of something*, which we have determined to be a constellation of objects, practices, and models in relation to a previously existing one, must be complemented by an innovation *toward something* that we are able to observe as a parameter of reference for the evaluation, justification, and diffusion of the innovation in the field in question. For instance, the focus on economic profit has been the prevalent parameter of reference since Schumpeter formulated the economic theory of innovation (cf. Schumpeter 1934).

---

19 Cultural models can include distinct 'visions of function and use' (computers for accounting, writing, or gaming) or new 'concepts of engineering and design' (telecommunication as 'one-way transport,' as 'one-to-many communication,' or as 'two-way media') (Rammert 2002: 178f.).

Schumpeter's innovation in economic theory shifted the perspective, temporally and in terms of content, from an allocation of resources geared toward short-term optimizing to novelties and recombinations of production factors that have a long-term impact. Market penetration, income from patents and licenses, return on investment, and other indicators confirm the still dominant focus on commercial success.[20]

If we look at other differentiated social spheres for principles similar to the ones that have proven successful in the economic sphere, we should be able to find references that function according to a comparable inner logic of their own. Following Max Weber would direct our attention to the pursuit of power in the sphere of politics, the pursuit of true knowledge in the sphere of science, the pursuit of that which accords with the law in jurisprudence, the pursuit of beauty in the arts, and the pursuit of sensual fulfillment in eroticism. In accordance with Luhmann, we could add up to another twelve self-referentially closed social subsystems such as the military, mass communication, education, health, sports, and the family (Schimank 2005: 154). What can be plausibly inferred from a theoretical point of view and can roughly be observed empirically in regard to the dominant criteria of orientation and selection in the context of the respective institutions and organizations also seems to apply, at first glance, with respect to the order of references for innovation at the macro level. Innovations in politics are guided by the reference of gaining power, be it by means of new bottom-up participation or legitimation procedures or new top-down types of policies and modes of governance; innovations in the arts distinguish themselves from new fashions according to the reference that they give rise to unprecedented aesthetic sensations.

However, our empirical case studies raise doubts about these neatly aligned guiding references associated with the social spheres. As indicated above, there is not really an abundance of evidence supporting the supposed unity and purity of references: Must regulatory innovation in accordance with Basel III to prevent the next banking crisis be seen as being more an innovation of the banking system guided by economic criteria or more an innovation in the capacity for political intervention in the economy guided by the desire to reclaim the power to act (cf. Jöstingmeier 2015)? When a new format or even a new genre such as 'jazz jam' or 'poetry slam' spreads from the sphere of the arts to science and mass communication, in terms of which references are we to describe the nature of this innovation (cf. Hill 2014)? If we can detect no significant difference in the orientations involved in creating new scientific devices and artistic installations but rather find similar

---

20 For a self-critical view of these indicators, see Smith (2005) and for a critical outside perspective, Braun-Thürmann (2012) and Bormann et al. (2012).

combinations of scientific-technical and aesthetic references, then what value does the dominant reference have as a means of distinction (cf. Stubbe 2015)? And if electro-mobility is to be rendered an object of innovation research, does it represent a scientific-technological innovation (e.g., in terms of developing battery technology and the architecture of complex socio-technical systems), an economic innovation (e.g., in terms of developing profitable business models for manufacturers and operators), a political innovation (toward a fundamental restructuring of mobility and energy provision), or an environmental innovation (toward sustainable mobility and lifestyles)? Or perhaps it is a mix of all of these, an innovation regime based on multi-referential orientations (cf. Stock 2015; Wentland 2014)?

One thing is evident: the number of references has increased, and not only on account of the increase in the number of differentiated spheres in society. Rather, the reflexivization of innovation seems to be the underlying driving force. One way that this can be understood is along the lines of the theory of reflexive modernization as an unintended side effect of the growth dynamics and autonomy of social subsystems (cf. Beck and Lau 2005). This reflexivity can be identified at the social-structural level (Beck and Holzer 2004: 165f.). It becomes apparent in the altered self-descriptions of the subsystems (e.g., the economy or science), in which additional references have been incorporated, yet not in the form of rules that determine when to stop but rather in terms of deceleration and balancing systems. We can interpret the current expanded self-descriptions of economic innovation as 'sustainable innovation' or 'social innovation' and of scientific innovation as 'responsible science and innovation' (RSI) as signs of this kind of reflexivity.[21]

The second type of reflexivization concerns the increase in reflection and knowledge on the part of actors who adopt a creative stance toward reflexive modernization and its consequences. We assume that this is a much more powerful source driving the increase in references and fields in which the 'reflexive creation of novelty' (Hutter et al. 2015) takes place and thus marks a point to begin our search for the conditions that account for the successful establishment and

---

21 The European Commission, which has recently labelled the European Union as an 'innovation union,' defined the concept of 'responsive innovation' in its Horizon 2020 action program as follows: RSI, or 'responsible research and innovation' (RRI), "means that societal actors work together during the whole research and innovation process in order to better align the process and its outcomes with the values, needs and expectations of European Society" (European Commission 2012: 3). More precisely, RSI is "a transparent interactive process by which societal actors and innovators become mutually responsive to each other with a view on the (ethical) acceptability, sustainability and societal desirability of the innovation process and its marketable products" (von Schomberg 2012: 50).

diffusion of innovation at the macro level. A variety of fields are evolving below the macro level because actors can draw on *given* references in an existing field as well as create and establish *new* references by combining existing ones in new ways. They follow neither a 'logic' of continuous functional differentiation at the level of subsystems nor a 'logic' in accordance with Bourdieu's fields of practice. It is rather that these fields of innovation evolve on the margins of and between social spheres in processes in which individuals, groups, and organizations engage in communication, cooperation, or conflict, centered on an opportunity or a problem, thus creating a field of collaboration, a conflict arena, or a common platform for action. Moreover, they also emerge at different levels of action in the form of intermediary institutions, transversal 'interstitial arenas' (Shinn 2006: 315), heterogeneous innovation networks (Powell et al. 1996), or other mixed communication settings[22] that cut across the various levels of action. As the second type of reflexivization is both a reproductive and a creative response to the problems of the first type, we can hold that it not only increases the possibilities and combinations of guiding references but at the same time creates an awareness of the variety of fields and levels for the practice of innovation.

5 Practical Reflexivity and the Situational Creation of Fields

Innovation research of a sort that is capable of transcending the narrow confines of innovation economics and is not content with merely attempting to compare economic, political, or cultural processes of innovation can also conceive of reflexivity in a third way. Once we adjust the sociological analysis to a 'flight above the clouds' (Luhmann 1995: 1), the reflexivity of innovation turns out to be, fully in line with Beck's reflexive modernization, a side effect of enhanced differentiation. If we direct our attention to the specific performance of the actors involved in innovation, the reflexivization of innovation must be understood as tactical and strategic—and at times creative and playful—acts of interrelating assumed and implied guiding principles. Yet if we turn to the 'ongoing accomplishment' (Gar-

---

22 Early examples of this are 'mediating bodies' such as 'value engineering teams,' 'scientific councils,' 'round table talks,' and 'project groups' in firms, which mediate between the different guiding 'rationalities' in four distinctly 'figurated' settings of corporate product innovation as a 'reflexive self-binding mode of controlling consequences' (Rammert 1988: 188f.), and 'conversation circles,' which, in the case of pharmaceutical patent law, serve to establish a 'structural coupling' between the economic and legal system (Hutter 1989: 94). For a current overview, see Mölders 2012: 488ff.

finkel 1967: VII) of innovation, the other two types of reflexivity appear to be a consequence of practical reflexivity: "an unavoidable feature of the way actions (...) are performed, made sense of and incorporated into social settings" (Lynch 2000: 26f.). Since acts of innovation—as any other practice—are always performed at a specific location and by heterogeneous but nevertheless specific individuals, they are invariably indexical, which is to say that the constitutive activities cannot be grasped and interpreted, neither by those involved nor by sociological observers, without taking the specific conditions in which they are performed into consideration. For instance, glossy brochures might mention that the discovery tours in the district of Wesel in North Rhine-Westphalia—which represent artistic interventions in the public sphere in which the towns and villages in the surrounding area of a West-German city are visited by foot, bike, or bus as part of the *Urbane Künste Ruhr* project (Ruhr Urban Arts; cf. Mohr 2013)—are not tourist attractions but an art initiative for the purpose of cultivating a greater appreciation for local expertise. The tour begins to unfold once a resident stands beside one of the highways and speaks of home. The ambiguous, intertextual, and hybrid references that render 'postwar modernity' accessible to experience are not inherent to the concept of home that he is referring to nor are they innate to highways; they are cited and interwoven with one another only in the course of the actual tour. They are indexical, inescapable.

Drawing on Schütz's thesis of the 'suppression of the primes' (Schütz 1964: 21), Garfinkel developed a praxeological concept of reflexivity by further elaborating and expanding on the idea of indexicality that was formulated in linguistics primarily to get a grasp on the logic of deictic expressions (here, there, then, now, you, I). The interpretation of an occurrence in accordance with an a priori typified world is not a matter of individual inclination but is itself rather the outcome of the practical efforts of the heterogeneous range of people involved to 'remedy'[23] indexical expressions—which is, however, never really accomplished and thus leads to ever-recurring attempts to do so. This happens as part of the activities themselves that constitute this practice: "[...] the activities whereby members produce and manage settings of organized everyday affairs are identical with members' procedures for making those settings 'accountable'" (Garfinkel 1967: 1).

Whatever practice is collectively performed by whomever, the heterogeneous assortment of people involved in accomplishing the practice employ the same

---

23 "Wherever and by whomever practical sociological reasoning is done, it seeks to remedy the indexical properties of practical discourse; it does so in the interest of demonstrating the rational accountability of everyday activities" (Garfinkel and Sacks 1970: 339).

means in *representing* it as they do in *producing* it. They do not have to explicitly state that the process of tinkering with the various installations in the robotics laboratory or the arrangements of the art installation involves figurational acts of configuring something that can later be displayed, tested, and described. They represent this through the same activities in which they engage in producing it. When they comment on their activities in the process, when they explain, demonstrate, and explicate what they are doing while they are doing it, then it is not this that constitutes the reflexivity of practice; such commentary are rather (additional)— acts of reflexivity (see also Passoth and Rowland 2014: 479; Reckwitz 2009: 177; on reflexivity as a characteristic feature of communicative action, see Knoblauch, this volume). Practical reflexivity is actually rather 'uninteresting' (Eickelpasch 1982: 16ff.); it is an inherent, inevitable part of everyday practice.

In the context of innovation and the creation of the new, it is exactly this uninteresting reflexivity of practice that actually becomes quite interesting. This is because the attempt to 'remedy' the situatedness of relevant activities operates on the basis of those involved referring to something that is known but not explicated. This something is a backdrop of anticipated orientations and meanings—"collective systems of meaning that remain implicit and unconscious" (Reckwitz 2009: 172, our translation)—that, by necessity, must stay vague and unspecified. In this way, from moment to moment, a collectively valid backdrop of social order is positioned, adjusted, and readjusted, thereby providing a framework of meaning to make sense of a practice beyond the specific local acts that constitute it.[24] The principles guiding action, such as those of the economy, the political, the arts, but also those principles underlying conventions, value systems, or only temporary agreements, do not structure events 'behind the backs' of those involved. It is rather that the actors bring them into play, sometimes more or less explicitly, sometimes vaguely, but always in ways that are effective in practice. To do so, the parties involved continuously and situationally construct new fields of potential references. This works, although not always reliably, provided that they can refer to the existent, the uniform, the well-known—that is, to a state of normality, albeit only an assumed one. As a matter of course, practical reflexivity then operates on the basis of more or less clearly defined guiding principles, against the backdrop of which things can be interpreted. It is precisely this that no longer works in cre-

---

24 "Limiting oneself to the narrow context of what is observable" (Nassehi 2006: 459, our translation) by no means implies that directing attention to concrete practice poses any fundamental conflict for an awareness of the translocal order of empirical settings; the issue here is rather that collective patterns of meaning, cultural codes, and social order are all perceived only as other specific practices, which are referred to in specific situations (cf. also Passoth 2011).

ating the new: The preference for the new, the unknown, the different, the deviant virtually forces one to refer to the familiar while at the same time relegating it to the status of being no longer relevant. In the context of creating the new, practical reflexivity means that the mechanisms and methods of creating and representing the new must invariably draw on an assumed system of order and at the same time transcend it—and this applies both in regard to the relations that are to be established and the references drawn upon.

The consequences of the two-stage concept of innovation outlined above, which makes it possible to distinguish novelty from innovation, become particularly evident when we look at innovation in practice. What already applies to the practical process of creating the new, of producing new relations between heterogeneous elements, has much greater consequences when it comes to the practical process of establishing the references that render new an innovation since only those novelties qualify as an innovation that become successfully established in society. However, in ongoing practice, the establishment of an innovation in society is always only a vague and open-ended possibility. The artistic interventions in the public sphere in the context of the *Urbane Künste Ruhr* project create "an awareness of the hidden potentials of the Ruhr region—the many vacancies in the inner cities, vast old industrial wasteland, or unused courtyards" (Mohr 2013, our translation); and, in the process of planning and implementation, they are always a potentially successful instrument of citizen involvement that can be copied and applied again, even though they are currently not yet realized. The experimental forms of mobility that have evolved around the already existing modes of electro-mobility are potential manifestations of a new mobility culture and a new energy future as are the various projections of the future that have grown around these forms and which are all woven into culturally specific narratives of mobility, even though this new culture and future, too, are presently not a reality.[25]

In the act of innovating, innovation is present as a proposal, as a novelty that could potentially be socially established. Yet which particular relations and references are given significance in specific innovation processes is neither clear nor uncontroversial: both are exactly the things that are coordinated in the act of innovating. For this purpose, those involved in processes of innovation construct fields of innovation that require determining the possibilities, limitations, and impossibilities of those relations and references that are considered to be potentially relevant. To do so, fields of innovation are aligned along the long-familiar major lines of differentiation such as the economic, the political, or the arts. But they

---

25 This applies as much to the practices of decision-makers in businesses and politics as it does to the practices of users, holdouts, and enthusiastic pioneers.

also bring new combinations and mixtures of such guiding principles into play that, if they prove to be useful, can serve to bridge the gaps between pieces of long-established knowledge. Fields of innovation can also be constructed so that the new, the other, and the deviant come into conflict with a whole range of existing guiding principles to a degree that new relations and references emerge and become established. For all the focus on the new and on exploring new relations, the fields constructed in the acts of innovating and in which references can be found are heterogeneous but not arbitrary. If we take a bird's-eye view, we see a rampant growth of fields of innovation offering a range of alternative references, fields that overlap, and fields that are combined with or pitted against one another, and must be coordinated and brought to life. Currently, this can be observed particularly well in the relation between climate research and energy policy or between the automotive industry and Germany's electro-mobility policy.

In this way, the analysis of innovation directs attention to a type of social coordination that is simply not geared toward clearly defined and distinctive social spheres but rather—transgressing the usual boundaries—toward situationally creating, practically combining, and reflexively mediating guiding principles that already exist, are assumed to exist, or are newly composed. The act of innovating is a virtually prototypical practice that builds bridges, makes connections, and combines that which is different while it also creates arenas of negotiation, conflict, and demarcation.

Once we adopt a view informed by a greater awareness of reflexive innovation, we notice that the case studies conducted in the context of the Research Training Group by no means simply fail to correspond with the clear-cut boundaries of social spheres; they are neither merely exceptional empirical instances of an innovation practice that is otherwise neatly sorted along the lines of the guiding distinctions of the economic, the political, and the arts, nor are there signs of dedifferentiation or that these references are becoming irrelevant. Rather, an approach to innovation research that investigates empirically the different relations and heterogeneous references that are produced, cited, and combined with and pitted against one another in the concrete practice of innovation provides insight into a form of social coordination that, depending on the situation, brings into play—again and again, in new and variable ways—both established references (of the economic, the political, or the arts) and occasionally even completely new ones in order to position something as entirely new and innovative.

It is precisely this focus on the new of whatever kind, which can be highlighted as that which is to be preferred over the already existent, the usual, the well-known, or some state of normality, let alone over the outdated, that renders innovation such a consequential form of coordination in contemporary society. Commitment to the new does not equate to complete openness and 'anything goes.' On the contrary, what it involves is a *commitment to variability*—the variability of that which has been proposed, established, and stabilized. A greater orientation toward the new demands a reflexive practice of innovation.

6   Fragmental Differentiation and the Practice of Innovation

The picture that is emerging at the end of these considerations is this: For the design of a research program that focuses on the practice and processes of innovation as a means of diagnosing contemporary society, observations of how differentiation at the macro level is changing its form are just as relevant as observations of the practices and orientations within and between the different fields.

The functional form of differentiation of guiding principles, communication media, and self-referential subsystems, which systems theorists in particular have identified as being the characteristic feature of modern societies, has gradually changed since the 1970s—not least in the course of recurring contact with changes on the ground, 'below the clouds,' and in critical contact with other observers operating at similar altitudes. In contrast to the focus on four functions and subsystems in Parsons' theory of society, Luhmann went on to radicalize and open up systems theory so as to allow for the emergence of new guiding distinctions and a larger number of subsystems in response to unsettling, pressing problems. In adopting the view 'from the ground,' the various researchers who collaborated in a research network with Ulrich Beck (cf. Beck and Lau 2004) seem to have taken the highly detailed maps and separation rules for the planning of flight routes seriously but were increasingly forced to take note of the practices of deviating from expected paths, transcending boundaries, and engaging in improvisation. Beck's 'theory and empirical reality of reflexive modernization' is able to demonstrate the limits of the functionally specified criteria of rationality that are operative in a range of social spheres—from economy, science, and politics to intimate and familial relationships—when it comes to applying them to address their own side effects. In regard to this 'reflexivity of side effects,' Beck and Lau observe, for instance, a 'logic' of 'both one and the other' as opposed to a code of 'either/or' and call for developing "complex reflexive solutions, (...) which do greater justice to the new uncertainties and ambivalences that pervade the macro and micro spheres alike" (Beck and Lau 2005: 114, our translation). What they describe as a mix of the basic principles of first modernity and the basic institutions of second modernity, we would describe from a vantage point that is more forward-looking, directed toward novelty, and more open to the variety of innovative practices. The reasons for this are both empirical and a matter of research strategy: A 'both-one-and-the-other' approach to research on the logic of first and second modernity fails to do justice to the new especially. A sociology that proceeds in this manner "is doomed to turn into an 'antique shop of industrial society' if it attempts to apply the concepts of first modernity to second modernity" (Reckwitz 2009: 170, our translation)—and this holds for sociology of innovation research as well. The objective should be to develop concepts for 'the next society,' which, as Baecker has demonstrated by using the focus on 'projects' as an example, must come to terms with forms of coordination that utilize the systems of order of first modernity yet systematically transcend them. "All function systems of modern society," Baecker argues (2007: 172, our translation), "are suitable models for this but are now combined into the most unlikely projects so that, although politics and economy, art and education, science and religion can still be distinguished, one must nevertheless acknowledge that in social movements, civic involvement, the conspiracy against the art market, and the belief in science one can only be separated from the other at the expense of the project." We have attempted to demonstrate that the focus on innovation in contemporary society is of a similar nature.

In our view, there is much to be said for a shift in the primacy of social differentiation toward a kind of 'fragmental differentiation' (Rammert 2006: 258ff.), the specifics of which have already been spelled out in detail elsewhere in terms of the transformation of science, industry, and politics representing a 'post-Schumpeterian mode of innovation' (Rammert 2000: 157ff.). Just as the primacy of functional differentiation in modern society has not resulted in the disappearance of segmented and hierarchical forms of social organization, the novel forms of fragmental differentiation will not fully displace the principles of functional differentiation. The adjective 'fragmental' implies a pragmatic opening up and mixing of functionally neatly separated guiding references and self-referential social spheres. It confronts the separate, parallel existence of differentiated spheres with fields and levels that are intertwined and overlap but, in spite of this apparent 'muddledness,' form an order that is reproduced in social practice. The fragmental regime does not operate on the basis of only one single refined parameter of reference or code but incorporates others as well. Via imitation and habitualization, this multi-referential orientation can congeal into local, field-specific codes that are commonly applied in the medium term and are composed of a reflexive mix of several other codes. The *fragmental* does not primarily follow a logic of abstract categorization and cartography along *functional* lines—like a political, economic, or climate map—but instead follows concrete, mixed movements: for instance, of people, media, and weapons to define and demarcate politico-geostrategic fields; or of money, patents, and brain drain to determine economic-scientific fields. The basic principle is not an endless process of subdividing entities into distinct and ever-more specialized units as in the case of functional differentiation; it proceeds more along the lines of the mechanisms of 'fractal distinction' and 'fractal differentiation' (Abbott 2001: 21f.), in which differentiation resembles a process of bifurcation that, after division and conflict, reincorporates parts of the subdued entity. In this way, the theory of fragmented differentiation, modeled after the design of fractal geometry, is able to reconstruct the references that emerge in the fragmented fields, in mixed combinations or refined to various degrees, as the re-emerging and reutilized guiding distinctions of functional differentiation.

According to the reading we are proposing here, the attention toward innovation in contemporary society enhanced in this way would be misinterpreted as being nothing more than a rhetorical intensification of the imperative of novelty in modernity. We would also be mistaken in viewing it as being merely an expression of the cultural preference for creativity, which has gained prevalence since the end of late modernity. Although both seem to be the case, it is not only the greater orientation toward *newness*—driving the numbers in the pool of imagined variants to heights that become difficult to keep track of—that can be grasped as a manifestation and driver of fragmental differentiation but first and foremost the reflexive orientation toward *innovation*, which is invariably geared toward the situational selection of promising new combinations of objects, projects, and practices—once defined as material relations—as well as toward potential fit with various social references. The increased orientation toward innovation is a manifestation of a transition of the primacy of differentiation at the macro level of society; together with a number of other forms of coordination that are gaining significance, it is indicative of the shortcomings of neatly separated lines of orientation. The more or less neatly sorted guiding principles of the economic, the political, law, science, and the arts that first modernity has institutionalized in enterprises, political parties, law firms, research institutes, and galleries and museums have not disappeared: not "all that is solid melts into air."[26]

But the greater orientation toward innovation *as such*—and not toward profitability, truth, or aesthetics—finds expression in the fact that contemporary society has a need for coordination between, beyond, and below these guiding principles. This need for coordination is also the driver of this transition to fragmental differentiation because, in the case of innovation, practical reflexivity virtually compels us to constantly reposition the guiding distinctions of functional differentiation: as being combinable, outdated, renewable, transgressable, or ignorable. The greater

---

26   Marx and Engels 1998: 38f.

drive toward *continuous* innovation disrupts habits, crosses established boundaries, mixes guiding references, and spreads to all spheres of society. It necessitates a reflexive practice of innovation and fragmental bifurcation, which gives rise to ever more fields of innovation; a reflexive practice of innovation is a new form of social coordination that brings us closer to the next type of society.

References

Abbott, Andrew. 2001. *Chaos of Disciplines*. Chicago: University of Chicago Press.
Baecker, Dirk. 2007. *Studien zur nächsten Gesellschaft*. Frankfurt a. M.: Suhrkamp.
Baur, Nina, Cristina Besio, and Maria Norkus. This volume. "Projectification of Science as an Organizational Innovation. A Figurational Sociological Perspective on Emergence, Diffusion and Impact."
Beck, Ulrich, Anthony Giddens, and Scott Lash. 1994. *Reflexive Modernization*, Cambridge: Polity Press.
Beck, Ulrich. 2006. *The Cosmopolitan Vision*. Cambridge, UK: Polity Press.
Beck, Ulrich and Boris Holzer. 2004. "Reflexivität und Reflexion." Pp. 165-192 in *Entgrenzung und Entscheidung*, edited by U. Beck and C. Lau. Frankfurt a. M.: Suhrkamp.
Beck, Ulrich and Christoph Lau, eds. 2004. *Entgrenzung und Entscheidung: Was ist neu an der Theorie reflexiver Modernisierung?* Frankfurt a. M.: Suhrkamp.
Beck, Ulrich and Christoph Lau. 2005. "Theorie und Empirie reflexiver Modernisierung: Von der Notwendigkeit und den Schwierigkeiten, einen historischen Gesellschaftswandel innerhalb der Moderne zu beobachten und zu begreifen." *Soziale Welt* 56(2/3): 107-135.
Blind, Knut and Stephan Gauch. 2009. "Research and Standardization in Nanotechnology: Evidence from Germany." *Journal of Technology Transfer* 34: 320-342.
Boltanski, Luc and Ève Chiapello. 2005. *The New Spirit of Capitalism*. London, New York: Verso.
Borman, Inka, René John, and Jens Aderhold, eds. 2012. *Indikatoren des Neuen. Innovation als Sozialmethodologie oder Sozialtechnologie?*. Wiesbaden: Springer VS.
Braun-Thürmann, Holger. 2012. "Innovationsindikatoren und das Hexeneinmaleins der Innovationspolitik." Pp. 17-37 in *Indikatoren des Neuen*, edited by I. Borman, R. John, and J. Aderhold. Wiesbaden: Springer VS.
Bröckling, Ulrich. 2004. "Kreativität." *Leviathan* 32(1): 130-134.
Christmann, Gabriela, Oliver Ibert, Johann Jessen, and Uwe-Jens Walther. This volume. "How Does Novelty Enter Spatial Planning? Conceptualizing Innovations in Planning and Research Strategies."
Dierks, Nicolas. 2015. *Endlose Erneuerung. Moderne Kultur und Ästhetik mit Wittgenstein und Adorno*. Paderborn: Wilhelm Fink Verlag.
Dolata, Ulrich. 2008. "Das Internet und die Transformation der Musikindustrie. Rekonstruktion und Erklärung eines unkontrollierten sektoralen Wandels." *Berliner Journal für Soziologie* 18(3): 344-369.
Eickelpasch, Rolf. 1982. "Das ethnomethodologische Programm einer 'radikalen' Soziologie." *Zeitschrift für Soziologie* 11(1): 7-27.
Esposito, Elena. 2003. "Vom Modell zur Mode. Medien und Formen der Nachahmung." *Soziale Systeme* 9(1): 88-104.
European Commission. 2012. *Responsible Research and Innovation. Europe's Ability to Respond to Societal Challenges*. Retrieved December 12, 2015 (https://ec.europa.eu/research/swafs/pdf/pub_public_engagement/responsible-research-and-innovation-leaflet_en.pdf).
Fagerberg, Jan, David C. Mowery, and Richard R. Nelson, eds. 2005. *The Oxford Handbook of Innovation*. Oxford: Oxford University Press.

Garfinkel, Harold. 1967. *Studies in Ethnomethodology*. Englewood Cliffs, N.J.: Longman Higher Education.
Garfinkel, Harold and Harvey Sacks. 1970. "On Formal Structures of Practical Actions." Pp. 338-366 in *Theoretical Sociology*, edited by J. C. McKinney and E. A. Tiryakian. New York: Appleton-Century-Crofts.
Garud, Raghu and Peter Karnøe, eds. 2001. *Path Dependence and Creation*. Mahwah, N.J.: Lawrence Erlbaum.
Gebelein, Paul, Martina Löw, and Thomas Paul. This volume. "'Flash Mobs' as Innovation. On a New Social Form of Technically Mediated Congregation."
Giddens, Anthony. 1990. *The Consequences of Modernity*. Cambridge: Polity Press.
Hage, Jerald and Marius Meeus, eds. 2006. *Innovation, Science, and Institutional Change: A Research Handbook*. Oxford: Oxford University Press.
Hill, Miira. 2014. *Embodiment of Science in Science Slams. A Case of Informal Public Science Communication*. Presentation held at Studying Science Communication. A Panel of the EASST14 Conference, Torun, Poland.
Hirsch-Kreinsen, Hartmut. 2014. "Wandel von Produktionsarbeit – Industriearbeit 4.0." *WSI-Mitteilungen* (6): 421-429.
Hutter, Michael. 1989. *Die Produktion von Recht. Eine selbstreferentielle Theorie der Wirtschaft, angewandt auf den Fall des Arzneimittelpatentrechts*. Tübingen: Mohr Siebeck.
Hutter, Michael. This volume. "The Role of Newness in the Experience Economy."
Hutter, Michael, Hubert Knoblauch, Werner Rammert, and Arnold Windeler. 2015. "Innovation Society Today. The Reflexive Creation of Novelty." *Historical Social Research* 40(3): 30-47.
Jöstingmeier, Marco. 2015. *Die Steuerung systemischer Risiken. Innovative Regulierung eines innovativen Problems?* (Unpublished dissertation). Berlin: TU Berlin.
Jungmann, Robert, Nina Baur, and Dzifa Ametowobla. 2015. "Grasping Processes of Innovation Empirically. A Call for Expanding the Methodological Toolkit. An Introduction." *Historical Social Research* 40(3): 7-29.
Kleemann, Frank, Kerstin Rieder, and Günter G. Voß. 2009. "Kunden als Innovatoren. Die betriebliche Nutzung privater Innovativität im Web 2.0 durch Crowdsourcing." *Wirtschaftspsychologie* 11(1): 28-35.
Knoblauch, Hubert. This volume. "Communicative Action, the New, and the Innovation Society."
Knorr-Cetina, Karin. 1992. "Zur Unterkomplexität der Differenzierungstheorie. Empirische Anfragen an die Systemtheorie." *Zeitschrift für Soziologie* 21(6): 406-419.
Köppel, Johann. This volume. "Germany's *Energiewende*: Path Disruption or Reinforcement of the Established Path?"
Landau, Friederike and Henning Mohr. 2015. "Interventionen als Kunst des urbanen Handelns? Rezension zu J. Laister, A. Lederer, and M. Makovec (eds.), Die Kunst des urbanen Handelns / The Art of Urban Intervention." *sub\urban. zeitschrift für kritische stadtforschung* 3(1): 173-178.
Liebl, Franz. This volume. "What Is Strategic Marketing in an Innovation Society? A Frame of Reference."
Lindemann, Gesa. 2011. "Differenzierung der modernen Gesellschaft. Eine grenzregimetheoretische Perspektive." Pp. 135-156 in *Soziale Differenzierung. Handlungsthe-*

oretische Zugänge in der Diskussion, edited by T. Schwinn, C. Kroneberg, and J. Greve. Wiesbaden: Springer VS.
Luhmann, Niklas. 1995. *Social Systems*. Stanford: Stanford University Press.
Lynch, Michael. 2000. "Against Reflexivity as an Academic Virtue and Source of Privileged Knowledge." *Theory, Culture & Society* 17(3): 26-54.
Marx, Karl and Friedrich Engels. 1998 [1848]. *The Communist Manifesto*. London: Penguin Press.
Mohr, Henning. 2013. "'Stadt selbst Machen' zwischen individueller Aneignung und politischer Verpflichtung. Zur zentralen Kontroverse des Symposiums MYCITY der Urbanen Künste Ruhr." *Common – Journal für Kunst & Öffentlichkeit* 3(3). Retrieved December 08, 2015 (http://commonthejournal.com/journal/kunst-zum-leben-aneignungals-strategie-zur-veraenderung-no-3/stadt-selbst-machen-zwischen-individueller-aneignung-und-politischer-verpflichtung-zur-zentralen-kontroverse-des-symposiums-mycity-der-urbanen-kuenste-ruhr/).
Mölders, Marc. 2012. "Differenzierung und Integration. Zur Aktualisierung einer kommunikationsbasierten Differenzierungstheorie." *Zeitschrift für Soziologie* 41(6): 478-494.
Nassehi, Armin. 2004. "Die Theorie funktionaler Differenzierung im Horizont ihrer Kritik." *Zeitschrift für Soziologie* 33(2): 98-118.
Nassehi, Armin. 2006. *Der soziologische Diskurs der Moderne*. Frankfurt a. M.: Suhrkamp.
Ogburn, William F. 1964. "Cultural Lag as Theory." Pp. 86-95 in *On Culture and Social Change, Selected Papers*, edited by W. F. Ogburn and O. D. Duncan. Chicago, London: University of Chicago Press.
Passoth, Jan-Hendrik. 2011. "Fragmentierung, Multiplizität und Symmetrie. Praxistheorien in postpluraler Attitüde." Pp. 259-278 in *Strukturentstehung durch Verflechtung. Akteur-Netzwerk-Theorie(n) und Automatismen*, edited by T. Conradi, H. Derwanz, and F. Muhle. Paderborn: Fink.
Passoth, Jan-Hendrik and Nicholas J. Rowland. 2014. "Beware of Allies! Notes on Analytical Hygiene in Actor-Network Account-making." *Qualitative Sociology* 36(4): 465-483.
Picot, Arnold and Stefan Hopf. This volume. "Innovation by the Numbers: Crowdsourcing in the Innovation Process."
Powell, Walther W., Kenneth W. Koput, and Laurel Smith-Doerr. 1996. "Interorganizational Collaboration and the Locus of Innovation: Networks of Learning in Biotechnology." *Administrative Science Quarterly* 41(1): 116-145.
Rammert, Werner. 1988. *Das Innovationsdilemma. Technikentwicklung im Unternehmen*. Opladen: Westdeutscher Verlag.
Rammert, Werner. 1990. "Telefon und Kommunikationskultur. Akzeptanz und Diffusion einer Technik im Vier-Länder-Vergleich." *Kölner Zeitschrift für Soziologie und Sozialpsychologie* 42(1): 20-40.
Rammert, Werner. 2000. "Auf dem Weg zu einer post-schumpeterianischen Innovationsweise. Institutionelle Differenzierung, reflexive Modernisierung und interaktive Vernetzung im Bereich der Technikentwicklung." Pp. 157-173 in *Technik aus soziologischer Perspektive (volume 2). Kultur, Innovation, Virtualität*, edited by W. Rammert. Wiesbaden: Springer VS.
Rammert, Werner. 2002. "The Cultural Shaping of Technologies and the Politics of Technodiversity." Pp. 173-194 in *Shaping Technology, Guiding Policy: Concepts, Spaces & Tools*, edited by K. H. Sørensen and R. Williams. Cheltenham, UK: Edward Elgar.

Rammert, Werner. 2006. "Two Styles of Knowing and Knowledge Regimes: Between 'Explicitation' and 'Exploration' under Conditions of Functional Specialization or Fragmental Distribution." Pp. 256-284 in *Innovation, Science, and Institutional Change*, edited by J. Hage and M. Meeus. Oxford: Oxford University Press.

Rammert, Werner. 2010. "Die Innovationen der Gesellschaft." Pp. 21-51 in *Soziale Innovationen. Auf dem Weg zu einem post-industriellen Innovationsparadigma*, edited by J. Howaldt and H. Jakobsen. Wiesbaden: Springer VS.

Rammert, Werner. 2014. "Vielfalt der Innovation und gesellschaftlicher Zusammenhalt." Pp. 619-639 in *Vielfalt und Zusammenhalt. Verhandlungen des 36. Kongresses der Deutschen Gesellschaft für Soziologie in Bochum und Dortmund 2012*, edited by M. Löw. Frankfurt a. M.: Campus.

Reckwitz, Andreas. 2009. "Praktiken der Reflexivität: Eine kulturtheoretische Perspektive auf hochmodernes Handeln." Pp. 169-182 in *Handeln unter Unsicherheit*, edited F. Böhle and M. Weihrich. Wiesbaden: Springer VS.

Reckwitz, Andreas. 2012. *Die Erfindung der Kreativität: Zum Prozess gesellschaftlicher Ästhetisierung*. Berlin: Suhrkamp.

Reckwitz, Andreas. This volume. "The Creativity *Dispositif* and the Social Regimes of the New."

Reichhardt, Sven. 2014. *Authentizität und Gemeinschaft. Linksalternatives Leben in den siebziger und frühen achtziger Jahren*. Frankfurt a. M.: Suhrkamp.

Schimank, Uwe. 1985. "Funktionale Differenzierung und reflexiver Subjektivismus – Zum Entsprechungsverhältnis von Gesellschafts- und Identitätsform." *Soziale Welt* 36(4): 447-465.

Schimank, Uwe. 2005. *Differenzierung und Integration der modernen Gesellschaft*. Wiesbaden: VS Verlag.

Schimank, Uwe. 2011. "Gesellschaftliche Differenzierungsdynamiken – ein Fünf-Fronten-Kampf." Pp. 261-284 in *Soziale Differenzierung. Handlungstheoretische Zugänge in der Diskussion*, edited by T. Schwinn, C. Kroneberg, and J. Greve. Wiesbaden: Springer VS.

Schimank, Uwe and Ute Volkmann. 2012. *Marketization of Society: Economizing the Non-Economic*. Welfare Societies Conference paper, Universität Bremen.

Schroth, Fabian. 2014a. *Experiments and Construction Processes of Climate Governance Arrangements*. Dissertation chapter presented for discussion at the Institute of Sociology research lab. Berlin: Technische Universität.

Schroth, Fabian. 2014b. *Mit CO2-Märkten experimentieren: Die Entstehung des Clean Development Mechanism aus pragmatistischer Perspektive*. Presentation held at the Fourth Open Conference of the International Politics Section, Magdeburg.

Schubert, Cornelius. This volume. "Social Innovation. A New Instrument for Social Change?"

Schulze, Gerhard. 1992. *Die Erlebnisgesellschaft: Kultursoziologie der Gegenwart*. Frankfurt a. M.: Campus.

Schumpeter, Joseph A. 1934 [1912]. *The Theory of Economic Development*. Cambridge, MA: Harvard University Press.

Schütz, Alfred. 1964. *Collected Papers (Volume I). The Problem of Social Reality*. The Hague, Boston, London: Martinus Nijhoff.

Schützeichel, Rainer. 2011. "'Doing Systems' – Eine handlungstheoretische Rekonstruktion funktionaler Differenzierung." Pp. 73-91 in *Soziale Differenzierung. Erkenntnisgewinne handlungstheoretischer Zugänge*, edited by T. Schwinn, C. Kroneberg, and J. Greve. Wiesbaden: Springer VS.

Shinn, Terry. 2006. "New Sources of Radical Innovation: Research, Technologies, Transversality, and Distributed Learning in a Post-Industrial Order." Pp. 313-333 in *Innovation, Science, and Institutional Change*, edited by J. Hage and M. Meeus. Oxford: Oxford University Press.

Sloterdijk, Peter. 2013. *You Must Change Your Life. On Anthropotechnics*. Cambridge: Polity Press.

Smith, Keith. 2005. "Measuring Innovation." Pp. 148-177 in *The Oxford Handbook of Innovation*, edited by J. Fagerberg, D. C. Mowery, and R. R. Nelson. Oxford: Oxford University Press.

Stock, Jessica. 2016. "Alltagsmobilität und die Ideologisierung des Klimawandels." Pp. 293-315 in *Zum gesellschaftlichen Umgang mit dem Klimawandel. Kooperationen und Kollisionen*, edited by C. Besio and G. Romano. Berlin: Nomos.

Stubbe, Julian. 2015. "Comparative Heuristics from an STS Perspective: Inquiring 'Novelty' in Material Practice." *Historical Social Research* 40(3): 109-129.

von Hippel, Eric. 1988. *Sources of Innovation*. Oxford: Oxford University Press.

von Hippel, Eric. 2005. *Democratizing Innovation*. Cambridge: MIT Press.

von Schomberg, René. 2012. "Prospects for Technology Assessment in a Framework of Responsible Research and Innovation." Pp. 39-61 in *Technikfolgen abschätzen lehren*, edited by M. Dusseldorp and R. Beecroft. Wiesbaden: Springer VS.

Voß, Jan-Peter. This volume. "Innovating Governance: Epistemic and Political Reflexivities in the Re-Making of Democracy."

Wentland, Alexander. 2014. *The Electric Future Re-imagined? Reshaping Cars, Infrastructures, and Society through the Electrification of Transportation*. Presentation held at Science Shaping the World of Tomorrow: Scientific Imagination and Development of Society, Antwerp, The Netherlands.

Windeler, Arnold. This volume. "Reflexive Innovation. On Innovation in Radicalized Modernity."

Wittgenstein, Ludwig 1999 (1953): *Philosophische Untersuchungen / Philosophical Investigations*. German & English. Oxford, UK: Blackwell Publishers.

Reflexive Innovation

On Innovation in Radicalized Modernity[1]

Arnold Windeler

1 Reflexive Innovation and Sociation Today: Definitions

Today, innovation as 'creative destruction' (Schumpeter 2003: 83) is becoming a social imperative that increasingly characterizes innovation societies far beyond their economies (Hutter et al., this volume). This development is accelerated through *reflexive innovations* that actors constitute in interactions drawing on modern institutions, systems of regulation, and the actors' capabilities. These specific conditions, both symbolic and material, influence which innovations are produced, advanced, and transformed and how this occurs, and these conditions themselves are again and again produced and reproduced in processes of innovation. In this essay, informed by structuration theory (Giddens 1984), I outline a practice-theoretical perspective of reflexive innovation as a defining feature of radically modern societies (cf. Giddens 1990a). I have systematically developed the concepts that underpin this perspective elsewhere (Windeler 2001, 2014). The present essay adopts an alternative perspective on innovation compared with established innovation research; it draws on Joseph Schumpeter but then addresses innovations in their relationship to society as being conveyed through social practices.

Since the 1960s, innovations have played an increasing role in shaping modern societies and have often been a topic of public and academic discourse, not least

---

1 I would like to thank Dzifa Ametowobla, Robert Jungmann, Uli Meyer, and Cornelius Schubert for their valuable input.

because prestigious universities and newly established research institutions have devoted attention to the issue (Fagerberg 2005; Godin 2012; Knoblauch, this volume). The prominent role of innovation is the source of the dynamics of renewal in modern societies: each individual innovation seems to be 'merely' a transition for other ones that are evolving. Everything is to be redone; everything seems improvable by innovation. Innovation becomes an imperative for action—even beyond the classic fields of business and science. Preserving the current state is relegated to the background, and what has been destroyed is suppressed (Erumban and Timmer 2012). As this takes its course, societies transform themselves into innovation societies, and innovation becomes a panacea for every socio-economic problem (Godin 2015: 7). This in turn focuses increased attention on innovations in politics, business, and society in general. The innovation imperative proves quite robust, while innovations themselves are not at issue even if they contribute, for instance, to financial, energy, and environmental crises. But innovations do not simply evolve on their own. To understand which ones are currently being generated, and how this happens and why, one needs an understanding of innovation that presupposes an understanding of innovation societies since innovations are recursively constituted on the basis of given social conditions.

Establishing such an understanding is, however, easier said than done, given that sociation in present-day society tends to be difficult to grasp and the concept of innovation has been at risk of completely losing its distinctiveness for some time now (ibid.). If we refuse to simply surrender to this diagnosis, a look at the perspectives that dominate the literature is of little avail. My approach to tackling this problem is inspired by Joseph Schumpeter's (2000: 51f.) famous definition of innovation as new combination of already existing resources, materials or means of production. I ask, how can innovations be explained in societal contexts?

Let us start with Schumpeter's social-philosophical sketch of a research program in which he defines the core of innovation in this way:

> The change [that identifies an innovation] *transmuting one imprinted form into another one* must represent a crack, a jerk, a leap […]. When starting from the old form, the new one must *not* be reachable by adaptation in small steps (Schumpeter 2005: 113, first emphasis A.W.).

With Joseph Schumpeter, the theoretical problem of innovation research can be formulated as follows: How can the transfer of one imprinted form into another be explained? He himself did not succeed in finding an answer to this question in his lifetime. As Markus C. Becker, Thorbjørn Knudsen, and James G. March (2006: 357) have argued, Schumpeter was never able to link his typology of new combinations to an understanding of the processes generating novelty. Thus, although Schumpeter saw combinations as involved in novelty, he found it difficult to provide any description of an inheritance mechanism that is any more precise than the word 'combination'.

Not that Schumpeter (2005) did not try. He made a total of three attempts, though he himself discarded them as inadequate. He tried to explain innovation through the entrepreneur's personality, through the depersonalized entrepreneurial function, and with reference to evolutionary theory. His verdict was that rationally and scientifically, "the *triad* 'indeterminacy, novelty, leap' remains unconquerable all the same" (ibid.: 117). At the end of his manuscript, however, he calls for further elaborating the aforementioned *triad*: "I think it is more correct to speak of a new task" (ibid.: 118).

I take up this task from a practice-theoretical perspective. In so doing, I follow Schumpeter more than just a little but then take a different route. I share his view that innovation addresses the transfer of 'imprinted forms into others', and that the problem of explaining innovations is not only one of imperfectly mastering the facts but rather refers to the theoretical inclusion of the *triad* that he mentions:

> To many, it will seem obvious to say that the 'in-explicability' of development [that means: of innovation] sketched above might perhaps just be an effect of the imperfect mastering of the facts, and will disappear with its perfection. Such an interpretation has obvious support, due to the fact that the better we master a state and the apprehensible factors of change, the sooner we develop an idea of things to come. Unfortunately, you do not reach the essence of the matter in this way (ibid.: 117).

What Schumpeter means by the 'essence of the matter' is that innovation—the leap from one imprinted form into another one that he diagnosed—cannot be deduced and remains *unforeseeable* (see also Ortmann 2016). This is highly plausible because it seems true for an astounding number of things in modern life: many things are created by someone stumbling upon something or 'accidents' happening (Kennedy 2016). But even if innovations are developed along innovation paths, their fundamental unpredictability may be reduced but cannot be completely eliminated (for a discussion of innovation paths, see, e.g., Garud and Karnøe 2001; U. Meyer 2016; Sydow et al. 2012; Windeler 2003). At the same time, it is important to note that even fortunate coincidences must be noticed and unexpected discoveries made. From a practice-theoretical perspective, serendipity cannot simply be reduced to discovery. What is needed for something to be discovered (and to be susceptible to discovery in the first place) is people's perspicacity, cleverness, attention, and activities as well as—often overlooked—social contexts that enable or even trigger discovery (Merton and Barber 2004). And grounded in this insight is the fact that innovations are not simply discovered but need to be constituted in social practices.

This shifts the focus to ways of understanding and analyzing innovations. And here there are alternatives to the ways by which both Schumpeter and the dominant practice of innovation research have approached the subject matter. The alternative presented here is the practice-theoretical approach that I propose and will discuss in more detail below.

Three paradigms characterize innovation research today: the paradigms of 'creation,' 'evolution,' and 'structure or institution.' Whereas some emphasize the role of artistic or technical ingenuity in creating the new—or, as Joseph Schumpeter initially did, the significance of entrepreneurs with certain character traits—others highlight the importance of mutations, emergence, coincidences, poor imitations, and the like—as Schumpeter did attempt to devise more generally (Becker and Knudsen 2002; Rammert 2014: 628f.; Windeler 2003). The literature on national innovation systems, by contrast, primarily has stressed structures and institutions, neglecting the actors' agency, whereas that on entrepreneurship—committed to the creation paradigm—has failed to consider structures and institutions and has concentrated on agency, of individuals and collectives (e.g., teams and organizations like start-ups; Autio et al. 2014; Zahra, Wright, and Abdelgawad 2014). What unites such analytical approaches are the basic paradigmatic assumptions regarding structure and actors deeply engrained within them. In this regard, I agree with the general objection formulated by Anthony Giddens:

> Explicitly or otherwise, such authors have tended to see in structural constraint a source of causation more or less equivalent to the operation of impersonal causal forces in nature. The range of 'free action' which agents have is restricted, as it were, by external forces that set strict limits to what they can achieve. The more that structural constraint is associated with a natural science model, paradoxically, the freer the agent appears [...]. The structural properties of social systems, in other words, are like the walls of a room from which an individual cannot escape but inside which he or she is able to move around at whim. Structuration theory replaces this view with one which holds that structure is implicated in that very 'freedom of action' which is treated as residual and unexplicated category in the various forms of 'structural sociology' (Giddens 1984: 174).

In the practice-theoretical perspective proposed here—in contrast to what structural, evolutionary, and institutional theories suggest—social requirements in the form of structures, structural features, and mechanisms are neither fixed and externally given nor forces that compel actors to act. Instead, they are *implicated* in acting and *restrict and enable* it at the same time when actors endogenize them in acting while drawing on the customary procedures and techniques used in applying requirements. Their latitude or 'freedom to innovate' is thus not simply externally given but recursively constituted on a recurrent basis by the actors in interactions. From this perspective, however, actors do *not* have the degree of freedom to act that structural, evolutionary, and institutional theories accord to them. Actors *cannot* (within the framework of given constraints) act more or less at will, for instance, *arbitrarily declaring something an innovation*; instead, their action is oriented by rules and resources that are activated in interaction and that indicate to them what one is expected to do in this context. Overall, this means that neither what actors do nor institutions, structures, and structural features can be seen as residual and not requiring further explanation.[2]

This raises the question of whether there are possibilities to overcome the deficits of established innovation research? I think there are. What I propose is at least a *shift in perspective* on innovation. This proposed shift places the focus on *social practices*—meaning regularized types of action or ongoing series of 'practical activities' (Giddens 1993: 81)—without losing sight of the institutions, structures, and actors involved, but also without according any one entity the central role per se, as is usually the case. As I show below, the practice-theoretical perspective considers innovation as something that is actively brought into the world, even if the results are not intended and at least to some extent elude planning and control. This is so because innovation is a social and therefore socially embedded process that is recursively produced and reproduced by actors under given circumstances, although not of their choosing, on which they nevertheless have some degree of influence. The practice-theoretical approach pursued here leads to a specific concept of innovation that differs fundamentally from the established understandings in at least seven aspects that I will discuss below and provides an analytical perspective that correlates with this concept, which I will outline thereafter.

First, the practice-theoretical perspective offers an alternative understanding of innovation compared to established innovation research by *decentering the subject* without completely departing from it. Actors (such as individuals or organizations) come to be viewed as agents who situationally produce and reproduce innovations

---

2 Even if given conditions have a certain 'objectivity' for individual actors, these conditions do not determine their actions, though they limit the range of options (Giddens 1984: 177), and rules and resources indicate to them how these are to be used appropriately. And if actors cannot resist social conditions and forces, this is always also because of their motives and the goals that they are pursuing (ibid: 178).

as innovations in interactions incorporating social practices (based on the rules and resources embedded in them). It is not only the subject that is decentered in this understanding of innovation. Innovation is specifically not addressed as the result of individual action alone, as the creativity paradigm would have it, nor is it viewed as something in which actors are negligible, as the evolutionary, structural, and institutional paradigms suggest. And what is at least as significant, the practice-theoretical approach offers an alternative understanding of innovation to that proposed by Joseph Schumpeter and a large part of innovation research. Innovation is understood as the transfer of one imprinted form into another one, constituted *as* innovation *in social interactions by knowledgeable agents referring to social practices.*

Second, this practice-theoretical perspective distinguishes between means of action and innovation. It assigns great significance to the means of action for innovation. This is so especially because a certain potential to cause, enhance, or prevent innovation as well as a certain performativity (Muniesa 2014) is inherent to such means.[3] At the same time, this perspective *decenters* the *social significance* of such means. It is perhaps surprising that this is entirely in line with Schumpeter (1934). For him, although an entrepreneur innovates by means of new or newly combined resources, materials, or means of production, the artifacts—or rather the means of action[4]—do not themselves transfer one imprinted form into another one. They can be results or moments of innovation processes, no more and no less. This understanding of means of action enables a closer focus on their significance, depending on their uses and on the characteristics of the types of innovation.

Third, this brings us to a new view of the *production and reproduction of innovations*. From a practice-theoretical perspective, actors constitute innovations as innovations in processes of interaction. Innovations thus *exist*, are present in time-space, *only in the form in which they are instantiated* and *coordinated* as *memory traces in social interactions*. Actors can focus on and advance an innovation. But determining from which point in time onward a change is to be considered an innovation or whether something that already exists must still be considered an

---

3 The means of action can trigger innovation even if they are not used, as illustrated by the example of the atomic bomb, which, although currently not in use, continues to initiate 'innovations in warfare' (Eden 2004).

4 I am using the concept of means of action and not the conventional, yet insufficiently defined, concept of 'artifact' commonly referred to in the innovation literature (e.g., Braun-Thürmann 2005: 6). In so doing, I am trying to avoid associations with Aristoteles' definition of the artifact, which considers artifacts as a means made for a certain purpose and explicitly presumes a maker or an author or a group of authors (Hilpinen 2011).

innovation—or still this *particular* innovation—is the product of recurrent interaction. An innovation is thus *neither* based only on the *perception of individuals nor* can it *be determined independently of how it is used and evaluated*. Thus this understanding differs from that of Schumpeter, who seems to assume precisely that when he states that "When starting from the old form, the new one must *not* be reachable by adaptation in small steps" (Schumpeter 2005: 113) or, in earlier work, claims that one can speak of an innovation in the modern economy when entrepreneurs "have employed existing means of production differently, more appropriately, more advantageously. [When] [t]hey have 'carried out new combinations'" (Schumpeter 1934: 132). From a practice-theoretical perspective, actors continuously produce and reproduce novelties as innovations (or refrain from doing so) by, for instance, producing and reproducing in their social practices a new product, method, or behavior as an innovation. This also implies that innovations do not always yield positive results, as Schumpeter assumes; they are therefore also not always desirable per se; they by no means always lead to more appropriate or more advantageous combinations of resources, materials, or means of production, although this may sometimes be the case. Furthermore, assessments of innovations often vary among actors depending on the individual situation. For the assessments themselves, it should be noted that the forms and criteria of valuation and evaluation (Lamont 2012) are also socially constituted. This being the case, they can turn out differently depending on context, varying, for instance, with the practices and criteria of relevant professional groups in the respective areas of activity.[5] It comes as no surprise that advocates and footdraggers, winners and losers certainly do not assess innovations nor the associated comparative advantages in the same way, be they economic or related to social prestige, the satisfaction of needs or something else (see also Rogers 2003: 15). And they not only diverge in their assessments but also in their ability to assert their positions. Actors thus recursively declare changes in form in the respective contexts to be innovations and apply their own individual assessments accordingly.[6] However, if the declaration of

---

5   The degree of novelty of the innovation and the means can vary, as well as the degree to which they are seen as things with which one can do things in a new way. Some novelties—such as organizations—make an imprint on entire eras of society, while others vanish again quite rapidly (such as, for instance, the Discman, which was once an innovative practice of music reception; see also Oudheusden et al. 2015; Tavassoli and Karlsson, 2015).

6   The possibility to declare something an innovation is constitutive of the innovation. That does not preclude that the declaration itself resembles more than 'innovation dust' (U. Meyer 2016) and simply varies what is known or even pretends that what is familiar is brand new, just as long as the accompanying claim that something is an

a change as an innovation is to attain social relevance, it must prove itself as such in social practices.

Fourth, this also entails a different understanding of the *diffusion of innovations*: innovations are not completed by the first act of the 'transfer of one imprinted form into another one', as traditionally assumed in the footsteps of Schumpeter (Fagerberg 2005). The idea of the diffusion of a *given* innovation that is possibly deviated from, which goes back to Everett Rogers (2003: 17), is replaced by a conception of diffusion as an *ongoing social production and reproduction of innovation*, during which both that which remains the same and that which changes are recursively produced, sustained, or possibly altered. Innovations, and the means of action and meanings with which they are associated, thus always have their own history and cannot be understood independently of it.

Fifth, another component of the practice-theoretical perspective on innovation involves the *embedding and embeddedness* of *innovations* in *ensembles of social practices*. As actors recursively construct innovations by drawing on social practices, they are always entangled in several social practices at once—and potentially in a variety of ways. Ensembles of social practices—which, besides practices of organized exploration and experimentation, can include many others, such as routines—are gaining significance for innovations and their extension in time and distanciation in space, depending on what is generated as an innovation, what means are required to do so, and which activities have been undertaken (Dodgson 2011). The network connections involved here among actors who are linked with each other by means of social practices, a connectedness that is mostly positively connoted in 'relational sociology' (Emirbayer 1997), can be highly ambivalent, es-

---

innovation is recognized as such in social practices. The declaration of something as an innovation is always accompanied by socially determined assignments of value and practices of evaluation (Antal, Hutter, and Stark 2015; Lamont 2012; Rammert 2014). Yet not all innovations are subject to discursive disputes; for instance, the use of the atomic bomb was not debated in this way, and other things—such as the changes in the form of traveling associated with rolling suitcases—are barely discussed or not discussed at all (I owe this juxtaposition to Raimund Hasse). In any case, innovations are always also based on more or less explicit attributions of meaning and evaluations that in turn are based on predetermined practices of declaration. In the process, what is new for some actors can be familiar to others. This is because, as James March and Herbert Simon already stated some time ago for organizations, "most innovations in an organization are a result of borrowing rather than invention" (March and Simon 1993: 209). Their statement also describes the mechanism by which perception and utilization of skills, developments, and means gain significance for innovations (Cohen and Levinthal 1990).

pecially for innovations.[7] Besides the often-proclaimed advantages, problems can also arise, for instance, information that is crucial to a business might be leaked to a competitor (Pahnke et al. 2015). Embedding innovations in ensembles of social practices means, furthermore, that innovations can influence, pave the way for, or trigger bundles and series of (other) innovations. Whether and to what extent existing innovations increase opportunities for others to come (Clausen et al. 2011) is just as relevant a question as how innovations mutually interact, that is, how they become part of, advance, displace, or generate other innovations—without it always being immediately clear or even unambiguously determinable who creates what or where the borderlines are between these processes. Innovations thus always construct both *continuities* and *changes in the hitherto customary*.

Sixth, innovations not only have a certain duration and spatial distribution; they also have *their time and their place while they contribute to creating them*. For example, innovations utilizing smartphones or mobile application software (apps) presuppose the existence of capital that is continuously on a quest for new, exploitable ideas, as well as the existence of the Web as a virtual 'place' for almost any form of transaction.

Seventh, innovations are *powerfully* produced and reproduced. Complex innovations in particular are prototypical examples of this. If one follows David Yoffie and Michael Cusumano (2015), for example, the success of the world's leading technology companies—Microsoft, Apple, and Intel—is based not least on the fact that they are capable of creating cross-industry platforms and ecosystems that en-

---

7 Exponents of structural network analysis have attributed networks of social relationships great significance for innovations and their diffusion. Mark Granovetter, for instance, emphasized 'weak ties' (Granovetter 1973, 1974) and Ronald Burt 'structural holes' (Burt 1992, 2005). Michel Ferrary and Mark Granovetter (2009) linked the robustness of the Silicon Valley innovation cluster first and foremost to venture capitalists and their connections with other actors. Yet actors of a 'clique' (with strong relationships among themselves) can under no circumstances ensure that all information flows in the same fashion. Information flow depends on what is at issue and which activities are linked (or not linked) with which practices in which ways. Moreover, not all actors are equally in the position of being able to actually articulate or use information in networks of relationships, precisely because networks of relationships feature these structural characteristics (Windeler 2001: 118ff.). Organizations, for instance, may be incapable of absorbing external ideas in spite of maintaining external relationships. The 'not invented here' syndrome is an example of this (Cohen and Levinthal 1990: 133). One can add to this networks of relationships among components (as in the case of technologies, for instance) that combine with the skills and abilities of actors and with space (Carlsson et al. 2002), as well as reflections on the performativity of networks (Healy 2015) or problems of developing appropriate indicators (Nelson et al. 2014).

able other producers to create products and services on the basis of an established technology that (other) actors can then appropriate as innovations. Michel Ferrary and Mark Granovetter (2009) report something similar when they show how venture capitalists together with other enterprises again and again pave the way for innovations in Silicon Valley in a controlled fashion. Occasionally, even national regulatory frameworks are revised or sites created, such as consortia, conference series, and the like, to enable innovations (Belt and Rip 1987; Schubert, Sydow, and Windeler 2013; Sydow et al. 2012). That said, innovations can yield results that even run counter to the interests of those who operate them. Furthermore, it is by no means always agreed who is able to appropriate the results (Dedrick, Kraemer, and Linden 2009). As a general rule, *innovations are* thus *contested* and accompanied by disputes. But this also applies more generally: "New ways threaten the old and those who are wedded to the old may prove highly intolerant" (Gardner 1981: 32)—and often for quite convincing reasons (Adner and Snow 2010; Ortmann et al. 1990). Nonetheless, innovations can also spread virtually unnoticed, as we see in the rolling suitcase example. Moreover, intended innovations can fail for a variety of reasons. Besides conflicts over (potential) consequences and ideologies, innovations can—as regards their performance and acceptance—fall far short of expectations or require capabilities that do not sufficiently exist. It is also true that "[i]f there is too much hype at the discovery stage and the product doesn't live up to the hype, that's one way of its becoming disappointing and abandoned, eventually" (Colapinto 2014: 18). Furthermore, the development of means that are constitutive for innovations can be unsuccessful or forbidden, their use even banned—as the example of the atom bomb teaches us. But innovations can also fail for entirely different reasons, as the 'not invented here' syndrome shows.

Drawing on the considerations above, I will define the practice-theoretical concept of innovation as follows: *innovation* is a change that social actors reflexively and recurrently produce and reproduce as a transfer of one imprinted form into another by drawing on social practices in their interactions. In innovation processes, social actors thus not only modify established forms. They reflexively and recurrently transmute imprinted forms into another in a particular manner. They create 'new' forms and destroy imprinted ones in socially proved ways. For social actors in innovation processes not only create, advance, and in some cases alter the mentioned transfer; in each case they also prove (and have to prove) the respective transfer as an innovation in social practices. In this way the constitution of innovations is intertwined with changes in social practices or even the production of new forms of activities in a particular context—that social actors view as outside the range of existing ones—that, in turn, influence the further constitution of innovations in time and space. In principle, anything to which an imprinted form can be attributed can be innovated—to whatever extent intended.[8] This applies, for instance, to objects, methods, procedures, regulations, forms of coordination (such as those characteristic of markets, organizations, or networks), and resource mobilization as well as to forms of signification, legitimation, and domination, types of capabilities, action fields, all the way to modes of sociation. Yet out of the sheer endless array of things that could be innovated only a selection actually become subject to innovation.[9]

To understand the social constitution of innovations and particularly that of innovations with a certain degree of complexity—one needs an analytical perspective that is able to include in the analysis institutional and structural requirements, regulations of social systems, and the capabilities of the actors involved to explain more exactly how innovations embedded in social contexts are produced

---

8   I am skeptical about the widely held assumption that, behind an innovation, there is always the intention of an actor or a group of actors to create an innovation (Godin 2015: 235). Not only do the participating actors differ, they also pursue different intentions. Furthermore, these innovations are occasionally put to uses that are quite different from what they were originally intended for, often producing effects that no one had considered (Gould and Vrba 1982; Villani et al. 2007). And for the actors it is often primarily about something other than innovations, such as economic, political, or other interests. Innovations can thus also be the unintended, unanticipated, or simultaneous result of actions otherwise motivated.

9   An example might illustrate what I mean when speaking of the highly selective realization of innovations. Our semiconductor study investigated innovation in the technology to manufacture computer chips (Sydow et al. 2012). In 2000, six alternative technological options were under discussion in this field of innovation. At the same time, people in the field agreed that for economic reasons there could be only one solution for the mass production of computer chips around the world. What is most interesting is how these options were narrowed down to that one solution. To make a complex story short, besides technical criteria regarding the feasibility and maturity of the technological alternatives, the globally leading researchers, employees of the corporations involved (such as Intel), system suppliers (such as ASML and Canon), and politicians included professional, economic, and political criteria in their assessments. The criteria were fed into a highly organized process of technology innovation on a global scale. A toolbox consisting of both field-specific and cross-cutting instruments and organizational arrangements was used to assess and coordinate collaboration in research and development as well as financing and manufacturing. This toolbox included (1) roadmaps for continuous planning, (2) conferences to exchange ideas, create shared viewpoints and means of legitimation, as well as establish agreement on collaborative research and political projects and survey and coordination tools, and (3) consortia such as SEMATECH (Lange et al. 2013; Schubert et al. 2013).

and reproduced than Schumpeter and many other innovation studies do.[10] Below I will present a practice-theoretical analytical framework that is informed by Anthony Giddens's structuration theory. The constitution of innovations is presented as a process that competent actors constitute by drawing on social practices; the interactions that they engage in reflect social institutions and regulations of social systems such as organizations (on this, see Figure 1 below). In Sections 2 to 4, I conceive of innovation societies as radically modern societies that are characterized at the level of social institutions by the modern principle of reflexivity, by the ensembles of driving forces of modern societies, and by sets of institutionalized positions. As further specifics of the social constitution of innovation in innovation societies, I highlight the general specifications of the conditions and the skills of the actors involved, which are shaped primarily by organizations, networks, and the fields of innovation. The specifics of the concrete issues of innovation I will not discuss further in this essay. Section 2 starts with *modern institutions*. Section 3 then discusses *structures* of social practices and the *skills of the parties involved*. Section 4 addresses the *regulation of social systems*, and Section 5 concludes with an outlook on *implications for innovation research* and the *development of the innovation society today*.

2 Reflexive Innovation and Institutions

In showing that creative destruction is an inherent feature of capitalist sociation, Schumpeter (2003) attributed significance to social context in the constitution of innovation. However, this insight is usually lacking in contemporary innovation

---

10 Innovations in the cultural sphere, for instance, address changed forms of signification that are used as innovations in social practices. In the political and economic sphere, innovations address changes in the form of domination that are utilized as innovations in social practices. In the political sphere, innovations principally pertain to changes in forms of shaping social time-spaces, the production and reproduction of bodies, associations of people, and life opportunities. In business, the issue is primarily about changes in forms of the power of disposition, in forms of use of the means of production (such as raw materials, the tools of production, and technologies), and in forms of the production and use of goods and services. In the field of law—for instance, in the context of prosecution or jurisprudence—innovations affect the transfer of the ingrained ways of making judgements and providing legitimation into other ways of doing so that are used as innovations in social practices (Giddens 1984: 33, 258). Innovations can, however, also combine references to different spheres of society and, in so doing, feature different points of reference (for the latter aspect, see also Rammert 2014 as well as Section 2.2 below).

studies. To understand innovation societies as contexts of reflexive innovation, I propose to choose a more general point of departure than Schumpeter did. Innovation societies today can be understood as radically modern societies, as societies characterized by the *modern principle of reflexivity* (Section 2.1). As radically modern societies, innovation societies are, contrary to Schumpeter's assumption, societies in which *capitalist economization* pervades not just the economy but all fields of action; together with *industrialization and rationalization*, it forms an integrated ensemble that acts as a driver of modern sociation (Section 2.2). Moreover, even in the process of innovation in the economy, it is not only entrepreneurs who play significant roles, as Schumpeter suggests. Rather, a number of different actors, embedded in ensembles, now assume institutional positions in innovation processes, among them also entrepreneurs in some areas (Section 2.3). My broader argument is that if we want to understand how innovations shape innovation societies today and are in turn shaped by them, we need to develop an understanding of the principles, drivers, and networks of positions presented in the next sections.

2.1 Reflexivity as a Principle of Modern Sociation and Innovation

Today, reflexivity is an institutional feature of modern societies and the innovations that they generate. By making this determination, I draw on a thought by Giddens (1990a), who contrasts the form of *reflexivity* observed in the modern era with traditional forms of sociation. Reflexivity is thus *not* an invention of modernity, but it develops a specific form in it:

> The reflexivity of modern social life consists in the fact that social practices are constantly examined and reformed in the light of incoming information about those very practices, thus constitutively altering their character (ibid.: 38).

What is special about the *modern principle of reflexivity* becomes apparent by contrasting it with traditional reflexivity. When actors act traditionally, they monitor, rationalize, and motivate their own actions and those of others as well as occurrences in terms of whether they provide a legitimate contribution to sustaining traditions or changing them in the spirit of these traditions. Exemplarily, Augustine's aphorism "Do not seek to understand in order to believe, but believe that thou mayest understand" refers to traditional actions. This is because he not only ties human knowledge and insight to faith but also sees the purpose of life in living in accordance with faith. In the modern era, this is completely different. The modern imperative is to *act in light of ever new information about social practices and how they might be organized differently*. Actors—just as observers—are thus called upon to act without protection by some higher order (such as religions) and on the basis of forms of order created by people (which can be potentially revised). The empirical validity of a reflexive order presumes actors who engage in reflexive action, who at least implicitly recognize these orders de facto, and who assume that they can procure suitable information if they wish to do so and that such information tends to provide an appropriate foundation for their involvement in events, activities, and relationships. We will discuss this in more detail shortly.

To say that actors act reflexively does *not necessarily* imply that they have a more comprehensive understanding of social issues or that all changes—including innovations—are equally likely. Actors always take into account only what they are paying attention to—and this is not independent of the actors' abilities and the conditions governing their actions. Moreover, they give meaning to what selectively occupies their attention in quite different ways as they recursively create, advance, and possibly change situations, circumstances, processes, and so on in the course of their actions. The information used in acting is anything but neutral simply because it is always *selectively* produced and reproduced—sometimes to a very high degree, for instance, in organizations. What is also crucial is that a large portion of the capacity to act is at the level of *practical skills*. Actors may know how one is expected to act under given conditions and show their understanding in their activities but may not necessarily be able to explain in detail why it is necessary to do so in this way under these circumstances. There is always much that actors do not grasp even to slightest extent and definitely not in depth—particularly under the conditions of radical modernity. The information and knowledge that actors use today, not least in innovation processes, necessarily require, for instance, expert knowledge that they for the most part cannot control independently. Modern-day actors are nevertheless expected to act competently; they are assumed to know how to exchange goods and services impersonally, work in teams, use airplanes, or live in high-rise buildings, and so on, and particularly how to collaborate with others to produce and reproduce innovations. That they do not know how all this works in detail does not mean that they do not act on the basis of their understanding and knowledge and express this in their activities. Further on, it does not exclude that they can give reasons why they do what they do, or did what they did, in a certain way and not differently. Their ability to do what they do presupposes confidence in, for instance, ensembles of technological achievements, expert knowledge, and (other) people (Giddens 1990a); it is furthermore based on practical knowledge and some degree of control (Sydow and Windeler 2003). From this it follows that it is interesting to whom or what actors in innovation processes pay attention, what they focus on, and in which way and why, and whether this produces, advances, or paves the way for (or impedes) alternatives, the new, and innovations (on reflexivity, see also the essay by Hubert Knoblauch in this volume).

Although contexts of action today continue to display different combinations of both modern and traditional conditions, and people certainly do not always act only in ways that qualify as modern, the modern principle of reflexivity is even further radicalized in the era of *reflexive modernity*. The social world is now more generally scrutinized and (re-)configured under the spotlight of a continuous stream of ever new information; the practices of valuation and evaluation themselves are also increasingly designed in a reflexive way. Exploring, testing, and experimenting while taking contexts and means of action into account that are different from those that are known and likewise making use of different capabilities than those that are usually employed becomes a permanent state. Actors are now increasingly required to act in a modern way and, in so doing, take practices of reflexive valuation and evaluation into consideration, assess both the given and that which deviates from it, and check it for usability. In this way, innovations today are produced and reproduced reflexively to a certain degree, rendering them reflexive innovations. Actors constitute this form of innovation recursively on the basis of a continuous stream of new information, which is systematically—and to some degree even strategically—generated about *conditions, consequences and ways in which actors recursively produce and reproduce innovations in time-space*. In this way, they not only continuously and systematically generate information and knowledge about innovations but observe and design innovations anew again and again in light of new information and new knowledge. *Reflexive innovation* thus refers to innovations that are borne by an incessant process of producing new information and knowledge. In principle, this amounts to a *pluralization* of possibilities for innovation, precisely because they are less determined by that which is familiar, customary, instilled, and constantly repeated.

The fundamental pluralization of possibilities for innovation under conditions of reflexive modernity is also based on actors recursively taking into account modern means of production and reproduction of the social, for instance, modern forms of dealing with times and spaces, symbolic tokens, technological achievements, and expert knowledge—or at least they are expected to do so to a certain degree. Modern ways of dealing with *times and spaces* are characterized by actors primarily coordinating activities and events in terms of measured times and spaces (Giddens 1990a: 14ff.; Gilbert-Walsh 2010; Koselleck 2000: 78ff.) in time-space and, on this basis, by reflexively connecting and/or decoupling and recombining the places, regions, and spaces in which they are produced and reproduced. In principle, modern-day actors can thus continuously dis-embed innovation activities and events from their respective contexts in new or altered ways by employing new or modified means of action and pursuing divergent aims and horizons, and then re-embed them in time-space and in activity and event streams that are reflexively linked (or decoupled) in varying ways. These re-embeddings can transcend the boundaries of individual social domains, national territories, or political-administrative units.[11] The possibilities for reflexive innovation are furthermore supported, enhanced, and complemented by modern forms of handling *symbolic tokens* (such as money), *technological achievements* (such as individual machines, technology platforms, or technologies combined in buildings or infrastructures) and through reflexive forms of the use of *expert knowledge* (such as that of professional groups) (Giddens 1990a: 27; Orlikowski and Scott 2008; Windeler 2014: 239ff.). Further adding to this—and conveyed, for instance, through consulting, Internet searches, and recruiting employees of various professions—are forms of observation, rationalization, and the inclusion of hitherto disregarded contexts, means of action, and skills. Today these are included systematically and not just 'experimentally.' Sometimes they are even designed to initiate or enhance innovations and generate alternative options. In addition, actors are to a certain degree expected to use information and knowledge about moods (Silver 2011), dispositions (Bourdieu 1977: 78 ff.), emotions (Nussbaum 2013), and the 'other of reason' (Böhme and Böhme 1985); this, too, is information, and this knowledge is also relevant to something happening or not happening (Windeler 2014: 234ff.). Moods and emotions can—as the performances of Steve Jobs, the former CEO of Apple, testify to—be used at least to increase the social significance of innovations and/or the opportunities for their exploitation. This means that change must not necessarily await suitable opportunities for it to become an innovation. To a certain degree, opportunities

---

11 Taylorist/Fordist forms of organizing production are prominent examples (Boyer and Freyssenet 2003). Current extensions of these modes of production are Industry 4.0, which envisions the digital transformation of industry, and logistic chains by means of which flows of goods and activities are coordinated on a global scale (Gereffi and Fernandez-Stark 2011). Globally coordinated research and development activities attest to the fact that nation states and policies defined by governments are not always at the center of attention, without, however, being irrelevant (Sydow et al. 2012). Places, as geographically situated physical settings, are reflexively related to one another, interconnected, and bound together in space via their utilization periods and (in time via the) time-bound chains of events that occur within their boundaries just as times, activities, and events are bound to spaces. Both places and interaction partners seem more easily replaceable in times of reflexive modernity, although they do not lose their significance completely owing to their specific characteristics or specific capacities, as long as the differences continue to be treated as relevant; some even gain in significance.

can also be (collectively) created—however, not always successfully. Moreover, innovations are by no means always a response to conditions of scarcity. Sometimes abundance and excess are the problem and one that calls for innovations of a special kind—for instance, how to deal with a surplus of data or information, individually and as a society (Abbott 2014).

That which has been established, no matter what it may be, even the most current innovation, tends to come under pressure in radicalized modernity, increasingly requiring specific justifications for it to be continued.[12] The complexity of innovation processes is in principle systematically enhanced through the pluralization of potentially and actually relevant conditions, consequences, and ways in which actors recursively produce and reproduce innovations in time and space. This complexity is selectively reduced, however, by employing expertise, trust, and social practices of dealing with these situations. The social practices of dealing with the universalizing radicalized principle of reflexivity drive modernity and keep it on the path of reflexivity while they also institutionalize the form of reflexive innovation, which in turn further develops and, in some instances, changes modern institutions in specific ways.

2.2 Reflexive Innovation and the *Trias* of Capitalist Economization, Industrialization, and Rationalization

Reflexive innovations are currently being created, advanced, and in some cases altered in innovation societies by drawing on *ensembles of modern institutions*—as practices that are deeply sedimented in time-space (Giddens 1979: 80)—rather than by only referring to, for instance, economic institutions—as Schumpeter supposes at least for the modern economy—or 'post-modern' institutions, however they may be defined (Giddens 1990a: 11f.). The ensembles of modern institutions are shaped in turn by the driving forces of modernity, as determined by Karl Marx, Émile Durkheim, and Max Weber, which today, however, are recurrently modified in a reflexive manner. Present-day innovation societies are driven, as the assumption goes, by reflexive forms of capitalist economization, industrialization, and rationalization.

The thesis of radical modernity, which I have adopted, and modified, from Anthony Giddens, is based on the idea that modernity is taking a new shape and that this process is mediated by forms of radicalized reflexivity. This is equally true,

---

12 Yet even traditions can be continued, but only on the basis of knowledge that is itself not reflected in traditions (Giddens 1990a: 36ff.; Windeler 2014: 283).

as I will claim, for the driving forces that characterize modernity and the innovation processes that come with it. The thesis I wish to propose is as follows. In accordance with Karl Marx, we live in a modernized *capitalist* society today in which—mediated by the reflexively advanced principle of *capital valorization*—the production of goods and accumulation of capital create incessant momentum, and *capitalist economization* forms the sociation and the innovation processes embedded therein, even beyond the sphere of the economy. Sociation and its dynamics—and here I draw on Émile Durkheim—is additionally characterized by processes of reflexive *industrialization*, that is, continuous processes of reflexively advanced forms of a *complex division of labor and industrial exploitation of nature*. Today, it is not least *rationalization*—as I intend to argue with reference to Max Weber—that leaves its imprint in reflexive form not only on innovation processes but also on sociation, its momentum, and on the ongoing disenchantment of the world. This means that actors today produce and reproduce *spheres of life* reflexively on the basis of science, modern technology, and bureaucracy and that this extends not only to the economy but also to politics, technology development, law, art, the military, and even to lifestyles and the individual conduct of life. In so doing, they are assessing future developments and necessary 'precautions' *on the basis of intersubjectively defined criteria* as opposed to criteria given through habits, customs, conventions, and traditions. Thereby, they *systematize*, at least to some degree, *by rigorously calculating* the information considered relevant for the purpose of rationalization and *calculate* social events mostly on the basis of *numbers* and *numerical* considerations. In this way, they methodically *control and shape* events, activities, and relationships in those spheres and in innovation processes on the basis of rather specific information and knowledge that is acquired while focusing on rationalization.

The reflexivity principle of modernity thus also accounts for the driving forces of modernity as defined by the classics of sociology and thus shape the basic conditions of innovation in a modified form. The driving forces, too, are (individually or in ensembles) reflexively created anew, sustained, and, as the case may be, transformed time and again. Practices of valuation and evaluation are moments in these processes as they help orient the reflexively linked (and decoupled) driving forces in present-day fields of action, co-create their reflexive manifestations and interconnections, and in turn are themselves shaped by the ensembles of driving forces. In these processes, it is their ongoing incorporation in social interaction that recurrently confers upon the driving forces (and their ensembles) their socially constituted power and adaptability.

Current debates have highlighted this. For some time now, a number of innovations have been triggered, for instance, through processes of reflexively driven 'marketization' in other areas of society (such as science or health) as well as arrangements at the interface of neoliberal capitalism and social market economy or have been influenced by these processes. Public disputes today about issues concerning the industrial exploitation of coal, oil, and gas or renewable energies, while being fed by information, expertise, and knowledge, are not only drawing a great deal of attention to the forms of industrial exploitation of nature but also often initiate innovations and shape the ways in which they are evaluated. Never-ending discourses on issues of intensifying bureaucratization and the need to reduce or transform it bear witness to the reflexive inclusion of the rationalization of the world in public as well as private communication and, at the same time, are subject to multifaceted innovations. What the debates, disputes, and discourses also make clear is that at issue here are ensembles of driving forces, for instance, when the matter in question is renewable energies and the criticism thereof. Individual driving forces can have a dominant impact on the formation of the institutions and structures and also innovations found in individual spheres, such as economization in the economy. However, when one force dominates, the others do not immediately become insignificant. It is rather that forces interacting in ways that match well improves their efficacy—without, however, determining what will happen or can happen.

2.3 Reflexively Institutionalized Positions, Position Practices, and Forms of Positioning

In today's innovation societies, reflexive innovations are further characterized by institutionalized actors, interactions, and relationships. Besides the entrepreneurs to whom Schumpeter referred, modern institutions play an important role in constituting other relevant actors of innovation, such as venture capitalists, regulatory actors, consumers, or users, any of whom may be involved in innovation processes. Whether these actors are individuals, organizations, nation states, or others, they not only operate under given institutional conditions, but they themselves are also institutionalized as innovation actors. Modern-day innovation processes thus feature reflexively institutionalized positions or roles—roles if the normative rights and obligations associated with positions are relatively clearly formulated. Institutionalized guidelines and ideas that indicate what it means to be an innovation actor in general and, for instance, a venture capitalist in particular are associated with requirements and ideas that specify what it means to act as such and to maintain relationships with others accordingly (this I will address in more detail below). These institutionalized requirements and ideas can also vary depending on the field of action. Innovation actors are thus not individual actors (e.g., individual entrepreneurs), as Schumpeter would have us believe, but actors that are institutionally embedded in networks of positions by which they are related to other actors and by which their activities are interrelated. In some contexts—such as in Silicon Valley—even the networks of positions are institutionalized.

The institutionalized forms of action that individual innovation actors or groups of actors in innovation processes are expected to display include financing or financial support (Ferrary and Granovetter 2009; Lange et al. 2013), signalizing, embedding, collective learning, and selection (Ferrary and Granovetter 2009), participation, and conflict resolution (Windeler and Wirth 2005), the creation of public awareness (Schubert et al. 2013), influence on legislative processes (Barley 2010), standardization and patent registration, valuation and evaluation (Lamont 2012), as well as the regulation of innovation in social systems such as organizations, networks, and fields of innovation. Additional activities to be mentioned here are generating and monitoring institutionally codified terms and meanings, legitimations, or forms of powerful implementation of innovations (or the prevention thereof).

People who hold positions monitor, control, and shape innovations. In so doing, they incorporate practices of valuation and evaluation that are institutionalized in fields of action, practices that today are often determined by professional groups or professions. Some act in the roles of authorized representatives or self-proclaimed 'guardians' and monitor compliance with institutionally defined guidelines. This usually results in struggles among actors over relevant practices, knowledge (bases), and relevant skills—for instance, between professional groups in the respective domains (Abbott 1988). Sometimes organizations such as associations, clubs, or inter-organizational governance units, which is what Neil Fligstein and Doug McAdam (2012) have written about, actively assume positions responsible for defining, monitoring, and generalizing the conditions that govern action in the field in question. Greenpeace represents such an organization for the environment. Fields of action thus cultivate patterns, established in time-space, of coordinated responsibilities and forms of conflict resolution and consensus building. The designations, assessments, and efficacy of positions may vary with the structural features of different sets of positions. New positions may even evolve by chance owing to fortunate circumstances, as the history of the emergence of venture capitalists in the USA illustrates (Kenney 2011). What positions actors occupy today is thus based on modern institutions, rules and resources, and the usual solutions predominant in the fields of action on the one hand and on the reflexive activities of positioning on the part of those involved, who in turn act on the basis of conditions regulated by social systems on the other.

In their activities, individuals, organizations, and nation states thus express modern ideas of actors and innovation actors—possibly of different kinds depending on the field of action—that identify them as universally 'responsible' and 'authorized' to contribute to shaping the world by means of institutionalized activities (J. W. Meyer 2008); however, today these ideas also require that they act reflexively, both individually and in coordination with others, and take into account the institutionalized patterns and ensembles of reflexively formed driving forces that are ingrained in positions, the actions associated with these positions (henceforth referred to as 'position actions'), and the contexts of interaction. Actors are thus authorized, legitimized, and prompted to create, advance, and possibly change innovations by drawing on the institutionalized forms of signification, legitimation, and domination ingrained in innovation practices as well as on the forms of coordination and regulation of innovations engaged in with others that are inherent to these practices. Which of the positions and actions in these positions—in interrelated ensembles of such positions and position actions—play a central role in individual innovation processes and which are more peripheral is a question to be answered empirically, as is that of who takes and can take which positions. Actors today are thus not only prompted—and this may differ depending on context—but also authorized in a socially recognized and legitimated manner to represent their own interests in innovation processes and beyond as well as to (responsibly) act as representatives for 'others.' This applies even to 'entities lacking agency'—such as ecosystems, animals, and plants as well as imagined actors such as fetuses or endangered languages or cultures—and to 'principles,' such as those of law and science, of the professions, or also of high culture or etiquette (J. W. Meyer 2008; Meyer, Boli, and Thomas 1987: 24f.; Meyer and Jepperson 2000: 62ff.). Whether innovation processes differ when they involve pursuing innovations of interested agents compared to those pursuing innovations of 'entities lacking agency' is an empirical question. What this extensive institutional authorization also does is to institutionally expand and restrict the possibilities for innovation at the same time. This makes a substantial contribution to socially constructing, restricting, and enabling the institutionalized pluralization of innovations and to further advancing the institutionalization of innovation societies.

The radicalized reflexivity principle, along with the driving forces of modernity and the institutionalized (ensembles of) positions, not only lends particular momentum to innovation processes to modernize but also plays a part in determining which innovations are generated (and which are not) and how this occurs. However, since institutions do not determine how actors act and since their social significance unfolds by actors taking them into account in acting, the extent to which modern institutions require innovations depends on how actors reflexively monitor, rationalize, and refer to them in their activities. A crucial factor in understanding innovation is thus how actors—coordinated with others—reflexively create, sustain, and possibly change innovations by drawing on modern institutions and which possible alignments of conditions and practices of innovation they develop in the process.[13] I will now discuss the conceptual foundation of how to analyze from a practice-theoretical perspective how actors take institutions into account in acting and lend them significance.

3 Reflexive Innovation, Structures, and Modern Actors

Joseph Schumpeter experimented all his life with different approaches to include the relationship between action and structure in innovation processes. Contemporary innovation discourse is also characterized by the paradigms of creation, evolution, and structure or institution, as I indicated at the outset of this essay. With this in mind, I propose an alternative approach to the problem of structure and action in innovation by drawing on Anthony Giddens. This approach substitutes the duality of structure for the dualism of action and structure prevalent in innovation research. In this alternative view, innovations are recursively produced and reproduced by actors in interactions and relationships in time-space. This is because actors—be they individuals, organizations, or nation states—constitute everything social (and thus also societies, innovations, and the actors themselves) by drawing on social practices while *actualizing* in interactions capabilities stored in traces of memory and forms of action used in social practices, which have evolved at the level of ensembles of societies and organizations (⇩ in Fig. 1). And in so doing, they *(re-)produce* (themselves as) actors as well as, for instance, organizations and society as a whole, including their institutionalized forms and conditions (⇧ in Fig. 1). From this it follows that actors always have some latitude; what actors do is fully determined neither by institutions nor by the requirements of social systems or situational circumstances. It is rather the rules and resources that are ingrained in social practices and actualized in interactions as well as the generalized capacity to act associated with them (which indicate to actors which capacity to act is usually implied in a certain set of rules and resources) that invariably enable actors

---

13 These alignments also extend beyond efficiency, effectiveness, or supposed functional necessities (Boli and Thomas 1997; DiMaggio and Powell 1983). According to John W. Meyer (2009), they result in a 'world polity' that nevertheless takes neither the reflexivity principle of radically modern societies adequately into account nor the specifics of the ensembles of modern institutions in different fields of action.

to act skillfully, precisely because they restrict the possibilities of action. On this basis, actors also create innovations recursively by actively engaging with a given world that they not only interpret but also co-create by using ensembles of social practices that mediate between actors and the world, without, however, controlling events in this way—and certainly not comprehensively.

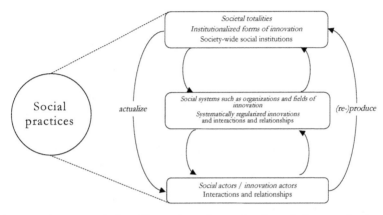

Figure 1 Social constitution of innovation—the practice-theoretical perspective (my own illustration).

Actors are confronted with *textures of conditions* in innovation processes. These textures are constituted, first, by actors recursively taking into account radical modern institutional conditions and forms of innovation (as discussed in Section 2), second, by the regulations of innovation activity that are primarily shaped in organizations, networks, and fields (which will be discussed in Section 4 below), and, third, by actors reflexively considering the situational conditions encountered in interaction situations. These textures of conditions are produced and reproduced, in ever-recurring cycles, as the medium and result of the social constitution of innovations outlined in Figure 1. Actors today are expected to command and express a certain *repertoire of reflexive skills*, mediated via the textures of conditions, particularly in innovation processes. It is assumed that actors involved in innovation reflexively and recursively take into account in appropriate ways content-related and procedural conditions and requirements (Windeler 2014). And when actors actualize and express suitable skills in the course of action, they not only demonstrate their understanding of events, they also prove themselves to be competent, even if their skills—as shown in Figure 1—are the product of social systems (Giddens 1990a: 79). What is decisive is this: even though the actors' knowledge is above all practical, their understanding and knowledge determined by society and always limited, and their information always selective and often inadequate, they use their understanding, information, and knowledge as their basis for action. Any explanation of innovation (or of the social in general) that were to ignore the actors' understanding of events and how they use this understanding in action is thus destined to fall short from the outset since that which is investigated includes what (other) actors have constituted as significant in action (Giddens 1984: 179, 213).[14]

> This is a mutual interpretative interplay between social science and those whose activities compose its subject matter—a 'double hermeneutic'. The theories and findings of the social sciences cannot be kept wholly separate from the universe of meaning and action which they are about (ibid.: xxxii f.).

But how do actors generate their ability to constitute innovations by drawing on existing textures of conditions? Actors recurrently produce and reproduce their capacity to act in innovation processes in time-space by recursively and reflexively monitoring, rationalizing, and motivating activities and observing and reflecting on events in these processes and beyond. They draw on actualized traces of memory that show repertoires of possible solutions, means of action, and forms of action envisioned in action (in innovation processes). This connects current action with earlier situations of action that one has experienced, learned about, or observed. In this process, actors recursively produce in interactions information, knowledge, and their understanding of innovations and how these three elements are socially embedded in time-space. This information, knowledge, and understanding is produced in the three dimensions of the social defined in structuration theory: *signification, legitimation,* and *domination* (ibid.: 29). As a result, actors have an understanding and knowledge—particularly for contexts that they are familiar with—of how to signify an innovation in the respective context and assign it meaning, evaluate it, and how to use material (such as nature, raw materials, and other material objects) and immaterial things (such as knowledge, social networks, and influence on peoples' opportunities in life) as a facility in a socially recognized way usually associated therewith. They can thus actively incorporate given re-

---

14 Actors can, for instance, use given requirements for different reasons and in different ways. They can, first, use them intentionally, second, because they consider their use natural, without explicitly associating interests with them, or, third, because they do not see any opportunities (so far) to change the situation that requires or suggests using the guidelines. One arrives at very different explanations, however, depending on what is the case.

quirements recursively in their actions. Unlike the common assumptions made by structural, institutional, and evolutionary approaches in innovation research, their actions are thus neither determined nor can they act at will within the framework of given requirements. Instead, rules and resources actualized in interactions as well as the perceived generalized capacity to act provide actors with orientations for acting competently under given conditions, suitably to the given framework, and by making use of their scope for action.

Rules and resources ingrained in innovation practices along with the generalized capacity to act offer actors the *techniques and generalizable procedures* usually employed in these practices as well as an idea of *the skills that one usually acquires by using them*. They indicate how to skillfully interact with others (in innovation processes) under given conditions—for instance, by including expert knowledge that largely exceeds one's own control—and thereby create, advance, and possibly change innovations as well as declare changes to be innovations. The rules and resources allow actors to signify changes as innovations with the help of interpretation schemes, evaluate them by applying norms, and influence them by using facilities, the means of which include symbolic tokens as well as technological achievements and expertise. The rules and resources of innovation combined with the generalized capacity to act to have *constitutive* and *generative* effects in social practices. This is because they enable actors to recursively produce and reproduce innovations, on a recurrent basis, in interaction with others, even if the capacities vary among actors and depend on the circumstances of action. They also allow actors to create new significations, legitimations, and ways of exercising domination as well as to generate new skills (for instance, in terms of creative monitoring, rationalizing, and acting). In addition, they make it possible to recombine existing techniques and procedures with commonly used capabilities—both systematically and playfully. The rules and resources together with the generalized capacity to act by employing them thus puts actors in a position not only to repeat existing things but also *to imagine new things, to 'design the future' by discovering, shaping, and attributing meaning* and *to develop ideas of whether and how one could realize what has been imagined*—for instance, to assess possibilities for generating innovations (see Beckert [2013] on the significance of imagined futures for capitalist economies and Popitz [2000] on the significance of creativity). In so doing, the imagined structures the realm of possibilities for a future present.

What is innovated and in which way is thus oriented, enabled, and restricted by what has been brought to mind reflexively. The way actors envision given requirements in action fundamentally contributes to shaping what is innovated and how that occurs. This is so because societies, organizations, networks and fields, and interactions—and hence all the levels of the social addressed in Figure 1—are oriented by ensembles of rules and resources that are ingrained in social practices, the generalized capacity to act that they represent, and traces of memory that actors recursively and mutually convey to each other in interaction (Windeler and Sydow 2001). That said, innovations may not be realized in some circumstances quite simply because they fall between the cracks of institutional, systemic, and situational attention, conditions impede them, or actors are simply overwhelmed or fail to develop sufficient interest in the change in question.

The social dimensions of signification, domination, and legitimation—conveyed via the rules and resources used in social practices of innovation—also constitute the *dimensions of innovation* and their *valuation and evaluation* (here I am expanding on Michèle Lamont's [2012] thoughts in this direction). They do so because not only meanings and evaluations but also forms of domination are always ingrained in innovations, innovation regimes, and the attribution of value. Thus, what needs to be determined is which significations, which evaluations, and which uses of which resources as well as which generalized capacity to act characterize individual innovations and how they interact in the individual contexts of given structural and institutional conditions. It is also interesting to identify which actors create, are able to use, and actually do use the realm of possibility for innovation, the evaluation of innovation, and the declaration of something as representing an innovation and in which ways they do so. This is so because the realms of possibility by no means determine action, as I have pointed out above, even though they may often not offer a great number of alternatives. What they most certainly do, however, is promote certain lines of action by selectively restricting the possibilities of action.

4 Regulation of Innovation: Organizations, Networks, and Fields of Innovation

Schumpeter did not discuss the production and reproduction of innovations in organizations in any depth. Innovation research on the whole is characterized by considerable gaps in this respect. On the one hand, there are numerous studies and reflections on innovation that neglect or even completely omit the so-called meso level of the social. On the other hand, there are a great number of studies that explicitly address organizations and networks in the context of innovations while forgetting the social embedding of organizations, networks, and fields. Both of these gaps need to be addressed, as innovation processes in innovation societies cannot be understood without including organizations and social institutions since actors take them into account in their actions.

Organizations and selected networks are important in innovation processes not only as actors, as I have made clear in Sections 2 and 3. Together with what we have referred to as fields of innovation, they constitute *institutionalized 'sites of innovation.'* As interwoven meso orders, they not only specify the institutional requirements at the level of society but, by what they regulate and what they do not, they also play a significant part in orchestrating the conditions under which actors produce and reproduce innovations. Through their systems of regulation, organizations, networks, and fields of innovation thus shape to a relevant extent what is done at any one time and which results these activities can potentially yield or not.[15] In this way, they specifically enable and restrict the ability to act of the actors involved in innovations—and thus the innovations themselves. When considering these systems of regulation, however, we must not forget that these regulations not only reflect modern institutions, social practices, and the ability of actors at the level of the social, as illustrated in Figure 1, but actors in turn, drawing on regulated social practices, also play a substantial role in forming the regulations themselves (see Figure 1 again).

What is (or is not) subject to reflexive regulation, in which way, and why in contexts of innovation is an empirical question. The empirical task is therefore to determine—as I have done elsewhere—what general conditions characterize the following aspects in the individual context of action:

(1) "the *selection* of actors, issues, action domains, means of action, and modes of time-space coordination—in the social system or in its environments,

(2) the *allocation* of means and time-spaces to actors, activities, events, and the settings of action,

(3) the *evaluation* of the relevant system occurrences,

(4) the *system integration* (or disintegration) of activities of present and absent actors as well as of artifacts, types of action, or technologies,

(5) the configuration of *orderings of positions and* of *positionings* of activities, tasks, issues, types of action sites, system units, procedures and programs, artifacts, and responsibilities, and what general conditions characterize

(6) the *constitution of the system borders* between units (e.g., departments) of the system as well to other systems. What is regulated is, for instance, activities

---

15 Some social systems (e.g., all organizations as well as selected inter-organizational networks) specifically develop the collective ability to regulate, transfer special tasks in the regulation of system events to individual actors (such as managers), and continually use the knowledge acquired to shape such regulations systematically. But even in organizations, it is *not solely* 'managers' who shape the order of the system but rather *all* actors relevant to the social system, yet not all to the same extent. Moreover, social systems are always confronted with the regulations of other social systems and their wider contexts.

of 'boundary spanners' or salesrooms, the management of resource flows, the access to system means, the use and dissemination of sensitive information, the inclusion of issues that are not part of the system, the permeability and surveillance of system borders, the ways of dealing with conflicts over the demarcation or shifting of borders, and the embedding of activities and events in contexts across systems or sub-systems" (Windeler 2014: 249ff., my translation).

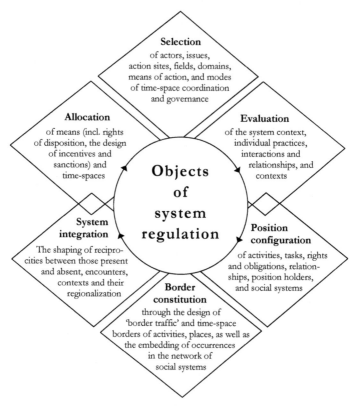

Figure 2   The objects of system regulation (Windeler 2014: 250, adapted).

The interlaced meso orders of organizations, networks, and fields, which are gaining increasing importance for innovation processes today, are not least a medium and result of social practices in which actors pave the way for innovations by cooperating in a regulated manner long before innovations become valuated and evaluated in markets or public discourse. Precisely because regulations of organizations, networks, and fields usually mutually determine each other in innovation processes, it is helpful to consider the structural characteristics of each of the respective orders separately.

Organizations—whether non-profit organizations, governmental organizations, or economic organizations—are considered by many to be the most significant innovation of mankind, not only because they are essential for the creation, implementation, and proliferation of capitalism, socialism, and democracy but also because they shape a great number of innovations (Böhme 2004: 28ff.; North, Wallis, and Weingast 2009; Weber 1978). Organizations are ascribed this significance in innovation processes particularly because they offer actors a specific, organizational form for the pursuit of innovations. It is a form that does *not* directly define the contents of the innovation itself but specifies a specific way of creating, sustaining, and possibly changing innovations. In specifying how to go about the task of innovation, organizations enable actors to jointly pursue innovations with others in an organized fashion and produce and reproduce innovation for other people (such as shareholders, members of an association, or citizens of a state) and for other purposes (e.g., to protect the basis of life) highly selectively and in a focused way. What is special about the organizational form of innovation results from organizations *coordinating the conditions of their reproduction highly reflexively* in time-space (Giddens 1990b: 302). This means organizations administer activities, events, and processes both within and outside of organizations in a highly reflexive manner. In this way, they not only constitute very specific conditions for innovations but also shape the modern principle of reflexivity to a significant degree and are in turn also shaped by this principle to a substantial extent. In innovation processes, organizations continuously generate, in a highly reflexive manner, selective information and knowledge, in accordance with the organization's specific focus of attention, about internal and external contexts of action, practices, and generalized skills and abilities that the organization deems relevant; they make use of this knowledge for administration, for the highly reflexive shaping of the conditions of action, and for organizational action in general. This implies that organizations are particularly well suited to meet the requirements of reflexive innovation and create innovations of this type—which, however, by no means precludes that the results can continue to be highly ambivalent, precisely because their reflexive focus tends to be systematically myopic toward much that they classify as less important. Modern-day organizations even transform themselves into reflexive organizations as a medium and result of actively embedding themselves in radical modernity and being embedded by the activities of other actors (Windeler 2015). If appropriately organized, they can expand their ability to regulate innovation processes, assume specific organizational roles in innovation processes, establish patterns of action expected in such roles, and actively contribute to shaping the specification of roles and positions in fields of action. At the same time, organizations' ability to act in innovation processes—despite the degree of agency that they are able to generate—should not be overestimated. There is much that does not even come into their organizational focus. There are also many things that go on in an organization that does not follow the same pattern throughout the organization; there may, for instance, be some variation among departments: one might be promoting an innovation while the other is undermining it. Overall, even highly powerful organizations cannot control innovation processes—let alone completely. But it is nonetheless also true that they can develop a specific ability to make use of innovations and can set conditions for innovations within and beyond the organization. In this respect, it is interesting, specifically for innovation studies, how organizations regulate and coordinate initial conditions for innovations and the processes of creating them. It is all the more astonishing that a great number of innovation studies pay very little attention to organizations.[16]

Let us now turn from individual organizations to inter-organizational networks. In *inter-organizational networks* organizations coordinate activities with other organizations and are essential for innovation throughout society today. They are characterized by the fact that they regulate and coordinate interactions and rela-

---

16 Three examples might briefly indicate the relevance of organization and organizations. One example is Facebook. It operates its communication platform very deliberately according to a fixed format, requiring that users submit to using all kinds of defined functions such as the so-called 'Like' button or to being targeted by advertising (Dolata 2015). In this way, Facebook has significantly influenced innovations in communication practices in recent years. The organizational arrangements of *research institutes* or *labs* also have a significant impact on innovations. This is because the lab is, unlike Karin Knorr Cetina (1988: 89, my translation) assumes, far more than just "a room that accommodates utensils and equipment for conducting [research] that scientists can combine to 'experiments.'" Labs and research institutes organize research. To this end, they usually select participants in a very deliberate way, determine topics and domains to be investigated, equip research teams with buildings, apparatuses, and other resources such as time and money, and define general conditions for the collaboration with other labs and actors. The same applies to *research-funding organizations* such as the German Research Association (DFG) or ministries involved in research funding: "In particular, what has gone overlooked in this discussion are organizational practices at the level of the funding source. Managers in research funding organizations like the National Science Foundation must translate broad agency goals into a multitude of operational decisions. How to choose the scientific fields to support? How to evaluate and select among proposals? How to manage ongoing research programs? These organizational practices undoubtedly affect the behavior of scientists in some way and may very well impact the rate and direction of scientific and inventive activity. This raises the questions: What practices matter and in what way?" (Colatat 2015: 874).

tionships among *more than two* organizations, which remain autonomous, primarily with a view to the *enduring sets of interrelationships* constituted between them (Windeler 2001: 231ff.). Inter-organizational networks are thus linked in a specific way with the organizations that support them, and practices and regulations at the network and organization level are recursively interwoven (Windeler and Sydow 2001). The recursive linking of organizational practices and regulations among participants in the network poses great challenges to the organizations involved and requires special abilities from them while at the same time opening up possibilities for them to expand their capacity to act (Battilana and Lee 2014; Bromley and Meyer 2017; Jandhyala and Phene 2015; Meyer and Rowan 1977; Parsons 1956, 1957; Pfeffer and Salancik 1978; Thompson 2004; Windeler 2001, 2014). By combining cooperation and competition in a particular way, they generate opportunities to make joint use of or generate resources in the network, to jointly cultivate markets, to collaboratively develop innovations, as well as to jointly influence the relevant contexts of action (e.g., to influence legislation [Barley 2010]) and to pursue collaborative strategies of exploitation or exploration (March 1991) of innovations (Windeler 2012).

If we look at settings such as Silicon Valley, it is obvious that, at the meso level, other contexts besides organizations and networks are systematically gaining significance today. Following Andrew Hoffman (1999), I propose including settings such as Silicon Valley as special *issue-based fields* since their theme is innovation. *Fields of innovation* develop around individual *innovation issues*, each of which is recursively constituted in the respective field—such as the innovation of industry regulations, production technologies, or forms of participation—in time-space (cf. DiMaggio and Powell 1983; Fligstein and McAdam 2012). Fields of innovation—as the Silicon Valley example demonstrates—are often colonized by various populations of actors (be they individuals, organizations, or social movements) that may be rooted in different spheres of society, nations, or cultures. They are also characterized by specific ensembles of regulations, structures, and actors with specific capacities to act. Fields of innovation's structures thus frequently refer not only to the forms of signification, legitimation, and domination that prevail in individual spheres of society; they sometimes combine these or weave them into new ensembles of structures and structural characteristics specific to the fields of innovation in question. Under the field of innovation's governance, social actors even from time to time combine the *most varied forms of regulation and coordination in parallel*, for instance, the type of regulation and coordination characteristic of markets, organizations, and networks. Social actors in these fields thus deliberately pursue innovation processes in ways that are different from what would be possible in markets, organizations, and networks alone. Fields of innovation hence oftentimes enable actors of varying origin (such as spheres of society, professional groups, and cultures) to pursue, generate, and advance innovations in a very specific way under the conditions of the respective field. This allows actors to make creative use of and recombine different systems of regulation and forms of coordination to create, advance, or possibly change innovations. Individual types of actors can hold central positions in fields of innovation—such as, for instance, venture capitalists in Silicon Valley or consortia like SEMATECH in the global semiconductor industry. The social significance of a field manifests itself in the interactions among participants and in the ideas, narratives, and practices specific to the field. This significance is also expressed in ensembles of field-specific, relationally linked (or decoupled) rules and resources, positions and position actions, and the degree of institutional life that they develop. As more recent studies show, the logics of fields play an elementary role, especially for young firms (Pahnke, Katila, and Eisenhardt 2015). But even disruptive developments need fields in which they can evolve in order to generate successful innovations (Ansari, Garud, and Kumaraswamy 2015). Often company specifics interact with specifics of industries or fields in processes of innovation (Barbosa, Faria, and Eirizy 2013; Windeler and Sydow 2001). Political-administrative units (such as nation states) can be of great significance for fields of innovation, but they need not be—as, for instance, our study on the semiconductor industry illustrates (Sydow et al. 2012). This relative autonomy lends fields of innovation their particular significance in a world in which political-administrative units are often losing significance—owing not least to the increasing (reflexive) development of fields of innovation themselves.[17]

5   Innovating as Reflexive Exploration and Experimentation

The practice-theoretical perspective developed here obviously does not provide the mechanism of innovation that Joseph Schumpeter was looking for, nor does it formulate a normative frame of reference that indicates what should be innovated

---

17   In the literature on sociation under the conditions of modernity, the prevalent ideas of a mechanistic, progressive, internal differentiation and functional specialization of society are not well suited to capture the processes that I have referred to in considering the creation of order in fields of action that cut across different spheres of society (Giddens 1990a: 21f.). This is not to say that we must reject these concepts completely, but we should probably put them into perspective by thinking of them more in terms of *possible* points of reference and *potential* results of social practices (for an alternative point of view, see Passoth and Rammert in this volume).

and in which way. It offers something different instead: a *theoretically informed view of innovation* that makes it possible to deconstruct innovation processes and sensitizes for the conditions, consequences, and practices of innovation in innovation societies today.

Innovating in radical modernity resembles, as I have tried to show, an ongoing reflexive process of exploration and experimentation under conditions of uncertainty and conditions that are given, yet also actively co-created. Ensembles of modern institutions, regulations, and actors' capabilities shape the realm of possibilities for innovation, each in their specific way, and produce a multitude of possibilities for reflexive innovation that become reality only in highly selective contexts that are also invariably determined by domination. This strips innovation of any apparent innocence and randomness and brings lines of conflict. One of them is that the imperative of innovation continuously summons one to innovate and question all that is given, whereas modern institutions and systems of regulation—particularly at the levels of ensembles of societies, organizations, networks, and fields of innovation—produce a certain uniformity, specifically when confronted with the fundamental uncertainties characteristic of radical modernity. And this prompts the question of what significance is actually accorded to the homogenization of practices, standardization, and regulation as well as to forms of signification, legitimation, and domination for innovation processes and the further development of the social context. Such processes of harmonization tend to decrease the spectrum of alternatives and increase the vulnerability to changing circumstances, which the financial, energy, and environmental crises as well as the often futile attempts to regulate them have demonstrated. At the same time, they tend to favor those who are able to set the conditions.

Under the conditions of a radicalized modernity, steering innovation processes often resembles 'driving by sight', or 'riding the juggernaut', as Giddens (1990a: 139) put it. This processional wagon, which weighs many tons and is used in Hindu processions honoring Krishna, has the characteristic that once it gets rolling, it develops enormous power and quite simply crushes people who oppose it or land under its wheels. It can serve as an image for the reflexive modern era and for reflexive innovations in innovation societies, which are marked by development processes that exhibit characteristics of a wagon such as the juggernaut, yet without heading for a predictable end. The obvious idea that any attempt to steer innovation is therefore completely in vain turns out to be short-sighted nonetheless: as humans, we are—precisely with the aid of modern institutions, regulations and forms of coordination as well as actor's modern capabilities—jointly able to steer innovations in desired directions for some time and to a certain degree. But that which is harnessed always threatens to get out of control and to go where its momentum takes it, irrespective of the will of those holding the reins. Reflexive action gains in significance in the process: precisely because control is always only partial, possibilities to steer things in desired directions gain strategic significance since this skill gives those who master it opportunities to gain a comparative advantage, even if they have to 'drive by sight' and repeatedly need to correct their course—which is easier for those who manage to keep their eyes on what is coming ahead of the current situation. By contrast, those who, for whatever reason, are unable to do so are largely at the mercy of what is to come. With this in mind, reflexive innovations also refer to radical forms of devaluation, disruption, and destruction. If the social challenges are to be met, what we need at the very least is the capacity for reflexivity in order to constitute appropriate, socially relevant reflexive innovations in time-space. The side effect of this is that exercising this capacity further advances the modern principle of reflexivity and the form of reflexive innovation.

The image of the juggernaut of innovation illustrates something else in a pointed manner: the *sovereignty trap* in the current mode of sociation. Organizations in particular are culturally summoned and empowered to act in a sovereign way, to produce and reproduce innovations on their own. When actors—from politics, business, or other spheres—claim to exercise sovereignty in their actions, individually or together with others, they are aggrandizing the actor, claiming credit for processes that they have long ceased to master or perhaps never have. Even so, the continuously asserted claim of sovereignty, also advanced in the media, implies that responsibility for the consequences of innovations, particularly the undesirable ones, can be attributed to them. This in turn prompts opponents to claim that they could do it better than those who maintain they have solved the task. This sets a vicious cycle in motion that alternates between the claimed sovereignty of being in control of innovation processes and the actual lack of such control—a process that can evolve into a spiral at increasing speed.

Much would be gained if alternatives were to become clear again and if a lack of alternatives would cease to dominate the picture. Also much would be won if, instead of painting the picture of an ideal, untainted world of successful innovation, there were a greater inclination to take into account the recursive relationship between innovation and society under the conditions of radical modernization and more attention were paid to the social processes involved in constituting the freedoms required for innovation. This is crucial since it is precisely under the conditions of reflexive modernity that innovations and the practices of their valuation and evaluation must be questioned reflexively. There may be no escape from the innovation society, but it is nevertheless worthwhile to communicate in society about substantial alternatives and alternative paths of innovation. It is also worthwhile to reach a common understanding in society for regulating innovation and to cultivate the art of reflexive innovation, particularly under the conditions of radical modernity. Regulation of any kind, however, resembles 'driving by sight' given that new regulations inscribe themselves into the textures of regulations, which not only mutually determine one another but also continuously evolve and sometimes transform themselves in the process. The moment they are established, they are again immediately confronted with new challenges. The foremost task of innovation research worthy of the name is thus to draw on theoretically informed analytical approaches to generate information about which ensembles of forces are advancing innovations today, in which settings, and how these ensembles are in turn driven forward by innovations, what consequences are associated with this process, and which alternatives could be realized and in which ways. I consider this task to be a collective one. What we need to do is refine theory perspectives, as the one presented here, that enable us to understand and explain how innovation societies are socially constituted.

References

Abbott, Andrew. 1988. *The Systems of Professions*. Chicago, London: University of Chicago Press.
Abbott, Andrew. 2014. "The Problem of Excess." *Sociological Theory* 32(1): 1-26.
Adner, Ron and Daniel Snow. 2010. "Old Technology Responses to New Technology Threats: Demand Heterogeneity and Technology Retreats." *Industrial and Corporate Change* 19(5): 1655-1675.
Ansari, Shahzad (Shaz), Raghu Garud, and Arun Kumaraswamy. 2015. "The Disruptor's Dilemma: TIVO and the U.S. Television Ecosystem." *Strategic Management Journal* 37(9): 1829-1853.
Antal, Ariane Berthoin, Michael Hutter, and David Stark, eds. 2015. *Moments of Valuation. Exploring Sites of Dissonance*. Oxford: Oxford University Press.
Autio, Erkko, Martin Kenney, Philippe Mustard, Don Siegele, and Mike Wright. 2014. "Entrepreneurial Innovation: The Importance of Context." *Research Policy* 43(7): 1097-1108.
Barbosa, Natália, Ana Paula Faria, and Vasco Eirizy. 2013. "Industry- and Firm-Specific Factors of Innovation Novelty." *Industrial and Corporate Change* 23(3): 865-902.
Barley, Stephen R. 2010. "Building an Institutional Field to Corral a Government: A Case to Set an Agenda for Organization Studies." *Organization Studies* 31(6): 777-805.
Battilana, Julie and Matthew Lee. 2014. "Advancing Research on Hybrid Organizing. Insights from the Study of Social Enterprises." *The Academy of Management Annals* 8(1): 397-441.
Becker, Markus C. and Thorbjørn Knudsen. 2002. "Schumpeter 1911: Farsighted Visions on Economic Development." *American Journal of Economics and Sociology* 61(2): 387-403.
Becker, Markus C., Thorbjørn Knudsen, and James G. March. 2006. "Schumpeter, Winter, and the Sources of Novelty." *Industrial and Corporate Change* 15(2): 353-371.
Beckert, Jens. 2013. "Imagined Futures: Fictional Expectations in the Economy." *Sociological Theory* 42(3): 219-240.
Belt, Henk van den and Arie Rip. 1987. "The Nelson-Winter-Dosi Model and Synthetic Dye Chemistry." Pp. 135-158 in *The Social Construction of Technological Systems: New Directions in the Sociology and History of Technology*, edited by W. E. Bijker, T. P. Hughes, and T. J. Pinch. Cambridge: MIT Press.
Böhme, Hartmut. 2004. "Einführung: Netzwerke. Zur Theorie und Geschichte einer Konstruktion." Pp. 17-36 in *Netzwerke. Eine Kulturtechnik der Moderne*, edited by J. Barkhoff, H. Böhme, and J. Riou. Cologne: Böhlau.
Böhme, Hartmut and Gernot Böhme. 1985. *Das Andere der Vernunft. Zur Entwicklung von Rationalitätsstrukturen am Beispiel Kants*. Frankfurt a. M.: Suhrkamp.
Boli, John and George M. Thomas. 1997. "World Culture in the World Polity: A Century of International Non-Governmental Organizations." *American Sociological Review* 62(2): 171-190.
Bourdieu, Pierre. 1977 [1972]. Outline of a Theory of Practice. Cambridge, New York: Cambridge University Press.
Boyer, Robert and Michel Freyssenet. 2003 [2000]. *Produktionsmodelle. Eine Typologie am Beispiel der Automobilindustrie*. Berlin: Edition Sigma.
Braun-Thürmann, Holger. 2005. *Innovation*. Bielefeld: transcript.

Bromley, Patricia and John W. Meyer. 2017. "'They Are All Organizations': The Cultural Roots of Blurring Between the Nonprofit, Business, and Government Sectors." *Administration & Society* 49(7): 939-966.

Burt, Ronald S. 1992. *Structural Holes. The Social Structure of Competition.* Cambridge: Harvard University Press.

Burt, Ronald S. 2005. *Brokerage and Closure: An Introduction to Social Capital.* Oxford: Oxford University Press.

Carlsson, Bo, Staffan Jacobsson, Magnus Holmén, and Annika Rickne. 2002. "Innovation Systems: Analytical and Methodological Issues." *Research Policy* 31(2): 233-245.

Clausen, Tommy, Mikko Pohjola, Koson Sapprasert, and Bart Verspagen. 2011. "Innovation Strategies as a Source of Persistent Innovation." *Industrial and Corporate Change* 21(3): 553-585.

Cohen, Wesley M. and Daniel A. Levinthal. 1990. "Absorptive Capacity: A New Perspective on Learning and Innovation." *Administrative Science Quarterly* 35(1): 128-152.

Colapinto, John. 2014. "Material Question. Graphene May Be the Most Remarkable Substance Ever Discovered. But What's It for?" *The New Yorker*, December 22. Retrieved April 18, 2017 (http://www.newyorker.com/magazine/2014/12/22/material-question).

Colatat, Phech. 2015. "An Organizational Perspective to Funding Science: Collaborator Novelty at DARPA." *Research Policy* 44(4): 874-887.

Dedrick, Jason, Kenneth L. Kraemer, and Greg Linden. 2009. "Who Profits from Innovation in Global Value Chains? A Study of the iPod and Notebook PCs." *Industrial and Corporate Change* 19(1): 81-116.

DiMaggio, Paul and Walter Powell. 1983. "The Iron Cage Revisited. Institutional Isomorphism and Collective Rationality in Organizational Fields." *American Sociological Review* 48(2): 147-160.

Dodgson, Mark. 2011. "Exploring New Combinations in Innovation and Entrepreneurship: Social Networks, Schumpeter, and the Case of Josiah Wedgwood (1730–1795)." *Industrial and Corporate Change* 20(4): 1119-1151.

Dolata, Ulrich. 2015. "Volatile Monopole, Konzentration und Innovationsstrategien." *Berliner Journal für Soziologie* 24(4): 505-529.

Eden, Lynn. 2004. *Whole World on Fire: Organizations, Knowledge, and Nuclear Weapons Devastation.* Ithaca, London: Cornell University Press.

Emirbayer, Mustafa. 1997. "Manifesto for a Relational Sociology." *American Journal of Sociology* 103(2): 281-317.

Erumban, Abdul Azeez and Marcel P. Timmer. 2012. "The Dark Side of Creative Destruction: Innovation and Retirement of Capital." *Industrial and Corporate Change* 21(5): 1149-1174.

Fagerberg, Jan. 2005. "Innovation. A Guide to the Literature." Pp. 1-26 in *The Oxford Handbook of Innovation*, edited by J. Fagerberg, D. G. Mowery, and R. R. Nelson. Oxford: Oxford University Press.

Ferrary, Michel and Mark Granovetter. 2009. "The Role of Venture Capital Firms in Silicon Valley's Complex Innovation Network." *Economy and Society* 38(2): 326-359.

Fligstein, Neil and Doug McAdam. 2012. *A Theory of Fields.* Oxford: Oxford University Press.

Gardner, John W. 1981 [1963]. *Self-Renewal: The Individual and the Innovative Society.* New York, London: W. W. Norton & Company.

Garud, Raghu and Peter Karnøe, eds. 2001. *Path Dependence and Creation*. Mahwah: Lawrence Erlbaum.
Gereffi, Gary and Karina Fernandez-Stark. 2011. *Global Value Chain Analysis. A Primer.* Durham: Center on Globalization, Governance & Competitiveness (CGGC), Duke University.
Giddens, Anthony. 1979. *Central Problems in Social Theory: Action, Structure, and Contradiction in Social Analysis*. Berkeley: University of California Press.
Giddens, Anthony. 1984. *The Constitution of Society. Outline of the Theory of Structuration*. Cambridge: Polity Press.
Giddens, Anthony. 1990a. *The Consequences of Modernity*. Cambridge: Polity Press.
Giddens, Anthony. 1990b. "Structuration Theory and Sociological Analysis." Pp. 297-315 in *Anthony Giddens. Consensus and Controversy*, edited by J. Clark, C. Modgil, and S. Modgil. London, New York, Philadelphia: Falmer.
Giddens, Anthony. 1993 [1976]. *New Rules of Sociological Method*. 2nd ed. Cambridge: Polity Press.
Gilbert-Walsh, James. 2010. "Revisiting the Concept of Time: Archaic Perplexity in Bergson and Heidegger." *Human Studies* 33(2/3): 173-190.
Godin, Benoît. 2012. "'Innovation Studies': The Invention of a Specialty." *Minerva* 50(4): 397-421.
Godin, Benoît. 2015. *Innovation Contested. The Idea of Innovation over the Centuries*. London: Routledge.
Gould, Stephen Jay and Elisabeth S. Vrba. 1982. "Exaptation—A Missing Term in the Science of Form." *Paleobiology* 8(1): 4-15.
Granovetter, Mark. 1973. "The Strength of Weak Ties." *American Journal of Sociology* 78(6): 1360-1380.
Granovetter, Mark. 1974. *Getting a Job. A Study of Contacts and Careers*. Cambridge: Harvard University Press.
Healy, Kieran. 2015. "The Performativity of Networks." *European Journal of Sociology* 56(2): 175-205.
Hilpinen, Risto. 2011. "Artifact." *The Stanford Encyclopedia of Philosophy* (Winter 2011 Edition), edited by E. N. Zalta. Retrieved April 18, 2017 (https://plato.stanford.edu/archives/win2011/entries/artifact/).
Hoffman, Andrew J. 1999. "Institutional Evolution and Change: Environmentalism and the U.S. Chemical Industry." *Academy of Management Journal* 42(4): 351-371.
Hutter, Michael, Hubert Knoblauch, Werner Rammert, and Arnold Windeler. This volume. "Innovation Society Today. The Reflexive Creation of Novelty."
Jandhyala, Srividya and Anupama Phene. 2015. "The Role of Intergovernmental Organizations in Cross-Border Knowledge Transfer and Innovation." *Administrative Science Quarterly* 60(4): 712-743.
Kennedy, Pagan. 2016. "How to Cultivate the Art of Serendipity." *The New York Times*, January 2. Retrieved April 18, 2017 (https://www.nytimes.com/2016/01/03/opinion/how-to-cultivate-the-art-of-serendipity.html).
Kenney, Martin. 2011. "How Venture Capital Became a Component of the US National System of Innovation." *Industrial and Corporate Change* 20(6): 1677-1723.
Knoblauch, Hubert. This volume. "Communicative Action, the New, and the Innovation Society."

Knorr Cetina, Karin. 1988. "Das naturwissenschaftliche Labor als 'Verdichtung' von Gesellschaft." *Zeitschrift für Soziologie* 17(2): 85-101.
Koselleck, Reinhart. 2000. *Zeitschichten. Studien zur Historik*. Frankfurt a. M.: Suhrkamp.
Lamont, Michèle. 2012. "Toward a Comparative Sociology of Valuation and Evaluation." In: *Annual Review of Sociology* 38(1): 201-221.
Lange, Knut, Gordon Müller-Seitz, Jörg Sydow, and Arnold Windeler. 2013. "Financing Innovations in Uncertain Networks. Filling in Roadmap Gaps in the Semiconductor Industry." *Research Policy* 42(3): 647-661.
March, James G. 1991. "Exploration and Exploitation in Organizational Learning." *Organization Science* 2(1): 71-87.
March, James G. and Herbert A. Simon. 1993 [1958]. *Organizations*. New York: Wiley-Blackwell.
Merton, Robert K. and Elinor Barber. 2004. *The Travels and Adventures of Serendipity. A Study in Sociological Semantics and the Sociology of Science*. Princeton: Princeton University Press.
Meyer, John W. 2009. *World Society: The Writings of John W. Meyer*, edited by G. S. Drori and G. Krücken. Oxford: Oxford University Press.
Meyer, John W. 2008. "Reflections on Institutional Theories of Organization." Pp. 790-811 in *Organizational Institutionalism*, edited by R. Greenwood, C. Oliver, K. Sahlin, and R. Suddaby. London: SAGE.
Meyer, John W., John Boli, and George M. Thomas. 1987. "Ontology and Rationalization in the Western Cultural Account." Pp. 12-37 in *Institutional Structure. Constituting State, Society, and the Individual*, edited by G. M. Thomas, J. W. Meyer, F. O. Ramirez, and J. Boli. Newbury Park: SAGE.
Meyer, John W. and Ronald L. Jepperson. 2000. "The 'Actors' of Modern Society: The Cultural Construction of Social Agency." *Sociological Theory* 18(1): 100-120.
Meyer, John W. and Brian Rowan. 1977. "Institutionalized Organizations: Formal Structure as Myth and Ceremony." *American Journal of Sociology* 83(2): 340-363.
Meyer, Uli. 2016. *Innovationspfade. Evolution und Institutionalisierung komplexer Technologie in organisationalen Feldern*. Wiesbaden: Springer VS.
Muniesa, Fabian. 2014. *The Provoked Economy. Economic Reality and the Performative Turn*. London: Routledge.
Nelson, Andrew, Andrew Earle, Jennifer Howard-Grenville, Julie Haack, and Doug Young. 2014. "Do Innovation Measures Actually Measure Innovation? Obliteration, Symbolic Adoption, and Other Finicky Challenges in Tracking Innovation Diffusion." *Research Policy* 43(6): 927-940.
North, Douglass C., John J. Wallis, and Barry R. Weingast. 2009. *Violence and Social Order. A Conceptual Framework for Interpreting Recorded Human History*. New York: Cambridge University Press.
Nussbaum, Martha. C. 2013. *Political Emotions: Why Love Matters for Justice*. Cambridge: Belknap Press of Harvard University Press.
Orlikowski, Wanda J. and Susan V. Scott. 2008. "Sociomateriality: Challenging the Separation of Technology, Work and Organization." *The Academy of Management Annals* 2(1): 433-474.

Ortmann, Günther. 2016. "Innovation: In Ketten tanzen." Pp. 237-248 in *Innovationsgesellschaft heute. Perspektiven, Felder und Fälle*, edited by W. Rammert, A. Windeler, H. Knoblauch, and M. Hutter. Wiesbaden: Springer VS.

Ortmann, Günther, Arnold Windeler, Albrecht Becker, and Hans-Joachim Schulz. 1990. *Computer und Macht in Organisationen. Mikropolitische Analysen.* Opladen: Westdeutscher Verlag.

Oudheusden, Michiel van, Nathan Charliera, Benedikt Rosskampa, and Pierre Delvenne. 2015. "Broadening, Deepening, and Governing Innovation: Flemish Technology Assessment in Historical and Socio-Political Perspective." *Research Policy* 44(10): 1877-1886.

Pahnke, Emily C., Riitta Katila, and Kathleen M. Eisenhardt. 2015. "Who Takes You to the Dance? How Partners' Institutional Logics Influence Innovation in Young Firms." *Administrative Science Quarterly* 60(4): 596-633.

Pahnke, Emily C., Rory McDonald, Dan Wang, and Benjamin Hallen. 2015. "Exposed: Venture Capital, Competitor Ties, and Entrepreneurial Innovation." *Academy of Management Journal* 58(5): 1334-1360.

Parsons, Talcott. 1956. "Suggestions for a Sociological Approach to the Theory of Organizations I." *Administrative Science Quarterly* 1(1): 63-85.

Parsons, Talcott. 1957. "Suggestions for a Sociological Approach to the Theory of Organizations II." *Administrative Science Quarterly* 1(2): 225-239.

Passoth Jan-Hendrik and Werner Rammert. This volume. "Fragmental Differentiation and the Practice of Innovation. Why Is There an Ever-Increasing Number of Fields of Innovation?"

Pfeffer, Jeffrey and Gerald R. Salancik. 1978. *The External Control of Organizations. A Resource Dependence Perspective.* New York: Harper & Row.

Popitz, Heinrich. 2000 [1997]. *Wege der Kreativität.* Tübingen: Mohr Siebeck.

Rammert, Werner. 2014. "Vielfalt der Innovation und gesellschaftlicher Zusammenhalt. Von der ökonomischen zur gesellschaftstheoretischen Perspektive." Pp. 619-639 in *Vielfalt und Zusammenhalt. Verhandlungen des 36. Kongresses der Deutschen Gesellschaft für Soziologie in Bochum und Dortmund 2012, Part 2*, edited by M. Löw. Frankfurt a. M.: Campus Verlag.

Rogers, Everett M. 2003 [1962]. *Diffusion of innovations.* 5th ed. New York: Free Press.

Schubert, Cornelius, Jörg Sydow, Arnold Windeler. 2013. "The Means of Managing Momentum: Bridging Technological Paths and Organisational Fields." *Research Policy* 42(8): 1389-1405.

Schumpeter, Joseph A. 1934 [1912]. *The Theory of Economic Development.* Cambridge: Harvard University Press.

Schumpeter, Joseph A. 2000 [1911]. "Entrepreneurship as Innovation." Pp. 51-75 in *Entrepreneurship. The Social Science View*, edited by R. Swedberg. Oxford: Oxford University Press.

Schumpeter, Joseph A. 2003 [1942]. *Capitalism, Socialism, and Democracy.* London, New York: Routledge.

Schumpeter, Joseph A. 2005 [1932]. "Development." *Journal of Economic Literature* 43(1): 108-120.

Silver, Daniel. 2011. "The Moodiness of Action." *Sociological Theory* 29(3): 199-222.

Sydow, Jörg and Arnold Windeler. 2003. "Knowledge, Trust and Control. Managing Tensions and Contradictions in a Regional Network of Service Firms." *International Studies of Management & Organization* 33(2): 69-99.

Sydow, Jörg, Arnold Windeler, Cornelius Schubert, and Guido Möllering. 2012. "Organizing R&D Consortia for Path Creation and Extension: The Case of Semiconductor Manufacturing Technologies." *Organization Studies* 33(7): 907-936.

Tavassoli, Sam and Charlie Karlsson. 2015. "Persistence of Various Types of Innovation Analyzed and Explained." *Research Policy* 44(10): 1887-1901.

Thompson, James D. 2004 [1967]. *Organizations in Action. Social Science Bases of Administrative Theory.* New Brunswick, London: Transaction Publishers.

Villani, Marco, Stefano Bonacini, Davide Ferrari, Roberto Serra, and David Lane. 2007. "An Agent-Based Model of Exaptive Processes." *European Management Review* 4(3): 141-151.

Weber, Max. 1978 [1922]. *Economy and Society.* Berkeley, Los Angeles: University of California Press.

Windeler, Arnold. 2001. *Unternehmungsnetzwerke. Konstitution und Strukturation.* Wiesbaden: Westdeutscher Verlag.

Windeler, Arnold. 2003. "Kreation technologischer Pfade: Ein strukturationstheoretischer Ansatz." *Managementforschung* 13: 295-328.

Windeler, Arnold. 2012. "Kooperation und Konkurrenz in Netzwerken. Theoretische Überlegungen zum Strukturwandel der Arbeitsorganisation." Pp. 23-50 in *Vertrauen und Kooperation in der Arbeitswelt*, edited by C. Schilcher, M. Will-Zocholl, and M. Ziegler. Wiesbaden: VS Verlag.

Windeler, Arnold. 2014. "Können und Kompetenzen von Individuen, Organisationen und Netzwerken. Eine praxistheoretische Perspektive." Pp. 225-301 in *Kompetenz. Sozialtheoretische Perspektiven*, edited by A. Windeler and J. Sydow. Wiesbaden: Springer VS.

Windeler, Arnold. 2015. "Organisationen in der radikalisierten Moderne: Herausforderungen." Pp. 173-188 in *Zur Zukunft der Organisationssoziologie*, edited by M. Apelt and U. Wilkesmann. Wiesbaden: Springer VS.

Windeler, Arnold and Jörg Sydow. 2001. "Project Networks and Changing Industry Practices. Collaborative Content Production in the German Television Industry." *Organization Studies* 22(6): 1035-1061.

Windeler, Arnold and Carsten Wirth. 2005. "Strukturation von Arbeitsregulation: eine relationale Mehrebenenperspektive." Pp. 163-191 in *Organisation von Arbeit*, edited by M. Faust, M. Funder, and M. Moldaschl. Munich, Mehring: Hampp.

Yoffie, David B. and Michael A. Cusumano. 2015. *Strategy Rules: Five Timeless Lessons from Bill Gates, Andy Grove, and Steve Jobs.* New York: Harper Collins.

Zahra, Shaker A., Mike Wright, and Sondos G. Abdelgawad. 2014. "Contextualization and the Advancement of Entrepreneurship Research." *International Small Business Journal* 32(5): 479-500.

Communicative Action, the New, and the Innovation Society[1]

Hubert Knoblauch

"Di doman' non c'é certezza" (*Lorenzo di Medici*)

1 Introduction

While writing this chapter I happened to read an article in a Berlin newspaper about a meeting of a group called *Berliner Innovation ConSensus*, comprising organizations such as Shell, Google, Deutsche Bank, and the Federal German Ministry of Education and Research. The goal of this consortium is solely to inspire innovation of whatever kind. In some respects this is precisely the topic that I will be discussing in this contribution.

My use of the term 'innovation society' borrows from the title of the Research Training Group *Innovation Society Today: The Reflexive Production of the New*, which is based at the Institute for Sociology of the Technical University Berlin. As this graduate research group is primarily devoted to empirical research on innovation processes in different social fields—science and technology, business and industry, art and culture, and politics and planning—the purpose of this essay is to clarify key concepts that were formulated in the first strategic report (Hutter et al. 2015, this volume). To achieve an idea of innovation processes that can be valid across different social fields, the following considerations necessitate a high level of abstraction. Moreover, as the various empirical investigations pursued in this context have not yet been completed, these considerations should be seen as very provisional. At the same time, however, I shall try to give a unified theoretical

---

[1] I would like to thank Lilli Braunisch, Anina Engelhardt, Miira Hill, Werner Rammert, and the Research Training Group for their comments.

framework to the concepts that have emerged from different contexts and, in doing so, contribute to constructing a sociological theory of innovation.

Since we are talking about defining concepts here, I should begin with a remark on methodology. The word 'innovation' is evidently not only the subject of scientific debate.

The Berlin Innovation ConSensus referred to above has already shown that it concerns a category in the social world as such, because 'innovation' is a key to economic success, money, and social status or, in the case of social innovation, to recognition, valuation, or support from other members of society. As members of society themselves use the concept of 'innovation,' it would actually be necessary to examine their use of the term systematically in a way suggested by the sociology of knowledge: to view the actors and their knowledge as a subject in its own right and to investigate their 'first-order constructs' (Schütz 1962). Although some initial attempts exist to explain innovations in terms of the sociology of knowledge in terms of a sociology-of-knowledge analysis of actor knowledge about innovation (MacCallum et al. 2009), there is still no study that investigates the discursive use of 'innovation' in a systematic way based on empirical principles.[2] Given the research so far, the use of the concept in intellectual discourse can therefore be summarized quite briefly.[3] The goal of the present work, however, is not to reconstruct the meaning of the concept for the actors but to construct the concept in a coherent conceptual context that allows us to investigate the ideas of the actors empirically, including the scientists who participate in the innovations on a practical level. Such a comprehensive concept must therefore be broader in scope and focus on the new as a communicative construction. This would allow us to include the actors involved in the innovation and their actions.

I would like to begin the first part of this chapter with a rough sketch of the relationship between the transformations of modern society and the semantic developments of the concept of innovation. To compensate for the lack of an empirically based concept, I would like to propose communicative constructivism as a theoretical framework for a sociological concept of innovation. This concept incorporates the category of reflexivity and reflexive innovation. Innovation will

---

2 Moulaert / Van Dyck (2013) formulate it as follows in their adaptation of sociology of knowledge: One must incorporate the concepts of planners and scientific advisors (who use scientific concepts as a basis themselves), to generate inductively a universal concept of innovation. In the majority of contexts they describe, the goal is more about reaching a consensus on what is new in each case than about creating a universal concept of (social) innovation.

3 I am relying here on Godin's works, which follow a similar but not explicitly stated methodological model as proposed by Koselleck (2006).

be defined as a form of active construction of the new, the communicative character of which reciprocally reflects the meaning of the new for other people and, in doing so, allows its dissemination by them (including its diffusion). The concept of communicative action enables us to make the analytic connection to the three dimensions of innovation—semantics, pragmatics, and grammar—and to differentiate between two concepts of the 'innovation society' that will be outlined at the end of this chapter.

2 Discourses and the Meaning of Innovation

Innovation is linked to the metaphysical question of whether there is really anything new under the sun, as Solomon once asked long ago in the Book of Ecclesiastes, or whether "the new happens in being", as in the ontology of the French philosopher Alain Badiou (2007: XXVII). However difficult it may be to decide between these two metaphysical questions, from a sociological viewpoint, transformation and the creation of the new is a process that occurs in every society. Whereas social theories that work with the concept of evolution explain the necessity of the new for the processes of selection, differentiation, and forced adaptation to the environment, historical concepts see society as a construction in the face of chaos. Even more specifically, the new appears as part of social theory. As we know, the traditional societies that dominated most of history were characterized by the attempt to erect barricades against the chaos of the new. Actions become traditional to create stability and defy the vagaries of change. Modern societies are distinguished by the fact that change is part of their self-description. This is why the sociology of Auguste Comte saw 'social dynamics' as being the second pillar alongside 'social statics,' the stabilized institutions of society.

Comte (1830) actually used the concept of innovation himself when, for example, he praised the Catholic Church for introducing a system of general education, calling it 'a great and happy social innovation.' As Godin (2008) shows, the concept of innovation was used in England and France from the beginning of the modern age, but however with a negative connotation, almost as an accusation. The word acquired a positive meaning only after 1789. We can therefore say that the meaning of the word 'innovation' was reversed at the beginning of the modern era. This reversal also applies to what has been described as social innovation. During the nineteenth century, social reformers, including business people (Godin 2012), were described as innovators—long before Schumpeter (1939) lauded their role in innovation. It seems to be a feature of modernity that innovation has become an explicit topic.[4] As far as the future became intraworldly (mundane) and lost its religious meaning (Minois 1996), and as far as modernity saw history as progress in time (Knoblauch 2005: 39), innovation became an intrinsic characteristic of modern society. In light of modernity's familiar and sometimes deplored tendency toward instrumentalism and rationality (Weber 1978), it is also hardly surprising that innovation was increasingly restricted to the spheres of science, technology, and business. It was in the economy that innovation was seen as an important concept, and it is science and technology that are regarded as key forces of innovation.

The discourses of innovation I refer to here (and which were reconstructed by Godin) are defined with explicit reference to the word 'innovation.'[5] Similarly to Koselleck's method of historical semantics (2006), we look at lexical associations with the word 'innovation' and note fundamental changes in associative patterns as an expression of historical semantic changes.

In his reconstruction of the discourse on innovation and social innovation, Godin convincingly argues that the reason for the success of the concept of innovation is that it resolves a particular form of tension. Whereas invention—and this applies to discovery and imitation as well—were generally mutually exclusive in the pre-modern age, the achievement of the concept of innovation is that it resolves this tension. As Tarde's theories (1962) show, for example, the concept of invention or discovery and the related processes demand something new and do so in a way that blatantly contradicts mere imitation. The concept of innovation, however, allows the resolution of the tension between the two concepts and enables us to connect them in a linear way: innovation requires a discovery, but it also means that an imitation, a copy, must follow on from the discovery—in other words, a reproduction and reproducibility of the discovery. This amalgamation of invention and imitation in the concept of innovation becomes very clear in different theories of innovation such as Rogers' famous theory of 'diffusions of innovations,' which was developed in the early 1960s (Rogers 1995). It was also around this time that political and economic support for innovation assumed recognizable forms. The practical commercial use of the concept of innovation increased dramatically at the beginning of the 1960s.[6]

---

4   One of the important indications of this is the *'querelle des anciens et des modernes'* that concerned the role of tradition and of continual renewal.

5   I would like to thank Anina Engelhardt for pointing out that Godin's reconstruction probably underestimates artistic movements. It should be emphasized that we still lack empirically based reconstructions of the discourse about the concept of innovation.

6   Peter Drucker was one of the first authors to offer a detailed exploration of innovation—and was also involved in initiating the international debate on the 'knowledge

Despite its relevance to the economy and to knowledge and technology management, innovation has not become a central category of sociology or other basic research. This has a number of consequences for sociological research, for the concept has not been defined in a conceptual sociological framework that is theoretically and empirically coherent. Instead, we are dealing with a concept that is used and influenced by sociologically examined actors who have a definite interest in innovation themselves (or, less often, who want to obstruct it). A concept of innovation founded on a sound sociological terminology has yet to be developed.

3 The Construction of the New

If we are looking for a sociological interpretation of innovation that lives up to the conceptual principles of sociology, it is useful to consider Rogers' widely discussed work. For Rogers (1995: 11), innovation means 'an idea, procedure, or project perceived as new by an individual or other unit of adoption.' Although Rogers does not follow up this aspect, his definition has very strong sociological implications: first, he emphasizes that innovation demands perception of novelty, and second, this presumes that the perspective of others plays a decisive role. This emphasis on recognition and other people categorically embeds innovation in a social relationship between the subject who actively constructs the new and the subject who perceives or adapts to it. As Mead has shown, these two perspectives can only be identical in borderline cases. We should note that in this situation the meaning of the new is not substantially defined but is essentially influenced by other people's perception. Here the concept of perception is probably not meant psychologically at all, for the new has to be *reciprocally* perceived—in other words, we are talking about an essentially *social phenomenon*. At the same time this definition has very strong *constructivist* implications: it assumes that something that is new is (co-)defined as new in other people's perception. This reveals that perception can by no means be regarded merely as passive sensory perception but, as I have indicated above, must encompass everything that becomes relevant at a sensory level in the process of social reciprocity. In fact, it covers everything that is *communicated*. Finally, we should add that we are not just talking about signs here. Like Schumpeter before him, Rogers explicitly emphasizes the importance of new processes, products, and therefore objects as well.

---

society' (Drucker 1969). The 'Sputnik shock' may be one of many reasons for the growth of interest in the technical future of society and in international coordination.

Even if Rogers pursued other ends, at least three of the abovementioned aspects are suitable for developing a sociological definition of innovation. If one takes one's own targets seriously, they must first and foremost acknowledge the differences between thinking, acting, and things, they must contain a concept of the sphere of social interaction or of intersubjective perception, and they must be able to grasp the relationship between the producer of a new thing and its recipients. These three aspects are also at the center of the communicative constructivism that I wish to propose as the framework for developing a sociological theory of innovation. As I do not have the space to expand on this here, I would simply like to outline the features that are particularly important for the theory of innovation. I would just like to point out that this approach advances the theory of social construction of reality established by Peter Berger and Thomas Luckmann (Berger and Luckmann 1966). However, whereas Berger und Luckmann use the basic concept of social action (borrowed from Weber), the concept of communicative action seems more appropriate to me. Although this follows on from Habermas' theory of communicative action (1984), it diverges from it in relation to several problematic points: it does not separate the instrumental rationality of the world of objects, of work, or, in the present case, of technological innovation from the communicative rationality of linguistic usage, of communication, and here, for example, of social innovation. Rather, communicative action is a type of reciprocal social action that is always connected to specific objectivations and is consequently linked just as much to other people as it is to objects.

As communicative constructivism has already been outlined elsewhere (Knoblauch 1995, 2013a; Keller, Knoblauch, and Reichertz 2013), in this chapter I would like to highlight only those aspects of key importance for the concept of innovation. Against the background of Habermas' work, it is absolutely essential to mention that communicative action describes the embodied performance of social actions because it can only become part of the experience (or the perception) of other actors through its embodiments. As communicative actions are oriented toward the responses of others, are tailored to them, and are dependent on them, we can describe them as fundamentally relational. And just like the concept of innovation that I have outlined, the performance of communicative actions necessarily involves a kind of objectivation.[7] Bodily performances that engender sounds are gestures that can already be described as objectivations, as well as reified and materialized objectifications produced by means of such embodied objectivations, such as signs, technologies, or things.

---

7   Objectivation is used here in the sense of Berger and Luckmann (1966).

In other words, communicative action corresponds to all semantic aspects of the sociological concept of innovation as described above. But the specific factor is still missing: the new, or innovation. What, then, is the new? The philosopher Boris Groys (2002) proposes possible answer to this question that was recently debated enthusiastically. In his essay on the 'cultural economy of the new,' he advanced the theory that the new resulted from new contextualizations and recontextualizations (Groys 2002: 50). While this may appear coherent, every communicative action could, in fact, be seen as a kind of recontextualization of meaning (Knoblauch 2001). Joas particularly emphasized this in his theory of creative action (Joas 1996). According to Joas, every action demands adaptation to the situation in relation to other people and objects; this adaptation is expressed in a kind of situated creativity. Suchman's (1987) concept of situated action took a similar track in considering the adaptation of action to the contingent circumstances of the respective situation. As events do not occur in the anticipated order, actors always have to act in a 'new' way, even when they are maintaining a sequential order that apparently remains unchanged. In arguing this, Suchman also included objects and technologies in situated action. For, as Latour (2005) rightly stressed, objects help to stabilize order. Yet objects are at the same time also unstable elements, particularly in relation to the new. This forces us to ask once again exactly what it is that comprises the new.

As I have already mentioned above, temporal semantics plays a role. The new is essentially derived from the distinction between 'old' and 'new.' This distinction presupposes, however, that we have a clear idea of what the old is. The definition of the new must therefore anticipate extensive knowledge as a background against which the new can be described as something new in the first place. If, however, we refuse to presuppose an omniscient system but one populated by actors with their limited knowledge, it seems more appropriate to begin by seeing the new simply as the other, as something different.[8] By 'new' we mean something that is distinct from knowledge and the typifications it involves.[9] We need to stress again that this distinction must be socially acknowledged; and moreover, the circle of universally assumed knowledge also forms the framework in which what has been differentiated from existing knowledge can be seen as new. In this process it is essential for the new that we express the observation of the difference of knowledge in temporal

---

8   Patent law makes the same assumption by relating recognition of the new to a fundamental totality, that of the recognized patents, which, although vast, is limited.
9   I am relying here on Schütz's contribution to the theory of creative action (Knoblauch 2013b).

semantics: 'new' is the different or strange thing that was previously regarded as not yet known.

We can illustrate this with an example. In an earlier study we examined visions of the future (Knoblauch and Schnettler 2000). We realized in the interviews with female visionaries who, to varying degrees, had visions of the future that the futurist quality of the visions itself was not, as such, a feature of the experiences the women described. The women had visions, but the fact that they referred to the future was not part of the vision itself (aside from apocalyptic prophesies). The futuristic aspect of the vision first emerged through retrospective narrative constructions: it was only after the envisaged event had occurred that these women were able to recognize (and reconstruct) that the visionary experience they had had before this event was a vision of the future (Schnettler 2004). Because knowledge about the future is embedded in the narrative construction here as well, it is easy to see that, even in retrospect, knowledge of the new does not have to be explicit (I will return to this issue below).

Consequently, the thesis is that to be able to talk about the new we must additionally consider the temporal semantics of difference (precisely because all action and every communication proceeds in time). As action has to be connected to a kind of semantics, we are necessarily dealing with communicative action. The new has to be communicated, and it has to be reciprocally understood in the communication in such a way that it can be accepted and passed on (diffused). Innovation is thus basically a reciprocally reflected communicative construction of the new as something new.

The special semantics that marks out the new can draw on the explicit discourses referred to in the first section. Its meaning as a goal for action is marked by the idea of progress influenced by the Enlightenment and formulated, for example, in Popper's notion of the accumulation of knowledge for science. The new, however, can also be understood in the framework of other models of time, as described by Mannheim (1979). As we know, for instance, the new of the dialectical idea of time is distinguished by the oppositional difference to what has already occurred. In my conclusion I shall return to the question of whether and which ideas of time are involved in the innovation society. Before that, however, we must clearly establish that the semantics of the new does not necessarily have to be tied to a linguistic lexical frame, nor even to the specificity of language, but can use other forms of objectivation instead.

4 Communicative Action and Reflexivity

In sociological terms, innovation is based on the orientation of reciprocal social communication to the new as something new. I shall call this social reciprocity 'reflexivity.' Reflexivity is an essential aspect of communicative action (Knoblauch 2001). This reflexivity is already expressed in our basic model of communicative construction of the new in the form of the 'as': the new 'as' something new. It indicates that the new is not merely existent or something that 'irrupts into being'; it must also be communicated as such. This communication must not necessarily be 'explicit': the new emerges not only by talking about it, such as through an institutional act that awards it the label 'innovative.'[10] New forms can develop in the course of actions as well and can be built into routines of action without us specifically giving them linguistic expression. Many elements of children's education by first-time parents consist of such 'social innovations.' This can also occur with ideas, objects, and subjects.

To understand how something can be regarded 'as new' without necessarily having to be attached the label as new, we need to clarify the concept of reflexivity that is contained in every 'as.' In the classical version of the theory of action, the concept of reflexivity means that agents can act consciously. As Schubert clearly shows (this volume), a second aspect of reflexivity can be identified. This aspect is highlighted by Beck and Lau (2005), who see the reflexive modern age as an epoch turned toward the results of modernity. In other words, reflexivity refers to the observation of the results of action. Giddens (1990) emphasizes a rather different aspect. He sees reflexivity in 'monitoring,' in observing what happens during the action. Whereas these ideas relate to the observation of actions by the individual acting person (or an acting collective), I would like to highlight another aspect that essentially belongs to communicative action: reflexivity in this other sense means the circumstance that actions have meaning not only for the agents but also for other people. We approach our actions so as to signal what we think or want to express or do; but these actions are reflexive because in this signaling they are oriented to other people (or to what we assume of other people). In other words, actions are reflexive to the extent that they are made comprehensible for other people. For this reason reflexivity is more of a characteristic of communicative action itself than of the actors as persons.[11]

---

10   Once again I must stress that I consider the terms 'implicit' and 'explicit' to be misleading because they are 'logocentric' in recognizing only language as a characteristic form of explication. See also Knoblauch (2005).

11   For the idea of this reflexivity as a constitutive element of agency, see Archer (2012).

In terms of the new, this means that it is not created by actors and their knowledge; instead, the new is part of a process of action that is aptly described by the word 'doing.' Innovation involves a kind of action that must be communicative to the extent that the new it contains must also be observable, comprehensible, and reasonable for others. In this situation the creation of the new necessarily occurs *in actu*. But the circumstance that the reflexive construction is part of a kind of communicative action also tells us that it can be institutionalized and fully become an innovation. This occurs through the patterns of reproduction of the action that emerge during institutionalization.[12] One aspect of institutionalization is the necessity to make the now-routinized action meaningful: in other words, to provide legitimation. And one aspect of innovation consists in legitimating the new as something new. This can occur through communicative processes of assessment and evaluation by which evaluation criteria are linked to specific actions, ideas, or products that are supposed to define 'newness' (Lamont 2012); it can also concern valorizations to which it is possible to ascribe an economic value (Hutter 2014).[13]

As innovation has to be recognized even if it appears in invisible forms (such as the emperor's new clothes), it requires communication, knowledge, institutional paths, and structures. If we subscribe to the idea that objects, technologies, and materials are part of social reality, as social constructivism and the actor-network theory propose, then every innovation can be seen as a social innovation. This is why, strictly speaking, social innovations are those intentional changes explicitly directed toward particular institutional characteristics of the social structure.[14] The social character of innovations not only includes knowledge of the new, including its evaluation, the relevant experts, and the related (specialist) communication, it also requires socially disseminated general knowledge about what is not new.

The advantage of the concept of communicative action is that it refers to innovation as part of actors' intentionality and that at the same time it relates, due to reflexivity, to 'communicative intentionality.' Communicative intentions refer to shared knowledge about the act of communication (see Levinson 1983: 15ff.).[15] In relation to innovation, this means that we can also include those forms of innova-

---

12   For the institutionalization process and legitimation, see Berger and Luckmann (1966).
13   Flichy (1995) emphasized that knowledge about innovation can be communicated in ways that are very clearly distinct from the explicit categories of language, for example, by pictures, films, and music.
14   Social innovation as the 'intentional, targeted new configuration of social practices emanating from specific actors' (Howaldt and Schwarz 2010: 89, my translation).
15   The concept is broadly congruent with what Searle and Tomasello have defined as 'shared intentionality.'

tion that are not explicitly described as such but function as such by virtue of their performance in practice.

5 Reflexive Innovation and Discursive Reflexivity

After considering the discourse about the concept of innovation (that is, what is defined as 'semantics' in the context of the Research Training Group) and clarifying its relationship to communicative action (that is, what the research group defines as 'pragmatics'), we can now focus on the aspect that the group defines as the 'grammar of innovation.' This is the dimension to which most of the actors in the social discourse about innovation refer. Innovation in relation to the actors refers to the social organization of communicative actions in which the new is created. This dimension is defined by the institutionalized and socially organized forms of social co-production of the new. From an analytical perspective we can regard organized forms in general as the result of communicative action. To put it more precisely, we can regard acting and knowledge as universal preconditions in the construction of the new; formal organizations, however, are the necessary (but not sufficient) specific preconditions for explaining a particular system of construction of the new that is defined as innovation (Windeler 2003). In the case of innovation there is the additional factor of the kind of organization that led to the connection between invention and imitation. Examples of this include the practice of registering technological innovations in the form of patents, which became established from 1910 onward. The emergence of research policy also played a particular role with its attempt to organize the targeted production of scientific and technical results. This received a special boost from the national-innovation-system programs pursued by some institutions in the 1980s and by the OECD from the 1990s onward. The monitoring and assessment has meanwhile become fairly standardized. It is these formal structures of social organization that we describe as the 'grammar' of innovation. They are now so complex that they have become a topic of research on the innovation society in their own right. This has been shown, for instance, by Garud and Gehman (2012), who used the example of sustainability to differentiate between the temporal, relational, and narrative dimensions of this 'grammar' while taking account of technologies and objects as well.

In this context we should always understand *innovation in the narrow emic sense* as the organized creation and communication of the new. As with any other kind of institutionalization, organized innovation requires specific legitimations (Ragu and Gehman, for instance, call them 'narratives') that explain to others what innovation (including as a novelty) consists of. As communicative action, such legitimations take the form of discourses in which the meaning of innovation can be socially negotiated, made obligatory, or disputed. Since we have so far only spoken about universal discourses in which the word 'innovation' appears, we are referring here to specific discourses in which the meaning of individual innovations is evaluated in order to assign a value to them (and definitely an economic value as well).

In terms of methodology we must extend the historical semantics as developed by Koselleck in two ways, each of which relates to the semantic field.[16] This semantic field usually encompasses a series of lexical units that are synonymous with innovation, overlap with it, or describe individual aspects and attributes, and that exhibit a particular ordering of proximity, distance, specificity, or universality that can be delimited from other types of semantics. On the one hand we must look for categories related to innovation, which means words in the semantic field of innovation such as 'creation,' 'renewal,' or 'novelty.' In my opinion, this semantic field is marked out by the concept of communicative construction of the new outlined above. For sociological purposes, on the other hand, we must consider the changes in diachronic and synchronic perspective (in other words, the connection between innovation and similar words in different institutional spheres, social groups, professions, regions, and so on). More detailed observation involves primarily concepts, expressions, and tropes that refer to the whole semantic field of innovation.

Discourses are explicit forms of semantically coded communication about a topic (for example, 'the new'). Discourses are therefore legitimating in a very fundamental sense because they not only communicate meaning but also create meaning by communicating about innovation and making it a topic.[17] The discourses that are about innovation mostly include the consequences of innovation. As the legitimizing discourses differ from the pragmatic processes in which the new is created,[18] they represent a particular form of reflexivity that we can call *discursive reflexivity*.

Discursive reflexivity distinguishes between organized innovation and the kind of reflexivity that implicitly appears in pragmatic actions. Ibert (2003: 23) offers an example of this with the observation that while innovation may appear every-

---

16 In doing this, however, we must also take into account visual discourses, the analysis of which probably requires a methodology of its own; see Traue (2013).
17 A more detailed exploration of the relationship between discourse and legitimation can be found in Knoblauch (2011).
18 Aesthetic theory has repeatedly shown us that this naturally applies to pure 'communicative innovation' as well, that is, the spoken word, writings, and visual objectifications.

where, as an explicit goal of planning it is a new and trailblazing phenomenon. Innovation becomes reflexive as a discourse in, for example, the academic field of Innovation Management that makes innovation in its institutionalized form an explicit topic of its communication. This also applies to debates about the relevance of innovation, the measurement of innovation, or the delimitation of innovation from other areas such as social innovation.

The reflexivity of organized innovation, however, is not explicitly limited to communicating in a discourse. Organized innovation, because it is institutionalized, finds expression in objectified forms: it can be based in hierarchical or heterogeneous organizations and be conducted by fiat in such a manner that it makes the new into a constituent '*idée directrice*' for these institutions. We simply have to look at the obvious example of science. In this case we expressly consider the question of the new (and how it arises) only in very rare cases—unless we belong to an institution explicitly concerned with innovation. All the same, we are under pressure to create something new because the institutional structure operates as a kind of framework that gives a direction to the institution's actions and at the same time serves as a semantic frame of reference for the 'right' actions.

Frameworks like this become explicit as relational factors when they are criticized. This is why scientists can demand as the last resort, so to speak, that the novelty of a research result be proved if they do not accept the practical routines (as the 'present state of research'). The same applies to technical matters in industrial research and development departments. Here, as in a series of other institutions, innovation can explicitly be an '*idée directrice*.' This applies, for example, to so-called 'innovation centers' as well as to start-ups and a series of institutions explicitly dedicated to innovation. In Berlin alone we can see the emergence of a growing number of organized centers for technical innovation (Siemens, Telekom, Google, etc.) as well as for environmental, cultural, or social innovation. These centers tackle special operational problems, but their special feature is that in addressing their problems they concentrate on innovation in general, specifically by creating discourses and forms of communication such as future talks, productive confrontation, experiment days, and the like.[19]

---

19 Using the example of social innovation in the city, Noack (2014) first suggests, and later shows in detail, that various levels can be distinguished more precisely: innovation itself (such as a new form of urban journalism), the process in which this innovating arises (for example, the aforementioned types of communication about innovation, the organizations in which this occurs, such as civic associations) and, finally, the organizational and financial structures that they are linked to innovations (e.g., urban institutions), acknowledge them, value, and evaluate it.

6 The Innovation Society

A.N. Whitehead once commented that the greatest invention of the 19th century was the invention of the method of invention (Godin 2008: 22). If we regard invention as the principle of the early and classical modern age, innovation appears as a characteristic of late modernity. This is especially evident in the mention of the word 'innovation' in the German language between 1800 and 2000 (see Figure 1).

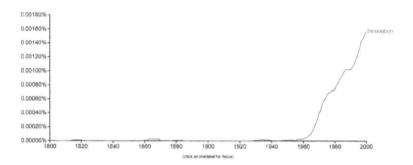

Figure 1 Incidence of the term 'innovation' in the German language segment of the 5.2 million books scanned by Google (source: https://books.google.com/ngrams/graph?content=innovation&year_start=1800&year_end=2000&corpus=20&smoothing=3&share=&direct_url=t1%3B%2Cinnovation%3B%2Cc0); retrieved July 28, 2017.

The institutionalization of innovation, its role in discourse, and the corresponding reflexivization throughout society seems to be an even more recent development for, as Steve Fuller remarked critically (2007: 103): "Innovation is the first global policy craze of the twenty-first century." In fact, the growing importance of innovation fosters the assumption that it is becoming a principle of action that influences today's society, thereby making it an innovation society. The question that increasingly comes to the fore is "how people cope when they are supposed to adjust to a society that constantly has to produce innovation to remain capable of surviving economically" (Kehrbaum 2009: 136, my translation). To cite Rammert, the innovation society means that "all areas [of social life] must permanently innovate and reciprocally coordinate reflexively with each other to do so." In this manner "innovation itself becomes the principle of integration into the future development of other areas that are self-innovating" (Rammert 2013: 13f., my translation).

As far as I can see, two different models emerge from the description of this kind of (still empirically untested) hypothesis of the development toward the innovation society. If we emphasize the institutional aspects of innovation, as most actors in the field do, the innovation society appears as an extension of a principle of action from the technical and scientific subsystem of society into other subsystems. Rammert (2008, 2010), for example, represents this view: Whereas the different social subsystems become increasingly fragmented, innovation becomes an overarching frame of reference that transcends its boundaries and has an impact on society as a whole beyond the individual systems. Innovation also alters its legitimation in this process. It is translated, so to speak, into the 'logic' of various subsystems and consequently contributes to further fragmentation.

From this perspective the concept of creativity also appears as a translation of innovation into the code of particular subsystems or social fields such as art, education, or mass media. In this process the concept of innovation still seems, despite translation, to draw on the rationality of science, technology, and economy, with the result that translation concepts such as 'creativity' are, we could say, only lexical substitutions for a semantics that remains unchanged.

In contrast to this idea we could formulate a different theoretical model of the innovation society. According to this model, creativity represents its own independent category that transcends the boundaries between different institutional areas and systems (Reckwitz 2017). In particular, ever since Florida's (2004) rapid dissemination of the concept, creativity seems to be a possible alternative to innovation. One reason for this could be that, following on from Rousseau's and the Romantic movement's ideas of subjectivity, creativity is increasingly being integrated into the educational programs of global educational systems as well. Creativity could actually become a code that displaces that of innovation.

Of course, there is no reason why innovation and creativity have to be opposed to each other as two alternative models; in fact, we could even surmise that creativity is, so to speak, the subjective form of appropriation or the form of subjectification of an innovation that not only extends across institutions but also empowers the subject.[20] But even if this coupling of innovation and creativity is possible and may currently be gaining general acceptance, we should still remember that from the perspective of theory of action, creativity and innovation indicate two different directions.

---

20 Nowotny (1995: 210f.) describes this aspect in the following manner: "Innovation, as the social side of creativity, means that it is a process through which individual creativity is communicated and thereby negotiated, transmitted and ultimately accepted or rejected."

7 Conclusion: The Action Structure of Innovation and Creativity

If innovation as a form of communicative action introduces something new into social reality, then what is characteristic of the new, as I have shown, is due to the communicative aspect of action. The temporality that is assumed in the new is, however, a universal aspect of action. This is because actions are distinguished by the fact that they are directed toward a design in the future, toward what Schütz (1962) called 'future exacti.' Even if, as I have already said, we do not yet have enough empirical research on this orientation to the future, we can follow Mannheim (1979: 190ff.) in differentiating between various models of future orientation or 'utopian mentality.' Mannheim identifies chiliasm as a key ideal type of utopian mentality oriented toward a completely different world; and the idea of the revolutionary upheaval of everything currently in existence is also a kind of utopian mentality. In contrast to a conservative ideology that is skeptical about innovation—which represents the third form of utopian mentality—Mannheim identified a fourth form: the liberal utopian consciousness that tries to achieve changes in incremental steps. This is the model that comes closest to the conception of the future in relation to innovation. Its proximity to the liberal model is highly plausible in terms of the sociology of knowledge, given that the more recent innovation trend coincides with the idea of the 'end of ideologies' after the fall of the Berlin Wall. Instead of the utopian desire to design new things, this is done step by step, even experimentally, so to speak. The 'destruction of the old' that Schumpeter emphasized is still directed at only a small segment, at special objects, technologies, or ideas. We can even question whether the idea of 'destruction' fits with the discourse of innovation at all, or whether evolutionary ideas of adaptation, improvement, and correction, which certainly have conservative features, are not more important instead. We can therefore surmise that innovation is a variation of the liberal idea of time. We are no longer talking about planned change and incremental steps (which imply the idea of progress); rather, this is about a reflexive change that monitors its change while performing the steps, or in other words, monitors its own changes.

Unlike innovation, which is characterized by a temporal difference between the old and the new, creativity highlights a different distinction. First, from a temporal perspective it does not aim for the new that emerges in reality but at the particular that emerges through the actors. In this sense it stresses the difference the subject makes. The important point is not, initially, that which is new in reality. Rather, it refers to the fact that something is done by a subject in its own way that makes it unmistakable and only new on a third perceptual plane. Whatever might be new about this becomes clear first of all with reference to the diversity of the subjective perspective. Even if the creating contained in creativity always has a temporal perspective, what emerges here as 'a new thing' is not essentially temporally defined.

Although the innovation society toys with creativity, we must reiterate that creativity and innovation involve two different approaches to orientations for action. This difference can definitely have consequences. As Esposito (2011) explains, innovation in modern society occurs as the diffusion of new things through imitation. Imitation is also a model linked to mass production and mass media. The mass media allow the things that have been newly created to be disseminated. By now, the spread of digital media makes detachment from mass production and the mass media easier and affects innovation because products can now be created by the subjects themselves. Even if the required means of production are relatively standardized, they allow the subjects to design their own products creatively without newness playing a role (even if it is claimed). The otherness that comes from this difference is then regarded as the new (an experience that we not infrequently have in science).

It is precisely this, of course, that is called into question when we are concerned with innovation that has to be proved. For this reason we must clarify whether what is subjectively seen as different can also be regarded as new. Independently of how this question is answered, we must sharply distinguish between two orientations, which can certainly coexist with each other in the innovation society or can be intertwined in conflict. However, whether they do this is an empirical question, the investigation of which actually presupposes the concept of the innovation society.

References

Archer, Margaret S. 2012. *The Reflexive Imperative in Late Modernity*. Cambridge: Cambridge University Press.
Badiou, Alain. 2007. *Being and Event*. London: Continuum.
Beck, Ulrich and Christoph Lau. 2005. "Theorie und Empirie reflexiver Modernisierung: Von der Notwendigkeit und den Schwierigkeiten, einen historischen Gesellschaftswandel innerhalb der Moderne zu beobachten und zu begreifen." *Soziale Welt* 56(2/3): 107-135.
Berger, Peter. L. and Thomas Luckmann. 1966. *The Social Construction of Reality*. New York: Free Press.
Comte, Auguste. 1830. *Cours de philosophie positive*. Paris: Rouen.
De ́Medici, Lorenzo. n.d. *Canti Carnascialeschi, Canzona di Bacco*. n.p.
Drucker, Peter. 1969. *The Age of Discontinuity. Guidelines for a Changing Society*. London: Heinemann.
Esposito, Elena. 2011. "Originality through Imitation: The Rationality of Fashion." *Organization Studies* 32(5): 603-613.
Flichy, Patrice. 1995. *L'innovation technique*. Paris: La Découverte.
Fuller, Steve. 2007. "Creativity in an Orwellian key." Pp. 97-114 in *Knowledge, Communication, and Creativity*, edited by A. Sales, M. Fournier. London: Sage.
Garud, Raghu and Joel Gehman. 2012. "Metatheoretical Perspective in Sustainability Journeys: Evolutionary, Relational and Durational." *Research Policy* 41(6): 980-995.
Giddens, Anthony. 1990. *The Consequences of Modernity*. Cambridge: Polity Press.
Godin, Benoît. 2008. *Innovation. The History of a Category* (Working Paper 1). Montréal: Project on the Intellectual History of Innovation. Retrieved September 01, 2015 (http://www.csiic.ca/PDF/IntellectualNo1. Pdf.).
Godin, Benoît. 2012. *Social Innovation. Utopias of Innovation from 1830 to the Present* (Working Paper 11). Montréal: Project on the Intellectual History of Innovation. Retrieved September 01, 2015 (http://scienceofsciencepolicy.net/publication/social-innovation-utopias-innovation-1830-present).
Groys, Boris. 2002. *Über das Neue. Versuch einer Kulturökonomie*. Frankfurt a. M.: Fischer.
Habermas, Jürgen. 1984. *Theory of Communicative Action Volume One: Reason and the Rationalization of Society*. Boston: Beacon Press.
Howaldt, Jürgen and Michael Schwarz. 2010. *"Soziale Innovation" im Fokus. Skizze eines gesellschaftsinspirierten Forschungskonzepts*. Bielefeld: transcript.
Hutter, Michael. 2014. "Cultural Conditions of Creation: A Communication-Centered Approach to Reckwitz' 'Creativity Dispositif.'" Pp. 32-47 in *Culture, Communication, and Creativity. Reframing the Relations of Media, Knowledge, and Innovation in Society*, edited by H. Knoblauch, M. Jacobs, and R. Tuma. Berlin: Lang.
Hutter, Michael, Hubert Knoblauch, Werner Rammert, and Arnold Windeler. 2015. "Innovation Society Today. The Reflexive Creation of Novelty." *Historical Social Research* 40(3): 30-47.
Ibert, Oliver. 2003. *Innovationsorientierte Planung. Verfahren und Strategien zur Organisation von Innovation*. Opladen: Leske & Budrich.
Joas, Hans. 1996. *The Creativity of Action*. Chicago: University of Chicago Press.

Kehrbaum, Tom. 2009. *Innovation als sozialer Prozess. Die Grounded Theory als Methodologie und Praxis der Innovationsforschung*. Wiesbaden: Springer VS.

Keller, Reiner, Hubert Knoblauch, and Jo Reichertz, eds. 2013. *Kommunikativer Konstruktivismus. Theoretische und empirische Arbeiten zu einem neuen wissenssoziologischen Ansatz*. Wiesbaden: Springer VS.

Knoblauch, Hubert. 1995. *Kommunikationskultur. Die kommunikative Konstruktion kultureller Kontexte*. Berlin, New York: De Gruyter.

Knoblauch, Hubert. 2001. "Communication, Contexts and Culture. A Communicative Constructivist Approach to Intercultural Communication." Pp. 3-33 in *Culture in Communication. Analyses of Intercultural Situations*, edited by A. Di Luzio, S. Günthner, and F. Orletti. Amsterdam: John Benjamins.

Knoblauch, Hubert. 2005. Wissenssoziologie. Constance: UVK.

Knoblauch, Hubert. 2011. "Diskurs, Kommunikation und Wissenssoziologie." Pp. 225-244 in *Handbuch sozialwissenschaftliche Diskursanalyse Band 1: Theorien und Methoden*, edited by A. Hirseland, R. Keller, W. Schneider, and W. Viehöver. Opladen: Leske & Budrich.

Knoblauch, Hubert. 2013a. "Grundbegriffe und Aufgaben des kommunikativen Konstruktivismus." Pp. 25-48 in *Kommunikativer Konstruktivismus. Theoretische und empirische Arbeiten zu einem neuen wissenssoziologischen Ansatz*, edited by R. Keller, H. Knoblauch, and J. Reichertz. Wiesbaden: Springer VS.

Knoblauch, Hubert. 2013b. "Projection, Imagination and Novelty. Towards a Theory of Creative Action based on Schütz." Pp. 31-50 in *The Interrelation of Phenomenology, Social Sciences and the Arts*, edited by J. Dreher & M. Barber. Dordrecht: Springer.

Knoblauch, Hubert and Bernt Schnettler. 2000. "Die Apokalypse findet nicht statt. Prophetische Zukunftsvisionen zum Ende des Jahrtausends in Deutschland." Pp. 26-30 in *Sieben Hügel. Bilder und Zeichen des 21. Jahrhunderts. Vol. V: Glauben*, edited by B.-M. Baumunk & E. M. Thimme. Berlin: Henschel-Verlag.

Kosellek, Reinhart. 2006. *Begriffsgeschichten. Studien zur Semantik und Pragmatik der politischen und sozialen Sprache*. Frankfurt a. M.: Suhrkamp.

Lamont, Michèle. 2012. "Toward a Comparative Sociology of Valuation and Evaluation." In: *Annual Review of Sociology* 38(1): 201-221.

Latour, Bruno. 2005. *Reassembling the Social: An Introduction to Actor-Network-Theory*. Oxford: Oxford University Press.

MacCallum, Diana, Frank Moulaert, Jean Hillier, and Serena Vicari Haddock, eds. 2009. *Social Innovation and Territorial Development*. Aldershot: Ashgate.

Mannheim, Karl. 1979 [1936]. *Ideology and Utopia*. London: Routledge.

Minois, Georges. 1996. *Histoire de l'avenir, des Prophètes à la prospective*. Paris: Fayard.

Moulaert, Frank and Barbara Van Dyck. 2013. "Framing Social Innovation Research: A Sociology of Knowledge Perspective." Pp. 466-480 in *The International Handbook on Social Innovation: Collective Action, Social Learning and Transdisciplinary Research*, edited by F. Moulaert, D. MacCallum, A. Mehmood, and A. Hamdouch. Cheltenham: Edward Elgar.

Noack, Anika. 2014. "'Anybody got an idea?' Communicative Forms, Roles and Legitimations in the Communicative Genesis and Negotiation of Social Innovation." Pp. 101-123 in *Culture, Communication, and Creativity. Reframing the Relations of Media, Knowl-*

edge, and Innovation in Society, edited by H. Knoblauch, M. Jacobs, and R. Tuma. Berlin: Lang.

Rammert, Werner. 2008. "Technik und Innovation." Pp. 291-319 in *Handbuch der Wirtschaftssoziologie*, edited by A. Maurer. Wiesbaden: VS Verlag für Sozialwissenschaften.

Rammert, Werner. 2010. "Die Innovationen der Gesellschaft." Pp. 21-51 in *Soziale Innovationen. Auf dem Weg zu einem post-industriellen Innovationsparadigma*, edited by J. Howaldt and H. Jakobsen. Wiesbaden: Springer VS.

Rammert, Werner. 2013. *Vielfalt der Innovation und gesellschaftlicher Zusammenhalt* (Working Papers 1-2013). Berlin: Technische Universität Berlin.

Reckwitz, Andreas. 2017. The Invention of Creativity. Modern Society and the Culture of the New. London: Polity.

Rogers, Everett M. 1995. *Diffusion of Innovations*. 4th ed. New York: Free Press.

Schnettler, Bernt. 2004. *Zukunftsvisionen. Transzendenzerfahrungen und Alltagswelt*. Constance: UVK.

Schubert, Cornelius. This volume. "Social Innovation. A New Instrument for Social Change?"

Schumpeter, Joseph A. 1939. *Business Cycles. A Theoretical, Historical, and Statistical Analysis of the Capitalist Process*. New York: McGraw-Hill.

Schütz, Alfred. 1962. "Common-Sense and Scientific Interpretation of Human Action." Pp. 3-47 in *Collected Papers I. The Problem of Social Reality*, edited by M. Natanson. The Hague: Nijhoff.

Suchman, Lucy. 1987. *Plans and Situated Actions*. Cambridge: CUP.

Tarde, Gabriel. 1962 [1890]. *The Laws of Imitation*. Gloucester, Mass: Smith.

Traue, Boris. 2013. "Visuelle Diskursanalyse. Ein programmatischer Vorschlag zur Untersuchung von Sicht- und Sagbarkeiten im Medienwandel." *Zeitschrift für Diskursforschung*, 2(1): 117-136.

Weber, Max. 1978 [1922]. *Economy and Society*. Berkeley, Los Angeles: University of California Press.

Windeler, Arnold. 2003. "Kreation technologischer Pfade: Ein strukturationstheoretischer Ansatz." *Managementforschung* 13: 295-328.

The Creativity *Dispositif* and the Social Regimes of the New

Andreas Reckwitz

1 Creativity from the Perspective of Social Theory

A sociological understanding of creativity can mean two things. Either creativity is grasped as an intrinsic characteristic and *prerequisite* of human action or the social world, or creativity is understood as a *product* of a very specific sociocultural constellation, primarily of modernity or postmodernity, that defines, promotes, and reinforces creativity in its own way. In both cases creativity is viewed from a sociological angle that is clearly different from that of the ubiquitous psychological discourse. Most psychological studies on creativity that have been conducted since J. P. Guilford's (1950) influential lecture to the American Psychological Association posit creativity as a universal—if perhaps unevenly distributed—faculty of the human mind (or brain) and its cognitive structures (see Runco 2007). As soon as creativity becomes the focus of sociology, however, this reduction to the cognitive dimension is bound to fall short.

Actually, this social dimension can relate to two wholly different constellations. At the level of general social theory, creativity can be understood as a structural feature of the social, as the inherent characteristic of practices, interactions, communication, or social processes that repeatedly and unpredictably bring about new kinds of events of their own accord. Thus, in a way, creativity can be said to predicate the social dimension. Informed by action theory, the work by Heinrich Popitz (1997) and Hans Joas (1996) points in this direction. In quite a different way, Gilles Deleuze and Félix Guattari's (1987) poststructuralist, postvitalistic theory of rhizomatic structures can be regarded as the kind of approach that stresses the inherent creativity of the social world (albeit without explicitly using the concept of creativity). Authors in the field of cultural studies, too, such as Paul Willis (1990), presuppose the experimental, even subversive potential of social practices and, hence, ultimately their inherent 'creativity.' For all their differences, these authors characteristically share a more or less emphatic normative identification with the creative dimension as something ostensibly natural in human beings, a trait of all that is alive, or a source of the political.

This perspective that social theory has on the phenomenon of creativity indisputably has its merits and serves as a necessary counterweight to explicit or latent structuralist approaches, which start from the assumption that social stability and reproduction are normal. I want to pursue a different path, however. In my understanding, creativity is not a universal trait of humanity or social practice but rather a very specific social, cultural, and historical product. As a subject of study, the phenomenon of creativity thus shifts from the realm of general social theory to the theory of modernity, historical sociology, and cultural sociology. From this perspective it is crucial to embed the understanding of creativity thoroughly and minutely in the historically specific social practices and discourses that bring it about.

Of course, there is a need in social theory for a vocabulary that acknowledges social reproduction and social change alike, a vocabulary that recognizes the repetition of sameness and the inception of the new as much as structuralizing forms of the social world. However, such a view easily does without the culturally loaded concept of creativity and by no means has to be linked with a modernistic glorification of the inception of the new and a complementary normative denigration of social repetitions.[1] One must in fact assume that social complexes of practices alternate between repetition and the emergence of novelties. A complete reproduction of the same is just as marginal a case as a complete break with the past in an utterly new event.

From the perspective of social theory and empirical sociology, however, other questions are more interesting: How is it that modernity, particularly late modernity (the phase since the 1970s and 1980s), has come to be marked by the ever greater prevalence of a social constellation that prioritizes and systematically promotes creativity? How and why have late-modern subjects learned to see themselves as 'creative' and to model themselves accordingly as a 'creative self'? How have vastly dissimilar social fields been restructured in a way that they follow a social

---

1   In my view, one of the key merits of a theory of social practices (see Giddens 1979; Reckwitz 2003) is that it places this dual character of repetition and normality at the core of the social world.

regime of the new, especially the aesthetically new? As I see it, the question of creativity is not really one of the 'human being' but rather one of modernity. My basic assumption is that a dynamic *dispositif* of creativity (the precursors of which date back centuries) emerged in Western societies during the 20th century and has intensified since the 1970s. As a *dispositif*, it crosses the boundaries between functionally differentiated systems, encompassing the arts as well as broad segments of the economy, the mass media, city planning, and areas of psychological counseling. Thus, late-modern society is changing direction toward a structure of expecting and producing the aesthetically new.

My perspective is, then, influenced by that of Michel Foucault (although he never showed much interest himself in the phenomenon of creativity). Just as Foucault's genealogical-archeological analysis of the *dispositif* of sexuality has a demystifying effect and decodes something seemingly natural as a sociocultural and historical constellation (see Foucault 1978), a comparable perspective on creativity can have a similar effect. How and along which path have Western social practices, discourses, and ways of subjectification internalized the form of the creative production and reception of the new to the point that it has since come to seem like a quasi-natural order of things?

A sociological analysis of the origin and current structures of the creativity *dispositif* is a complex task. The available space confines me to providing an analytical framework consisting of four basic assumptions.

1. The creative complex of contemporary society is a highly specific version of what I call social regimes of the new in modernity: a regime of the aesthetically new.
2. This regime of the aesthetically new requires clarification of the terms of aesthetic practices and of aesthetization, which prove to be essential for a sociology of the present.
3. The creativity *dispositif* can be understood as a specific constellation of sociality composed of producers, the audience, things, and elements that manage attention.
4. The social field of modern art is a structural prototype of the creativity *dispositif*.

This backdrop allows me to summarize my argument, namely, that the culturalization of society, condensed in the *dispositif* of creativity, has come to represent the model that has succeeded the classic industrial, scientist 'innovation society.' It also permits me to develop a corresponding heuristic framework for analyzing social regimes of the new in modernity, particularly late modernity.

2 Regimes of the New

In the framework of the creativity *dispositif*, the status of a familiar core element of structure and semantics in modern societies changes fundamentally: the new.[2] It is a classical diagnosis to say that modern society in its institutions and semantics is essentially oriented not to traditional repetition but rather to dynamic self-change, that it always has an inherent preference for the new as opposed to the old. Ever since its emergence in the late 18th century, modern society has tried to promote the new at the political, economic, scientific, technical, and artistic levels in every way, be it political revolutions and reforms, technical inventions, the circulation of commodities, or artistic originality.[3] The new is not necessarily oriented to progress or thinking in terms of 'absolute breaks.' Rather it is based on a temporal matrix that distinguishes between the past, present, and future as distinct and prefers the new to the old.

However, a regime of the new does not have just a temporal connotation but a phenomenalistic and social one as well. At the level of phenomena, the new sets what is different apart from what is the same. In social terms, the new points to what deviates as opposed to what is normal and normatively expected. Whether at the temporal or the social level, the new never exists objectively. It is always a function of frequently contested observational and perceptual schemata. 'Social regimes of the new,' as shown to be characteristic for modern society, are now ensembles of practices, discourses, manners of subjectification, and systems of artifacts, which do not only observe the new and prefer it but which are also keen on promoting and actively bringing it about, escalating it, and intensifying it.

In terms of ideal types, one can distinguish between three different modern forms of the new. They follow upon each other in rough sequence, without the older ones completely vanishing. They are the regime of the new as a stage (New I),

---

2   In parts 1 through 4 of this essay, I draw on passages from *The Invention of Creativity—Modern Society and the Culture of the New* (Reckwitz 2017), particularly from the first and second chapters.

3   For a classical treatment of semantics, see Koselleck (2004). Although the diagnosis that modern society is oriented to the new is familiar, analysis of social regimes of the new is still awaiting the formulation of a comprehensive sociological research program that goes beyond the classical research area that focuses on processes of technological innovation. Werner Rammert (2010) clearly pointed out the necessity of such a detailed analytic approach—on which the *Innovationsgesellschaft heute* research training group builds. In principle, I am inclined to agree, but at this general level I prefer using the term *regimes of newness* and exploiting the difference between the two concepts.

the regime of the new in the sense of escalation and intensification (New II), and the regime of the new as a kind of stimulus (New III). To put it succinctly, these regimes of dynamization have three corresponding models of modernity: the modernity of perfection, the modernity of progress, and aesthetic modernity. The first regime of the new aspires to a stage at which an old constellation is replaced by a new, more progressive and more rational one once and for all. The new appears as something absolutely and clearly novel, revolutionary. After passing through this stage, after the new has been achieved, it no longer needs anything fundamentally new; at most it only requires incremental improvements. This model is the one on which political revolution is based. In the New I constellation, the new is thus subordinate to the goal of politico-moral progress, which finally appears.

The regime of the new in the sense of escalation and intensification, New II, is different. In that constellation the aim is to produce the new in a continuous, eternal process. Scientific development of technical solutions is characteristic of this regime, but it also includes economic innovation in the market. The concept of escalation encompasses quantitative increases and qualitative leaps. In any case, the constellation of New II is characterized by the fact that the individual act of the new contains the normative aspiration of improvement and that this sequence of improvement is infinite.

The regime of the new as aesthetic stimulus, New III, which proves to be a key part of the creativity *dispositif*, is organized differently than either of the two other regimes. It, too, is about the dynamic production of a sequence of new acts that are infinite, but the value of the new is largely divested of its progressive connotations. The value of the new consists not in its integration into a sequence of progress but rather in its momentary aesthetic stimulus, which is repeatedly replaced by the next different sensual, affective quality. It is not progress or intensification but rather the movement itself, the succession of stimuli, that is of interest and normative priority. The new determines itself essentially by its sheer difference to past, old events, by its difference in the sense of being other than what is identical, and by its difference as a welcome departure from the usual. The new is thus the *relatively* new as an event. It does not demarcate a structural break. As part of the regime of the aesthetically new, the new shares a semantic field with the interesting, surprising, and original.

The regime of the New III does not imply a concept of progress or intensification. Instead, it is based on a pure concept of difference devoid of normative connotations and with an affective character. The production of the new no longer follows the model of political revolution or that of technological invention but rather the creation of objects or atmospheres that stimulate the senses and meanings and that are emotionally operative, as is the case for the first time in modern art.

3 Processes of Aesthetization

If the creativity *dispositif* can be basically understood as a social regime of the aesthetically new in the sense of New III, then what can one take 'aesthetic' and 'aesthetic practices' to mean? Indeed, the creativity *dispositif* drives a process of aesthetization as radical as it is specific. But what is the aesthetic, and what are aesthetizations? The word *aisthesis* originally referred to the entire gamut of sensory perception. A discriminating use of the term, however, does not equate aesthetic with sensory perception as a whole but instead draws on a basic intuition of classical aesthetics. As I understand it, the aesthetic refers to sensuous processes as denoting dynamic processes that have become disengaged from their purposive-rational, pragmatic embedding. Aisthesis as the totality of all sensory perception can then be distinguished from aesthetic perception in particular (see Seel 1996). The specific nature of aesthetic perceptions is that they are beholden to being ends in themselves and that they are self-referential.

This contemporary understanding of aesthetic should be freed from the classical coupling to good taste, beauty, contemplation, and the autonomous sphere of art.[4] The crucial point about aesthetic perceptions is not whether they are beautiful or ugly, harmonious or dissonant, introverted or pleasurably exciting but rather that they are not subordinated to purposive rationality and their cognitive acts of mere information processing. They must instead possess their own dynamic and an orientation to being acted upon. Aesthetic practices are thus found not only in art or the natural environment—the classical cases of the bourgeois philosophical aesthetic—but also at the sports stadium or on a tourist trip; in fashion design, interior decoration, and gastronomy; in sexuality and eroticism; and in 'creative work.' Aesthetic perceptions include still another dimension in a specific way, namely, they are not purely sensory activity but rather also contain a considerable degree of affectivity, a spontaneous and self-referential emotional involvement of the subject. Aesthetic phenomena always encompass a double of 'perceptions and affections' (Deleuze and Guattari 1994: 132). Aesthetic sensory perceptions include a specific affective response of the subject through an object; a situation; a mood, state of mind, or arousal; an enthusiastic, concerned, or placid feeling.

---

4   The notion of restricting aesthetics to beauty is still defended in some sociological diagnoses, as in Lipovetsky and Serroy (2013). However, I dissociate myself from the concept's complete abstraction as found in Welsch (1996). He relates aesthetics to contingency situations in general, thus dissolving the tie to sensory perceptions and affects.

A praxeological look at sensuousness and affective response is central to a sociological understanding of the aesthetic dimension. Two aggregate conditions of the aesthetic dimension can be distinguished from each other in this context: aesthetic episodes and aesthetic practices. In aesthetic episodes an aesthetic perception momentarily and unpredictably appears; a subject is affected by an object, thereby breaking the cycle of expedience. Then the moment disappears. In aesthetic practices, by contrast, aesthetic perceptions or objects are repeatedly evoked for such a perception in a routine or habitual manner. Aesthetic practices thus always contain frequently implied aesthetic knowledge, cultural schemata that guide the production and reception of aesthetic events. Such an understanding of the aesthetic emphasizes an aspect of social practice long marginalized by rationalist philosophy and sociology. The antonym of the aesthetic that refers to spontaneous sensory perception and affective response is instrumental and rule-based action in which sensory perception surfaces only secondarily as cognitive information processing. In this context affects, too, appear to be subordinated to the rationality or normativity of the action context, which ideally is neutral in terms of affect.

This background to the understanding of the aesthetic can clarify the contours of the phenomenon of social aesthetization,[5] which involves a precise, definable structural change. In processes of aesthetization, the share of aesthetic practices as a whole within society expands at the expense of primarily nonaesthetic, instrumental, and normative practices. The exact form and direction of the aesthetization can vary greatly. In reality, aesthetization lends weight to the meaning of 'pure' aesthetic practices but also increases hybrid practices. Instrumental or normative practices, too, are encompassing ever more elements of aesthetic practices (as in the work process or a partnership). The distinctive feature of the creativity *dispositif* is that it imposes an aesthetization oriented to the production and reception of *new* aesthetic events. As stated above, modern society has always structurally driven novelty at the political and technological levels as well. Conversely, vastly different types of society have always had aesthetic practices oriented not to originality but rather to repetition and ritualization.[6] The creativity *dispositif* focuses the aesthetic on novelty and focuses the regime of novelty on the aesthetic. It marks an overlap between aesthetizations and the social regimes of the new (see Figure 1).

---

5   Schulze (1992) presented a related concept of aesthetization. However, it focuses on the way that aesthetic practices are received, that is, on their consumption-oriented aspect.
6   A classic place in this respect is indisputably the aesthetic of ancient Japan and China (see Jullien 2010; also Han 2011), (source: own illustration).

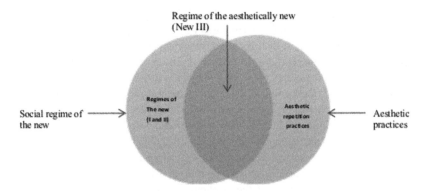

Figure 1 Regimes of the new and aesthetization (source: own illustration).

4 Aesthetic Socialities: Creators, Audiences, Structures of Attention

The discussion thus far has shown that a specific structure of sociality is characteristic of the creativity *dispositif*. I generally assume that the social has no fixed suprahistorical structure but rather coalesces from historically specific and different forms. Now, the sociality of the creativity *dispositif* does not have a structure of simple interactions or communications at its core, nor is it sustained by a normative system of rules or a structure of exchange between actors driven by some rational purpose—all 'classical' forms of the social world that have been extensively discussed in sociology. Essentially, I am talking about a form of the social that is characterized by a relation between aesthetic producers or creators, an audience, and objects. On the one hand, there have to be practices oriented to the production of aesthetically new entities and sustained by corresponding individuals or collective 'creators.' On the other hand, there has to be an audience interested primarily in the aesthetic appropriation of objects and events. Practices and audience are linked through material cultural objects.

The creativity *dispositif*'s form of aesthetization is coupled to a particular production ethos, that of the creative. It requires that the aesthetically new be brought about by a subject or other agent, such as a collective or practice itself. Processes of aesthetization that take place in the context of the creativity *dispositif* thereby go beyond the scope of what Guy Debord (1970) understood as being meant by a 'society of the spectacle' with passive consumers. Within the *dispositif*, institutions and subjects are in fact confronted by the imperative of having to mobilize creative potential and produce new aesthetic objects and events: works of art, cultural aesthetic goods, services, media formats and innovations, transformations of urban space, and self-presentations in social networks. The creators in this scenario differ from the producers in industrialized society, who were producers of types. Instead, I am talking about the productive creation of singularities, of unique, new kinds of things.

However, the creative producers depend on an audience as a second, complementary entity. The aesthetic stimulus provided by the new demands an audience that notes the novelty of the new and allows itself to be impressed by it. Ultimately, there is no such thing as 'the new' as an objective fact. It depends on a corresponding form of attention and valuation that focuses solely on the new and distinguishes it from the old. Niklas Luhmann (1990) justifiably pointed out that the social fields of modern society all cultivate achievement functions and audience functions alike. In the case of the creativity *dispositif*, however, the audience maintains a special form. The audience relates to what it observes, receives, and uses not in terms of processing information but rather in terms of the symbolic, sensory, and emotional excitability. The late-modern audience is essentially an aesthetically interested one.

Producers before an audience are always producers of performative acts. They 'perform' in front of an audience. In that relationship, however, audience and producers are linked with each other by a third entity: objects. The audience's interest is in the aesthetic objects, which must have a sensually perceptible materiality, and they are cultural and aesthetic conveyors of meaning and affect. Aesthetic objects include things that can be experienced through sight or touch (images, apparel, or furniture), hearing (tones, music), or taste or smell (food). They can be spatially complex aesthetic surroundings (e.g., urban spaces). Lastly, the subject's body itself can become an aesthetic object before the audience (as in theater and film).

The triad consisting of producers, audience, and objects is held together by a specific coordinating mechanism: the distribution of attention. The audience is a source of collective attention that sooner or later settles on certain objects and shifts away from others. In social practice, actors inevitably attend only to a limited set of phenomena, though. Now, in the context of the creativity *dispositif*, attention is directed by the guiding criterion: the new. Events that the observers perceive as novel tend to appear worthy of interest and have a chance of retaining their attention for a while in order to produce an aesthetic effect. The management of the audience's attention is thus a key coordination problem of the late-modern social world (see Figure 2).

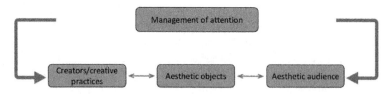

Figure 2 Sociality of the creativity *dispositif* (source: own illustration).

5 The Field of Art as a Blueprint

Aesthetic practices and aesthetization, a social regime of the aesthetically new and emotionally fascinating, a constellation of creators, audience, objects, and structures of attention—it is remarkable that the social field of art, the blueprint provided by the social field for all these structural features of the creativity *dispositif*, has tended to be marginalized by sociological analysis (on this point see also Menger 2006). But all these features characterized the field of modern art when it originated around 1800, although its initial form was quite specific.

5.1 Modern art constitutes a social ensemble keyed to bringing about aesthetically oriented practices (i.e., those entailed in the production and reception of aesthetic events) in as absolute a form as possible. They consist in practices serving spontaneous sensuousness and affective response absolved of all rational purpose. The practices in modern art are attempts to establish art's autonomy through various strategies and methods that differentiate the purely aesthetic from both the moral, normative realm and rational purpose as well as from the 'impure aesthetic' dimension (e.g., the popular and kitsch) and the crafts. Although these attempts to establish the arts as an independent sphere of pure aesthetics ostensibly hinder the later spread of aesthetic practices beyond art, it is crucial to see that the attempts to separate aesthetic experiences sharply from instrumental actions thereby make it possible to escalate and intensify the former. This radical project of achieving an 'absolute aesthetic' by diversifying the field of art is what has enabled aesthetic events to retain their amazing attraction in modern times.

5.2 The aesthetic practices of modern art are tied into a social regime of the aesthetically new, the aim of which is to evoke a constant series of novel aesthetic events, that is, new kinds of works of art offering different sensual and emotional surprises. This regime of novelty has characterized modern art (as opposed to premodern art, including neoclassical works) since 1780 and was discursively prepared through the positioning of the 'aesthetics of genius' against the classical 'aesthetics of rules.' Whereas in the aesthetics of rules the artist's task is to apply and perfect the use of the rules of ideal art and, hence, to engage in the reproduction of the old and the universal, the new aesthetic invents the artist as a creator of original works that cannot be derived from generally accepted patterns.

5.3 The field of art is characterized by a form of the social world in which aesthetic producers and an aesthetic audience rely on each other. The field of art models the figure of the artist as a 'creative producer' credited with the competence to bring aesthetically new work into the world. The field of art simultaneously cultivates the role of an aesthetically sensitized audience to complement the producer of originality. At root, the sociality of art is thereby one of neither rational production nor intersubjective interaction or exchange. It is rather about the social process of producing sensory, semiotic, and emotional stimuli for an audience. The field of art invents both of the subject's positions that characterize the creativity *dispositif*: the creative subject and the aesthetic recipient. From the outset, the field of art has also generated its own mechanisms for distributing attention: 'agencies of consecration' (Bourdieu 1984: 1) such as literary and art critique and academic canonization but also disputes between different organs that manage attention (via secessions, for example).

6 Culturalization of Society and Regimes of Innovation

My basic argument is that late-modern society is marked largely by social practices that operate through structural features of the creativity *dispositif*, through a social regime of the aesthetically new, and through a sociality of creative producers, audiences, artifacts, and structures of attention. These structural traits are discernible in many (though not all) social fields of contemporary society, no doubt especially in the economy and the mass media. They are apparent, too, in cultural ways of life. The hegemonic late-modern way of life is not only directed by 'individualization'; rather, given its principal representatives (the academic middle class), it systematically adopts the everyday ethos of a successful, 'creative' way of life. This diagnosis can be the point of departure for a comprehensive research program that traces the different manifestations, consequences, and inherent contradictions of the creative *dispositif* in different fields, milieus, and spatial contexts (local, national, and global).[7]

---

7   In more detail, I traced back the genealogy of the creativity *dispositif* in Reckwitz (2017).

How do such a line of reasoning and a research program of this kind relate to the assumption that modern society is an 'innovation society' (Hutter et al., this volume)? Of course, the answer to this question depends on how one conceptualizes the relation between innovation and creativity. In principle there are two possibilities. Either one takes innovation to be the general term encompassing any orientation to the new. In that case, the orientation to the aesthetically new is a specific subset of this general orientation. Or one treats the regimes of innovation and creativity as competing sociostructural forms of the new. As I see it, the latter assumption is more informative and heuristically more promising than the former, particularly because a third, already broadly formulated concept—the 'social regime of the new'—is available in addition to innovation and creativity. Drawing on all three concepts, one might posit the following hypothesis for a theory of modern society: In various social fields since the late 18th century, modern society has been generally and gradually shifting to social regimes of the new that emphasize and promote novelty at the expense of the traditional. It should be stressed that, in the genealogy of human societies, this shift to an antitraditionalist regime of novelty is a historically unlikely and highly unusual process. However, the exact form of the regime of the new differs from one period to the next, from bourgeois modernity to organized modernity to late modernity.[8] In bourgeois modernity the spread of the social regimes of the new represents a very uneven and initially rather slow process that emanated from discrete urban islands of modernization and gained momentum in the course of the 19th century. During bourgeois modernity, this basically progressive dynamic is still accompanied by widespread social practices that do *not* readily submit to such a social regime of the new and persist in a logic of repetition instead (e.g., in agriculture or Christian religious communities but also in the classical bourgeois way of life). In 'repetition regimes' of this kind, the new is suspect as it were. They are, by and large, traditional societies, where novel, deviant elements are systematically eliminated in favor of the received 'identical' structures, with a habitual or ritualized repetition of social practice being the goal—which is, of course, never completely accomplished.

The social regimes of the new are arrayed against these practices of repetition. Aside from examples that model the 'new as a stage' in a process, especially in the form of revolutionary practices that prepare bourgeois political revolutions,[9]

---

8 See Reckwitz (2006) on this periodization.
9 Clearly, New I is not really suited to establishing a corresponding regime in the long run, for achieving the desired stage would attain the revolutionary goal. Thus, the practices of New I tend to have a preparatory character. They are about eventually achieving the conditions in which a leap to the desired stage—usually a revolutionary

these social regimes have been primarily those modeled on the new conceived of as escalation and intensification (New II). Technological progress and its effects on economic markets and consumption habits are their backbone. Since the early 20th century, however, it is organized modernity—called 'industrial society' as an ideal type in sociology and seen as shaping 'Fordism' in post-Marxist terms—that has provided the actual sociohistorical context of such domination of technological self-intensification. Organized modernity can be understood as a prime example of an innovation society in that it subjugates broad swathes of society to the 'regime of innovation.'

I wish to use such a regime to paraphrase a novelty regime that sets store by material innovations as instrumental improvements that correspond to the model of technological progress of the New II kind. This type of society is built around the industrial mass production of capital goods and consumer goods that is regularly perfected through technological innovations in production processes as well as in consumer goods.[10] It is no contradiction to observe that most of industrialized society's work activities—in accordance with principles of efficiency—continue to consist in repetitive practices, albeit less in ritualized or habitual ones than in routines stemming from the rehearsal of formal rules.[11] An industrial society of this kind, a type that did not prevail throughout Western societies until the late

---

overthrow—is possible (as in the phases preceding the revolutions of 1789, 1848, and 1917). The status of the socialist movements in the late 19th century is interesting in this context. They initially seemed to be working merely to prepare a revolutionary situation (New I). Except for the movement in Russia, they then shifted to working on incremental reforms as part of the mainstream democracies (New II). In organized modernity, however, the focus of this incrementalist reform work is still often the imagined achievement of a final stage (meaning, in this example, the welfare state offering rights typically associated with civil society).

10 This argument is the point of departure for the broad movement of classic sociological research on innovation. See David (1975), Edquist (1997), and Braun-Thürmann (2005) to name only a few of the sources to consult.

11 I see the following differences between habitual, routinized, and ritualized practices of repetition: *Habitual* repetition rests from the outset on implicit knowledge, especially knowledge transmitted by behavioral imitation. In contrast, *routinized* repetition is based on the communication of formal rules (e.g., principles of efficiency in an organization structured according to a division of labor) that eventually lead to routinized practice (on the difference between habit and routine with respect to practices, see Bongaerts 2007). Lastly, *ritualized* repetition is a repetition marked in a culturally specific way and framed as valuable (e.g., a religious ceremony or a seasonal celebration). In a narrative woven from the theory of modernization, the routinized practices of repetition presumably gain relevance at the expense of the habitual and ritualized ones. Nevertheless, both latter kinds of repetition still exist today.

19th century, has been inextricably linked to the Fordist model of mass consumption since the early 20th century. Technological advance is not confined primarily to industry. Through productivity increases and new functional consumer goods, it reaches the mass of consumers. Accordingly, the cultural imaginary of the Fordist consumer society is dominated by a combined ideal of technological progress and affluent society, that is, mass prosperity.

The innovation society—or better, social complexes structured on criteria of the innovation society—thus basically correspond to the pattern of the New II social regime. Since the 1970s, though, the social fields and milieus of Western societies have been shifting increasingly toward the social regime of New III. In post- or late modernity they have been organizing more and more as a regime of the aesthetically new. One could simply speak of a 'creative society' or 'creativity society,' but to avoid the misleading normative connotations of such a label, I speak instead of a culturalization of society, specifically, a culturalization that has the creativity *dispositif* at its center.[12] In this context, I take culturalization to mean a structural shift in which the specific patterns and rules of the cultural field, essentially the arts, are expanding into society at large. In terms of ideal types, the form of orientation to the new in culturalized society, which is both a postindustrial and post-Fordist one, differs fundamentally from that of the classic industrial society of the Fordist kind dominated by innovation. The pattern of material, functional escalation of technological solutions is juxtaposed with the interplay of differences stemming from cultural, aesthetic stimuli as the new key engine of social dynamics. A paradigm of 'inventions' is being replaced by one of 'originalities.' Culturalized society is

---

12 My approach to the theory of modernity thus diverges from that in Hutter et al. (this volume) and the DFG Research Training Group *Innovation Society Today: Reflexive Production of Novelty* at the Technical University of Berlin and informs a research program with a different accent (though it does overlap with that of the research training group). Whereas their research program starts from the assumption that the special nature of late modernity is to be sought in the reflexivity that comes to characterize the orientation to innovation, I see the more basic structural change as lying in the cultural and aesthetic shift represented by the regime of the new. Of course, I do not wish to dispute that the existing regimes of innovation are becoming 'reflexive.' (In passing, it is also interesting to note how the regimes of the aesthetically new are likewise structured reflexively, as with aesthetic management; see Guillet de Monthoux 2004). Rather, I am thinking of a fundamentally changed perspective on modernity and postmodernity that permits examination of other phenomena that cannot be accounted for by the theory of reflexive modernization as discussed by Ulrich Beck (see Lash's justified critique of Beck and Giddens in Beck, Giddens, and Lash 1994). The idea that industrial society is giving way to the reflexive knowledge society is rooted in the old narrative of modernization theory. What is increasingly permeating the old industrial and knowledge society is, from my viewpoint, a culturalization of society.

no longer classical industrial society, but the labels of knowledge society or service society do not capture its nature, either. Both of the latter terms remain cast in the logic of the industrial society. Rather, at the economic center of late-modern society stands *cultural production*, that is, the manufacture, distribution, and consumption of semiotic-aesthetic objects *and* services.[13]

In principle, the regime of innovation and the regime of the aesthetically new differ in structure (see Table 1). In the former, affect is reduced; in the production and reception of the latter, it is highly charged. By the same token, the normative ideal of technological progress and prosperity that characterizes the regime of innovation contrasts with the ideal of quality of life and self-realization in the regime of the aesthetically new, which centers on aesthetic creation of and by the individual. The regime of innovation stands for standardized production and consumption, the regime of the aesthetically new for the pluralized production and consumption of 'singularities.' The regime of innovation places the primary emphasis on technical knowledge as a resource and on the engineer as the agent (with the ultimate ideal being the 'inventor'); the regime of the aesthetically new stresses cultural (semiotic-narrative and aesthetic) knowledge and introduces the ideal of the creative subject, with the successful 'artist' at the apex.

Table 1 Two ideal types of social regime in the creativity *dispositif.*

Innovation	The aesthetically new
Functional, technical innovations as escalation or intensification	Culturally aesthetic novelties as change of stimulation
Industrialized society	Culturalization of society
Technical knowledge/industrial production	Cultural knowledge/cultural production
Affect neutrality	Affect intensity
Engineer/'inventor'	Creative spirit/'artist'
Standardization	Pluralization/singularities
Technological progress/prosperity	Successful self-realization/quality of life
Bureaucracy	Market for goods, market for attention
Supplier/customer	Creator/audience

---

13 On contributions to such a diagnosis of culturalization (related primarily to the economy), see Lash and Urry (1994), Menger (2006), and Hutter (2011). In many ways, of course, the theories of postmodernity (e.g., Jameson 1991) provide important background to this kind of perspective, but given the spread of the creative economy and digital media since the turn of the millennium, the culturalization of society is structurally yet again another step removed from what the postmodern authors of the 1980s were able to perceive.

There are additional structural differences as well. In a way, the dominance of the regime of innovation fosters bureaucratic structures that correspond to Max Weber's model of formal rationalism, particularly in the broad field of mass production organized around efficiency, whereas the regime of the aesthetically new is inseparably linked with a spread of market structures. Overproduction of constantly new cultural events and things leads to stiff competition for the uncertain attention of consumers and recipients.[14] Although the regime of innovation has audience-related functions, as in academia, its structure resembles in many respects that of suppliers (standardized goods generally recognized as necessary) and customers, which contrasts with the culturalized society's structure of creators and recipients/consumers. Lastly, the orientation that the social fields have to innovation corresponds in classical industrial society to a logic of progress also at the level of biography and life course—upward social mobility and a biographical logic of ascending phases of life. By contrast, culturalized society corresponds much more to nonlinear biographies and life courses (and, hence, to the ideal of flexibility; see Reckwitz 2006, section 4.2). In that context, constant and successful 'creation' by and of the individual is a goal and a demand of the subject at work, during leisure time, and in the private sphere.

Of course, both the logic of industrial society, which informs a regime of innovation, and the culturalized logic associated with a regime of the aesthetically new are ideal types. In sociohistorical reality the one logic has not completely displaced the other; rather, their weighting has shifted. This observation means two things. First, the logic of industrial society in its day, from 1880 to 1970, was never total. Vestiges of repetition regimes (e.g., logics of probation, cyclical treatment, and generational legacy) or remobilizations of repetition regimes exist in scattered fields and milieus in organized modernity (as in late modernity, too). But aside from that fact, initial elements of culturalization and aesthetization—and, hence, precursory formats of the creativity *dispositif*—are discernible in Fordism as well. They are apparent, for instance, in the early creative industries and the approaches of a consumer society that broke through the confines of mass consumption oriented merely to utility (see Reckwitz 2006: chapter 3). Second, there persist in late-modern society—for instance, in the capital-goods industry and healthcare—powerful complexes of an innovation regime in which the imperative of innovation is clearly broadening and firmly taking root. Another example is the continuous innovation in organizations, which is increasingly undermining the practices of repetition that once constituted their Fordist structures. In some respects, the 'new' logic of the aesthetically new is competing in late-modern society with the 'old'

---

14 See Menger (2014) on this important point.

logic of innovation. To some degree, both logics are also combining unpredictably in areas such as economics, the media, urban development, and the way people lead their lives. The goal of an empirical research agenda for analyzing the regime of the new in contemporary society should consist precisely in elaborating on this simultaneity of nonsimultaneities between the advanced regimes of the aesthetically new, the regimes of innovation, and the established or recently mobilized regimes of repetition and should closely examine the structural and cultural conflicts as well as the hybridizations that arise from them (see Table 2).[15]

Table 2 Historical overview of the regime of the new and the old.

Type of Modernity	Dominant Trend	Secondary Trends
Bourgeois	Gradual spread of innovation regimes	Strong repetition regimes Revolutionary practices
Organized	Innovation regimes	Regimes of the aesthetically new Repetition regimes
Late	Regimes of the aesthetically new	Innovation regimes Repetition regimes

---

15 Special attention should be devoted also to those hybrid artifacts in which technology and aesthetics are coupled, as is the case for no small amount of contemporary consumer goods, such as automobiles, housing, and media equipment.

References

Beck, Ulrich, Anthony Giddens, and Scott Lash, eds. 1994. *Reflexive Modernization: Politics, Tradition and Aesthetics in the Modern Social Order.* Cambridge: Polity Press.
Bongaerts, Gregor. 2007. "Soziale Praxis und Verhalten—Überlegungen zum Practice Turn in Social Theory." *Zeitschrift für Soziologie* 36(4): 246-260.
Bourdieu, Pierre. 1984. "The Market of Symbolic Goods." Ch. 3 in *The Field of Cultural Production: Essays on Art and Literature.* New York: Columbia University Press.
Braun-Thürmann, Holger. 2005. *Innovation.* Bielefeld: transcript.
David, Paul A. 1975. *Technical Choice, Innovation, and Economic Growth: Essays on American and British Experience in the Nineteenth Century.* London: Cambridge University Press.
Debord, Guy. 1970. *The Society of the Spectacle.* Detroit: Black & Red.
Deleuze, Gilles and Felix Guattari. 1987. *A Thousand Plateaus. Capitalism and Schizophrenia.* Minneapolis: University of Minnesota Press.
Deleuze, Gilles and Felix Guattari. 1994. *What is Philosophy?* New York: Columbia University Press.
Edquist, Charles, ed. 1997. *Systems of Innovation: Technologies, Institutions and Organizations.* London: Pinter.
Foucault, Michel. 1978. *The History of Sexuality, Volume 1: An Introduction.* New York: Pantheon Books.
Giddens, Anthony. 1979. *Central Problems in Social Theory: Action, Structure, and Contradiction.* Berkeley: University of California Press.
Guilford, Joy P. 1950. "Creativity." *American Psychologist* 5(9): 444-454.
Guillet de Monthoux, Pierre. 2004. *The Art Firm: Aesthetic Management and Metaphysical Marketing.* Stanford: Stanford University Press.
Han, Byung-Chul. 2011. *Shanzhai. Dekonstruktion auf Chinesisch.* Berlin: Merve Verlag.
Hutter, Michael. 2011. "Experience Goods." Pp. 211-215 in *A Handbook of Cultural Economics*, edited by R. Towse. 2nd ed. Cheltenham: Edward Elgar.
Hutter, Michael, Hubert Knoblauch, Werner Rammert, and Arnold Windeler. This volume. "Innovation Society Today. The Reflexive Creation of Novelty."
Jameson, Fredric. 1991. *Postmodernity, or, the Cultural Logic of Late Capitalism.* Durham: Duke University Press.
Joas, Hans. 1996. *The Creativity of Action.* Chicago: University of Chicago Press.
Jullien, François. 2010. *In Praise of Blandness: Proceeding from Chinese Thought and Aesthetics.* Berlin: Merve Verlag.
Koselleck, Reinhart. 2004. *Futures Past. On the Semantics of Historical Time.* New York: Columbia University Press.
Lash, Scott and John Urry. 1994. *Economies of Signs and Space.* London: SAGE.
Lipovetsky, Gilles and Jean Serroy. 2013. *L'Esthétisation du monde. Vivre à l'âge du capitalisme artiste.* Paris: Gallimard.
Luhmann, Niklas. 1990. *Political Theory in the Welfare State.* Berlin: De Gruyter.
Menger, Pierre-Michel. 2006 [2002]. *Kunst und Brot. Die Metamorphosen des Arbeitnehmers.* Constance: UVK.
Menger, Pierre-Michel. 2014 [2009]. *The Economics of Creativity: Art and Achievement under Uncertainty.* Cambridge: Harvard University Press.

Popitz, Heinrich. 1997. *Wege der Kreativität*. Tübingen: Mohr Siebeck.
Rammert, Werner. 2010. "Die Innovationen der Gesellschaft." Pp. 21-51 in *Soziale Innovationen. Auf dem Weg zu einem post-industriellen Innovationsparadigma*, edited by J. Howaldt and H. Jakobsen. Wiesbaden: Springer VS.
Reckwitz, Andreas. 2003. "Grundelemente einer Theorie sozialer Praktiken. Eine sozialtheoretische Perspektive." *Zeitschrift für Soziologie* 32(4): 282-301.
Reckwitz, Andreas. 2006. *Das hybride Subjekt. Eine Theorie der Subjektkulturen von der bürgerlichen Moderne zur Postmoderne*. Weilerswist: Velbrück Wissenschaft.
Reckwitz, Andreas. 2017. *The Invention of Creativity. Modern Society and the Culture of the New*. London: Polity.
Runco, Mark A. 2007. *Creativity. Theories and Themes: Research, Development, and Practice*. Amsterdam: Academic Press.
Schulze, Gerhard. 1992. *Die Erlebnisgesellschaft: Kultursoziologie der Gegenwart*. Frankfurt a. M.: Campus.
Seel, Martin. 1996. "Ästhetik und Aisthetik. Über einige Besonderheiten ästhetischer Wahrnehmung—mit einem Anhang über den Zeitraum der Landschaft." Pp. 36-69 in *Ethisch-ästhetische Studien*, edited by M. Seel. Frankfurt a. M.: Suhrkamp.
Welsch, Wolfgang. 1996. "Ästhetisierungsprozesse—Phänomene, Unterscheidungen, Perspektiven." Pp. 9-61 in *Grenzgänge der Ästhetik*, edited by W. Welsch. Stuttgart: Reclam.
Willis, Paul. E. 1990. *Common Culture: Symbolic Work at Play in the Everyday Cultures of the Young*. Boulder: Westview Press.

Part II
Between Economy and Culture

The Role of Newness
in the Experience Economy

Michael Hutter

1 Introduction

Since the 1990s, there has been great interest in publications that indicate that increased leisure time and income are making experience an ever more important factor across all of society, particularly in the economy. Building on such observations, Schulze (1992) introduced the *Erlebnisgesellschaft* (experience society) as a key concept of what in the subtitle of his book he called a 'cultural sociology of the present.'[1] Pine and Gilmore (1999) sketched out an experience economy in their eponymous book. Despite initial interest in the notion, however, it faltered, possibly because the term is morally loaded. An orientation toward experience was equated with hedonism, narcissism, and irresponsibility.

The same period witnessed the emergence of the notion of the creative economy. In 1985 this notion did not yet exist, but universities have since established departments under this label, and the creative economy has become a sector for which statistical indicators are being updated annually worldwide. As this chapter shows, an intense academic debate is raging over whether the concept of the creative economy is focusing attention on economic considerations in the cultural sphere, that is, whether it is leading to an 'economization of culture.'

Both nomenclatures revolve around the same phenomenon: people, sometimes organizations as well, pay for the opportunity to have experiences through products such as concerts, novels, theme parks, or apparel. The first thing that strikes an

---

1 All English translations of specific terms are my own unless otherwise noted.

observer is the relatively consistent ability of producers to deliver surprising variants of what they offer. It seems more worthwhile, though, to look at the differently distributed abilities in society to turn the products into physically and symbolically mediated experiences that register in a person's mind and become memories. Most of these experiences take place in interactions with other people or while one is watching and listening to the successful interplay of teams and ensembles.

I start by tracing the history of this chapter's two key notions—the creative economy and the experience economy—because the ambiguities and misunderstandings surrounding them reveal the complex nature of the social process. I then show the aesthetic and commercial dimensions of the continuous provision of cultural experiences. These observations document the significance of novelty as an end in itself. The ensuing discussion leads to another, new understanding of societal renewal and change.

2 A Conceptual History of the Creative Economy

In 1998, the British Department for Culture, Media and Sport published a report entitled *Creative Industries Mapping Document*, which identified 13 kinds of activities that, taken together, constitute the creative industries. The market volume and number of employees for which each of these activities accounted were tallied to show the scope and the growth of the sector. The department then proposed strategies to promote this sector, which were implemented by a Creative Industries Task Force in the following years. The second edition of this report appeared in 2001, after which time political priorities changed. But the newly created category of creative industries had long since been copied and adapted around the world.

The background to this development begins with the critical response of French media experts to the position taken by Adorno (2002), who had introduced the term 'culture industry' (*Kulturindustrie*) to castigate the way commercial actors were exploiting aesthetic processes (see also Adorno 1992: chapter 3).[2] Miège (1989) countered that valuable aesthetic innovations could indeed come of the industrialized production of cultural goods such as films or books. Even before the appearance of Miège's publication, this argument had been taken up by cultural policy experts of the British Labour Party. Actors at the local and city levels used the point to draw a link between the traditional mechanical industries, the production spaces of which had been abandoned, and the new workers in artistic and related fields, who needed spaces for rehearsals, performances, and other forms

---

2   The reception refers predominantly to the use of the term in Adorno (1984).

of collective work (Garnham 1987).³ So it was that the culture industry became the cultural industries, which henceforth were identified as the drivers of future prosperity. This construct became a component of municipal strategies in cities controlled by Labour. After the conservative government under Margaret Thatcher dissolved the Greater London Council in 1985, the first projects geared specifically toward these industries appeared in Sheffield and Manchester under the direction of a specially created development agency. Tony Blair, who was to serve as the Labour prime minister of the United Kingdom from 1997 to 2007, took this cultural policy program into his election campaign in 1997. However, yet another significant semantic shift occurred. The concept of cultural industries belonged to the program of Old Labour, from which New Labor wanted to set itself apart while seeking to attract a new, young, culturally interested segment of the voting public. The term therefore changed from 'cultural' to 'creative,' from the past-oriented reference to culture to the future-oriented notion of creating something that has never been seen before. Symptomatically, the Department of National Heritage became the Department for Culture, Media and Sport after the Labour Party won the national elections. The new name essentially includes all the sectors treated in this text as part of the experience economy.

The adjective 'creative' had several careers in the first decade of this millennium: Charles Landry (2000) propagated the term *creative city*, John Howkins (2001) the *creative economy*, and Richard Florida (2002) the *creative class*, for whose members cities were expected to provide attractive work and leisure activities. The ensuing worldwide enthusiasm for such development strategies culminated in 2008 at the Creative Cities Summit 2.0 in Detroit, Michigan, where these three authors appeared together on a 'super-panel.'⁴

The same decade saw the appearance of creative-industries reports for cities, regions, and countries around the world. The definitions used in these documents differed in some of their details, but they had a common core. The resemblances surface, for example, in UNESCO's *Creative Economy Report 2013* (Figure 1).

---

3   For overviews, see Cunningham (2001), Hesmondhalgh (2005), and Pratt (2005).
4   "The highlight of the conference was an *überpanel* of the creativity movement's most energetic proselytizers" (Peck 2011: 57).

1. DCMS Model	2. Symbolic Texts Model	3. Concentric Circles Model	
Advertising	Core cultural industries	Core creative arts	Wider cultural industries
Architecture	Advertising	Literature	Heritage services
Art and antiques market	Film	Music	Publishing
Crafts	Internet	Performing arts	Sound recording
Design	Music	Visual arts	Television and radio
Fashion	Publishing		Video and computer games
Film and video	Television and radio	Other core cultural industries	
Music	Video and computer games		Related industries
Performing arts	Peripheral cultural industries	Film	Advertising
Publishing	Creative arts	Museums and libraries	Architecture
Software	Borderline cultural industries		Design
Television and radio	Consumer electronics		Fashion
Video and computer games	Fashion		
	Software		
	Sport		

4. WIPO Copyright Model		5. UNESCO Institute for Statistics Model	6. Americans for the Arts Model
Core copyright industries	Interdependent copyright industries	Industries in core cultural domains	Advertising
Advertising	Blank recording material	Museums, galleries, libraries	Architecture
Collecting societies	Consumer electronics	Performing arts	Arts schools and services
Film and video	Musical instruments	Festivals	Design
Music	Paper	Visual arts, crafts	Film
Performing arts	Photocopiers, photographic equipment	Design	Museums, zoos
Publishing		Publishing	Music
Software		Television, radio	Performing arts
Television and radio		Film and video	Publishing
Visual and graphic art		Photography	Television and radio
		Interactive media	Visual arts
Partial copyright industries		Industries in expanded cultural domains	
Architecture		Musical instruments	
Clothing, footwear		Sound equipment	
Design		Architecture	
Fashion		Advertising	
Household goods		Printing equipment	
Toys		Software	
		Audiovisual hardware	

Figure 1 Six classification models for the Creative Economy. Source: UNESCO, *Creative Economy Report* 2013 (2013: 22).

Initial attempts to have the sector include parts of software production have since been discontinued. The sector includes gastronomy and other lifestyle areas, particularly in reports from Asia. In this context, there seems to be a clash between the two semantic fields of culture—between a diversified field of sensuous-symbolic activities and a shared understanding of life throughout society.

As a term and a concept, the creative industries were enjoying tremendous success among policy-makers and academics, but critics raised their voices at the same time. They pointed out that 'culture' had disappeared, taking with it the reference to shared aesthetic values. Furthermore, the very broad use of the concept of industries was tainted with notions of entrepreneurship and claims to ownership (O'Connor 2000; O'Connor and Oakley 2015; Pratt 2005). As a result, composite terms that suggested a dichotomy, such as 'cultural and creative industries' (Söndermann et al. 2009), became common. East Asian countries had referred to *cultural industries* from the outset. Although their basic strategic focus on commercial market volume is particularly evident, that emphasis nevertheless fell under the broad umbrella of national culture, the inclusiveness of which is virtually second nature to the population within it.

Another terminological shift occurred from *creative industries* to *creative economy*. The switch from 'industry' to 'economy' sufficed to mask the work relations that often lead to the exploitation of creative resources. The creative economy, or cultural and creative economy, thereby becomes an objectified field in which sensuous-symbolic activities take place and which attracts particular attention because of its special character and potential. At least such is the intention behind the use of this term by United Nations organizations, especially the United Nations Conference on Trade and Development (UNCTAD) and UNESCO.[5] In addition, the term *creative economy* is also sometimes used to refer only to commercially provided art and media products.[6]

The uniquely emotional and value-laden difference between the semantic ranges of the two adjectives 'creative' and 'cultural' has become ever clearer and more detailed over the course of the past three decades. The argument for attributing independent significance to cultural events stems from two different epistemic sources. One is the particular variety of neo-Marxist social theory still cultivated in universities in Britain and the Commonwealth. According to this line of thought, access to symbolic capital must be politically assured. The state is therefore responsible for providing culture that fosters community-building values. The other epistemic source, informed by cultural anthropology, posits that aesthetic

---

5   See UNCTAD (2008) and UNESCO (2013). Andy Pratt and David Throsby are among the leading authors of both these reports. Pratt explained, "At UNESCO when we did the latest report they only retained the name 'creative economy' for the 'brand value' and recognition. The consensus was to call it the cultural economy ... The final iteration would be to return to talking of the cultural sector" (A. Pratt, personal communication, November 19, 2014).

6   Retrieved February 13, 2015, from the website of the Berlin Chamber of Trade and Commerce (IHK Berlin) (http://www.ihk-berlin.de/branchen/Kreativwirtschaft/ Branchen_der_Kultur-_und_Kreativwirtschaft/).

cultures are imaginary communities that are constantly being renewed and thereby sustained in self-made and in purchased experience games.

Such aesthetic experiences can be observed and described from the perspective of the players and the audience. In the German sociological literature published on this subject, the only writer to have made a mark is Gerhard Schulze (1992). The reasons he identified for the increase in the experience of everyday aesthetics are similar to those identified above. However, his proposal met with little understanding. Schulze's representation of shared, playful interactions did not gain currency, and experiences—in the sense of sensations—were narrowly interpreted as noninstrumental individual activities. Likewise, in the vein of neo-Marxist ideology that builds on Adorno, experiences were conceived of as the newest cunning of capitalist exploiters seeking to lure buyers away from other, culturally superior activities.[7]

Publications in English use the terms *experience, experience goods*, and *experience economy* primarily in applied management discourses. Joseph Pine and James Gilmore may have a claim to having invented the term *experience economy*, calling for it in 1999 to succeed the service economy. This part of the economy offers products that buyers choose for the experience they promise to provide. The authors distinguish between four segments in the range of experience on offer: 'educational,' 'escapist,' 'esthetic,' and 'entertainment.'[8] The experiences that these authors describe therefore go beyond aesthetic experiences, although the three other segments of experience are compatible with an aesthetic dimension. Recent publications have consistently referred to Pine and Gilmore (1999). The suggestively titled publication by Albert Boswijk and his coauthors, *The Experience Economy: A New Perspective*, is entrepreneurial in its own way (Boswijk, Thijssen, and Peelen 2007). This book, which was self-published in 2007 by the European Center for the Experience Economy in Amsterdam, addresses a wide spectrum of areas in which meaningful experiences are offered. They extend from retail tourism and the hospitality industry to wellness and healthcare. The authors position the cocreating process, which involves the user of the experience as participant and codesigner, at the center of their approach. They expect to see successful business models proliferate in this rapidly expanding sector of the economy.

---

7   See Lonsway (2009), Holbrook and Hirschman (1982), and Lury (1996). The term *experience good* has also been introduced in the macroeconomic literature. However, the definition there refers to goods such as washing machines for which an initial 'experience' provides certainty about the product's performance (Hutter 2011a).

8   See Pine and Gilmore (1999: xix). New interpretations of this classic work are found in Sundbo and Sørensen (2013a) and Michelsen (2014).

A broad discussion about the creative industries has emerged in Scandinavia, where economists take the experiences of users or consumers as their point of departure. Commercial utility remains uppermost in the minds of the researchers, but they take the sector's interdisciplinary demands into account.[9] They also note the overlaps between *experience* and *creative industries*. Trine Bille and Mark Lorenzen (2008) have related experience industries to artistic creativity. For example, they classified music and theater as creative experience areas; restaurants, sports, and pornographic products as experience areas. Design and advertising were placed in the creative areas. The result is a concentric circle model in which the high-culture arts occupy the center and media products and products with direct sensory appeal are relegated to the periphery or excluded entirely. All in all, these authors are rather skeptical about expanding the economic vocabulary to include the category of experience as a way to understand the development of the creative economy (Bille 2012).

At best, recognizable evidence that the field of economics has taken the experience dimension on board surfaces in discussions with managers and entrepreneurs, who must engage in very practical and pragmatic ways with performances for their customers. General macroeconomic analyses retain their emphasis on the creative potential of producers to shape symbolic media in ways that lead to aesthetic experiences.

3 A Sociology of Aesthetic Experiences

Experiences, in particular shared experiences, are used in all differentiated spheres of values. Religious ceremonies are experiences in which the emotions of the participants range from a vague feeling of solemnity to a physical trance. In Christianity, the belief in the resurrection of Jesus as a historically imagined but actually impossible event is fundamental. This event is not experienced directly by the believers, but the celebration of this miracle nevertheless makes them share in it together. In the legal sphere, the collective experience of the process of arriving at a verdict is possible even in austere functional courtrooms. Other kinds of collective experiences are turned to in the sphere of political power. References to military victories or defeats are indirect ways of entering the imagination space of people over whom power is exercised. Parliamentary debates, elections, parades, and memorial events are direct means of doing so. When it comes to the experi-

---

9   The handbook by Sundbo and Sørensen (2013b) is particularly broad. See also Power (2009).

ence economy, however, the most interesting events are those that occur in the aesthetically coded sphere of 'culture.'

This sphere is about the representation of the world, or, more precisely, particular parts of it, including the self-image projected by the participants. This representation happens in an event that the participants each perceive, take in, and remember (or forget) as an experience. Such representations reach far beyond the possibilities and concerns of the elite arts. They operate with symbolic means that can be experienced with the physical senses and which occasion different kinds of enjoyment.[10] However, enjoyment results only if the experience is more than one that is just being repeated exactly. The representation and, hence, the reception of the representation must constantly change. Alteration of the user's disposition and setting might suffice for that purpose, but users eventually expect new configurations of symbols, whether they be a novel, film, videogame, sports match, travel route, or cooking recipe. These configurations of symbols are components of games that perpetuate and renew themselves continually and engage people as players or observers. It is these experiences that constantly bubble up in the cultural sphere and that reach their spectators, and often their players, through 'experience markets.'[11]

Gerhard Schulze coined the term 'experience market' (*Erlebnismarkt*) in 1992 in a chapter he dedicated to the notion in his book *Die Erlebnisgesellschaft* (The Experience Society). His analysis, which he illustrated and substantiated with descriptive statistical studies conducted in the vicinity of Nuremberg, pointed to the same features that remain worth studying today. Schulze characterized the episodes in which experience occurs as 'everyday aesthetics' (*alltagsästhetisch*, 1992: 98f.) if they occur routinely, are motivated by the intention to experience something, and are selected from alternatives.[12] Everyday aesthetics is therefore "a play of sign and meaning" (ibid.: 96). Whereas such play used to be something unusual, everydayness (*Alltäglichkeit*) and the intention to experience something are sufficient conditions today (ibid.: 100). But everydayness does not imply simplicity. The whole experience is a configuration of signs and meanings for the interpretation of which the producer can offer the participants some help at best,

---

10 Schulze (1992) distinguished between contemplation (*Kontemplation*), congeniality (*Gemütlichkeit*), and tension (*Spannung*). He attributes them to specific social milieus (ibid.: 108) but later blurs these classifications (Schulze 2013).

11 For a discussion of the play metaphor as a heuristic for autonomous valuation processes, see Hutter (2015: chapter 1).

12 "Aesthetically ordinary episodes often consist in the appropriation of signs that the subject decodes in a manner that he or she calls 'beautiful'" (Schulze 1992: 712).

but disappointments cannot be avoided. Aesthetic signs turn up constantly and can be selected by facilitators and participants for experience-related patterns and intentions. Furthermore, recordings can be made, they can be copied and replayed as often as desired.

Taking the participant's perspective, as outlined here, on the experiences that are constantly offered and selected lets us draw conclusions as to how innovation is conceived in this sector. The participants find themselves in a stream of incessant novelty that virtually consists of their bodily experiences and mental recollections.[13] The participants discover themselves there as new and changeable. They engage in the mode of exploration, as Thévenot (2014) would say, without straying too far from the regime of familiarity (ibid.: 135). They seek familiar surprises (Hutter 2011b). This form of novelty as a permanent flow of variations, some of which are repeated and finally stabilized, corresponds to the evolutionary algorithm of change. It differs from change conceived of as innovation steps (see also the contributions by Reckwitz and Windeler, this volume). In that tradition, innovations are defined as changes that are oriented toward a previously defined objective and whose success can therefore be measured against the degree to which that objective is achieved. Novel experiences, by contrast, bear their own inherent value. It lies within the new, surprising, moving, boring, everyday aesthetic experiences themselves. The steps involved in such value creation, however, take place within the context of social and material conditions. Hence, advances in innovation also keep occurring in markets of the experience economy. The technological infrastructure in which symbolic content is configured, distributed, and presented in ways that can be sensually experienced definitely follows a logic of planned improvement in technical artifacts.

Value creation has two meanings in this context. In the aesthetic experience itself there lies a sensuous-symbolic value for which operationalizations of 'quality' must be found in the communication among the participants. The production of this quality is usually attributed to an individual creator, although other participants are aware of their own contribution. Value creation also occurs when the participants gain access to the experiential constructs through a market. In those cases, operationalizations of commercial value are agreed upon and payable in sums of money. I address both kinds of value creation, starting with aesthetic value in this section and continuing with commercial value in the next.

---

13   Schulze refers to 'subjects' consisting of the "systems called body and consciousness" (Schulze 1992: 734). He thereby alludes to processes that take place inside the participants.

The variety of reasons why people seek experiences for themselves and for others invites one to identify different criteria for categorization. Schulze applies schemes attached to specific milieus (see footnote 8 above) and finds particular 'variants of experience orientation' (Schulze 1992: 165) in each of them. These variations refer to different dimensions of meaning. They occur substantively, temporally, and socially. Furthermore, each dimension is internally structured according to another difference; this results in six categories to which illustrations of specific offers of experience can be assigned.

The *material* dimension consists of an external and an internal category. Fictional narratives, with their dramatic storylines and familiar endings, represent the external world. Furnished rooms let participants experience internal situations. The *temporal* dimension differentiates between past and future. Preserved and accessible historical monuments awaken memories, and carefully produced and placed advertising messages are construed as promises for the future. The distinction made in the *social* dimension is between *ego* and *alter*. The subject sets him- or herself apart by means of status goods, which may range from a certain brand of car and designer handbag to tattoos. All the experience orientations interact. Shortcomings in one dimension or the other are sensed and compensated for. Furthermore, many variations of experience satisfy several dimensions of meaning. Together they generate the craving for sensation-seeking and event excitement for which people willingly pay.

Twenty years after Schulze, Reckwitz (2017) developed a theory of the experience society; it mentioned Schulze's earlier work but made little use of it. Reckwitz centered his analysis on the aesthetic dimension of experiences and related it to the dynamic of the new (see also Reckwitz, this volume). Like Schulze, he extended the aesthetic dimension beyond the elite arts. The decoupling of the autonomous sphere of the arts from the traditional sphere is historically relevant. The decisive characteristic is self-referentiality, which is experienced as an affective, and therefore somatic and mental, stimulus. To satisfy the desire for these aesthetic stimuli, a "particular social regime of attention" has been institutionalized "that enables one to repeatedly refresh attention for new stimuli" (Reckwitz 2017: 40). He identified five 'agents of aesthetization' that have promoted development toward 'aesthetic capitalism' (his version of the experience society): the expansionism of art, the media revolutions, capitalization, the expansion of objects, and the focus on subjects (ibid.: chapter 1). In the context of these developments, industrial capitalism has been transformed to aesthetic capitalism. The dominant orientation toward the new, which Schulze noted and which Reckwitz treated as a primary force, turns the experience society into the innovation society, where the boundaries between fashions, novelties, and innovations has indeed become fluid.

4 Features of the Experience Economy

This now raises the question of the kind of economy that corresponds to the changed demands that arise from the understanding of the experience society outlined above. In response to the vortex of desires, aesthetic experiences are prepared and presented in a form for which either the players or the observers and listeners are willing to part with their money.[14] When the experience begins, when the cup match kicks off, or when someone pushes the 'Play' button, the phase of commodification ends (see Kopytoff 1986).

The similarity of experience orientations might permit the cost advantages of mass production, but it cannot obscure the fact that the experiences are collective goods. They are produced and enjoyed together. Yet when they become available in some recorded and prepared form, that form often becomes endlessly replicable. This situation results in problems that are well known in economic theories of public goods. There are several reasons why people hesitate to offer goods that consist primarily of information. One is that the potential participants hope others will cover the costs of the shared experience. Another is that the effect of the new signs and symbols is hard to predict. A third reason is that the exploitation of successful experience products depends on a legal institution of material property that is ill suited to immaterial goods (see Hutter 2000, 2006).

Attention is thus shifting back to what is happening in the creative economy, in which all cultural and creative industries are clustered. But the focus now extends beyond the perspective of the creator and provider of an experiential good. Eyes are turning instead to the remembered and hoped-for experiences of the players and observers of sensuous-symbolically designed games, in which each move represents something and can thereby be recognized, experienced, and remembered. How do the prevalent subsectors of the creative economy fit with the experience orientations of the participants? And how do the roles differ between those who earn money from these games and those who pay for them?

According to the classification established by Pratt and Throsby (UNCTAD 2008), the creative economy falls into four categories. The first contains the markets for traditional culture, such as the various applied arts, which use traditional materials and patterns, and the provision of national heritage. The products and

---

14 Gabriel Tarde has already pointed out the basic role of desire: "Economic progress supposes two things: on the one hand, a growing number of different desires, for, without a difference in desires, no exchange is possible, ... On the other hand, a growing number of similar exemplars of each desire taken separately, for, without this similitude, no industry is possible" (as quoted in Latour and Lépinay 2010: 35).

services for this column are mostly state funded, but markets have nevertheless been established. Traditional culture also includes gastronomy. Shared meals are necessarily a sensuous-symbolic experience. It is possible to heighten the nature of the experience significantly by increasing the investment into it, thus leading to prices that are comparable to those of opera tickets and designer suits. Participants in markets of traditional culture seek experiences that are memorable and that provide a sense of belonging. The second category encompasses genres in which original artworks are created and attract attention. The participants read invented and documented stories, they listen to concerts, they go to plays and sculpture exhibitions, they walk around parks and unique buildings. They thereby experience status-positioning, they personally partake in aspects of worlds in which they do not normally reside, and they can present themselves in relation to the works they have encountered. The third category contains all the products that use media for recording, broadcasting, and diffusing content. They range from newspapers, radio, film, and television to audiovisual material in digital form. The products in this category are always copies of works that belong to the category of original culture. In terms of monetary volume, the use of industrial or digital reproduction techniques generates by far the greatest portion of experience products. This category is oriented toward stories in which people can experience tension and surprise and toward large game platforms that offer opportunities for identification and participation, from which the audience can derive feelings of belonging. Lastly, the fourth category encompasses four different basic services that shape the environment: services in object design, architecture, fashion, and advertising.[15] Advertising's orientation toward promises is evident, whereas spaces of experience and status-positioning are dominant in the other three categories.

The considerations discussed above indicate that a fifth category should be added to the experience economy. It encompasses games, such as sports, games of chance, and tourism, all of which only initially appear to lack an aesthetic dimension. Sports matches have an unusually high capacity to generate feelings of excitement and belonging, even when the game is transmitted only on tiny screens or via a sportscaster's voice. Games of pure chance are actually about playing against nature, but they are organized and offered in a social way so that the promised opportunities to win keep reigniting desires. Every trip that is not confined to a specific purpose or routine is a sequence of experiences, carefully arranged and

---

15 Actually, the costs of raw materials and supplies for the entire processing industry, from construction to the automotive sector, should be included in the creative industry. After all, it is the creation of experience that makes the investment in production attractive.

enriched by multiple additional services. A successful trip offers a spectrum of experience values, from exclusivity to belonging, from tales worth telling to stays in hotels and unusual spaces such as beaches or cathedrals, and from memories of past civilizations to the hope of possibly seeing the mountain peak that is still enshrouded by clouds.

The roles of the players and participants in the various experience markets are more diverse than the simple distinction between sellers and buyers would suggest. Aesthetic problems are situationally resolved in shifting constellations of players with different skills and experiences. Take, for instance, a documentary film that has reached a large city's arthouse cinemas for several weeks of screening. A film crew, led by a director, found and filmed the raw pictures and sound; the post-production team edited the material into a reproducible standard length film of about 100 minutes. Public funding institutions and private investors have contributed to financing the film, as have the media hardware companies involved in its production so as to enhance their reputation among hobbyist filmmakers. The film will then be offered for a while to the network of screens (i.e., movie theaters) that various companies manage. At the same time, advertising agencies and information media try to pique public interest in the film. The viewers pay to gain access to the film experience, first by buying tickets, then by buying DVDs and subscriptions to streaming platforms (assuming that they own equipment on which to play the film). The viewers talk among each other; some also contact the production team or travel to the country in which the images were made. Maybe the film will be shown on television, financed by subscription fees or by advertising companies that use the film content as a way of drawing attention to their products.

Coproduction and cocreation thereby achieve a remarkable level of complexity, which then generates unavoidable variation. In turn, variation is symptomatic of the sectors or rather of the kinds of experience games that are set in motion across the five categories and are constantly supplied with new variations in game moves. In aesthetic capitalism—the economic form of the experience society—new products for stimulating aesthetic experiences play a major, ever-growing role.

5   Dealing with Novelty in the Innovation Society

Future change and self-development of the experience society depend on the extent to which the commercial games through which user communities are provided with options for experience are able to adapt to the specificities of cultural games. That success relates to cultural policy as a discrete field of collective design (see Flew 2012). It also relates to new forms of collaboration and contractual conditions between products and consumers of experience.[16] Especially significant in the legal sphere is the adaptation of basic legal concepts, particularly those relating to tangible property rights (see Handke 2010).

In these fields, which are peripheral to actual experiences but which nevertheless affect them, it is possible to formulate objectives that intentional innovative activities can aim to meet. The actors continue to operate within the familiar stepwise innovation paradigm, just as they do when developing hardware technologies. However, within the individual game processes, in which players and their public keep having new aesthetic experiences, novelty is not a means to an end but an end in itself. The game and the players come into being during play. They achieve and change their identity over the course of rounds in the game, in keeping with the experience typically associated with tradition, art, media, creative achievement, sport, games of chance, and travel. With evolutionary inevitability, variations of novelty lead to new practices of play, which in turn establish themselves in altered playing communities and thereby continue value creation in the transformed society. While conducting social or economic analyses of the innovation society, one therefore has good reason not only to observe ways to improve the world but also to keep an eye on social activities that relate to the inward-oriented quest for experience and joy.

---

16 Caves (2000) laid the groundwork for such agreements in his discussion of incomplete contracts in the creative industries.

References

Adorno, Theodor W. 1984. *Aesthetic Theory*. London: Routledge and Kegan Paul.
Adorno, Theodor W. 2002. "The Culture Industry: Enlightenment as Mass Deception." Pp. 94-136 in *Dialectic of Enlightenment. Philosophical Fragments*, edited by M. Horkheimer and T. W. Adorno. Stanford: Stanford University Press.
Adorno, Theodor W. 1992. *The Culture Industry: Selected Essays on Mass Culture*. London: Routledge.
Bille, Trine. 2012. "The Scandinavian Approach to the Experience Economy—Does it Make Sense?" *International Journal of Cultural Policy* 18(1): 93-110.
Bille, Trine and Mark Lorenzen. 2008. *Den danske oplevelsesøkonomi: Afgrænsning, økonomisk betydning og vækstmuligheder*. Frederiksberg: Samfundslitteratur.
Boswijk, Albert, Thomas Thijssen, and Ed Peelen. 2007. *The Experience Economy. A New Perspective*. Amsterdam: Pearson Education.
Caves, Richard E. 2000. *Creative Industries: Contracts Between Art and Commerce*. Cambridge: Harvard University Press.
Cunningham, Stuart. 2001. "From Cultural to Creative Industries: Theory, Industry and Policy Implications." *Culturelink* (102): 19-32.
Flew, Terry. 2012. *The Creative Industries: Culture and Policy*. Thousand Oaks: SAGE.
Florida, Richard. 2002. *The Rise of the Creative Class*. New York: Basic Books.
Garnham, Nicholas. 1987. "Concepts of Culture: Public Policy and the Cultural Industries." *Cultural Studies* 1(1): 23-37.
Handke, Christian. 2010. *The Creative Destruction of Copyright: Innovation in the Record Industry and Digital Copying*. Erasmus Universiteit Rotterdam. Retrieved January 19, 2017 (https://ssrn.com/abstract=1630343 or http://dx.doi.org/10.2139/ssrn.1630343).
Hesmondhalgh, David. 2005. "Media and Cultural Policy as Public Policy and Cultural Policy." *The International Journal of Cultural Policy* 11(1): 95-109.
Holbrook, Morris B. and Elizabeth C. Hirschman. 1982. "The Experiential Aspects of Consumption: Consumer Fantasies, Feelings, and Fun." *The Journal of Consumer Research* 9(2): 132-140.
Howkins, John. 2001. *The Creative Economy*. New York: Penguin Press.
Hutter, Michael. 2000. "Besonderheiten der digitalen Wirtschaft—Herausforderungen an die Theorie." *WISU—das Wirtschaftsstudium* (12): 1659-1665.
Hutter, Michael. 2006. *Neue Medienökonomik*. Munich: Fink.
Hutter, Michael. 2011a. "Experience Goods." Pp. 211-215 in *Handbook of Cultural Economics*, edited by R. Towse. Cheltenham: Edward Elgar.
Hutter, Michael. 2011b. "Infinite Surprises: On the Stabilization of Value in the Creative Industries." Pp. 201-222 in *The Worth of Goods: Valuation and Pricing in the Economy*, edited by J. Beckert and P. Aspers. London: Oxford University Press.
Hutter, Michael. 2015. *The Rise of the Joyful Economy: Artistic Invention and Economic Growth from Brunelleschi to Murakami*. London: Routledge.
Kopytoff, Igor. 1986. "The Cultural Biography of Things: Commoditization as a Process." Pp. 64-91 in *The Social Life of Things: Commodities in Cultural Perspective*, edited by A. Appadurai. Cambridge: Cambridge University Press.
Landry, Charles. 2000. *The Creative City: A Toolkit for Urban Innovators*. Near Stroud: Comedia.

Latour, Bruno and Vincent A. Lépinay. 2010. *The Science of Passionate Interests: An Introduction to Gabriel Tarde's Economic Anthropology*. Chicago: University of Chicago Press.
Lonsway, Brian. 2009. *Making Leisure Work: Architecture and the Experience Economy*. London: Routledge.
Lury, Celia. 1996. *Consumer Culture*. Cambridge: Polity.
Michelsen, Anders. 2014. "The Visual Experience Economy: What Kind of Economics? On the Topologies of Aesthetic Capitalism." Pp. 63-88 in *Aesthetic Capitalism*, edited by P. Murphy and E. de la Fuente. Leiden: Brill.
Miège, Bernard. 1989. *The Capitalization of Cultural Production*. New York: International General.
O'Connor, Justin. 2000. "The Definition of the Cultural Industries." *The European Journal of Arts Education* 2(3): 15-27.
O'Connor, Justin and Kate Oakley, eds. 2015. *The Routledge Companion to the Cultural Industries*. London: Routledge.
Peck, Jamie. 2011. "Creative Moments: Working Culture, Through Municipal Socialism and Neoliberal Urbanism." Pp. 41-70 in *Mobile Urbanism: Cities and Policymaking in the Global Age*, edited by E. McCann and K. Ward. Minneapolis: University of Minnesota Press.
Pine, B. Joseph II and James H. Gilmore. 1999. *The Experience Economy: Work is Theatre and Every Business a Stage*. Boston: Harvard Business School Press.
Power, Dominic. 2009. "Culture, Creativity and Experience in Nordic and Scandinavian Cultural Policy." *International Journal of Cultural Policy* 15(4): 445-460.
Pratt, Andy C. 2005. "Cultural Industries and Public Policy: An Oxymoron?" *International Journal of Cultural Policy* 11(1): 31-44.
Reckwitz, Andreas. 2017. *The Invention of Creativity. Modern Society and the Culture of the New*. London: Polity (First German edition: 2012).
Schulze, Gerhard. 1992. *Die Erlebnisgesellschaft. Kultursoziologie der Gegenwart*. Frankfurt a. M.: Campus.
Schulze, Gerhard. 2013. "The Experience Market." Pp. 98-121 in *Handbook on the Experience Economy*, edited by J. Sundbo and F. Sørensen. Cheltenham: Edward Elgar.
Söndermann, Michael, Christoph Backes, Olaf Arndt, and Daniel Brünink. 2009. *Endbericht: Kultur- und Kreativwirtschaft*. Berlin: Bundesministerium für Wirtschaft und Technologie.
Sundbo, Jo and Flemming Sørensen. 2013a. "Introduction to the Experience Economy." Pp. 1-20 in *Handbook on the Experience Economy*, edited by J. Sundbo and F. Sørensen. Cheltenham: Edward Elgar.
Sundbo, Jo and Flemming Sørensen, eds. 2013b. *Handbook on the Experience Economy*. Cheltenham: Edward Elgar.
Thévenot, Laurent. 2014. "Community-Engaged Art in Practice." Pp. 132-150 in *Artistic practices*, edited by T. Zembylas. London: Routledge.
UNCTAD. 2008. *Creative Economy Report 2008*. New York: United Nations Conference on Trade and Development.
UNESCO. 2013. *Creative Economy Report 2013. Special Edition: Widening Local Development Pathways*. New York, Paris: United Nations Development Programme.

What Is Strategic Marketing in an Innovation Society?

A Frame of Reference

Franz Liebl

1 An Uncharted Territory

At first glance the concept and subdiscipline of strategic marketing seem well established in marketing theory and practice. A closer look reveals something else, however. Adopted from the Anglo-American literature (Aaker 1984), the term has existed in translation in the German-speaking countries for some 25 years, having gained currency through Raffée and Wiedmann's (1985) highly regarded eponymous volume of conference papers, yet there is still no clearly recognizable, systematic understanding of market-oriented strategic management.

The chief reason is that strategic management, marketing, and consumer research—the three disciplinary fields capable of making the key contributions to genuine strategic marketing—are developing as parallel worlds with minimal substantive or cultural ties. One might even say that strategic marketing is an uncharted territory between these three disciplines (see Figure 1).

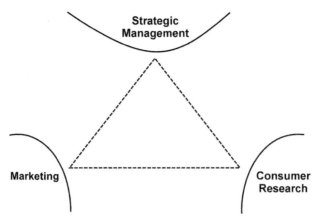

Figure 1 Strategic marketing as uncharted territory between the disciplines (source: own illustration).

Although extensive studies in the sociology of science would be needed to shed light on the reasons for this 'Bermuda Triangle,' its existence is quite obvious in international scientific discourse. This chapter aims to identify the underdeveloped connections between the various areas (section 2). It then develops a frame of reference for genuine strategic marketing (section 3) with an eye to revealing the reciprocal relationships between the constitutive elements so that they become accessible for use.

The conditions of advanced individualization, which become manifest in particular ways in an innovation society, pose particularly great challenges to strategic marketing. However, this fact is not necessarily a disadvantage, as shown below; the conditions of advanced individualization simultaneously pave the way for moving in a promising direction. The frame of reference is primarily geared to innovative practices in society in general and among consumers and clients in particular. It prompts a search for relevant sources that can appropriately tie such innovative activity back to entrepreneurial, strategic action.

2 Parallel Disciplinary Worlds

This section begins with a presentation of the central issues of the discourses in the different disciplines and shows how their different focal points make it difficult to establish mutual connections. Such an overview requires a case-by-case reconstruction of individual schools of thought in each of the disciplines, an exercise undertaken only to the extent necessary for treating the question posed in the title of this chapter.

2.1 Strategic Management: Strategy without Customers

The discourses of strategic management are the point of departure for this analysis. Their primary focus on organizational research eclipses the relevance of the client perspective almost entirely. The literature does include a few key articles based explicitly on the client's viewpoint (especially Abell 1980; Porter 1980, 1985, 1996), but the substantive thrust of the approaches involved differs from those of consumer research in that the need for an empathic method—especially an analysis of the customers' life-worlds and imaginations—is not critically examined. For example, the contributions by Porter reflect the premise that mere external observation will reveal customer dispositions and values and that conventional, standardized kinds of market research suffice to create customer value (Band 1991; Gale 1994; Stahl and Bounds 1991). Arguably, the turning point in such argumentation did not come until the 21st century, when Prahalad (2000) stated that strategic management had long lost sight of customers and that value for both customers and companies is created right at the interface between the two. The role of empathic forms of consumer research in strategic management has since been substantively and procedurally strengthened, thereby resulting in methodological concepts for supporting strategy development (e.g., Liebl and Rughase 2002; Osterwalder and Pigneur 2010).

2.2 Consumer Research: Strategy as *Persona Non Grata*

The fact that disciplinary boundaries are marked not only by the difference between language-games but at least as much by specific attitudes indicates the relationship between consumer research and the various fields of business administration, especially strategic management and marketing. Consumer researchers, given their disciplinary backgrounds in sociology, ethnology, or cultural studies, attach little importance to the commercial use made of their research results. In fact, such practical application even avowedly contradicts the objectives of their fields because it would mean an exploitation of their own work and, above all, of the persons they study. Consumer researchers therefore frown upon following up on the strategic implications of their exploration of their subjects' life-worlds, particularly such questions as what the findings about consumer dispositions mean for the development of new products, the design of communication campaigns, business-model innovation, or the use of innovative technologies.

2.3 Marketing: Strategy as a Vacuum

For decades critical questions have repeatedly arisen, not least in the marketing discourse itself, as to why marketing's contribution to the field of strategy is perceived as virtually nonexistent (Day 1992; Varadarajan 1992). This is true with respect to both management theory and business practice. Literature published in German notes "what a weak position marketing has at the level of senior management" and states that "it contributes little" of strategic value (Scharrer 2011: 1, my translation). Indeed, the marketing discipline has never developed a viable concept of strategy or shown recognizable interest in issues of general management and leadership.

Three other aspects occupy center stage in the discipline instead.

- First, marketing is still understood as a defined toolkit for managing all kinds of exchange relationships, as had once been suggested by Bagozzi (1975).
- Second, because marketing intended to represent an antidote to the formerly predominant production-and-sales orientation, it turned attention to customers. The idea was to make them the starting point for business planning and marketing decisions. The notion of 'customer centricity' conveyed this orientation (Keith 1960), as did Levitt's (1960) famous article on 'marketing myopia.' Marketing saw itself as more than just a function of advertising. Ideally, its express objective was not only to communicate the company's view externally to the customers but, above all, to make the needs of the customers known internally within the company (Strong and Harris 2004).
- Third, Kotler spearheaded a broadening of the perspective on marketing by showing that the marketing function, like finance and human resource management, existed in nonbusiness organizations as well (Kotler and Levy 1969). Under the moniker 'social marketing,' Kotler and Zaltman (1971) applied marketing concepts to social movements or NGOs, whereby themes and issues were treated like products and segments of the public were analogous to customer groups. The authors even suggested the same toolkit used for the marketing process, with the classic four Ps (i.e., product, price, promotion, place) as the variables for managing the 'marketing mix' of political parties, public administration, or social movements. This development was prototypical for creating a plethora of marketing subdisciplines—marketing hybrids such as ecomarket-

ing, micromarketing, macromarketing, and B2B marketing—with the aim of legitimating and further expanding the marketing discipline. Without any irony, Hunt characterized the key concern of marketing as "*marketing* marketing to nonmarketers" (1976: 24, italics in the original text).

This logic of expansion continued with a kind of 'strategic turn' to 'strategic marketing' that emerged in the 1980s. Strictly speaking, it was only a relabeling of a purportedly novel—and thus for theory and practice extremely attractive—discourse about strategic planning and strategic management. In other words, strategic marketing contributed nothing new to concepts of strategic planning. Marketing merely borrowed the analytical and planning instruments developed by its neighboring fields and used them for its own toolkit: portfolio analysis, SWOT (strengths, weaknesses, opportunities, threats) analysis, lifecycle analysis, gap analysis, and experience curve (see the chapters in Raffée and Wiedmann 1985). At the same time, the prevailing orientation in marketing ceded way to a recognizably antithetical element—competition as a kind of alternative model to customer focus. Taking on board the notion of competition represented one of the major conceptual advances in the early phase of strategic thinking. It implied recognition that competition, too, existed and that the outcomes of one's own decisions—one's own competitive strategy—must always be regarded as a result influenced by the decisions and strategies of competitors. For marketing, this tradeoff between customer focus and competitor focus gave rise to a conflict that triggered years of ultimately fruitless discussion about which paradigm to follow. It is moot whether this debate had anything to do with the fact that the term *strategic marketing* was finally superseded by the expression *market-oriented management* (see Meffert 1988, for example). The proponents of market-oriented management subsequently took ever less notice of the discourses on strategic management and focused instead on their instrumental perspective and their disciplinary toolkit (e.g., Day 1992; Varadarajan 1992).

Precisely that functionalist, instrumental understanding, or rather misunderstanding, of strategy is at work when reviews of strategic marketing's state of the art (e.g., Varadarajan 2010) assert that strategic marketing and marketing strategy are still considered interchangeable or that the conception and application of a marketing strategy is the primary interest of strategic marketing. In that kind of logic, marketing strategy is not considered from the perspective of business strategy or top management but at the subordinate level of functional strategy or functional areas (see Hanssmann 1995). All in all, the prevalent term *strategic marketing* suggests a strategic turn that did not exist. Instead of addressing the concerns of top management, the discussion in marketing has been much more about satisfying the need to formulate the domains of the discipline as generally as possible and about staking out its own claims broadly. Brown characterized the resulting relationship marketing as a pleonasm that merely repackages the old notion of customer centricity (1998: 42f.).

Another basic characteristic of marketing as a discipline is that its dominant research paradigm is largely shaped by that of the natural sciences. Marketing is conceived of as a 'science' with a quantitative orientation, standardized research methods, and large samples. In the 1990s, this mainstream paradigm came under fire from representatives of 'postmodern marketing' (Brown 1995) who argued for the introduction of postmodern notions such as 'plurality,' 'ambiguity,' 'multiple perspectives,' and 'fragmentation.' To the extent that postmodernity was about moving into the age of leave-taking, postmodern marketing's clarion call was to dispense with monistic concepts rooted in the fiction of singularity, especially expressions such as *the* core of a brand, *the* USP (unique selling proposition), and *the* target group. In the same vein, postmodern thinking in this field entailed taking leave of research approaches rooted in the natural sciences and thus designed to study universal 'laws of the marketplace.' Scholars sought to transfer postmodern research strategies to consumer research. They therefore favored interpretive and nonstandardized instead of positivist and standardized methods of data collection and used small samples or case studies coupled with a high number of observations from each subject, aiming at what Geertz called 'thick description' (1971: 3 and passim).

In summary, the strategically indisputable merit of postmodern marketing consisted in having correctly recognized and treated individualization as the key challenge (see especially Gabriel and Lang 1995, 2009) and in having given qualitative research an appropriate place in the analysis of customers and consumers. In that respect, old-school strategic marketing had a notable shortcoming: it did not address advanced individualization. Another correct conclusion at which postmodernists arrived lay in their critique of the manifestations of marketing's uncontrolled diversification (Brown 1998).

Although the turmoil caused by the deconstruction of mainstream marketing was necessary and fruitful, the project of postmodern marketing has remained incomplete. Relevant questions have been posed, but not all the strategically necessary ones. Furthermore, the challenging demands have not gone beyond the domain of marketing. There is a degree of irony in the fact that the undisciplined aspects of postmodern marketing accommodated disciplinary boundaries so comfortably. The project has remained incomplete precisely because of its confinement to ironies and deconstructions, as successful and brilliant as they no doubt have been. Nevertheless, if the claim of 'market-oriented management' is taken seriously in a setting dominated by advanced individualization and ubiquitous commitment to innovation, then a methodological and procedural reconstruction beyond deconstruction is needed to come to grips with the task of shaping the field. In other words, it is necessary to conceptualize a kind of post-postmodern marketing that can become genuine, contemporary strategic marketing. Such a strategy-oriented approach must lead to conclusions other than those by Brown (2001), who, in a post-ironic turn, postulated a reversion of marketing to the old production-and-sales orientation.

3 A Framework for Innovation-Oriented Strategic Marketing

I can now outline the research and development program of an innovation-oriented strategic marketing: mapping and colonizing the uncharted territory described in the previous sections. Below, I present a framework with which to move forward while doing justice to that landscape's advanced state of individualization with its individualized customer behavior and under the conditions of the innovation society. This framework is based on an entrepreneurial view.

3.1 Foundations

In the wake of Schumpeter's (1934) concept of entrepreneurship, the field of business administration has been oriented to innovation. Nonetheless, the topic long played only a secondary role in strategic management, seldom being discussed in detail (e.g., Ansoff, Declerck, and Hayes 1976). Only recently has an entrepreneurial view figured in strategic management, with strategic innovation squarely on its agenda. The point of departure for innovation-oriented strategic marketing comprises two dimensions (see also Liebl and Düllo 2015: 65-68).

- The *competitive dimension* aims to create differentiation from competition. Instead of pursuing strategy development for purposes of adaptation or optimization within a given set of restrictions, the current discussion takes an entrepreneurial view (see especially Liebl 2003; Smith and Cao 2007; SMS 2000) and focuses on strategic innovation—or more precisely, the innovation of the business model (e.g., Doz 2007; Eden and Ackermann 2007). In essence, this reorientation implies the creation of new markets and new business models and the introduction of new rules of the game into markets. It is at this juncture

that Spinosa, Flores, and Dreyfus (1997), who saw entrepreneurship itself as a form of sociocultural innovation, made an important contribution. They did not consider all forms of business activity to be entrepreneurship. They emphasized that such innovations begin with something that can be understood as an anomaly that the entrepreneur identifies in the lifeworlds of customers or consumers. Unlike other observers, the entrepreneur does not dismiss the anomaly but rather creates a new kind of product that opens new 'worlds' to the future customers or consumers. Spinosa et al. used the term *worlds* in Heidegger's (2010) sense to mean the reciprocal relationship between an object (or product), the particular ways of using it, and the identities of the users. By disclosing new worlds, an innovation may have a significant impact on the identities of the users. Spinosa et al. therefore concluded that entrepreneurs provide 'history-making' (1997: 16-33) through their innovations and the attendant cultivation, not only from an economic but also from a social and cultural perspective.
- The *political dimension* relates to securing the organization's degrees of freedom in order to preserve its scope of strategic action in the future. This political space for a company is determined by the expectations of its stakeholders (e.g., government, society, media, and nongovernmental organizations) and the degree of legitimacy or acceptance that these actors accord to the organization's business activity.

Unlike conventional marketing, which is characterized by an instrumental orientation, strategic marketing in an innovation society is both problem and goal oriented. It is about agenda-building (the identification of issues that may be strategically relevant to the organization) and strategy development (the development and implementation of strategic options) through innovation activities appropriate to the organization. Figure 2 outlines the frame of reference for strategic marketing. The general goals are stated on the right-hand side. The processes for achieving them are shown in the lower right quadrant.

Why is it appropriate to speak of a frame of reference instead of 'theory' or 'model'? According to Minsky (1975), a frame of reference is a mental analytical structure underpinned by a particular view of the world. That view sets the conditions for the relevant cognitive elements and operators, such as basic assumptions about reality, categories for classifying phenomena, and the analytical instruments (Shrivastava and Mitroff 1983). Porter emphasized that formulating and using frames of reference, or 'frameworks' (1991: 97f.), is especially appropriate as a kind of prototheory when a comprehensive theory is not yet available, when generalizing hypotheses are still empirically untested, or when general quantifiable models cannot be formulated and validated given the specificity of individual

What Is Strategic Marketing in an Innovation Society?

corporate contexts and the usually vague database. Such conditions must usually be reckoned with in strategic management and strategic marketing. Nevertheless, this sort of restriction is not necessarily a disadvantage, for the framework's most important function in processes of strategy development and agenda-building is to enable the participants to pose new, and better, strategic questions.

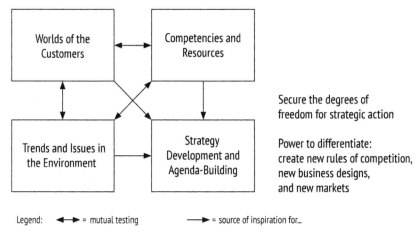

Figure 2 Frame of reference for strategic marketing (source: Liebl and Düllo 2015: 73).

The strategic framework depicted in Figure 2 therefore highlights the fields that offer relevant points of departure for entrepreneurial strategic action. From the entrepreneurial point of view, the formulation of strategic options is based essentially on three bodies, or sources, of knowledge.

- The first one consists of the *customers' worlds*, which are pivotal for considering competitive advantage; by 'worlds' of the customers, I mean not only their lifeworlds but also their mental orientations (e.g., imaginations, desires, expectations, phantasies). Porter (1985) pointed out that the precondition for every differentiation on the market is that the customer initially perceives a difference and then appreciates it properly. A radical change of perspective is required to reconstruct those parts of a customer's world that are relevant to the company's business (or business model). Under the conditions of an innovation society, the study and reconstruction of the customers' worlds take on particular significance because the innovation activities of customers and consumers come to the foreground. Understanding innovations in buying and consumption

becomes the basis for developing strategic options in general and innovations of business models in particular.
- Insofar as the entrepreneurial view also encompasses the resource-based view, the second body of knowledge needed for the formulation of strategic options centers on the *company's competencies and resources*. Strategic innovation then entails combining, recombining, using, and interpreting competencies and resources in new ways.
- The third source of knowledge is *trends and issues in the corporate environment*, which reflect changed or new attributions of meaning and practices created by single or collective actors in that environment. Such actors thereby in effect become stakeholders of the organization because their actions and interpretations have a bearing on it. Eyerman and Jamison (1991) anticipated the concept of an innovation society when they ascribed a key place to groups that bring about, or at least express, symptoms of change. New social movements and post-traditional communities from youth culture are especially conspicuous examples of collective actors driving sociocultural innovation. They can also be regarded as *cognitive* communities because they create new bodies of knowledge that eventually culminate in changed value systems.

The monodirectional arrows in Figure 2 symbolize that each of these three bodies of knowledge can become a source of inspiration for strategic options and innovations. The bidirectional arrows mean that the impulses stemming from each of these fields need to be tested against the other two to ensure coherence in the strategy process. For example, the worlds of customers can provide points of departure for developing new kinds of products and services. Obviously, though, the ideas can be implemented only if the organization has the necessary competencies and resources to do so. This coordination applies *mutatis mutandis* to options in the other fields of knowledge as well.

In summary, the entrepreneurial goal or challenge in an innovation society is to ensure that the innovative potential of customers (consumer innovation) and that of the cognitive communities in society (trends and issues) are appropriately addressed by innovations in the company's own business model. The soft term 'address' is deliberately chosen because it encompasses causality in both directions. It expresses a thoroughly realistic view reflected in Drucker's mildly ironic observation:

> When a new venture does succeed, more often than not it is in a market other than the one it was originally intended to serve, with products and services not quite those with which it had set out, bought in large part by customers it did not even think of

when it started, and used for a host of purposes besides the ones for which the products were first designed (1985: 173).

Entrepreneurial behavior can thus be appropriately grasped as an experimental process rather than as a sequence of analysis, planning, and subsequent implementation. Sarasvathy called this approach to identifying and creating opportunities 'effectuation' and described the underlying logic as follows:

> The distinguishing characteristic between causation and effectuation is in the set of choices: choosing between means to create a particular effect, versus choosing between many possible effects using a particular set of means. Whereas causation models consist of many-to-one mappings, effectuation models involve one-to-many mappings (2001: 245).

Likewise, Chia and Holt used the metaphor 'wayfinding' (2009: 159-185) to characterize the essence of strategic action taken by companies under the fluid conditions of individualization and an innovation society. By contrast, strategic marketing initially considered strategy and planning to be virtually identical.

3.2 A New Way of Dealing with the New

The mechanics of reinterpreting and reallocating resources for business-model innovation are well understood, and multifaceted creative techniques (e.g., contradiction-oriented innovation strategy) have been conceived to support those processes. Henceforth, attention must shift to identifying and understanding innovation activities that occur outside the organization. In other words, the challenge lies primarily in identifying and developing the sources of 'the new' (Groys 2008: 23-42) that indicate where customers and cognitive communities are generating innovations. Such sources can serve as stimuli for the process of strategy development.

The extent to which the new will be disseminated, expanded, and, ultimately, valued can be clarified only later in the process, for it is an expression of entrepreneurial behavior to provide for such change on a broad basis, that is, to work toward a normalization (Link 1999) of that change. As Spinosa et al. (1997) emphasized, entrepreneurship does not consist in riding on the coattails of sociocultural change but rather in actively and decisively driving it forward. Strategic action in general and strategic marketing in particular build on a notion of the strategic that Gälweiler called 'potential for success' (1987: 26-46). According to this line of thinking, strategy is about capturing potential for success that is first identified or created and then exploited. By contrast, strategic marketing as originally understood focused primarily on competition, so it fixated on what already existed. Whereas the new represents potential, normalization entails making full use of this potential. The former chief designer at Renault, Patrick Le Quément, articulated the entrepreneurial implications of such an orientation toward potential for success for contemporary strategic marketing. According to Büschemann (1999), Le Quément does not believe that it is possible to come up with innovative concepts by asking consumers what they want. It is much more a matter of giving customers what they would like to have but did not know they were looking for, something they say they have always wanted when they finally get it.

But where does the new come from? In the wake of research by Barnett (1953), Koestler (1964), and Groys (2014), an array of cultural practices has been identified as sources of the new. Among the most important ones, some of which overlap, are *bricolage*, *détournement*, postproduction, recoding, cultural hacking, jamming, nonintentional design, fandalism, mashup, transgression, deviation, hybridization, and cross-appropriation. As Mathews and Wacker (2003) pointed out, they all have something illegitimate about them, at least initially—a violation of a rule, a deviation from the norm. Characterizations such as 'subversive' and 'interventionist' surface, too, although they are not analytically helpful (Liebl 2014). In other words, contemporary strategic marketing seeks out what is bizarre today and could become mainstream tomorrow. From this stance, it appears more purposeful to conceive of innovation as bizarreness in a process of normalization than to use the conventional notions of invention and diffusion.

Instead of pursuing trend research disguised as diffusion research, strategic marketing that operates under the conditions of an innovation society therefore needs a management system that resembles a 'cabinet of curiosities.' Finding the items for this special collection means engaging in what Diederichsen called the 'cultural production of originality' (1996: 162), including literature, art, design, and music. Equally important are 'popular' offshoots and varieties like pop music, comics, and other crossover genres, which attract particular attention because of their function as avant-garde media, not because of their presumably wide distribution. Seeking the new in such sources makes sense because, as Groys (2014) pointed out, the criteria for justifying the inclusion of particular artworks in cultural archives have been changing since the beginning of the 20th century. The deciding factor is no longer masterful craftsmanship or beauty but rather the innovativeness of a work. This shift has turned the sphere of art into a kind of professionalized zone of innovation. Mathews and Wacker may be overoptimistic when they state that "at its heart, all art is inherently deviant" (2003: 112). But research in this area has identified a wide range of features and functions that are provided by cultural products of originality in all genres and that are key to contemporary strategic marketing. Cultural products of originality serve as a

- sociocultural seismograph with a different or higher-than-normal sensitivity,
- formulation of future scenarios, creation of prototypes, articulation of issues that cannot yet be comprehended sufficiently with scientific language-games,
- means of provocation for artists as actors of social change and mobilization, and
- reservoir of cultural themes, including the production of new linkages between them.

(For an overview, see Liebl and Düllo 2015; Liebl and Schwarz 2012.) The curator Pontus Hultén recapitulated these special features pithily: "science deals with what already exists; art deals with what does not yet exist" (1995: 29, my translation).

Such a management system, however, requires approaching and using the cultural production of originality differently than has been the case in discussions about arts in business. Take, for example, the use of fiction as an alternative form of trend research (building on Hutter 1991), which is just the 'simple case' of an art form based on written texts. But even that verbal art form poses no small challenge. It calls for the development of appropriate approaches to and methods for reading the texts in order to serve as a resource for innovation-centered strategic marketing. A literary analysis of a fictional text, such as a novel, would presumably yield little of strategic value. By the same token, the standard kind of content analysis used in media-monitoring would not do justice to the novel as a genre. Hence, there is a need for some third type of reading that, informed by literary and cultural expertise, could generate strategic insights from fictional texts. The various aspects of such a method are spelled out in detail by Schwarz (2011) and Liebl and Schwarz (2012).

Similarly, strategically relevant art needs to be identified and studied for its implications (Schwarz and Liebl 2013). In terms of strategic marketing, the purpose cannot be only to make employees 'somehow more creative' but rather to find in artworks traces of strategic innovation (i.e., consumption-related innovation, trends, issues, and recombinations of resources). It is thus not about the essence of art per se but about strategically relevant works of art and their strategic implications. Bauer (2006) discussed the cultural strategies of innovation that come from works that attempt to bring about economic, cultural, or social change. The subtitle he gave his dissertation—*What Strategic Management Can Learn from Contemporary Fine Art*—provides a useful, focused program for developing the concept of such strategic art. The value of this approach is readily apparent because it addresses a question that has long occupied management research and practice: Where are the contexts from which organizations can learn and adopt ideas? This approach dovetails with the theory of entrepreneurship put forward by Spinosa et al. (1997), which posits that the entrepreneur's role is to effect cultural innovation and to do so decisively by using techniques of cross-appropriation. Seeing not only an aesthetic and economic but also a strategic value in artworks is completely consistent with this theory of entrepreneurship, which underlies contemporary, innovation-centered strategic marketing.

References

Aaker, David A. 1984. *Strategic Market Management*. New York: John Wiley and Sons.
Abell, Derek F. 1980. *Defining the Business. The Starting Point of Strategic Planning*. Englewood Cliffs, NJ: Prentice-Hall.
Ansoff, H. Igor, Roger P. Declerck, and Robert L. Hayes. 1976. "From Strategic Planning to Strategic Management." Pp. 39-78 in *From Strategic Planning to Strategic Management*, edited by H. I. Ansoff, R. P. Declerck, and R. L. Hayes. New York: Wiley.
Bagozzi, Richard P. 1975. "Marketing as Exchange." *Journal of Marketing* 39(4): 32-39.
Band, William A. 1991. *Creating Value for Customers: Designing and Implementing a Total Corporate Strategy*. New York: Wiley.
Barnett, Homer G. 1953. *Innovation: The Basis of Cultural Change*. New York: McGraw-Hill.
Bauer, Thomas. 2006. *Cultural Innovation: What Strategic Management Can Learn from Contemporary Fine Art* (Dissertation). Witten: Universität Witten/Herdecke.
Brown, Stephen. 1995. *Postmodern Marketing*. London: Routledge.
Brown, Stephen. 1998. "Postmodernism: The End of Marketing." Pp. 27-57 in *Rethinking Marketing: Towards Critical Marketing Accountings*, edited by D. Brownlie, M. Saren, R. Wensley, and R. Whittington. London: SAGE.
Brown, Stephen. 2001. *Marketing—The Retro Revolution*. London: SAGE.
Büschemann, Karl-Heinz. 1999. "Dem Zeitgeist auf der Spur: Was der Kunde nicht will, aber immer wollte—Designer Patrick Le Quément verhilft Renault zu erfolgreichen Autos und einem modernen Image." *Süddeutsche Zeitung*, December 20, p. 29.
Chia, Robert C. H. and Robin Holt. 2009. *Strategy without Design: The Silent Efficacy of Indirect Action*. Cambridge: Cambridge University Press.
Day, George S. 1992. "Marketing's Contribution to the Strategy Dialogue." *Journal of the Academy of Marketing Science* 20(4): 323-329.
Diederichsen, Diedrich. 1996. *Politische Korrekturen*. Cologne: Kiepenheuer & Witsch.
Doz, Yves. 2007. *Strategic Agility and Corporate Renewal*. Paper presented at the Academy of Management Conference, 3-8 August, Philadelphia, PA.
Drucker, Peter F. 1985. *Innovation and Entrepreneurship: Practice and Principles*. New York: Harper & Row.
Eden, Colin and Fran Ackermann. 2007. *The Resource Based View: Theory and Practice*. Paper presented at the Academy of Management Conference, 3-8 August, Philadelphia, PA.
Eyerman, Ron and Andrew Jamison. 1991. *Social Movements—A Cognitive Approach*. Pennsylvania: Penn State University Press.
Gabriel, Yiannis and Tim Lang. 1995. *The Unmanageable Consumer: Contemporary Consumption and Its Fragmentation*. London: SAGE.
Gabriel, Yiannis and Tim Lang. 2009. "New Faces and New Masks of Today's Consumer." *Journal of Consumer Culture* 8(3): 312-341.
Gälweiler, Aloys. 1987. *Strategische Unternehmensführung*. Frankfurt a. M.: Campus.
Gale, Bradley T. 1994. *Managing Customer Value*. New York: Simon & Schuster.
Geertz, Clifford. 1971. "Thick Description: Toward an Interpretive Theory of Culture." Pp.3-30 in *Interpretation of Cultures: Selected Essays*. New York: Basic Books.
Groys, Boris. 2014. *On the New*. London: Verso.

Groys, Boris. 2008. *Art Power*. Cambridge, MA: MIT Press.
Hanssmann, Friedrich. 1995. *Quantitative Betriebswirtschaftslehre—Lehrbuch der modellgestützten Unternehmensplanung*. 4th ed. Munich: Oldenbourg.
Heidegger, Martin. 1979. *Being and Time*. Albany, NY: SUNY Press.
Hultén, Pontus. 1995. "Warum werden Museen so geliebt, Herr Hultén? Ein Interview von Gerd Presler." *Frankfurter Allgemeine Magazin*, January 6, pp. 28-29.
Hunt, Shelby D. 1976. "The Nature and Scope of Marketing." *Journal of Marketing* 40(3): 17-28.
Hutter, Michael. 1991. "Literatur als Quelle wirtschaftlichen Wachstums." *Internationales Archiv für Sozialgeschichte der deutschen Literatur* 16(2): 1-50.
Keith, Robert J. 1960. "The Marketing Revolution." *Journal of Marketing* 24(3): 35-38.
Koestler, Arthur. 1964. *The Act of Creation*. London: Penguin.
Kotler, Philip and Sidney J. Levy. 1969. "Broadening the Concept of Marketing." *Journal of Marketing* 33(1): 10-15.
Kotler, Philip and Gerald Zaltman. 1971. "Social Marketing: An Approach to Planned Social Change." *Journal of Marketing* 35(3): 3-12.
Levitt, Theodore. 1960. "Marketing Myopia." *Harvard Business Review* 38(4): 45-56.
Liebl, Franz. 2003. "What Is Strategic Knowledge Management Anyway?" Pp. 314-325 in *KMAC 2003—The Knowledge Management Aston Conference 2003*, edited by J. S. Edwards. Birmingham: The OR Society.
Liebl, Franz. 2014. "Strategische Subversion: Wofür?—Wogegen?" *Earnest & Algernon* (8): 106-109.
Liebl, Franz and Thomas Düllo. 2015. *Strategie als Kultivierung: Grundlagen—Methoden—Prozesse*. Berlin: Logos Verlag.
Liebl, Franz and Olaf G. Rughase. 2002. "Storylistening." *gdi impuls* 20(3.02): 34-39.
Liebl, Franz and Jan O. Schwarz. 2012. "'Art Facts': Zur Nutzung kultureller Originalitätsproduktion für die Strategische Frühaufklärung." Pp. 276-301 in *FOCUS-Jahrbuch 2012: Prognosen, Trend- und Zukunftsforschung*, editey by W. J. Koschnik. Munich: Focus Magazin Verlag.
Link, Jürgen. 1999. *Versuch über den Normalismus: Wie Normalität produziert wird*. 2nd rev. and exp. ed. Opladen: Westdeutscher Verlag.
Mathews, Ryan and Watts Wacker. 2003. *The Deviant's Advantage: How Fringe Ideas Create Mass Markets*. London: Random House.
Meffert, Heribert. 1988. *Strategische Unternehmensführung und Marketing. Beiträge zur marktorientierten Unternehmenspolitik*. Wiesbaden: Gabler.
Minsky, Marvin. 1975. "A Framework for Representing Knowledge." Pp. 211-277 in *The Psychology of Computer Vision*, edited by P. H. Winston. New York: McGraw-Hill.
Osterwalder, Alexander and Yves Pigneur. 2010. *Business Model Generation: A Handbook for Visionaries, Game Changers, and Challengers*. New York: Wiley.
Porter, Michael E. 1980. *Competitive Strategy—Techniques for Analyzing Industries and Competitors*. New York: Free Press.
Porter, Michael E. 1985. *Competitive Advantage—Creating and Sustaining Superior Performance*. New York: Free Press.
Porter, Michael E. 1991. "Towards a Dynamic Theory of Strategy." *Strategic Management Journal* 12(S2): 95-117.
Porter, Michael E. 1996. "What Is Strategy?" *Harvard Business Review* 74(6): 61-78.

Prahalad, Coimbatore K. 2000. *What's New About the New Economy*. Presentation to the plenary session at the Strategic Management Society Conference 'Strategy in the Entrepreneurial Millennium,' 15-18 October, Vancouver, B.C.

Raffée, Hans and Klaus-Peter Wiedmann, eds. 1985. *Strategisches Marketing*. Stuttgart: Poeschel.

Sarasvathy, Saras D. 2001. "Causation and Effectuation: Toward a Theoretical Shift from Economic Inevitability to Entrepreneurial Contingency." *Academy of Management Review* 26(2): 243-263.

Scharrer, Jürgen. 2011. "Marketing hat zu wenig zu melden. Studie von Heidrick & Struggles / Berater fordern stärkere strategische Rolle der Marketingchefs." *Horizont*, March 24, p. 1.

Schumpeter, Joseph A. 1934 [1912]. *The Theory of Economic Development*. Cambridge, MA: Harvard University Press.

Schwarz, Jan O. 2011. *Quellcode der Zukunft: Literatur in der Strategischen Frühaufklärung*. Berlin: Logos.

Schwarz, Jan O. and Franz Liebl. 2013. "Cultural Products and Their Implications for Business Models: Why Science Fiction Needs Socio-Cultural Fiction." *Futures* 50: 66-73.

Shrivastava, Paul and Ian I. Mitroff. 1983. "Frames of Reference Managers Use: A Study in Applied Sociology of Knowledge." Pp. 161-182 in *Advances in Strategic Management, Vol. 1*, edited by R. Lamb. Greenwich, CT: JAI Press.

Smith, Ken G. and Qing Cao. 2007. "An Entrepreneurial Perspective on the Firm—Environment Relationship." *Strategic Entrepreneurship Journal* 1(3-4): 329-344.

SMS Strategic Management Society. 2000. *20th Annual International Conference Call for Panel, Paper, and Poster Proposals "Strategy in the Entrepreneurial Millennium."* Vancouver, B.C.

Spinosa, Charles, Fernando Flores, and Hubert L. Dreyfus. 1997. *Disclosing New Worlds: Entrepreneurship, Democratic Action, and the Cultivation of Solidarity*. Cambridge: MIT Press.

Stahl, Michael J. and Gregory M. Bounds. 1991. *Competing Globally through Customer Value: The Management of Strategic Suprasystems*. Westport: Quorum Books.

Strong, Carolyn A. and Lloyd C. Harris. 2004. "The Drivers of Orientation: An Exploration of Relational, Human Resource and Procedural Tactics." *Journal of Strategic Marketing* 12(3): 183-204.

Varadarajan, P. Rajan. 1992. "Marketing's Contribution to Strategy: The View from a Different Looking Glass." *Journal of the Academy of Marketing Science* 20(4): 323-343.

Varadarajan, P. Rajan. 2010. "Strategic Marketing and Marketing Strategy: Domain, Definition, Fundamental Issues and Foundational Premises." *Journal of the Academy of Marketing Science* 38(2): 119-140.

Innovation by the Numbers

Crowdsourcing in the Innovation Process

Arnold Picot and Stefan Hopf

1 Crowdsourcing: Leveraging the Power of Many

Since 2006, when the US journalist Jeff Howe first used the term *crowdsourcing*—a neologistic portmanteau of 'crowd' and 'outsourcing'—to denote a division of labor in which tasks are delegated to countless masses by means of a (usually web-based) public appeal (see Howe 2006, 2008), crowdsourcing as a new form of organization has met with a rapid rise in scholarly interest. Yet the basic organizational principle is nothing new. Numerous historic examples describe a very similar phenomenon. Early Renaissance architects puzzled over how to construct the Santa Maria del Fiore Cathedral in Florence for half a century until a goldsmith and a clockmaker proposed a solution in response to a public announcement in 1418 (Boudreau, Lacetera, and Lakhani 2011). In 18th-century Britain, anyone who contributed to more accurate and therefore safer methods of maritime navigation was entitled to large monetary rewards under the Longitude Act of 1714 (Spencer 2012). And in 1879, philologist James Murray appealed to his readership to assist in the documentation of the English language, a voluminous undertaking that was to be collected in the *Oxford English Dictionary*, still a seminal reference work to this day (Lanxon 2011).

When comparing present-day crowdsourcing with these historic examples of collective problem solving, the most prominent difference lies in the digitization and accompanying dematerialization of products and services (Negroponte 1995; Picot, Reichwald, and Wigand 2008). Information and communications technologies (ICTs) that are now widely available in the economy and society—in conjunction with collaboration platforms—also greatly facilitate sharing and networking among suitable experts. As value chains become more and more immaterial, digital collaboration processes have grown and quickened in terms of range, applications, quality, and speed, thereby engendering new forms of support for innovation and novel ways to integrate different actors in these processes (Brabham 2013). Crowdsourcing is currently implemented for an incredibly diverse array of problems—from simple, predefined tasks such as the de-duplication of yellow page listings to highly complex challenges such as optimizing the landing of a Mars probe in its descent through the Red Planet's atmosphere.

Figure 1 illustrates the heightened interest in crowdsourcing among the global scientific community, starting from Jeff Howe's original definition in his 2006 article *The Rise of Crowdsourcing* followed by his comprehensive book titled *Crowdsourcing: Why the Power of the Crowd Is Driving the Future of Business* shortly thereafter in 2008. Generally speaking, research related to crowdsourcing started to spike around 2010.

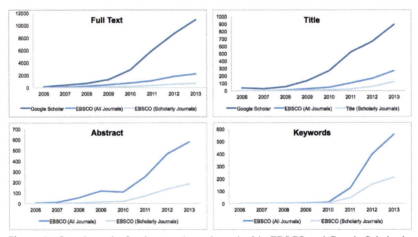

Figure 1   Search results for the term 'crowdsourcing' in EBSCO and Google Scholar by year (source: our own research).

The increasingly heterogeneous forms of crowdsourcing mentioned above have ultimately led to two basic perspectives on how to define crowdsourcing and classify its applications.

In their wide-ranging literature review of 209 publications, including 40 original definitions, Estellés-Arolas and González-Ladrón-de-Guevara (2012) proposed an integrative definition of crowdsourcing:

Innovation by the Numbers

Crowdsourcing is a type of participative online activity in which an individual, an institution, a non-profit organization, or company proposes to a group of individuals of varying knowledge, heterogeneity, and number, via a flexible open call, the voluntary undertaking of a task. The undertaking of the task, of variable complexity and modularity, and in which the crowd should participate bringing their work, money, knowledge and/or experience, always entails mutual benefit. The user will receive the satisfaction of a given type of need, be it economic, social recognition, self-esteem, or the development of individual skills, while the crowdsourcer will obtain and utilize to their advantage what the user has brought to the venture, whose form will depend on the type of activity undertaken. (ibid.: 197)

The authors distinguish three dimensions of crowdsourcing, each with its own lines of inquiry (ibid.: 191): (1) crowd (Who forms the crowd? What is the task at hand? What does it get in return?), (2) initiator (Who is the initiator? What result does the initiator receive?), and (3) process (How is the process structured? Which type of call is used? Which medium is used?).

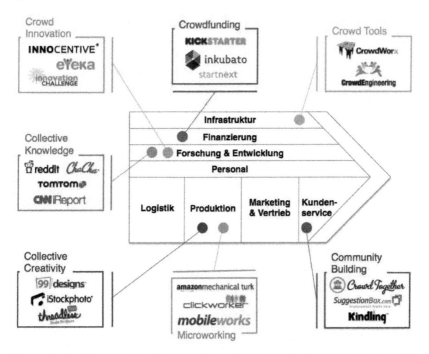

Figure 2 Basic forms and applications of crowdsourcing in business organizations with examples of service providers (source: Picot and Hopf 2013).

This comprehensive and inclusive understanding often stands in contrast to various other crowdsourcing definitions with different levels of abstraction; these distinctions are usually linked to specific crowdsourcing applications. In terms of classifying different applications, one possibility is to match crowdsourcing forms with the value-adding activities of business organizations (see Figure 2).

This systematic differentiation of basic crowdsourcing forms is neither mutually exclusive nor exhaustive since new forms and applications are constantly emerging and several, at times substantial, overlaps can be found between basic types of crowdsourcing and related terms and phenomena (e.g., collaborative innovation, collective intelligence, user innovation; see also Franke and Piller 2004; von Hippel 2005; Malone, Laubacher, and Dellarocas 2009). Based on the overview in Figure 2, we can, however, discern the following basic forms of crowdsourcing with a view to potential applications (Picot and Hopf 2013):

- *Crowd innovation*: Integration of external resources to generate, develop, and implement new ideas.
- *Crowdfunding*: Funding of projects or business ventures through numerous contributions from different sources, usually in the form of silent partnerships.
- *Crowd tools*: Applications, platforms, and tools that enable the collaboration, communication, and sharing of tasks between different actors.
- *Community building*: Active integration of individuals in thematic communities.
- *Microwork*: The process of splitting tasks into the smallest possible work packages and delegating them to a virtual workforce.
- *Collective creativity*: Utilization of creative crowd talent to produce various types of original content.
- *Collective knowledge*: Extraction of information and knowledge for primarily commercial purposes.

In the following article, our specific emphasis will be on crowd innovation and the question of how crowdsourcing can be used to generate or support innovation. We will also touch on crowdsourcing aspects from neighboring fields where relevant.

In the next section (2), we start by clarifying the relationship between crowd innovation and open innovation before going on to discuss the economic significance of the apparent shift from manufacturer-centered innovation to customer-centered and collaborative approaches to the production of novelty. We continue by exploring different manifestations of crowd innovation and their role in the innovation process. In section 3, we outline further topics and needs for research and, finally, present our conclusions in section 4.

2 Crowdsourcing Innovation

Crowdsourcing integrates external actors into the innovation process and can therefore be viewed as a specific type of open innovation (2.1). In this section, we discuss the emerging paradigm that can be found in this new development (2.2) and examine different forms and examples of crowd innovation and how they relate to the innovation process (2.3).

2.1 Crowd Innovation as a Category of Open Innovation

Opinions vary when it comes to which paradigm (open innovation, open source, etc.) supplies the best fit for crowdsourcing activities (Erickson 2013). Most authors view crowdsourcing as part of open innovation (Chesbrough 2003) since both concepts describe "an innovation-related task awarded through an open call to a network of customers, users, and other stakeholders" (Picot and Hopf 2013: 28, our translation; see also Piller and Reichwald 2009). Crowdsourcing can be applied in countless settings, which makes a nuanced analysis of its characteristics all the more essential. Crowdsourcing activities in the microwork sector, for example, are seldom innovation-related and can thus be relegated to the categories of production and outsourcing. Our focus in the present context lies on crowd innovation, which can be visualized as the common ground between two sets of activities—in this case open innovation and crowdsourcing (see Figure 3), from which it follows that not all open innovation activities can necessarily be considered crowd innovation. Involving a lead user in the innovation process (von Hippel 1986), for instance, is not a crowd-based form of open innovation. Returning to our initial definition, crowd innovation occurs when the search for new ideas and solutions is directed towards a larger and generally unrestricted audience. In this sense, crowd innovation is more 'open' than certain forms of open innovation.

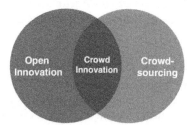

Figure 3 Crowd innovation as the intersection between open innovation and crowdsourcing (source: Picot and Hopf 2013).

In the past, the dominant model for the organized production of novelty was the so-called 'closed innovation model,' which centered on in-house production by specific manufacturers. Open innovation activities, in contrast, are essentially characterized by the fact that they occur mainly outside, and not within, organizations (see Figure 4).

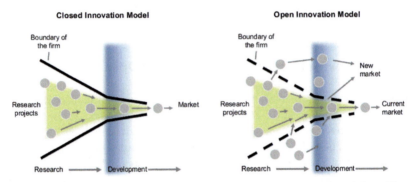

Figure 4 Closed and open innovation models at a glance (source: adapted from Chesbrough 2003).

The open innovation model reflects the active 'relaxing' of organizational boundaries so that external (and internal) ideas can be channeled through internal (and external) development processes and, finally, to the point of maturity and marketability (Chesbrough 2003). In addition to growing competitive pressure, an increasingly global labor market, and greater economic uncertainty (Huff, Möslein, and Reichwald 2013), this development is driven by technological progress (Baldwin and von Hippel 2011), which is a key condition for the cost-effective use of crowd innovation.

2.2 Economic Analysis of the Paradigm Shift from Manufacturer-to Customer-Centered and Collaborative Innovation

Organizations use crowd innovation, a novel form of customer-centered and collaborative innovation based on crowdsourcing, in their innovation processes for a wide variety of applications. The model developed by Baldwin and von Hippel (2011) provides an economically oriented, dynamic explanation for why innovation is sourced from crowds, individuals, or organizations (see Figures 5 and 6).

Innovation by the Numbers

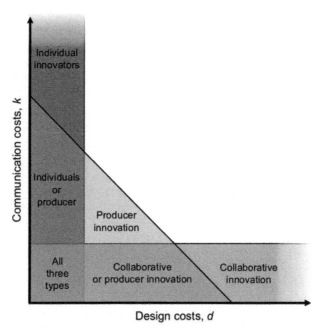

Figure 5 Feasibility of innovation approaches in relation to communication and design costs (source: adapted from Baldwin and von Hippel 2011).

This model describes possible approaches to innovation in relation to two dimensions: *communication costs* (associated with the exchange of information during the innovation process) and *design costs* (associated with the development of specifications and the definition, processing, and integration of tasks to implement a design). According to the model, innovation is sourced from individuals when design costs are low. Communication costs are insignificant in this case because individual innovators do not require extensive interaction to complete their work. Collaborative innovation, on the other hand, is the preferred sourcing option when communication costs are low, since this form of problem solving requires intensive multilateral communication. Design costs in this case are largely insignificant since individual innovators only make up a small portion of these costs. In-house innovation is especially suitable for innovation projects that involve both non-negligible communication and design costs, which, unlike for individual innovation and collaborative innovation, only make sense economically with the coordination mechanisms available in an organization.

We can model the paradigm shift from manufacturer- to customer-centered and collaborative innovation by adopting a dynamic view of exogenous changes and their theoretical implications. Significant performance gains (described, for example, by Moore's law, Kryder's law, and Nielsen's law) and inexpensively available information and communications technology are two main drivers behind this shift (e.g., Baldwin and von Hippel 2011; Afuah and Tucci 2012; Villarroel 2013). These developments significantly reduce communication and design costs and thereby considerably expand the spectrum of possibilities for individual innovation and collaborative innovation. This can increasingly lead to what is known as the 'producer squeeze problem' (Villarroel 2013: 184). In other words, in-house innovation remains economically superior only for a small spectrum of innovations (see Figure 6).

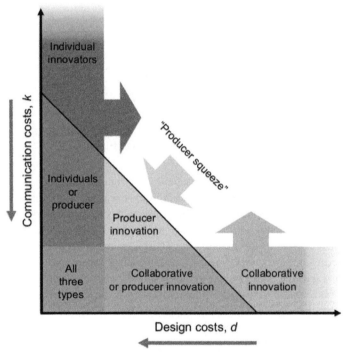

Figure 6 Shift in feasibility for different innovation approaches based on reduced communication and design costs resulting from technological advancements (source: adapted from Villarroel 2013; Baldwin and von Hippel 2011).

To address this problem, many companies are now trying to integrate individual innovation and collaborative innovation into their innovation process. Crowdsourcing in its various modalities offers a way to co-opt these economically attractive forms of innovation and use them for in-house innovation processes. As a 'solution to distant search' (Afuah and Tucci 2012: 355), crowdsourcing can be leveraged to find more cost-effective solutions, above all thanks to inexpensive access to a large number of volunteer problem solvers worldwide who already possess the required expertise or even the required solution (Afuah and Tucci 2012).

2.3 Crowdsourcing: Typical Forms and Applications for Innovation

Crowdsourcing can be leveraged as a highly versatile tool in the various phases of innovation. For simplicity's sake as well as to demonstrate different applications of crowdsourcing, we will assume a linear model of innovation with five phases: idea generation, concept development, prototyping, product/market testing, and market launch (e.g., Kupsch, Marr, and Picot 1991; Cooper and Kleinschmidt 1991; Piller and Reichwald 2009). Crowdsourcing activities geared toward innovation can be grouped into three main categories (e.g., Boudreau and Lakhani 2013; Picot and Hopf 2013):

- Crowd contests: Open calls announcing a specific problem along with an award (financial or other) for the best solution. This form of crowdsourcing is best suited to generating a broad spectrum of ideas and approaches for complex and novel challenges (examples include Kaggle, TopCoder, and InnoCentive).
- Crowd collaborative communities: Collective endeavors characterized by the collection and aggregation of different contributions into a coherent result. This form requires a desired outcome to be specified at the outset. Collaboration often occurs based on a platform and typically relies on non-monetary, intrinsic motivation (examples are Linux, test IO, and OpenIDEO).
- Crowd complementors: Complementary innovations that supplement an existing product or service, mostly by means of a dedicated platform or an existing standard and without the explicit specification of a problem (examples are Apple App Store, Mozilla Firefox add-ons, and Ford's OpenXC project).

As an IT-supported process innovation, different developments—technological, economic, social, and political—can result in the continuous adaptation and expansion of crowdsourcing and its described forms. The different types of crowd innovation can generally be employed throughout the entire innovation process, often sequentially or in hybrid combinations. In addition to crowd innovation, the other basic forms of crowdsourcing mentioned above (e.g., crowdfunding to finance an innovation or microwork to implement precisely specified tasks in product testing) may be employed in the innovation process (see Figure 7). We will continue by presenting some possible applications of crowd innovation which, in keeping with our focus on innovation and in the spirit of the Latin term *innovatio*, can prompt the renewal of existing concepts, behavior, or things (Schachtner 2001).

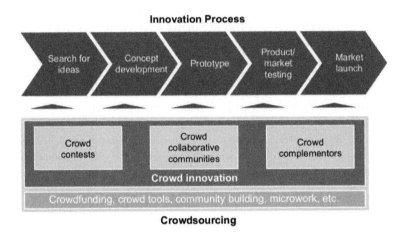

Figure 7 Crowdsourcing in the innovation process (source: adapted from Reichwald and Piller 2009).

"All innovation starts with the search for ideas" (Piller and Reichwald 2009: 124, our translation). Because companies start by gathering as many ideas as possible, crowd innovation is particularly useful in this phase since crowdsourcing can be utilized as an online-based 'broadcast search' to maximize the search radius and the number of individuals that can be addressed (Afuah and Tucci 2012). Dell's IdeaStorm can be viewed as a hybrid crowdsourcing-based example that mixes crowd complementors and crowd collaborative communities. In Dell's own words, IdeaStorm aims "to give a direct voice to our customers and an avenue to have online 'brainstorm' sessions to allow you the customer to share ideas and collaborate with one another and Dell. Our goal through IdeaStorm is to hear what new products or services you'd like to see Dell develop."[1] According to this description,

---

1   http://www.ideastorm.com, retrieved October 6, 2014.

the primary goal of the platform lies in generating new ideas for products and services through collaboration between customers and Dell employees (e.g., through voting and comment functions). In the period from February 2007 to June 2009, a total of 8,801 ideas were generated on this platform by 4,285 individuals, of which 348 ideas (about 4%) were ultimately implemented (Bayus 2013). Whether these numbers actually translate into economic success is largely unclear. In light of the fact that Dell offers a mere USD 1,000 for the intellectual property rights to an idea (though proof of such a transaction having occurred has yet to be seen) with no further financial commitments to the makers of ideas that are chosen and implemented, it is rather safe to conclude that the platform is generally profitable (ibid.). More problematic, however, seems to be the long-term commitment of users since on average they tend to submit only one (rarely successful) idea. Most ideas selected for implementation come from the relatively small group of 'serial ideators' (users who proposed more than one successful idea during the period under investigation); the idea stream from these users, and with it the innovative potential of the crowd, tends to decrease over time (ibid.). An additional study on the general quality of crowdsourced ideas confirms that, when compared to input from professional engineers and designers, the conceptual contributions received in crowd contests are superior in terms of novelty and usability, though generally lacking in terms of feasibility (Poetz and Schreiner 2012). Crowdsourcing's potential for idea generation is already apparent in the sheer numbers that it mobilizes, in line with the basic principle: "the wisdom of the crowd is proportional to their size" (The Economist 2012). What is more important, however, is how these ideas can be used to generate real added value (monetary and otherwise) (Afuah and Tucci 2012, 2013; Bloodgood 2013).

The phase of *concept development* comprises central research and development activities, including idea visualization, feasibility analysis, and general concept evaluation (Piller and Reichwald 2009). A well-known example of the use of crowd innovation in this phase is InnoCentive, a platform for "innovation solutions from the world's smartest people, who compete to provide ideas and solutions to important business, social, policy, scientific, and technical challenges."[2] Organized as a *crowd contest*, InnoCentive enables businesses to announce specific challenges (much like a broad collection of specifications) as an open call or 'broadcast' (Afuah and Tucci 2012) and to grant monetary rewards to the best solutions. To work on any of these challenges, individuals need to accept a call-specific agreement, which defines items such as the evaluation process and criteria, as well as intellectual property rules and the award. Calls on this platform

---

2   https://www.innocentive.com, retrieved October 6, 2014.

range from relatively simple and clearly delineated problems to highly complex and abstract challenges from diverse application fields. The National Aeronautics and Space Administration (NASA), for example, used the platform to search for a useful secondary function for dead weight, known in technical terms as 'balance mass,' which is discarded by Mars landers to facilitate entry and landing. NASA's objective was to equip the probes with an alternative balance mass that "should perform some type of scientific or technological function adding to our knowledge base"[3] (e.g., sensors that collect atmospheric data). Since its posting on September 20, 2014, exactly 2,108 'active solvers' contributed their ideas to this challenge, which was open for two months (until November 21, 2014). Afuah and Tucci summarized the major advantage of crowdsourcing for the *concept development phase* as providing the 'solution to a distant search' (2012: 355). This solution enables a 'distant search' (ibid.; i.e., the search for a solution that lies beyond a current and immediate skill set), often bound up with considerable costs for an individual or an organization (such as the acquisition of relevant expertise, the evaluation of various solutions and providers, and even good old-fashioned trial and error), to be transformed into a 'local search' (ibid.). The task of problem solving is thus transferred to numerous self-selecting individuals with the required expertise and perhaps even a viable solution. This presents a far more efficient and effective solution to the problem-solving process itself (Afuah and Tucci 2012). One example is a challenge posted on Kaggle—a similar crowd contest site—by the German multinational chemical and pharmaceutical company Merck. A computer scientist with no domain expertise in pharma proposed the winning solution, which employed machine-learning software to identify promising chemicals for new drugs (Markoff 2013). This form of crowd-based distant search (ibid.: 355) eliminated the costly prospect of overhauling the company's drug discovery process.

Once the initial idea is found, it is transformed, in the *prototype* phase, into a fully functional model (Piller and Reichwald 2009). As discussed in section 2.2 (see Figures 5 and 6 as well as Baldwin and von Hippel 2011), technical developments in areas such as computer-aided design (CAD), 3D printing, and rapid prototyping software have significantly reduced the costs of design. This makes crowdsourcing a cost-effective alternative for prototype creation. In the field of software development, one example is TopCoder, marketed as "the world's largest crowdsourcing development, design, and data science platform" with just under 700,000 users.[4] This crowd contest platform is used to post calls for the development of various software prototypes. Here, too, the calls contain a specific descrip-

---

3 ibid., Challenge ID: 9933607.
4 https://www.topcoder.com, retrieved October 6, 2014.

tion of a problem, which is delegated to users in the form of a contest. After the submission deadline, an internal TopCoder review board selects the best prototype in a peer review process. Further examples of crowd-based prototyping can be found in open source software development by crowd collaborative communities (e.g., Linux or the Apache HTTP Server Project; see, e.g., Brügge et al. 2004; Picot and Fiedler 2008). One key advantage of crowd-based prototyping lies in the possibility of modularization, in other words, using TopCoder to divide a customer's problem into numerous small work packages, also known as 'hyperspecialization' (Malone, Laubacher, and Johns 2011). Different packages can thus be completed in parallel and users can specialize in specific tasks or problems, which can then be completed more efficiently over time. On the whole, this not only increases the quality of contributions but can also lead to significant advantages in terms of costs, lead time, and flexibility (Lakhani, Garvin, and Lonstein 2010; Malone et al. 2011).

In the *product and market testing* phase, the prototype "moves into the production system, where it is usually manufactured in small quantities for a test market" (Piller and Reichwald 2009: 126, our translation). During this phase, *crowd innovation* is primarily implemented to test software-based prototypes. Small quantities have ceased to be a necessary restriction in this case since digital goods can be produced and distributed at a marginal cost. The combination of digital products and services with virtually unlimited test subjects through crowdsourcing results in completely new possibilities. As a crowd collaborative community, the German company test IO (formerly testcloud), for instance, offers "tailor-made, scalable, and cost-efficient crowdsourced software testing solutions for businesses. Our services include all types of explorative, functional, and usability tests for software: websites, mobile apps, and enterprise software" by over 8,000 testers in 40 languages.[5] In an increasingly global economy and society, these new possibilities mean it is not only possible to recruit testers worldwide but also to test products and services in specific markets and cultures and adapt them to local requirements. Another advantage of crowdsourcing solutions that accompany the entire innovation process is that conventional product and market testing might no longer be necessary when the innovation in question is a product of that same market (i.e., the crowd) (Piller and Reichwald 2009). Here we can cite Quirky, a company that picks up on ideas from inventors, offers support during the development and manufacturing process, and sells the products on its website in return for a portion of the sales.[6] Because the market is involved in the innovation process and therefore

---

5   See https://www.test.io, retrieved May 5, 2016.
6   See https://www.quirky.com, retrieved October 6, 2014.

the selection of promising ideas from the get-go,[7] it becomes conceivable to skip product and market testing altogether.

The *market launch* phase involves "price setting, the selection and combination of suitable distribution channels, brand and communication management, and sales staff training" (Piller and Reichwald 2009: 126, our translation). Crowd innovation in this phase can be aptly illustrated by the German T-shirt company Spreadshirt, whose business model relies on a crowd collaborative community whereby members can design and purchase T-shirts or sell their own designs.[8] The process starts with creative designs, which users adapt to different formats (e.g., T-shirts, mobile phone cases, tote bags). Users can sell the final products on the Spreadshirt platform. When it is time for the market launch, users play a key role "by recruiting friends to buy their products, posing as models for the online catalog, and spreading the word about the brand" (ibid., our translation). Another application of crowdsourcing during the market launch process can be found in what are known as 'predictive markets' (e.g., Spann and Skiera 2009), or virtual settings in which the crowd's bets on future events can be used as indicators of actual outcomes (Wolfers and Zitewitz 2004). Hewlett-Packard, for example, employed predictive markets that resulted in more accurate estimates of printer sales than the company's internal numbers (Plott and Chen 2002). For Siemens, the crowd predicted the delayed completion of a software solution, contrary to traditional planning and projection methods (Ortner 1998). Predictive markets can ultimately be used in most, if not all, fields: from predictions involving economic data to political elections to flu outbreaks. Crowdworx, a German software company and maker of "the leading prediction market software for companies"[9] promises more accurate predictions, faster results, and improved cost-effectiveness than conventional market research and expert polling. Three main aspects are behind these improvements. First, under the right circumstances, groups can be remarkably intelligent, "and are often smarter than the smartest people in them" (Surowiecki 2005: XIII), a phenomenon that has also been referred to as 'collective intelligence' or the 'wisdom of the crowds' (e.g., Malone et al. 2009). Second, competition, including that from predictive markets, can lead to an effective aggregation of asymmetrically distributed information and therefore to information efficiency (Hayek 1945). Third,

---

7   In the Web 2.0 context, this is sometimes referred to as 'perpetual beta,' an expression that describes an early, and often regular, long-term involvement of users in the development of software programs (e.g., O'Reilly 2009).
8   See https://www.spreadshirt.com, retrieved October 6, 2014.
9   See https://www.crowdworx.com/prediction-market-software-consulting-companies/, retrieved October 6, 2014.

with the Internet and the widespread diffusion of information and communication technologies in our current economy and society, organizations have the means to access and integrate a broad audience in the innovation process (Hubbard 2010).

The examples presented here illustrate just some of the various ways in which crowdsourcing can be applied to the innovation process. Continuing technological progress will most likely result in even more options as novel forms of technical support emerge or new segments of the global population join the digital crowd (e.g., Narula et al. 2011). With these dynamic developments come new questions and needs for research, which we will briefly outline in the next section.

3 Selected Research Issues and Needs

As an innovation that pertains to processes in organizations, crowdsourcing has an interdisciplinary and multifaceted character. It is not only applied in vastly different fields but is also the subject of varied analyses in innovation research. The result is a broad field of research in which different disciplines such as economics, humanities, law, and engineering have identified and pursued relevant issues related to the growing phenomenon of crowdsourcing, both within the actual innovation context and beyond. We will discuss some of these crowdsourcing-related topics and issues in these established academic fields in the sections that follow: organizational process and distinct forms (3.1), challenges and tasks (3.2), value creation and intellectual property (3.3), and employment (3.4).

3.1 Organizational Process and Distinct Forms

A process perspective on crowdsourcing as a conduit for innovation opens up various options for research. These are related, for instance, to how to design and optimize the organizational process or to different forms of crowdsourcing that can emerge with increasingly stable processes (e.g., the previously described crowd contests, crowd collaborative communities, and crowd complementors in the field of innovation). In their literature survey, Kittur et al. (2013) classified different lines of organizational research according to three dimensions (process, computer support, and individuals), which are outlined below.

The process perspective includes the following topics and needs for research:

- *Workflow organization*: Complex crowdsourced tasks often require workflows that operate in parallel. Collaborative crowdsourcing approaches in particular can result in complex dependencies between individual tasks and create the need for sophisticated means of integration. One major need for research will therefore lie in an analysis of changes in workflow organization along with the effects on quality and the need for new management approaches to coordinate between internal workers and an undefined number of external actors.
- *Task allocation*: Tasks can be distributed by a central entity or assigned through self-selection. In the best-case scenario, users receive tasks that correspond with their specific expertise, coupled with suitable incentives. Accordingly, and in light of notable improvements in task-routing algorithms that effectively match content and users (e.g., matching procedures on dating or job platforms), researchers can analyze which forms of task allocation are best suited to specific problems or jobs.
- *Hierarchy*: Researchers might investigate the extent to which traditional company hierarchies, including corresponding management structures, can be advantageous for self-organization, task description, and task allocation in the crowdsourcing process.
- *Real-time (collaborative) activities*: Crowdsourcing provides fast access to a large and flexible workforce—a major advantage. This makes the question of real-time assembly and organization interesting for research: If it can be done, which approaches seem promising?
- *Synchronous collaboration*: For many tasks, rapid attention and processing is crucial to success. Through access to a global workforce, crowdsourcing can be used to complete jobs in record time. This form of collaboration requires a precise understanding of how different cultural or socioeconomic aspects can affect virtual collaboration and which measures may be taken to ensure effective and efficient synchronous collaboration.
- *Quality assurance*: For distributed, highly granular work products, quality assurance is seen as a key challenge for certain forms of crowdsourcing. It can either be achieved through a precise definition of jobs or through a post hoc analysis of results. Although complex algorithms can cover certain parts of the quality assurance process, researchers can still analyze appropriate peer review procedures or other quality assurance concepts as well as optimal approaches for implementation. When tasks are less clearly defined, topics such as the criteria and procedures used to determine award winners can be addressed within a quality assurance framework.

Computer support in the crowdsourcing process has brought up a number of further questions and a growing need for research. Advancements in the field of artificial intelligence (AI) in particular create new possibilities that could lead to significant improvements in the crowdsourcing process:

- *Crowd support for artificial intelligence*: Crowdsourcing can be used to improve algorithms. Users can help train functions such as object recognition for self-driving cars (e.g., recognize people, even as partial images, on photos). Topics and relevant research in this area pertain to how users might provide content-based support for AI development and how to 'harness the crowd' for this purpose.
- *Artificial intelligence in support of the crowd*: There are numerous possibilities for using AI in the crowdsourcing process. Researchers could especially focus on the conditions under which AI can provide content-based and organizational support for the crowdsourcing process, effectively replacing human activity. This includes aspects related to AI-based process optimization and the automated request for human intervention.
- *Crowdsourcing platforms*: Platforms match 'task creators' and 'task solvers.' Design is therefore a significant aspect for crowdsourcing platforms and the crowdsourcing process. Some examples of platform providers (companies that provide platforms as a service) were briefly discussed in section 1 as crowd tools. Researchers could continue to analyze the dynamics of platform development and their underlying algorithms, which are subject to a steady stream of technological advancements.

Finally, the crowdsourcing process also depends on individuals, who can appear as clients or users/workers, among other roles. When it comes to ensuring appropriate conditions for the latter to complete their chosen or assigned jobs, we can also identify a number of specific research questions and topics:

- *Job design*: Work announced on crowdsourcing platforms is highly granular and often monotonous over time owing to its repetitive character. Although this level of granularity and the precise specification of tasks can make sense in terms of efficiency, keeping workers motivated and satisfied might prove difficult in the long term. For research, the main question then is how to integrate crowdsourcing processes at different granularity levels and within a larger context while still preserving efficiency. Topics in this case largely correspond with those addressed in the Taylorism debate (e.g., Picot 1990).

- *Reputation and referral mechanisms*: Certain mechanisms such as employer references and certificates provide important signals that simplify the recruiting process considerably for employers and employees alike. Crowdsourcing invokes an increasingly homogeneous repertoire of mechanisms, all of which ultimately boil down to a trade-off between sourcing from the anonymous crowd, an option with low transaction costs, and the selective recruiting of distinctly qualified experts. This trade-off should be subject to a more thorough analysis to develop suitable reputation and referral mechanisms.
- *Motivation and remuneration*: Workers participate in crowdsourcing activities for a wide variety of reasons and their efforts should be rewarded accordingly. On the basis of findings from psychological, sociological, and management research, different motives should be identified and paired with heterogeneous (i.e., not exclusively monetary) remuneration mechanisms. Studies analyzing the open source movement (e.g., Lakhani and von Hippel 2003; Brügge et al. 2004) have already laid some of the groundwork.

Frequently occurring combinations of crowdsourcing processes, computer support, and individual factors result in distinct organizational forms of crowdsourcing (integrative sourcing without remuneration, selective sourcing with crowd assessment, etc.; see, e.g., Geiger et al. 2011). Identifying these forms will enable the further structuring and integration of various research efforts that analyze the organization of crowdsourcing processes.

3.2   Problems, Challenges, and Tasks for Crowdsourcing

An efficient design of crowdsourcing activities requires a comprehensive understanding of potential tasks and challenges as well as related implications for the organization of crowdsourcing processes. Despite the general increase in crowdsourcing research, there are only a few approaches that have attempted to classify these activities. Brabham (2013) and Gadiraju, Kawase, and Dietze (2014) have provided initial suggestions and classification schemes at different levels of abstraction. Gadiraju et al. (ibid.) has proposed an empirical approach based on an analysis of 1,000 users registered on the crowdsourcing platform CrowdFlower.[10] Their approach provides a sufficiently granular classification of potential challenges and tasks that can be addressed by crowdsourcing:

---

10   See https://www.crowdflower.com, retrieved October 6, 2014.

- *Information search:* In this task category, searching for and analyzing information (e.g., the most inexpensive flight for a specific date) is delegated to the crowd.
- *Verification and validation:* Questions in this area can involve the verification of certain aspects depending on given parameters or the confirmation of certain information. This might include online identity checks to determine, for instance, whether Twitter users are humans or Internet bots.
- *Interpretation and analysis:* This type of task primarily draws on the wisdom of the many by summarizing the interpretation and analysis of users into the most representative result possible. One example is classifying reviews as either 'positive' or 'negative'.
- *Content generation:* Crowdsourcing tasks in this area involve generating new content (e.g., translations).
- *Surveys:* Crowdsourcing-based surveys can be employed to collect target-group-specific information, for instance, data on a certain cohort of students.
- *Content retrieval:* This category involves the simple retrieval of information such as a video.

Additional research on the classification of potential challenges and tasks delegated to crowds should endeavor to consolidate and integrate previous results and relate them to optimal organizational processes while considering key criteria such as efficiency. The contextual consideration of relevant problems and tasks requires a detailed analysis of potential classifications. In the context of innovation, for example, content generation (ibid.) should be assigned further subcategories in light of the extremely varied content types it contains (e.g., developing solution proposals for pre-structured problems, generating novel ideas, designing complementary innovations) as well as the requirements this entails for the organization of crowdsourcing processes.

3.3 Value Creation and Intellectual Property

Crowdsourcing's value-creating potential can be seen in its increasing use in the economy and society. Nonetheless, there is not enough systematic research on the objectification of this value (e.g., Afuah and Tucci 2012, 2013; Bloodgood 2013), widely believed to be a "fundamental factor that firms should consider first and foremost when engaging in the decision of how to problem solve" (Bloodgood 2013: 456). Meanwhile, the value produced by crowdsourcing activities can be examined on different levels and based on context-dependent value concepts. On the micro level, for instance, the monetary value of an individual task such as the crowd-based translation of a text passage can be determined in comparison to a professional service provider. On the macro level, in contrast, the strategic value of an invention generated through crowdsourcing can be assessed in terms of its significance in creating a competitive advantage. Some initial thematic and methodological considerations can be found in the work of authors such as Poetz and Schreier (2012); they provided a qualitative comparison of crowdsourced product ideas versus those of professional designers and highlight the absorptive capacity of companies to profit from numerous ideas (see Blohm 2013).

Value creation is closely tied to the issue of a suitable approach to intellectual property in the crowdsourcing process. Protective measures used in traditional innovation contexts such as strict confidentiality, shielding off internal processes from competitors and customers, as well as the accumulation of large IP portfolios, cannot be easily implemented in an innovation process characterized by involving as many people as possible (e.g., Brügge et al. 2004; Lakhani and Panetta 2007). Different methods do exist to deal with intellectual property in crowdsourcing processes, yet more work still needs to be done on best practices in this area. T-shirt designers on the platform Threadless[11] agree to turn over all copyright entitlements to Threadless in return for a monetary payment, for example. InnoCentive,[12] a platform for crowdsourcing innovative ideas, enables both submitting parties and 'solvers' to remain anonymous to protect IP so that no links can be drawn to company-specific research and development activities. The legal complexity of transferring collaboratively generated intellectual property also results in solvers on InnoCentive not being permitted to work together to find solutions to problems (or 'challenges'). This imposes a considerable restriction on the innovative potential of the crowd. Research in this area—in keeping with the principles of open innovation—should strive to identify conditions that foster openness, transparency, suitable incentives, and especially close collaboration while also protecting intellectual property (Lakhani and Panetta 2007).

---

11 See https://www.threadless.com, retrieved October 6, 2014.
12 See https://www.innocentive.com, retrieved October 6, 2014.

4 Conclusion

Crowdsourcing can be applied to innovation in a variety of ways. Its potential forms and applications are subject to a dynamic process of change, above all due to technological advancements, a situation that generates numerous questions and issues for research. Chesbrough (2003) describes an emergent paradigm of "open innovation" characterized by a shift from manufacturer-centered innovation to customer-oriented and collaborative innovation; activities in this area are also poised to become more economical owing to falling costs of communication and design. Crowdsourcing is not only an option for cost savings but also holds significant potential for innovation. Various topics in this innovation context, including the organization process, problems and tasks delegated to crowdsourcing, value creation, incentives, and intellectual property, will help tap into its well of potential.

References

Afuah, Allan and Christopher L. Tucci. 2012. "Crowdsourcing as a Solution to Distant Search." *Academy of Management Review* 37(3): 355-375.
Afuah, Allen and Christopher L. Tucci. 2013. "Value Capture and Crowdsourcing." *Academy of Management Review* 38(3): 457-460.
Baldwin, Carliss Y. and Eric von Hippel. 2011. "Modeling a Paradigm Shift: From Producer Innovation to User and Open Collaborative Innovation." *Organization Science* 22(6): 1399-1417.
Bayus, Barry L. 2013. "Crowdsourcing New Product Ideas over Time: An Analysis of the Dell IdeaStorm Community." *Management Science* 59(1): 226-244.
Blohm, Ivo. 2013. *Open Innovation Communities. Absorptive Capacity und kollektive Ideenbewertung*. Wiesbaden: Springer Gabler.
Bloodgood, James. 2013. "Crowdsourcing: Useful for Problem Solving, But What About Value Capture?" *Academy of Management Review* 38(3): 455-457.
Boudreau, Kevin J., Nicola Lacetera, and Karim R. Lakhani. 2011. "Incentives and Problem Uncertainty in Innovation Contests: An Empirical Analysis." *Management Science* 57(5): 843-863.
Boudreau, Kevin J. and Karim R. Lakhani. 2013. "Using the Crowd as an Innovation Partner." *Havard Business Review* 91(4): 60-69.
Brabham, Daren C. 2013. *Crowdsourcing*. Cambridge: MIT Press.
Brügge, Bernd, Dietmar Harhoff, Arnold Picot, Oliver Creighton, Marina Fiedler, and Joachim Henkel. 2004. *Open-Source-Software: Eine ökonomische und technische Analyse*. Berlin, Heidelberg: Springer.
Chesbrough, Henry. 2003. "The Era of Open Innovation." *Sloan Management Review* 44(4): 35-41.
Cooper, Robert G. and Elko J. Kleinschmidt. 1991. "New Product Processes at Leading Industrial Firms." *Industrial Marketing Management* 20(2): 137-147.
Erickson, Lisa B. 2013. "Hanging with the Right Crowd: Crowdsourcing as a New Business Practice for Innovation, Productivity, Knowledge Capture, and Marketing." PhD dissertation, College of Information Sciences and Technology, Pennsylvania State University.
Estellés-Arolas, Enrique and Fernando González-Ladrón-de-Guevara. 2012. "Towards an Integrated Crowdsourcing Definition." *Journal of Information Science* 38(2): 189-200.
Franke, Nikolaus and Frank Piller. 2004. "Value Creation by Toolkits for User Innovation and Design: The Case of the Watch Market." *Journal of Product Innovation Management* 21(6): 401-415.
Gadiraju, Ujwal, Ricardo Kawase, and Stefan Dietze. 2014. "A Taxonomy of Microtasks on the Web." In *Proceedings of the 25th ACM conference on Hypertext and Social Media*, Santiago, Chile, September 1–4, 2014.
Geiger, David, Stefan Seedorf, Thimo Schulze, Robert C. Nickerson, and Martin Schader. 2011. "Managing the Crowd: Towards a Taxonomy of Crowdsourcing Processes." In *Proceedings of the 17th Americas Conference on Information Systems (AMCIS)*, Detroit, Michigan, August 4–7, 2011.
Hayek, Friedrich A. 1945. "The Use of Knowledge in Society." *The American Economic Review* 35(4): 519-530.

von Hippel, Eric. 1986. "Lead Users: A Source of Novel Product Concepts." *Management Science* 32(7): 791-805.
von Hippel, Eric. 2005. "Democratizing Innovation: The Evolving Phenomenon of User Innovation." *Journal für Betriebswirtschaft* 55(1): 63-78.
Howe, Jeff. 2006. "The Rise of Crowdsourcing." *Wired Magazine* 14(6): 1-4.
Howe, Jeff. 2008. *Crowdsourcing: Why the Power of the Crowd Is Driving the Future of Business*. New York: Three Rivers Press.
Hubbard, Douglas W. 2010. *How to Measure Anything: Finding the Value of Intangibles in Business*. Hoboken: John Wiley & Sons.
Huff, Anne S., Kathrin M. Möslein, and Ralf Reichwald, eds. 2013. *Leading Open Innovation*. Cambridge: The MIT Press.
Kittur, Aniket, Jeffrey V. Nickerson, Michael S. Bernstein, Elizabeth M. Gerber, Aaron Shaw, John Zimmerman, Matthew Lease, and John J. Horton. 2013. "The Future of Crowd Work." In *Proceedings of the 2013 conference on Computer Supported Cooperative Work, San Antonio, Texas, February 2, 2013*. New York: ACM.
Kupsch, Peter U., Rainer Marr, and Arnold Picot. 1991. "Innovationswirtschaft." Pp. 1069-1156 in *Industriebetriebslehre*, edited by E. Heinen. Wiesbaden: Gabler.
Lakhani, Karim R., David A. Garvin, and Eric Lonstein. 2010. "TopCoder (A): Developing Software through Crowdsourcing." *Harvard Business School General Management Unit Case, No. 610-632*.
Lakhani, Karim R. and Eric von Hippel. 2003. "How Open Source Software Works: 'Free' User-to-User Assistance." *Research Policy* 32(6): 923-943.
Lakhani, Karim R. and Jill A. Panetta. 2007. "The Principles of Distributed Innovation." *Innovations* 2(3): 97-112.
Lanxon, Nate. 2011. "How the Oxford English Dictionary Started out like Wikipedia." *Wired*, January 13, 2011. Retrieved October 6, 2014 (http://www.wired.co.uk/news/archive/2011-01/13/the-oxford-english-wiktionary).
Malone, Thomas W., Robert J. Laubacher, and Chrysanthos Dellarocas. 2009. *Harnessing Crowds: Mapping the Genome of Collective Intelligence*. Cambridge: MIT Sloan School of Management.
Malone, Thomas W., Robert J. Laubacher, and Tammy Johns. 2011. "The Age of Hyperspecialization." *Harvard Business Review* 89(7-8): 56-65.
Markoff, John. 2013. "Scientists See Promise in Deep-Learning Process." *New York Times*, November 24, 2012. Retrieved October 6, 2014 (http://www.nytimes.com/2012/11/24/science/scientists-see-advances-in-deep-learning-a-part-of-artificial-intelligence.html?pagewanted=all&_r=0).
Narula, Prayag, Philipp Gutheim, David Rolnitzky, Arnand Kulkarni, and Bjoern Hartmann. 2011. "MobileWorks: A Mobile Crowdsourcing Platform for Workers at the Bottom of the Pyramid." In *Proceedings of the 3rd Human Computation Workshop*, San Francisco, California, August 8, 2011.
Negroponte, Nicholas. 1995. *Being Digital*. New York: Alfred A. Knopf.
O'Reilly, Tim. 2009. *What is Web 2.0*. Cologne: O'Reilly.
Ortner, Gerhard. 1998. *Forecasting Markets: An Industrial Application, Part II* (Working Paper). Vienna: Technische Universität Wien.

Picot, Arnold. 1990. "Division of Labour and Responsibilities." Pp. 745-752 in *Handbook of German Business Management*, edited by E. Grochla, E. Gaugler, and H. E. Büschgen. Berlin, Heidelberg: Springer.

Picot, Arnold and Marina Fiedler. 2008. "Open Source Software und proprietäre Software. Funktions- und Nachahmungsschutz oder Offenheit?" Pp. 165-185 in *Geistiges Eigentum: Schutzrecht oder Ausbeutungstitel?* edited by O. Depenheuer & K. N. Pfeifer. Berlin, Heidelberg: Springer.

Picot, Arnold and Stefan Hopf. 2013. "Grundformen des Crowdsourcing und ihre Bedeutung im Innovationsprozess." *IM+io—Fachzeitschrift für Innovation, Organisation und Management* 3: 24-32.

Picot, Arnold, Ralf Reichwald, and Rolf Wigand. 2008. *Information, Organization and Management*. Berlin, Heidelberg: Springer.

Piller, Frank and Ralf Reichwald. 2009. "Interaktive Wertschöpfung und Open Innovation." Pp. 187-201 in *Innovationsführerschaft durch Open Innovation*, edited by A. Picot and S. Döblin. Berlin, Heidelberg: Springer.

Plott, Charles R. and Kay-Yut Chen. 2002. *Information Aggregation Mechanisms: Concept, Design and Implementation for a Sales Forecasting Problem* (Social Science Working Paper 1131). Pasadena: California Institute of Technology.

Poetz, Marion K. and Martin Schreier. 2012. "The Value of Crowdsourcing: Can Users Really Compete with Professionals in Generating New Product Ideas?" *Journal of Product Innovation Management* 29(2): 245-256.

Schachtner, Konrad. 2001. Ideenmanagement im Produktinnovationsprozess. Zum wirtschaftlichen Einsatz der Informationstechnologie. Wiesbaden: Deutscher Universitätsverlag.

Spann, Martin and Bernd Skiera. 2009. "Sports Forecasting: A Comparison of the Forecast Accuracy of Prediction Markets, Betting Odds and Tipsters." *Journal of Forecasting* 28(1): 55-72.

Spencer, Robin W. 2012. "Open Innovation in the Eighteenth Century: The Longitude Problem." *Research-Technology Management* 55(4): 39-43.

Surowiecki, James. 2005. *The Wisdom of Crowds*. New York: Anchor Books.

The Economist 2012. "Don't bet on it." Retrieved October 6, 2014. (http://www.economist.com/news/finance-and-economics/21567382-intrade-retreats-american-regulators-dont-bet-it).

Villarroel, J. Andrei. 2013. "Strategic Crowdsourcing." Pp. 171-200 in *Leading Open Innovation*, edited by A. S. Huff, K. M. Möslein, and R. Reichwald. Cambridge: The MIT Press.

Wolfers, Justin and Eric Zitzewitz. 2004. "Prediction Markets." *Journal of Economic Perspectives* 18(2): 107-126.

The Berlin Innovation Panel

History, First Results, and Outlook

Knut Blind

1 Background

Innovations have been significant to economic development for centuries. In recent decades innovations have become the drivers of economic growth and hence also generators of employment. The importance of innovation has increased in economies with stagnating populations because process innovations have made it possible to improve productivity on the supply side, with product innovations stimulating the demand side. In addition, innovations also help solve environmental problems, and new markets are developing for environmental technologies. Newly industrialized and developing countries in particular benefit from environmental innovations.

The emergence of an innovation requires extensive interaction between various actors and institutions in technical and social processes. In addition to the companies that produce goods and services, innovation processes involve scientific organizations and universities, the users of the new technology or product, as well as political decision-makers. The regional context, with its overall regulatory conditions, labor supply, research institutions, specific economic structure and business networks, and demographic characteristics, thus influences the generation of innovations.

The institutions responsible for innovation policy have therefore begun to collect information about these regional conditions. Since the turn of this century, for instance, the European Commission has been gathering data on innovation as part of the *European Innovation Scoreboard* in order to track the progress of the member states toward achieving the objective of investing 3% of the EU's GDP in R&D. A similar reporting system, the Regional Innovation Scoreboards, was subsequently established for European regions, although the availability and completeness of documentation of many indicators relating to the research, development, and innovation activities in the regions still lag behind the corresponding domestic information that exists in the member countries.

The purpose of these initiatives at the European level is to observe the innovation that is taking place in the member countries and the regions alike to gain a clearer picture of their position in the national and regional competition as places of innovation and as business locations. This benchmarking can also yield information about needs to adapt innovation policies and to evaluate initiatives that have already been launched.

The first section of this chapter draws on a feasibility study to describe the history of the Berlin Innovation Panel, the world's first longitudinal study of innovation activities in a specific city. The second section presents some of the currently available results. The final section addresses the first measures of innovation policy that have been derived from the study.

2 Feasibility Study

The Department of Innovation Economics at the Technische Universität Berlin (TU Berlin) was commissioned by the Technologiestiftung Berlin (Berlin Technology Foundation) to conduct a study on the feasibility of developing a Berlin Innovation Panel. One of the first steps in that undertaking was to compare Berlin with other metropolitan regions by analyzing secondary statistics.[1] The second step entailed examining ways to monitor innovation and fields of competence thoroughly (see Blind, Wachsen, and Weber 2011).

2.1 Innovation Potential and Performance: Berlin Compared to Other Metropolitan Regions

A comprehensive set of indicators drawn from available secondary data was used to document the innovation potential and performance of Germany's metropolitan regions. The term *metropolitan region* (BBSR—Bundesamt für Bauwesen und Raumordnung 2009) refers to a large city that is closely knitted with its surround-

---

1 For detailed results, see Blind and Wachsen (2014).

ing areas (including rural ones) and distinguished by its size, prominent national role, and tight integration into the global urban system. It is noted for its economic strength, its efficient infrastructure, the presence of political and economic decision-makers, a large labor pool, and potentially strong demand.

To measure the innovation potential and performance of the metropolitan regions under study, indicators that differentiate the input from the output side of the innovation system were used. This distinction made it possible to assess both the effort required to generate innovation and the success of that investment. The indicators referred to research and development (R&D); employment in highly innovative sectors, which was derived from data on the number of highly qualified employees and the university graduates in specific disciplines; the number of new businesses created in selected innovative sectors; and the number of patent applications.

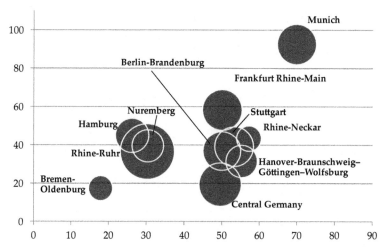

Figure 1 Innovation potential and performance of the metropolitan regions in Germany normalized into intervals between 0 and 100. The volume corresponds to the size of each region in terms of the number of persons with a job that entails mandatory social security coverage. Source: Blind and Wachsen (2014: 138).

The results of all the regions that were compared were quite diverse (see Figure 1). Overall, Munich scored highest on both the input and output indicators, coming out on top for 10 of the 26 indicators and scoring lowest on none. Other metropolitan regions had strengths only in specific areas. Stuttgart, with its strong economic sector, posted the highest level of research spending and largest number of researchers. The Saxony Triangle, the area that spans the border between Saxony and Saxony-Anhalt, was well positioned in publicly funded research and showed the highest level of R&D spending in research institutions and universities. Rhine-Main and Rhine-Neckar had a particularly well-qualified, knowledge-intensive service sector and a large number of university graduates. The strengths of Berlin-Brandenburg lay in the R&D personnel in public research institutions and in its position as Europe's leader in technology patents in the sciences. The weakest region in terms of concentration and indicator levels was Bremen-Oldenburg.

2.2 Results of the Feasibility Study

The feasibility study explored the possibilities of assessing Berlin's fields of competence. The first step was to identify ways to analyze secondary statistical data with a compilation of indicators of Berlin's innovation policy. The second step was to identify and assess the possibilities of gathering primary data on innovation performance in the fields of competence and in Berlin as a whole. The objective was to create a comprehensive analytical framework for continual monitoring that would track progress and regression in Berlin's innovation strategy.

The comparative analysis of the metropolitan regions revealed a broad spectrum of information gleaned from available data on innovation potential and innovation performance. The use of existing innovation surveys and official statistics offered several advantages. It permitted the comparison of results across regions and over time because the data were collected in Germany with the same instruments and with reproducible sampling at regular intervals. Furthermore, international harmonization made it possible to relate the benchmarks and their development to the European context. The required information was based on secondary sources, so it was possible with manageable effort to generate policy-relevant information about the innovation activities of the capital-city region of Berlin-Brandenburg with respect to Berlin. Strengths and weaknesses could then become immediately apparent through interregional comparison.

The advantages of this approach must be weighed against two drawbacks. First, it is not currently possible for innovation indicators to capture all the structures and processes that matter for innovation. For example, there are few appropriate indicators available to describe the diffusion of innovations. Second, two problems of demarcation arise from the use of existing datasets. Not all information can be acquired at the required level of regional specificity from the available statistics, and the regional attribution of some benchmarks is problematic. In addition to the difficulty of regional demarcation, there is the problem of specifying the industrial sectors involved. The scope of the sample usually used for nationwide data collection in Germany generates only a tiny number of company cases at the regional level. Therefore, such surveys permit only a very rough breakdown by economic sector, and particularly innovative sectors often tend not to fit into the usual classification of economic sectors.

The feasibility study highlighted significant gaps in Berlin's innovation monitoring despite the large body of relevant work on the subject. Efforts were made to find ways of closing these gaps both for the fields of competence and for the overall innovation system. The feasibility study gave rise to recommendations with different time horizons for these two areas of focus.

2.2.1 Monitoring Fields of Competence

- The monitoring of fields of competence in a consistent, practicable manner that permits comprehensive longitudinal comparisons between regions and segments of economic sectors is possible only by differentiating between economic sectors. To assure comparability, one should include only those classes of economic sectors that fall completely within a given field of competence and reflect the key areas of the fields, most of which are dominated by engineering.
- To ensure that the fields of competence are depicted in the most appropriate way, the demarcations of the economic sectors are to be continuously checked and, if necessary, adapted with the assistance of internal and external experts.
- The monitoring of fields of competence fits into comparably designed cluster monitoring, which reveals the significance that the dynamic core of those fields has for the overall cluster. Methodologically, this approach simultaneously addresses the difficulty posed by inability to depict the size of the fields of competence. The size of the *clusters* makes their demarcation much easier.
- Employment growth and business fluctuation can serve as central indicators for the monitoring. These data can be obtained from the business register and the statistics of Germany's Federal Employment Agency (Bundesagentur für Arbeit). They are to be assessed for dynamics and comparisons.
- Additional information such as turnover and gross value added, which require detailed calculations, is to be generated once a year for the fields of competence and the depiction of the fields of competence that these data permit.
- Some segments of the economic sectors cannot be depicted even approximately with this method, so their inclusion is to be based on nationwide industry reports and focused surveys.

2.2.2 Developing a Berlin Innovation Panel: Short-Term Recommendations

- Developing a panel survey of the Berlin economy calls for a long-term perspective. To reap the greatest benefit with manageable effort in the short term, expand on the Mannheim innovation panel to make it applicable in Berlin.
- Have the scientific panel initiated by a well-established Berlin research institution that has its own academic interest in the results of the survey.
- To ensure synergies for the assessment of the innovation activities, relate the results of the company panel to the scientific survey and to the monitoring of the field of competency.

2.2.3 Developing a Berlin Innovation Panel: Long-Term Recommendations

- Have an external institution conduct the survey in a manner in keeping with the requirements of the Berlin innovation monitoring. This approach will assure the flexibility necessary for adapting to specific information needs.
- Perform simultaneous surveys among industry and public research institutions to facilitate detailed analysis of issues surrounding the transfer of knowledge and technology.
- Orient the design of the survey instrument also to the specific needs of the various bodies that shape Berlin's economic, science, technology, and innovation policies.

3 History and Method of the Berlin Innovation Panel[2]

In keeping with the short-term recommendations for creating a Berlin Innovation Panel, the Innovation Survey 2012 for Berlin was conducted by the Center for European Economic Research (ZEW—Zentrum für Europäische Wirtschaftsforschung) for and in cooperation with the Chair of Innovation Economics at the TU Berlin. Technologiestiftung Berlin was not involved.

The methods used in the survey were the same as those in the German Innovation Survey that has been conducted annually by the ZEW for the Federal Ministry for Research and Education (BMBF—Bundesministerium für Bildung und Forschung) for more than 20 years. The Innovation Survey 2012 for Berlin en-

---

2 See Rammer and Horn (2013: 10f.).

compassed all Berlin-registered companies that have five or more employees and operate in industry or knowledge-intensive services. The survey was conducted from the end of February to mid-August 2012. The gross sample for Berlin included nearly 5,000 companies, of which about 1,000 came from the main portion of the German Innovation Survey and more than 4,000 from the expanded sample for the 2012 Berlin Innovation Survey. Just under 1,000 companies of the gross sample (18%) were considered neutral dropouts because at the time they were either no longer economically active, did not belong to the target population, or could not be reached despite numerous attempts to contact them by mail and phone. Proper responses were received from over 800 companies, which amounts to a response rate of 20% of the corrected sample after removal of the neutral dropouts. Of the companies that did not participate, almost 1,000 were contacted by phone about a few of the indicators of innovation activity so as to control for the possible distortion of the data from the participating companies. Information from over 1,700 companies, 42% of the sample, flowed into the analysis. The survey of the nonparticipating companies was completed in September 2012.

The results of the survey were extrapolated for the total number of companies in Berlin with five or more employees in the target sectors covered by the survey. This projection was conducted separately for fifteen groups of sectors and six sizes of companies (based on numbers of employees). Data on the number of companies, the number of employees, and the level of turnover in the total population were obtained from a special analysis of the company register conducted by the Statistical Office for Berlin-Brandenburg (Amt für Statistik Berlin-Brandenburg). The data in the company register referred to 2010, so it had to be extended to 2011. In addition, various adaptations were made to adjust the methodological parameters of the German Innovation Survey for the purpose of this survey:

- The public research institutions were removed from the R&D sector.
- The turnover figures for the financial services were adjusted to the gross earnings from interest and commissions.
- Individual large companies in Berlin that were not legally independent entities were included.
- Activities were removed if conducted outside Berlin by large companies with headquarters in Berlin but only a small part of their activities in Germany there.
- The number of self-employed persons was added to the employment figures.

The total population of the Innovation Survey for Berlin encompassed about 5,250 companies, accounting for about 263,000 employees and a turnover of €94 billion.

4 Results of the First Survey, 2012[3]

Berlin's economy proved to be much more innovation oriented than other economies in Germany, a finding that contradicts past economic weakness and reflects the improving trend that has been taking place for years. The percentage of surveyed companies that had introduced new products or processes (the innovator contingent) was 60% in 2011, 10 percentage points above the corresponding rate for Germany as a whole. However, this finding did not apply equally to all companies in the survey. The large companies scored lower on most of the innovation benchmarks. Small and medium-sized companies were particularly active innovators in both industry and services. The highest rates of innovation in Berlin were found in the electrical industry (84%), software and data processing (82%), and R&D services (91%). Compared with Germany as a whole, the following sectors showed a clearly higher level of innovation in Berlin: energy, water, and waste management; engineering and architecture; consumer-goods manufacturing; wood, paper, and printing; financial services; the electrical industry, measurement technology, and optics; food, beverages, and tobacco; and consulting. Economic sectors in which Berlin had significantly lower levels of innovation than in Germany as a whole were only found in the metal and stoneware industry and, surprisingly, the creative services. The overall higher level of innovation in Berlin companies applied to both product and process innovations.

In absolute figures the Berlin economy spent about €2.79 billion for product and process innovations in 2011, or about 3% of the turnover and hence 10% less than the corresponding figure (3.3%) for the German economy in total. This lower intensity of innovation in 2011 was due primarily to the lower level of investment in innovation projects, which accounted for €0.63 billion or 0.7% of the turnover. The rate was 0.9% for the German economy as a whole. The rate for R&D expenditures was very similar. Berlin companies spent €1.67 billion on R&D in 2011, or 1.8% of the turnover. The proportion of R&D expenditure was therefore as high as for Germany overall. Berlin small and medium-sized companies were found to have an above-average level of R&D, whereas large companies in Berlin reinvested a smaller percentage of their turnover in innovation projects than large companies did in Germany as a whole. This finding held for industry and the service sector alike.

The market results that Berlin-based companies achieved with their product innovations were lower than those for the Germany economy. In 2011, new products accounted for 14% of Berlin's economy's turnover compared with 17.4% in the

---

3   See Rammer and Horn (2013: 8ff.).

German economy as a whole. The lower level of returns on product innovation was attributable almost entirely to the major industrial companies and was largely due to structural conditions. The figure for Germany as a whole was strongly affected by the automobile industry and the high share of its turnover accounted for by new products, but that sector's role in Berlin is negligible. The greatest proportion of Berlin's turnover attributable to new products was found in the machine-tool and automotive manufacturing sector (40%), followed by the electrical industry (37%) and consulting (25%). Compared with the corresponding data on Germany as a whole, consulting, architecture, and engineering offices had a very high proportion of new products, whereas the sectors of software and data processing; food, beverages, and tobacco; and metal, glass, and stoneware were significantly lower than the comparable data on Germany. Lower turnover results for innovation also appeared for two kinds of products: novelties on the market (2.2% in Berlin versus 3.8% in Germany) and novelties in product mix (2.8% in Berlin versus 3.2% in Germany). The differences were smaller for process innovations than for product innovations. In 2011, process innovation led to a cost reduction of 3.7% in Berlin (4.0% in Germany) and contributed to a 2.6% increase in turnover thanks to quality improvements in Berlin (2.9% in Germany).

The consistent pursuit of independent R&D activities played a greater role in Berlin companies than in Germany as a whole. In 2011, 29% of the companies continuously conducted research, nine percentage points more than the German average. This result is primarily attributable to the higher level of R&D research by small and medium-sized industrial companies in Berlin. The share of companies engaged in research is also higher in Berlin (14%) than for all of Germany (12%).

From 2009 through 2011, 15% of the companies in Berlin commissioned third parties for research; the corresponding figure for companies in the rest of Germany was 13%. The greater openness to innovation processes in Berlin becomes even more apparent from the figures for participation in partnerships with other companies and institutions that pursue innovation. In Berlin 37% of companies participated in such partnerships compared to 30% of the companies in Germany overall. The higher level in Berlin is attributable primarily to companies in the service sector and to the greater extent of utilizing customers and Berlin's many scientific institutions as partners. For example, 19% of Berlin companies worked with scientific partners on innovations between 2009 and 2011, compared to 11% of companies in Germany as a whole.

A comparison of Berlin's results with those of five other metropolitan regions in Germany (Hamburg, Munich, Cologne-Düsseldorf, Frankfurt, and Stuttgart) shows that the higher level of willingness to innovate in Berlin is a phenomenon characteristic of a major city. In the other big cities, too, the share of innovative companies (63%) was much higher than in Germany overall and actually even surpassed the level in Berlin (60%). The companies in the comparable cities also had a significantly higher intensity of innovation (expenditures for innovation accounting for 5.7% of turnover) and notably higher values for all the indicators of success (including an 18.6% share of turnover from new products). Further analyses reveal, however, that the higher innovation performance in the other metropolitan centers stemmed primarily from structural conditions, as the sectorial constellation and the corporate structures there were much more oriented toward innovation than was the case in Berlin. When one controls for structural differences, the Berlin companies were shown to have significantly exceeded companies in the other metropolitan regions in terms of willingness to introduce product innovations and thus have proved to be much more successful innovators than their peers in the other locations. When controlled for structural conditions, the inclination of Berlin companies to undertake process innovations was also higher and was especially oriented toward cost reduction.

5 Comparison of Results over Four Years

To build on the results of the first survey, further surveys were conducted in 2013, 2014, and 2015, thereby making it possible to compare findings over four years and perhaps identify initial structural changes.

Whereas the share of companies that introduced product or process innovation over the past three years dipped slightly below the level in 2012 across Germany, Berlin's rate (50%) remained higher than the national average (45%) and equal to that in other major German cities (see Figure 2).

A closer look at the four-year trend that the survey shows reveals very different patterns. The percentage of innovators in small and medium-sized companies in Berlin remained constant or declined, but between the first and fourth year of the survey it grew in companies with more than 250 employees (see Figure 3). The reasons for these changes lay in the dynamic growth of small, innovative companies, which increased the intensity of innovation in the categories with more than 250 employees. In addition, well-established large companies in Berlin, such as Daimler AG, increased their innovation activities. For Germany (see Figure 4), a weakness in innovation surfaced in all companies except those with more than 1,000 employees. Berlin companies in the software and data-processing sector and in R&D continued to be particularly strong innovators (see Figure 5).

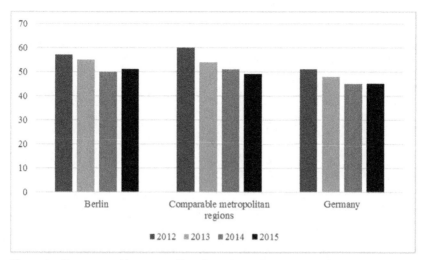

Figure 2 Percentage of innovators. Data from the Berlin Innovation Surveys 2012–2015, Center for European Economic Research (ZEW). Source: my graph.

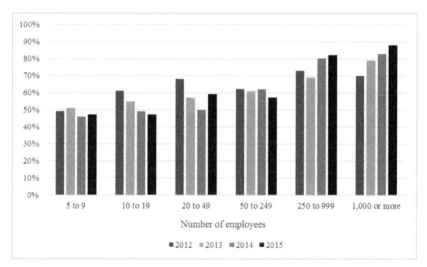

Figure 3 Innovators in Berlin by company size. Data from the Berlin Innovation Surveys 2012–2015, Center for European Economic Research (ZEW). Source: my graph.

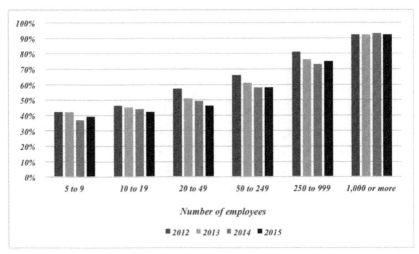

Figure 4 Innovators in Germany by company size. Data from the Berlin Innovation Surveys 2012–2015, Center for European Economic Research (ZEW). Source: my graph.

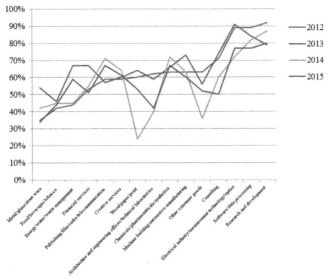

Figure 5 Innovators in Berlin by economic sector. Data from the Berlin Innovation Surveys 2012–2015, Center for European Economic Research (ZEW). Source: my graph.

6 Selected Results from the 2014 Survey and Challenges for Innovation Policy

The 2014 survey focused on the financing of innovations.[4] The responses showed that about 21% of Berlin companies did not pursue innovation activities between 2011 and 2013 for lack of financial means to do so. Financing was less of a problem for German companies as a whole than for those in Berlin.

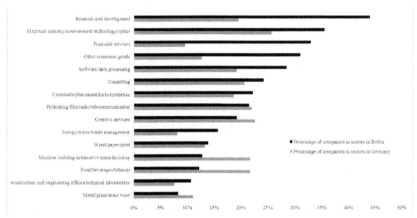

Figure 6 Percentage of companies in sectors in Berlin (black bars) and Germany (gray bars) that did not engage in innovation activities for lack of financial resources in 2013 separated by industry. Based on the Berlin Innovation Survey 2014 (Koglin 2015: 27), Center for European Economic Research (ZEW).

Only 17% of companies in Germany reported lack of funding as a barrier to innovation in this period.[5] This problem particularly hampered innovation at companies in two innovative and important areas of the service industry in Berlin, with 44% of R&D companies and 28% of software companies reporting that the lack of funding had definitely impeded their innovation activities. Financial bottlenecks clearly limited companies in the electrical industry, measurement technology, and optics in their efforts to take their innovation activities forward. Berlin companies

---

4   See the full report by the Technologiestiftung Berlin (Koglin 2015).
5   The most recent survey inquired about innovation barriers in general and revealed that companies in Berlin reported fewer problems in all categories except for lack of external resources; see the full report by Technologiestiftung Berlin (Kahl 2016). These results confirm the validity of the survey.

encountered far more difficulty in financing innovation than their counterparts in the German sample. However, the data is inconclusive as to whether the difference was mostly attributable to a better financial situation in other parts of Germany or to lower innovation ambitions. It was stated by 35% of the companies in Berlin but only by 28% of those in Germany as a whole that they would have striven for additional innovation had more funding been available. Companies in R&D (60%), software and data processing (51%), and the electrical industry (46%) in particular would have been interested in pursuing additional innovation activities. These results suggest that companies already engaged in innovation would expand their planned activities if sufficient funding were available and that companies not yet actively innovating would begin doing so. At the same time, easier access to external funding was less attractive to companies than having their own funding to invest.

7 The Berlin Innovation Panel in the Context of the Policy Cycle of Innovation Financing

The experience with the Berlin Innovation Panel can be interpreted in light of the first phases of Lasswell's (1951) model of policy cycles. The innovation surveys helped identify the problem that Berlin companies suffer from heavier financing restrictions than do companies in the rest of Germany. Unlike the classic policy cycle, this problem was not addressed by policy-makers or by interest groups; it emerged as a byproduct of a study prompted by scientific motives. After the problem had been identified and empirically verified, it was placed onto the political agenda by the Berlin Senate Department for Economics, Technology, and Research (Senatsverwaltung für Wirtschaft, Technologie und Forschung) in response to the Senate of Berlin's administrative decision to address the financial restrictions by creating a €35 million statewide program to finance innovation. The plan, however, was announced in March 2015 as a general investment program before the results of the innovation survey were actually published.

The next phase in the policy cycle, namely, the formulation and implementation of policy, was to occur after the release of the report in March 2015. In February 2016, on the basis of the proposal by the Senate Department for Economics, Technology, and Research, the Senate of Berlin decided to start the program 'Berlin Innovativ' with a budget of €10 million for two years. It aims to provide companies with up to 500 employees cheap loans for investments, particularly those related to innovation. In the future, the implementation of this program to promote innovation financing should be evaluated to determine whether the measure was acted on effectively and efficiently, the answer to which will lie at least partly in the results provided by future waves of innovation surveys. The policy cycle will end with the termination of the program after the problems of financing innovations in Berlin's economy have been resolved. With such a development being rather unlikely, however, an evaluation will probably identify the need for adjustments and thus place the topic back onto the political agenda. This step will then lead to a continuation or adjustment—that is, a redefinition—of the original program and an amendment of the existing rules or the creation of new ones.

8   Outlook

With a feasibility study and an academically driven innovation study as a point of departure, the Berlin Innovation Panel has fully established itself. It entered its fifth year in 2016. The results of the survey's most recent wave served to initiate a government program to promote funding for innovation, thus justifying the performance of a long-term study and providing evidence of the survey's usefulness for addressing specific questions of innovation policy. The fixed costs for undertaking a long-term observation have already been covered, and the practical utility of an innovation study focused on a city has been proven. The cost-benefit calculation for continuing the survey in the years that lie ahead is thus very convincing. Moreover, the innovation survey's potential is far from exhausted, as the additional data it has already collected can be combined with external data sources such as patent applications.

The Berlin Innovation Panel has a great deal to offer beyond generating considerations specifically about Berlin. It can be used as a feasibility study for other metropolitan regions as well, and its results can serve as a reference point for comparisons between metropolitan regions or cities. Discussions are underway to this effect. If other cities were to decide to conduct their own analogous innovation surveys, it would enhance the value of the Berlin Innovation Panel even more for its home city because it would be possible to improve currently available comparisons between cities.

If several city-specific innovation surveys were conducted in parallel, comparative analysis could identify the potential implications for the various phases of the policy cycle. Lastly, continuation and replication of the Berlin Innovation Panel in other German cities and even in cities in other European countries would respond to Shapira, Smits, and Kuhlmann's (2010) call for innovation researchers to position themselves actively as contributors to successful improvements in innovation policy.

References

BBSR—Bundesamt für Bauwesen und Raumordnung, ed. 2009. *Positionierung europäischer Metropolregionen in Deutschland*. Bonn: BBSR. Retrieved January 23, 2017 (http://www.bbsr.bund.de/BBSR/DE/Veroeffentlichungen/BerichteKompakt/2009/DL_3_2009.pdf;jsessionid=02E495DCA019E5EA9A70E872373CC3F7.live11292?__blob=publicationFile&v=2).

Blind, Knut, Eva Wachsen, and Mike Weber. 2011. *Innovative Metropolregion: Entwicklung eines Berliner Innovationspanels*. Berlin: Universitätsverlag der TU Berlin.

Blind, Knut and Eva Wachsen. 2014. "Innovation—Metropolregionen im Vergleich." Pp. 212-140 in *Pionier-Regionen der Zukunft: Innovation, Qualität und Kooperation*, edited by H. Pechlaner and C. Reuter. Wiesbaden: Springer Gabler.

Kahl, Julian. 2016. *Innovationserhebung Berlin (2015): Innovationsverhalten der Berliner Wirtschaft*. Berlin: Technologiestiftung Berlin. Retrieved January 23, 2017 (https://www.technologiestiftung-berlin.de/fileadmin/daten/media/publikationen/160602_InnovationserhebungBerlin2015.pdf).

Koglin, Gesa. 2015. *Innovationserhebung Berlin 2014: Innovationsverhalten der Berliner Wirtschaft*. Berlin: Technologiestiftung Berlin. Retrieved January 23, 2017 (http://www.businesslocationcenter.de/imperia/md/blc/service/download/content/innovationserhebung-berlin.pdf).

Lasswell, Harold. 1951. "The Policy Orientation." Pp. 3-15 in *The Policy Sciences*, edited by D. Lerner and H. Lasswell. Stanford: Stanford University Press.

Rammer, Christian and Nellie Horn. 2013. *Innovationsbericht Berlin 2013: Innovationsverhalten der Unternehmen im Land Berlin im Vergleich zu anderen Metropolstädten in Deutschland*. Mannheim: ZEW—Zentrum für Europäische Wirtschaftsforschung. Retrieved January 23, 2017 (http://ftp.zew.de/pub/zew-docs/docus/dokumentation1302.pdf).

Shapira, Philip, Ruud E. Smits, and Stefan Kuhlmann. 2010. "An Outlook on Innovation Policy, Theory and Practice." Pp. 449-466 in *The Theory and Practice of Innovation Policy*, edited by R. E. Smits, S. Kuhlmann, and P. Shapira. Cheltenham: Edward Elgar.

Part III
Between Politics, Planning, and Social Movements

'Flash Mobs' as Innovation

On a New Social Form of Technically Mediated Congregation

Paul Gebelein, Martina Löw and Thomas Paul[1]

> "The issues that divide or unite people in society are settled not only in the institutions and practices of politics proper, but also, and less obviously, in tangible arrangements of steel and concrete, wires and semiconductors, nuts and bolts." (Winner 1980: 29)

1 Introduction

People congregate. This is a phenomenon as old as humanity itself. How gatherings come about, get organized, and actually happen depends on their specific time and place in history. Just like society or—with fewer preconditions—social co-existence in general, they are subject to ongoing transformations. How people come together, interact, and possibly congregate as a group, in public, semi-public, or private spaces, is governed by things such as social norms, legal regulations, and political issues as well as by the given constellation of people in a certain territory, that is, the arrangement of residential and commercial space or specific mobility habits. Congregating involves three phases: preparation, the actual gathering, and feedback. The first phase involves preparation work, especially mobilizing participants. Then, people congregate in a real gathering at a given location. The feed-

---

1   Writing this paper was made possible by the financial support from the German Research Foundation (DFG) as part of the Collaborative Research Centre CRC 1053 *MAKI – Multi-Mechanisms Adaptation for the Future Internet*. The present essay documents results from the subproject C04 *User-centered perspective*. The authors wish to thank Peter Noller, who directed the ethnographic field research for the Leipzig flash mob and made valuable contributions to the research design. They would also like to thank Katherin Wagenknecht and Matthias Schulz for their dedicated work and Matthias Krügl for producing the graphics. Wolfgang Effelsberg and Thorsten Strufe were also important collaborators at various points throughout the project; they provided keen insights related to content and process.

back phase has to do with resonance; it determines how the gathering is received and interpreted.

It has been a little over a decade since we first witnessed a social form that claims to be an innovation (Rammert 2010) in its own right: the flash mob. This phenomenon involves the intentional and systematic creation of a new form of congregation. In this essay we explore how the practice of 'doing innovation' (Hutter et al., this volume) takes place in flash mobs. Our analytical focus lies on the first and second phases: mobilization and on-site performance. As we will show, as a cultural innovation, flash mobs are contingent upon simultaneous innovations in the use of space and technology. More pointedly, the success of the flash mob as a social form is literally *built* on the systematic coupling of new spatial arrangements and innovative communication technologies.

2 The Emergence of Flash Mobs

Flash mobs, as they have come to be known, are a new form of congregation that dates back to 2003. The year is no coincidence: Text messaging technology and mailing lists had become popular among creatives in New York; a new object had cropped up in the search for the 'next big thing' (cf. Heaney 2005). As described by scene members (for instance, on Wikipedia or in *A Flashmob Manifesto2*) ever since the first 'flash mob' initiated by Bill Wasik on June 3, 2003, in New York, the element of surprise has been a strong part of this new meetup genre (see Hutter 2011 on the relevance of surprise in innovation). Informed insiders gather at a designated place where they encounter unsuspecting bystanders. Acting in concert, these insiders radically transform the situation, lending it new meaning based on mutual knowledge. The result is a situational tension occurring along the boundary that separates the on-site public and participants, the knowing and unknowing, inductees and outsiders. The invisible line in this case is constituted by access to knowledge. What ensues can be interpreted as entertainment, an attraction, irritation, or perhaps even a threat.

In retrospect, Bill Wasik described the idea in an interview with Francis Heaney as follows: "The original idea was to create an email that would get forwarded around in some funny way, or that would get people to come to a show that would turn out to be something different or surprising . . . [T]he idea was that the people

---

2 http://web.archive.org/web/20081228204422/http://aglomerarispontane.weblog.ro/2004-12-05/20168/Manifestul-Aglomerarilor-Spontane---A-Flashmob-Manifesto.html; retrieved January 6, 2017.

themselves would become the show, and that just by responding to this random email, they would, in a sense, create something." (Heaney 2005) According to Wasik, the first flash mob took place in front of Claire's Accessories, a small chain store near Astor Place in Manhattan. Or it almost did. Wasik reports that police appeared on the scene shortly before the scheduled time and prevented people from convening in front of the store. "[T]hey're not letting anybody stand in front of the store. They made it look as if a terrorist had threatened to wage jihad against Claire's Accessories." (ibid.)

The first flash mob failed because authorities caught wind of the organizers' plans. The source of this leak never emerged. For his second attempt, Wasik modified the preliminaries so that potential participants would only receive the location details shortly before the event. "So for Mob #2, I hit on the notion of meeting in pre-mob locations, and then people would come through at the last minute and hand out flyers with the mob location. That worked fine for the second mob, which was at Macy's." (ibid.)

Ever since their inception, flash mobs have pursued alternate forms of constituting space, some of which conflicted with established practices. In June 2003, less than two years after September 11, 2001, in a charged atmosphere fueled by fears of further terrorist attacks, this divisive potential led to the deployment of law enforcement officials. The second flash mob avoided this outcome by tweaking the preparation phase. However, the organizers (those who handed out flyers) were clearly identifiable.

> "I didn't want it to seem like there was a leader. The project grew when people took it on as their own and forwarded the emails; that was what made the idea work. So it was sad having to resort to the pre-mob location, because then there had to be people who were clearly in on the planning, walking around with the flyers." (ibid.)

This situation changed with the use of text messaging and OSNs (online social networks). The technologies allowed the organizers to take a back seat since the new technical channels enabled the distribution of relevant information. Passing out flyers in person and on site became a thing of the past.

This new technique for initiating gatherings started to gain traction and circulate rather quickly. 'Flash mobs' sprang up in all parts of the world with sufficient technological savvy and resources. Different variants began to develop. Whereas the first flash mobs were organized as spontaneous happenings with no purpose other than to interrupt routines and entertain participants, more and more of these events began to align themselves with certain goals, frequently political. As a new format for political activity, flash mobs are also often ascribed political objectives. Such was the case with 'smart mobs' and their underlying concept (Rheingold 2003). As a result, recreational and family-friendly examples of this form of congregation coexist with contemporary forms of protest such as the Egyptian 'Twitter revolution' (cf. Gerbaudo 2012) or even violent acts in the USA that have received public attention in recent years.[3]

In the present context, we concentrate our analysis on a recreational flash mob that took place in Leipzig in 2012, 2013, and 2014. Our empirical material is comprised of participant observation data from 2013 and 2014, talks with participants on site, and photographs and videos of the events. Event pages used to organize or mobilize participants for the mob were also analyzed.[4] We employed a method that uses an integrated Firefox browser add-on consisting of a 'crawler' (Cho and Garcia-Molina 2000; Heydon and Najork 1999; Boldi et al. 2004) and a 'parser' (Charniak 2000). The crawler reads the entire event page; in the process it mimics human interaction with web browsers. This intervention is necessary because Facebook suppresses automated access systems.[5] Data is then transferred to the parser. The parser analyzes the event page structure and stores all posts, comments, 'likes,' shared content, and RSVPs ('Interested' or 'Going' responses) in a database. The author and time of posting can be determined for every piece of information. The challenge, then, is to weed out irrelevant data (design elements, standard information such as legal notices, or advertising). Once we had our data in a structured format we were able to apply descriptive and probabilistic methods

---

3   On March 24, 2010, *New York Times* investigative correspondent Ian Urbina wrote: "But these so-called flash mobs have taken a more aggressive and raucous turn here as hundreds of teenagers have been converging downtown for a ritual that is part bullying, part running of the bulls: sprinting down the block, the teenagers sometimes pause to brawl with one another, assault pedestrians or vandalize property." (Urbina, Ian. 2010. "Mobs Are Born as Word Grows by Text Message." *New York Times*. Retrieved January 6, 2017: http://www.nytimes.com/2010/03/25/us/25mobs.html). On August 2012, Scott Paulson took a similar direction in an article for CBSPhilly: "By the summer of 2011, flash mobs were making big city and national headlines for their criminal aspects—and the same has continued in the summer of 2012. Via social networking, crowds of youth coordinate to show up to a location and very often do something extremely harmful and illegal. No longer is participating in a flash mob simply a teenage or young adult pastime for the bored, but a mission with criminal intent." (Paulson, Scott. 2012. "Opinion: Media Covers Up Violence of Flash Mobs." *CBSPhilly*. Retrieved January 6, 2017: http://philadelphia.cbslocal.com/2012/08/02/media-covers-up-violence-of-flash-mobs/). For an investigation of young people's perspectives on flash mobs in Kansas City, see Houston et al. (2013).
4   We only collected and analyzed Facebook data that is publicly accessible to users.
5   This is due to the data-based business model applied by Facebook, which restricts data access to competitors such as Google+, LinkedIn, ello, etc.

and visualize the results. In our research project, we combined sociological and computer-science-based expertise at this juncture so that we could also benefit from computer-science methods for our sociological inquiry.

3   Mobilization and Online Activity

Shortly before 3 p.m. on June 15, 2013, visitors to Leipzig's Augustusplatz, located on the city's east end, were privy to the following scene: The square became a scene of bustling activity, filling up with an unusual number of people. This number accelerated and finally peaked, but no one seemed to leave. It appeared as though the square itself was their goal. A glance at the throng revealed no signs of an impending event. Just before the clock struck the hour, plastic bottles in hand, a few people started to blow soap bubbles that floated above the crowd. Taken in context, it is an unusual activity to find happening at more than one or two places in a public space. At three o'clock sharp, the bells in the Kroch Tower tolled and a sea of iridescent bubbles erupted over the crowd. On this June afternoon, Augustusplatz played host to its first *Seifenblasenflashmob* (Soap Bubble Flash Mob).

For people to congregate at a location, some prior organization is required, in other words, successful mobilization. Individuals or groups are usually in charge of this process. The task is to inform potential participants about the event and why they should participate. Traditionally, this preparation work happens as information is passed along in (overlapping) friendship circles, communities or scenes, or by organizations. Publically available media such as newspapers, radio, and television also play a decisive role. The mobilization process for the flash mob in our study was primarily based on use of the online platform Facebook. Facebook utilizes communication among friends and acquaintances and takes it one step further to enable 1:n communication (one to many) and limited[6] n:n communication (many to many).[7]

---

6   This communication is limited because Facebook's business model has a strong impact on how information is shared. 'Personalized advertising' is usually the keyword in this context; however, because the practice could actually be described as personalized information channeling, far more wide-ranging types of persuasion and influence should be discussed in this context (see Ochs and Löw 2012). Kramer, Guillory, and Hancock (2014) have illustrated how this type of influence occurs.
7   Current research has examined how information actually spreads in OSNs such as Facebook or Twitter. See, e.g., Bakshy et al. (2012) and Romero, Meeder, and Kleinberg (2011).

Generally speaking, to initiate a gathering, providing a time and a place on a public Facebook event page is all that is required. This information can circulate through friend networks and, once it reaches enough potential visitors who are willing to meet at the designated time and place, the task of mobilization is complete. What determines the successful circulation of this kind of information? To answer this key question, it can be assumed that information is spread on the basis of social acceptance, the interests of those involved, and the structural properties of the social network. The extent of this circulation and ultimately whether or not a flash mob will actually occur is difficult to predict on the basis of these data alone.[8]

As a communication medium, the Internet provides many examples of activities and events that were a resounding—although unexpected—success, along with flops that no one thought would fail. When something does generate attention, the crucial moment occurs with the transition from online to offline activity. This critical point always harbors the possibility of failure. A case in point is protests on Facebook against the resignation of Karl-Theodor zu Guttenberg as Germany's defense minister in March 2011.[9] Despite thousands of online supporters, this articulation of support never translated into any sizable physical gathering in an urban context.

The Soap Bubble Flash Mobs in 2013 and 2014 in Leipzig were organized using Facebook event pages on which initiators announced the location, time, and desired behavior (to make soap bubbles at the first toll of the Kroch Tower bells). Figure 1 shows a screenshot of the Facebook event page.

---

8   Here current research looks at the ex post recognition of major events. Chierichetti et al. (2014) examined how the 2010 Soccer World Cup in South Africa, the 2011 Academy Awards, and the 2011 Super Bowl were reflected in Twitter streams.

9   See the Facebook group: *Wir wollen Guttenberg zurück* (Bring back Guttenburg) (https://de-de.facebook.com/zuGuttenBACK; retrieved November 10, 2014).

'Flash Mobs' as Innovation 231

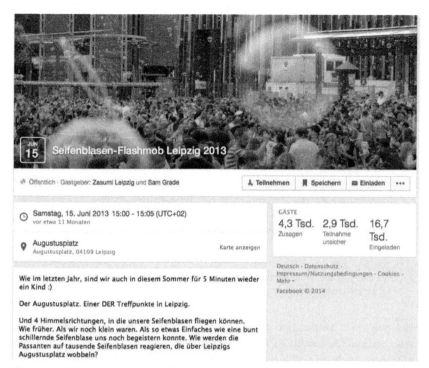

Figure 1 Screenshot of the 2013 Soap Bubble Flash Mob Facebook site (source: https://www.facebook.com).

The announcement reads:

"Just like last year, come join us in being a kid again for 5 minutes. :)

The place: Augustusplatz. One of THE places to meet up in Leipzig.

Soap bubbles floating in all directions.

Like old times, when we were little. When we could still find happiness in simple things like rainbow-colored bubbles. How will people react to thousands of soap bubbles floating above Leipzig's Augustusplatz?"

The event page announcement then continues with the following text:

"Equipment:
Anything goes as long as it makes soap bubbles: bubble guns, Pustefix bottles, bubble machines, etc.
Date: Saturday, June 15, 2013

Schedule:
Before 3:00 p.m.: Gather on and around Augustusplatz, in front of the opera house or in the surrounding streets.

3:00 p.m. sharp: Everyone blows bubbles
3:05 p.m. sharp: Everyone disperses

We'll start when we hear the Kroch Tower bells.
Important: The flash mob will only happen in fair weather—no rain or strong winds.

Come join us!
Let's enjoy the moment when confusion turns into smiles and laughter.
And please spread the word.... we want to break the 6,000 mark from 2012!!! :)"

Not only does the description specify the time and place but also the preferred schedule and the conditions for the event (weather). To justify this form of congregation that breaks with everyday routine, the initiators also supply a narrative framework: "being a kid again for 5 minutes." Anticipated consequences of watching "confusion turn into smiles and laughter" are included as well.

This type of event page makes it possible for Facebook account holders to send invitations to an event and, in doing so, draw attention to it. Invitees can go on to invite others from their own list of friends. The result is a recruiting process that snowballs through different friend networks, all the while gathering momentum. The event page is public; all users can add posts and comments. Figure 2 shows a 'wall' segment from the 2013 Soap Bubble Flash Mob page. The owner of the page can send messages to all event participants. In addition, a counter shows how many people have been invited as well as how many have indicated definite plans to attend or at least their interest in the event. Confirmations are posted in the newsfeeds of users' friends, thereby resulting in more publicity within individual friend networks. In the best-case scenario for an event, a self-reinforcing feedback loop emerges.

'Flash Mobs' as Innovation 233

Figure 2 Wall segment from the 2013 Soap Bubble Flash Mob (source: https://www.facebook.com).

The 2013 Soap Bubble Flash Mob was not the first of its kind in Leipzig. A well-attended event preceded it the year before; a similarly successful gathering followed in June 2014. On the basis of this recurrence, one might assume that (nostalgic) memories played a role in the mobilization process. Initiators would then be able to count on and motivate 'repeat participants.' In actuality, a comparison of the names and unique identification numbers (UINs) of individuals who confirmed their attendance on Facebook in 2013 and 2014 reveals little overlap in participants between the two years.

The Venn diagram in Figure 3 quantifies the overlap between 2013 and 2014 for Facebook users who said they would participate in the Soap Bubble Flash Mob on the event page. Only 724 participants from the first year announced their plans to participate again in 2014. One might argue that participants from 2013 might not have felt the need to broadcast their interest in the event more than once on Facebook. Official estimates of the crowd and our impressions in the field, however, indicate that the sum of online participants for both years (2013 + 2014 + overlap = 8,132 participants) clearly exceeds the actual number of participants in 2014 (between 3,000 and 4,000). The number of participants on Facebook and the number on Augustusplatz were, in fact, roughly the same, making it safe to conclude that most Facebook users did not decide to keep quiet about their plans. During our interactions with participants in the field and according to our analysis of their online communication, we discovered that many participants were either curious or expected the event to be a source of 'family fun.' The first motive can be satisfied with one visit; the second is more likely to recur.

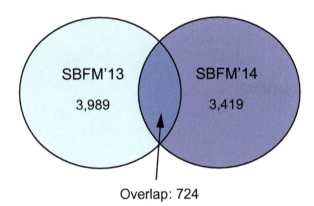

Figure 3 Overlap in confirmed attendance for SBFM '13 and SBFM '14 on Facebook (source: our research).

When Facebook users indicate their plans to attend an event, they generate positive press and help circulate the event announcement. The 'Going' button harbors a dual advantage: By clicking it, users represent themselves as active individuals and link themselves personally to the event and its image. Moreover, users become promoters and lend their support to event initiators in the process. Paolo Gerbaudo (2012) describes the initiators of these types of events as 'choreographers.' Neither ostensible leaders nor organizers, choreographers instead remain in the background doing a job that consists largely of 'scene-setting' or defining the event's framework. The choreographer's role is highly uncertain. Their initiative needs to receive enough positive feedback to get the ball rolling in the mobilization phase and to reach the critical mass for an event to happen offline. In addition to information such as the time and place, event instructions, and options to signalize participation, the Facebook event page also contains posts and comments. When users confirm their attendance or express interest, Facebook automatically posts their choice on the event page. Plotting all wall events (i.e., posts and comments) on a timeline results in an activity history such as the one shown in Figure 4.

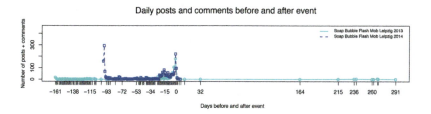

Figure 4 Activity history for the SBFM '13 and SBFM '14 (0: day of the flash mob) (source: our research).

The graph shows online activity for the 2013 Soap Bubble Flash Mob (SBFM '13) and 2014 Soap Bubble Flash Mob (SBFM '14) on the Facebook event page starting from the page creation date until 291 days (for SBFM '13) or 9 days (for SBFM '14) past the event. Increased activity can be observed at the start, which is attributable to the setup required for the event page and related activities as well as to initial publicity efforts. This initial activity spurt is much stronger in 2014 than in the previous year. Activity increases two weeks before the event and peaks on event day itself, after which there is a considerable ebb. Then, more than 260 days after the event, we see a slight increase in activity. This coincides with the announcement of the 2014 Soap Bubble Flash Mob: The 2013 event page receives increased traffic from curious users, for instance, who want to see how the event played out in the past. The crucial observation here is that the bulk of activity, consisting of attendance signals, posts, and comments, is concentrated shortly before the event.

The strongest activity occurs on the day of the event. A flash mob is governed by a precise choreography. Figure 5a provides a visualization of online activity for the period from 48 hours before to 48 hours after the start of the event (at 3 p.m.). Activity in the hours leading up to the event remains consistently high. Less activity can be observed from −16 hours (11 p.m.) to −9 hours (6 a.m.) owing to the time of day. The activity pattern increases during daylight hours on the eve of the flash mob and into the evening. Before that (from −32 hours) another dip can be seen at night. An enlarged view (Figure 5b) shows a strong drop in page activity with the start of the flash mob in both 2013 and 2014. At this moment, the center of activity and attention shifted to Augustusplatz in Leipzig. Facebook is crucial for the preparation phase; for the actual event, however, it is secondary. During the flash mob and for some time thereafter, the participants are focused on their immediate surroundings, which they often observe through the media of film and photography. The Soap Bubble Flash Mob lasted longer than the originally planned five minutes, but after 30 minutes the square had all but emptied again. In 2013, online activity picks up again after 75 minutes, whereas in 2014 it resumes as little as 15 minutes into the flash mob itself, that is, between 3:15 and 3:30 p.m. This shift is significant and might be linked to a more widespread use of the Facebook app on smartphones.

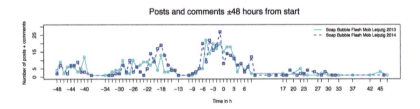

Figure 5a Activity history two days before and two days after the event (0: day of the flash mob) (source: our research).

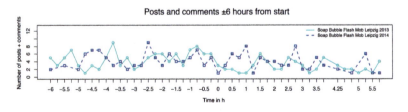

Figure 5b Detailed view of activity on the day of the event, shown in 15-minute intervals (−6 to +6 hours, 0: start of the flash mob) (source: our research).

Technology, as can be seen here, has an enabling function in the accomplishment of a flash mob by providing the necessary conditions for communication and mobilization. The introduction of mailing lists, mobile text messages, and Facebook as an online social network in 2004 all converged to enable information sharing among several different contacts at once, in a form that is discrete. Information can be spread *and concealed* on a large scale. These prerequisites make it possible to hail a new social form as an innovation: fleeting, subject-based gatherings that stir up their surroundings (and entertain participants). From a similar vantage point, Paolo Gerbaudo has argued that social media technology (Twitter, Facebook, etc.) has a unifying effect in the face of the increasing commercialization and fragmentation of society: "In front of this situation of crisis of public space, social media have become emotional conduits for reconstructing a sense of togetherness among a spatially dispersed constituency, so as to facilitate its physical coming together in public space" (Gerbaudo 2012: 159).

Social media are thus ascribed the ability to reconstruct social relationships and information flows, thereby generating new possibilities for congregating and, in the process, for constituting space. They compensate for the diminished importance of co-presence, which Stefan Hirschauer already described for the anonymity of major cities in 1999: "socio-spatial compression (urbanization) and geographic mobility have all but erased the meaning of co-presence as an opportunity for interaction" (Hirschauer 1999: 240, our translation). The mediatization of communicative action (Krotz 2001) opens up new forms of social contact in modern society.

As an innovative form of congregation, flash mobs are only possible, however, because they satisfy two spatial conditions: they specify an event location, and this site is where the participating actors create a shared space. Once they arrive, they are 'on site' and constitute the space through their form of congregation and associated social practices. They do not gather on Facebook but (in this case) on a square in Leipzig, which—preformed by activities on Facebook—is imbued with meaning as well as recorded and reinforced by the practices of photography and filming. In the wake of the gathering, several photos taken on site make their way onto Facebook, bringing the process full circle.

4 On Site

The Soap Bubble Flash Mob in Leipzig happened on the northern end of Augustusplatz. In the center of the square lies a large, round, low-lying fountain with a jet that shoots out of the center and an oversized yellow duck. Four turquoise glass cylinders mark the entry and exit points leading to a parking garage. The square is enclosed by streets to the south and west; a wall to the east and the Leipzig Opera House with an open staircase to the north. Figure 6 and Figure 7 show the progression of the 2013 and 2014 Soap Bubble Flash Mobs.[10]

Most people arrived at the square from the pedestrian zone at the southwest corner (always shown in the top right corner of the photos) and left in the same direction. This corner therefore contains the strongest concentration of people.

Comparing the image compositions in the two figures, the distribution of visitors in 2014 is skewed slightly more to the east (to the left in the photos). In 2014 a major coffee producer held a large-scale promotion event on Augustusplatz that day, which posed an obstacle to flash mob participants who were attempting to gather at the southeast corner of the square.

There were no pre-event indications on site; all participants knew about the flash mob through online media. Facebook assumes an enabling role for such events: the platform enables the coordinated, reflexive accomplishment of this form of congregation, which is perceived as new and innovative. Augustusplatz provided the physical space for the flash mob. The 'innovative' part of this congregating practice is ascribed to the moment of surprise that occurs when a public materializes that has hitherto only existed online. The performance happened without cues—no posters, no signposts. About 20 minutes before 3 p.m., passersby started to trickle onto the square, slowly at first, and then in growing numbers until a crowd formed. Then, a layer of soap bubbles suddenly erupted from the masses. Twenty or so minutes later, the square was more or less restored to its original state. The soap bubble cloud sparked a fundamental change in the situation on site: bubbles suddenly commanded the space. People who had been occupied with an afternoon stroll, taking a short break, or shopping were reassigned to the role of observers. But this transformation happened without shouts, songs, commands, or any other signals that might have indicated coordinated activity. In this case, the 'choreographers' or 'soft leaders' (Gerbaudo 2012: 134ff.) remained hidden and could not be made out through careful observation or by asking around in the crowd.

---

10 The photos shown here are screenshots of a video shot from the balcony of the Leipzig Opera building.

'Flash Mobs' as Innovation

Figure 6 2013 Soap Bubble Flash Mob progression; view from the Leipzig Opera balcony (chronologically from top left to bottom right) (source: our research).

Figure 7 2014 Soap Bubble Flash Mob progression; view from the Leipzig Opera balcony (chronologically from top left to bottom right) (source: our research).

This novel form of surprise gathering did not create a sense of community—there were no conversations on site or online comments to attest to a more enduring form of sociality. Few people returned to the event the following year. What the

Soap Bubble Flash Mob did provide is a stage for self-expression. Despite its ostensible neutrality, the event attempted to promote an ideal ("being a kid again for 5 minutes," see Figure 1) and create a platform for new experiences. Surprise and irritation were no longer adequate sources of legitimation for the event. Even for a non-political flash mob as in our case, legitimation comes from a framing narrative: "Like old times, when we were little. When we could still find happiness in simple things like rainbow-colored bubbles. How will people react to thousands of soap bubbles floating above Leipzig's Augustusplatz?" (cf. Figure 1)

The framing narrative in this case expresses a longing for the past, for childhood, for simple pleasures coupled with the desire to generate a public reaction. Organizers expected, as they described elsewhere in the announcement, to see looks of confusion and happiness among the crowd (see the announcement text in section 3). Similar to Facebook activity, the goal was to share good times with friends; but the flash mob also had a public dimension that went beyond this circle of friends. Participants wanted to be seen and—at least at the level of legitimation—be a source of happiness and surprise.

Clicking on an event page is a simple act with minimal commitment. The actual *doing* of innovation, that is, on-site participation in a flash mob, is more demanding. First, enough friends need to communicate their intent to show up and participate. The actual encounter and shared experience can only happen on site. To fully benefit from the event means having been there. Only then is it possible to appear in the photos that are uploaded and shared. Only then can participants be tagged, thereby increasing their visibility among friends. And only then can they write comments that demonstrate their firsthand expertise and insider status.

On the square during the SBFM, the casual observer could also have seen a number of individuals interspersed among the crowd with pens and notepads recording the physical proximity of groups, along with salient features of their social background. They turned out to be market researchers who investigate these types of events to sell stand space to companies interested in targeted marketing campaigns. That most likely also explains the presence of coffee producer Jacobs at the event. Jacobs promoted its coffee specifically for the event with the claim 'Closer with every cup' (*Jede Tasse bringt uns näher*), as can be seen on the vertical banner in Figure 8 below. This adept strategy speaks to what Paolo Gerbaudo identifies as a central dimension of gatherings organized online: "[S]ocial media have become emotional conduits for reconstructing a sense of togetherness among a spatially dispersed constituency" (ibid.: 159). The coffee producer attempted to address this 'sense of togetherness' that is associated with Facebook but rarely carries over into real life. The message is this: what better to bridge this gap than the age-old cultural practice of chatting over coffee?

'Flash Mobs' as Innovation

Figure 8 'Closer with every cup' (*Jede Tasse bringt uns näher*) (source: our image).

This practice of leaderless congregation specifies boundaries. It defines what is part of the gathering and what lies outside, that is, the limits of the constituted space, through shared knowledge, common practices, and accepted ideas, rules, goals, and emotions (cf. Schatzki 2002; Shove, Pantzar, and Watson 2012). In other words, anyone who has the required knowledge and is capable of reproducing the prescribed behavior can cross over and become part of the space. However, as leaderless congregations, there are no social roles or structures in flash mobs that enable a 'group stance' toward those who join the space. If someone does not abide by the flash mob's rules, the only conceivable—yet relatively improbable—negative on-site reactions to these crossovers would be a spontaneous dissolution, thus causing a breakdown in the constituted space or a radical redefinition of the situation, for example, through a spontaneous protest. The coffee producer exploited the improbability of sanctions from the flash mob and strategically positioned its stands at the corner of Augustusplatz (regarding markets and networks see also Lamla 2008).

5   'Flash Mobs' as a New Social Form of Technically Mediated Congregation. Discussion and Summary

Flash mobs are a relatively new social form that has only emerged in recent years. They are innovative in a dual sense: through their specific mediatization and through their institutionalization of surprise (which is both novel and unexpected) as a constitutive element. Having teased out these key elements, a flash mob can be summed up as a well-planned public surprise for general audiences. Whatever occurs when participants 'happen' to meet has an element of spontaneity, its unexpectedness serves, first, as a source of consternation and reflection among observers and, second, as a source of enjoyment for participants. This new social form is enabled by the effective use of modern communication technology (starting with e-mail, then text messages, and finally Facebook) to mobilize participants. Nonetheless, running counter to the claim that flash mobs are the product of technological innovation, embodied in phrases such as the 'Twitter revolution,' our empirical analysis shows that both technology *and* space are wielded in novel ways to generate an innovative practice. Facebook enables the effective mobilization of participants. It is a technical environment that shapes social practice, allows people to communicate in certain patterns, and distributes information on the basis of algorithmic rules.

On site at the flash mob, however, Facebook relinquishes its primary role. As a specific means of recruiting, electronic networks do contribute to the constitution of the space by eliminating the need for signs or organizers. On-site practices and the space produced by a flash mob are therefore systematically linked to the online life of the event before and after its instantiation in the real world. Facebook furnishes the platform for a reflexive, coordinated flash mob. The distribution of relevant information is based on sophisticated algorithms that enable highly successful recruiting using very brief comments and announcements. Yet the flash mob itself materializes on site through new forms of structuring space (cf. Löw 2001: 158ff.; Gebelein 2015). Flash mobs are temporary interventions in institutionalized spatial arrangements. They displace existing constellations and enable a new and different experience of the square. The unexpected space that emerges is meant to be temporary and is therefore also fragile. By dispensing with on-site leadership, the space becomes more democratic; the job of organizing is delegated to the online media. Compared to other forms of congregation (demonstrations, parades, rallies), the main focus is not about a sustained sense of community or strengthening group identity, but instead self-expression, entertainment, and a break from everyday norms. This site-based happening exhibits similarities with practices in sport subcultures such as skateboarding or parkour: people stake their own temporary space and seek out interesting niches, unusual paths, and innovative forms of movement. The aspects of mobilization, managing knowledge and unknowns, and on-site photos and video distinguish the flash mob from sport cultures among urban youth.

In terms of similarities, small groups standing within sight and admiring the soap bubbles of their neighbors, without direct interaction, can be likened to the casual scanning, 'likes,' and shares that happen on Facebook.[11] The peaceful ebb and flow of visitors as they populate and depopulate the square, assured of their next steps, provides the basis for innovative action; the surprise can now be served up to the uninitiated. The initiated, however, are sometimes not only participants but also their own audience. Flash mobs are staged with the purpose of observing the surprise. Cameras are also used to observe and record fellow participants. Just as on Facebook, the same people can (or must) play two different roles—actor and audience. This duality creates a backdoor for commercial exploitation or even appropriation since this form of knowledge can be usurped and applied for gain.

---

11 On the issue of how technology shapes social relations in subtle ways, see Kaminski and Gelhard 2014.

References

Bakshy, Eytan, Itamar Rosenn, Cameron Marlow, and Lada Adamic. 2012. "The Role of Social Networks in Information Diffusion." Pp. 519-528 in *Proceedings of the 21st international conference on World Wide Web (WWW-12)*, Lyon, France, April 16-20, 2012.

Boldi, Paolo, Bruno Codenotti, Massimo Santini, and Sebastiano Vigna. 2004. "Ubicrawler: A Scalable Fully Distributed Web Crawler." *Software: Practice and Experience* 34(8): 711-726.

Charniak, Eugene. 2000. "A Maximum-Entropy-Inspired Parser." Pp. 132-139 in *Proceedings of the 1st North American chapter of the Association for Computational Linguistics conference (NAACL-00)*, Washington, Seattle, April 29-May 04, 2000.

Chierichetti, Flavio, Jon Kleinberg, Ravi Kumar, Mohammad Mahdian, and Sandeep Pandey. 2014. "Event Detection via Communication Pattern Analysis." Pp. 51-60 in *Proceedings of the 8th International AAAI Conference of Weblogs and Social Media (ICWSM-14)*, Ann Arbor, Michigan, June 1-4, 2014.

Cho, Junghoo and Hector Garcia-Molina. 2000. "The Evolution of the Web and Implications for an Incremental Crawler." Pp. 200-209 in *Proceedings of the 26th International Conference on Very Large Databases (VLDB-00)*, Cairo, Egypt, September 10-14, 2000.

Gebelein, Paul. 2015. *Flächen - Bahnen - Knoten. Geocaching als Praktik der Raumerzeugung*. Bielefeld: transcript.

Gerbaudo, Paolo. 2012. *Tweet and the Streets. Social Media and Contemporary Activism*. London: Pluto Press.

Heaney, Francis. 2005. "The Short Life of Flash Mobs - Interview with Bill Wasik." Stay Free! Magazine. Retrieved January 18, 2016 (http://www.alternet.org/story/26807/the_short_life_of_flash_mobs).

Heydon, Allan and Marc Najork. 1999. "Mercator: A Scalable, Extensible Web Crawler." *World Wide Web* 2(4): 219-229.

Hirschauer, Stefan. 1999. "Die Praxis der Fremdheit und die Minimierung von Anwesenheit. Eine Fahrstuhlfahrt.*" Soziale Welt* 50(3): 221-246.

Houston, J. Brian, Hyunjin Seo, Leigh A. T. Knight, Emily J. Kennedy, Joshua Hawthorne, and Sara L. Trask. 2013. "Urban Youth's Perspectives on Flash Mobs." *Journal of Applied Communication Research* 41(3): 236-252.

Hutter, Michael, Hubert Knoblauch, Werner Rammert, and Arnold Windeler. This volume. "Innovation Society Today. The Reflexive Creation of Novelty."

Hutter, Michael. 2011. "Infinite Surprises: On the Stabilization of Value in the Creative Industries." Pp. 201-220 in *The Worth of Goods. Valuation and Pricing in the Economy*, edited by J. Becker and P. Aspers. Oxford: Oxford University Press.

Kaminski, Andreas and Andreas Gelhard, eds. 2014. *Zur Philosophie informeller Technisierung*. Darmstadt: WBG.

Kramer, Adam D. I., Jamie E. Guillory, and Jeffrey T. Hancock. 2014. "Experimental Evidence of Massive-Scale Emotional Contagion Through Social Networks." *Proceedings of the National Academy of Sciences of the United States of America* 111(24): 8788-8790.

Krotz, Friedrich. 2001. *Die Mediatisierung des kommunikativen Handelns. Der Wandel von Alltag und sozialen Beziehungen, Kultur und Gesellschaft durch die Medien*. Opladen: Westdeutscher Verlag.

Lamla, Jörn. 2008. "Markt-Vergemeinschaftung im Internet. Das Fallbeispiel einer Shopping- und Meinungsplattform." Pp. 170-185 in *Posttraditionale Gemeinschaften. Theoretische und ethnographische Erkundungen*, edited by R. Hitzler, A. Honer, and M. Pfadenhauer. Wiesbaden: VS Verlag.

Löw, Martina. 2001. *Raumsoziologie*. Frankfurt a. M.: Suhrkamp.

Ochs, Carsten and Martina Löw. 2012. "Un/Faire Informationspraktiken: Internet Privacy aus sozialwissenschaftlicher Perspektive." Pp. 15-62 in *Internet Privacy. Eine multidisziplinäre Bestandsaufnahme/A Multidisciplinary Analysis*, edited by J. Buchmann. Heidelberg: Springer Vieweg.

Rammert, Werner. 2010. "Die Innovationen der Gesellschaft." Pp. 21-51 in *Soziale Innovationen. Auf dem Weg zu einem post-industriellen Innovationsparadigma*, edited by J. Howaldt and H. Jakobsen. Wiesbaden: Springer VS.

Rheingold, Howard. 2003. *Smart Mobs. The Next Social Revolution*. Cambridge: Perseus.

Romero, Daniel M., Brendan Meeder, and Jon Kleinberg. 2011. "Differences in the Mechanics of Information Diffusion Across Topics: Idioms, Political Hashtags, and Complex Contagion on Twitter." Pp. 695-704 *in Proceedings of the 20th International Conference on World Wide Web (WWW '11)*, Hyderabad, India, March 28-April 01, 2011.

Schatzki, Theodore. 2002. *The Site of the Social: A Philosophical Account of the Constitution of Social Life and Change*. University Park: Pennsylvania State University Press.

Shove, Elizabeth, Mika Pantzar, and Matt Watson. 2012. *The Dynamics of Social Practice*. London: SAGE.

Winner, Langdon. 1980. Do Artifacts Have Politics? *Daedalus* 109(1): 121-136.

# How Does Novelty Enter Spatial Planning?

Conceptualizing Innovations in
Planning and Research Strategies

Gabriela Christmann, Oliver Ibert, Johann Jessen
and Uwe-Jens Walther

1   Introduction

Since its emergence in the second half of the 19th century, spatial planning has been assigned the task of shaping and structuring spaces (typically defined along the lines of administrative units) and regulating spatial development in the various dimensions of space as a natural, built, infrastructural, economic, and social environment. The ways in which this task has been approached, how and which *goals* have been set, and what *procedures* have been applied to pursue them has also always been subject to reorientation and change. This chapter addresses such instances of reorientation in spatial planning that are not perceived as simply improving upon and refining established routines but as representing fundamental changes that break with these routines. At the heart of this chapter is thus the question of whether—and, if so, how—such changes in spatial planning can be grasped as innovations. We begin by discussing in what respect groundbreaking changes in the practice of planning that the practitioners perceive as radical can meaningfully be interpreted as innovations (section 2). Transferring the concept of innovation from its traditional usage in economic and technological contexts to the sphere of institutionally embedded political-administrative practices requires a few modifications in terms of extending it toward a more comprehensive concept of 'societal innovation' (Rammert 2010: 24; Hutter et al., this volume), which we will discuss in section 3. We further pursue the question of how innovation in planning can be examined empirically. For this purpose, we outline the design of our research project *Innovations in Planning: How Does Novelty Enter Spatial*

247

Planning? (*InnoPlan* for short) (section 4).[1] We present our initial findings from the project in section 5. We focus on one of the project's research questions and show how the actors involved reflexively and/or intentionally advance the innovations in planning examined in our study (section 6).

2 Previous Perspectives on Change in Spatial Planning Practice. On Problems with the Notion of Change and the Potential of the Concept of Innovation

Even today, it is rather unusual to systematically apply the social scientific concept of innovation to the field of urban and regional spatial development. In the international discourse on spatial planning, the concept of innovation is generally considered to be an economic issue. In common understanding planning is concerned with innovation only to the extent that planning has to accommodate entrepreneurial initiatives from the private sector in specific ways (e.g., by designating and developing areas for knowledge-intensive industries or by planning creative urban districts) owing to enhanced innovativeness being a requirement of the economy. This is a line of reasoning that has been pursued under the heading of 'creative planning' (Bayliss 2004; Kunzmann 2004). Authors that have used this concept in reference to new developments in planning as such—for instance, the revival of 'strategic planning' (Healey 1997; Albrechts 2004)—have done so in a rather loose sense. In these cases, the concept of innovation is not at the center of attention, and there is a lack of any systematic discussion of theories of innovation.

The 'policy mobility' approach in critical geography (McFarlane 2006; Peck and Theodore 2010) features some parallels to the way the issue of innovation is dealt with in planning. This more recent strand of research is preoccupied with how new approaches and strategies in local policy-making spread internationally (e.g., the instrument of business improvement districts that was developed in the

---

1   The project *Innovations in Planning: How Does Novelty Enter Spatial Planning?* has been funded by the German Research Foundation (DFG). It has been conducted at the Leibniz Institute for Research on Society and Space (IRS) in Erkner and at the University of Stuttgart. It was launched on October 1, 2013 and completed at the end of March 2016. The principal investigators were Gabriela B. Christmann, Oliver Ibert, Johann Jessen, and Uwe-Jens Walther. Gabriela B. Christmann and Uwe-Jens Walther are also senior members of the DFG Research Training Group called *Innovation Society Today: The Reflexive Creation of Novelty*. The *InnoPlan* project team further consists of Franz Füg, Thomas Honeck, Oliver Koczy, and Daniela Zupan, who were working on their dissertations in this context.

USA or the beacon strategies geared toward achieving a 'Bilbao effect'; cf. McCann and Ward 2010) and which systematic modifications they undergo as they are transferred from one territorial context to another. Although the protagonists in this debate do not speak of 'social innovation' (they would probably even reject the term), this discourse is relevant to the question of innovation in planning that we are concerned with here in that it makes explicit reference to the spatial and social diffusion of new practices, which, according to Schumpeter, is a key feature of innovation. However, this discourse has been blind to our key issue, namely, the emergence of new policies and practices in planning. Rather, the focus remains restricted on the process of diffusion and on the question of how new practices are implemented in and adapted to local settings. Moreover, the diffusion of policies is critically interpreted as an act of exercising power in terms of societal globalization by which dominant political and economic centers of power expand their spheres of influence and, in so doing, subject an ever-growing number of countries and people to their logic (Peck and Theodore 2010). In contrast to this approach, we do not want to rule out the idea that there might be potential for the reform and improvement of political planning practice as inherent in and connected with the emergence and establishment of novel approaches (often displacing the previously dominant ones).

Even though planning-theory discourse over the past two decades has presented a picture that is extraordinarily multifaceted and difficult to map, one can identify some recurring observations in the large body of literature in terms of changes in the content of spatial planning:

Action orientation: Planning has extended its repertoire from the classic approach of setting the framework to implementing plans. This has become evident in the turn to (large-scale) project-based planning, the formation of public-private partnerships, and the establishment of development agencies.

Reduction of hierarchy: Planning acts less and less frequently on the premise of an authoritarian state that directs the individual actions underlying spatial development by means of a politics of command and control. A characteristic feature of the new types of planning is that the actors of public planning limit their role to that of process initiators, mediators, or simple participants, and in this role they seek to convince the private actors.

Informalization: New types of planning rely less on traditional formal instruments, such as laws, statutes, or planning approval procedures. They are replaced by private contracts and informal (handshake) agreements.

New spheres of action: In multilevel planning systems, the levels between the firmly institutionalized strata of administration are gaining particular significance. At the top, the influence of programs adopted at the EU level is growing in importance. At the regional level, functional spheres of action are emerging for implementing higher-level programs.

Marketing and identity management: New planning strategies increasingly involve elements of identity management, marketing, and the mobilization of attention and resources. These are all aspects that converge in new strategies for a festivalization of urban and regional planning.

Compared to the traditional understanding of planning, this has led to a substantial broadening of planning tasks, both in terms of procedures and content. Interestingly, the planning sciences have perceived these developments conceptually as a process of 'change,' yet not as change in planning *as such* but rather—and this is remarkable—as change in the planning *environment*. We will demonstrate this by the example of two influential books by Selle (2005) and Wiechmann (2008). In his book, Klaus Selle (2005) is specifically interested in public actors' contributions to spatial development and, apart from planning, sees these contributions to be in tasks of the kind that he calls 'development' and 'regulation.' Thorsten Wiechmann (2008), by contrast, focuses on tasks related to regional strategy development and observes that applying the instruments of planning in the traditional sense is only one of several possible modes of strategy development and, moreover, not ideally suited to all situations, particularly those that are complex, dynamic, and difficult to control (Wiechmann 2010).

Both authors underrate the possibility that the planning profession *itself* could also be a proactive driver of change. It is instead assumed that the planning system primarily responds to external change in a reactive manner. A theoretical-conceptual grasp of the agency that pushes change remains implicit in their analyses. Therefore, they adhere to a traditional concept of planning (comprehensive information, clearly defined goals, setting the framework for action, separation between public measures in preparation for action and private implementation) in spite of the changes observed in practice and focus their attention on the interaction between traditional planning and other types of action.

Our approach, however, focuses on the scope of action that creates opportunities to bring about change in spatial planning, for instance, via learning processes or by adopting a reflexive stance in dealing with existing practices. For this reason, we start from a generic concept of planning that is comprehensive enough to ensure that new practices are no longer confused with an absence of planning but are understood as new modes of planning: First, we conceive of planning as a type of social action that raises claims of applying a higher standard of rationality (Siebel 2006). We speak of planning whenever actors systematically take into account and consciously reflect on the consequences of action directed at the future in a professional (and not simply commonsensical) manner. Second, we take planning to refer to a specific mode of decision-making. Luhmann defined planning as 'deciding on decisions' (1971: 67, our translation). Decision-based models of planning employ two levels of decision-making: 'operational decision-making,' which occurs in the course of concrete action, and 'the premises of decision-making' (i.e., the formulation of the principles) upon which operational decisions are based (Faludi 1985; Mayer 1999). The rationality of planning is also the result of deliberately adjusting the interplay between the premises of decision-making and operational decisions, that is to say, the relation between preparation and spontaneity (Suchman 1987). The field of application that we have in mind in our discussion of this generic type of planning action is the shaping, ordering, and development of spatial structures. In terms of the agents of planning, we focus on all actors that are involved in making planning decisions in this field of application. These actors will mostly be members of public administrations and policy-makers but to an increasing degree actors from civil society and the economic sphere as well. This conception of planning is specific enough to clearly define the field of activities in question, yet open enough to capture changes that are the product of the planning process itself.

Against this backdrop, we suggest employing the concept of innovation to better grasp the proactive, intentional, and reflexive action of the actors in the planning system. In this vein, we conceive of innovations in planning as emergent effects that arise from the interplay of a changing planning environment and learning processes among people, professions, organizations, and political actors. A change in the planning environment certainly explains why things change, but this perspective alone does not let us understand in which direction these changes evolve and how they take shape as new practices. This requires taking practitioners' intentions, learning processes, and freedom to make choices into account.

In our view, turning to the concept of innovation is moreover not only appropriate for theoretical and conceptual reasons but might also be of relevance to applied research. A better understanding of how novelty enters spatial planning can be expected to improve our ability to organize such processes and design appropriate institutional frameworks to support them. However, this requires that we first understand innovative action in spatial planning.

3 Some Thoughts on the Concept of Innovation in the Context of Spatial Planning

From the late 1930s onward, social aspects of innovations were almost exclusively considered in the context of technological and economic development—in the sense that new technologies and business models could be successful only to the extent that they could be effectively incorporated into social practices. Only very recently, in the late 1990s did they appear on the agenda of the social sciences as an object of research in their own right (cf. Gillwald 2000). Since then, the social sciences have taken into account the fact that practices breaking with previous routines are found not only in technology and the economy but in other areas of life as well. They can occur, for instance, in people's everyday lives (e.g., communal living arrangements) or in the way urban planners handle their everyday tasks. According to Rammert (2010), social innovations—in addition to technological, economic, scientific, artistic, and other innovations—are part of what can be described by the umbrella term 'societal innovation'. Even though he lists and treats social innovations separately from other types of innovations (e.g., economic, technological) for analytical reasons, there can be no doubt that social innovations must invariably be considered an integral element of other innovations, such as those of an economic, technological, artistic, political, or any other nature. Social innovations typically occur as 'prerequisites, concomitants, or consequences' of other innovations (cf. Zapf 1989: 177, our translation; also Ogburn 1937).

When one considers the concept of social innovation, closer inspection of what constitutes 'the social' is in order. Two different usages can be distinguished (cf. Howaldt and Schwarz 2010: 10). A normative use of the term prevails in the international research literature in particular (cf. Moulaert et al. 2013). In this literature, social innovations are conceived of as novel practices and solutions to achieve socially highly valued and desirable objectives. The term refers to approaches that offer new, morally superior solutions to social problems. We, by contrast, prefer an analytical conception of the term that bears no such normative connotations. We understand social innovations in a very basic sense—and this is in accordance with the second, analytical, usage—as new ways of or solutions to organizing social processes. We fully agree with Zapf, who perceives social innovations as "new ways of achieving objectives, in particular, new forms of organization, new modes of regulation, new lifestyles" (Zapf 1989: 177, our translation).

Another characteristic feature according to Zapf (ibid.) is that social innovations "change the direction of social change, solve problems in better ways than previous practices," and "for this reason are worth imitating and institutionalizing." The aspects of novelty, 'better' solutions, imitation, institutionalization, and their repercussions on social change will be addressed and reconceptualized below in accordance with our own understanding of innovation in the context of planning. Moreover, we will clarify other important features of and issues related to innovative action such as intentionality versus non-intentionality, linearity versus non-linearity, the implementation of new ideas in practice, and the spatial diffusion of new practices.

Novelty—a social construction: A key criterion for identifying innovations is novelty. According to Zapf, something is 'new' when it is done differently from the way it was usually done before. It represents a deviation from or a break with common practice. However, it is not specified how new a mode of action or a solution must be or how much it must deviate from the previous practice to qualify as a social innovation. This is, of course, a question that is difficult to answer in principle since any deviation must connect with something familiar to gain social acceptance. Thus, even though a certain degree of novelty is a key feature of social innovation, a new combination of familiar elements (Schumpeter 1934)—or also the rediscovery of old ones and their transfer to new situations or contexts, including new spatial settings—might play a role as well (Gillwald 2000: 10f.). We therefore conceive of the newness in the nature of an innovation as a 'relative novelty' (ibid.), although it must nevertheless involve some type of 'break' with the customary. 'Absolute novelty' exists only in a historical perspective, specifically when something comes into being for the first time.

Drawing on Braun-Thürmann (2005: 6), we further assume that a deviating practice becomes a novelty only once third parties perceive it as such and experience it as an improvement over the previous situation. Whether something qualifies as new or not is therefore also a matter of collective perception in a society. With this in mind, we conceive of (social) innovations as social constructions—and this in two specific respects: in the form of subjects who establish a different way of doing things and in the form of third parties who perceive something that is different to be a 'novelty' or 'innovation.' Rammert's definition of novelty combines these two dimensions:

> Novelties are to refer to all variations that, temporally, set themselves apart from previous variants and are consequently also redefined at the semantic level as being new; that, materially, evolve or are produced as a modification of one or several elements or a combination thereof and as something of a different and previously unknown kind; and that, socially, represent deviations from normality that are accepted, upon conflict among interested parties, as an improvement and are incorporated into the body of institutional rules as a new normality or even transform them. (Rammert 2010: 45, our translation)

'Better' solutions—a first-order construction: In Zapf's definition (1989: 177), social innovations are 'better at solving problems than previous practices.' This formulation is misleading in that it suggests that this assessment of being a 'better solution' is a matter of the researcher's judgment. We avoid making such judgments yet take into consideration that the motive underlying social actors' pursuit of innovations is to develop solutions that are 'better' or 'more suitable' than ex-

isting ones. Of course, what social actors perceive as being 'better' than the established practice will invariably depend on the specific social frame of reference that defines what qualifies as an 'improvement.' We thus conceive of the actors' perceptions of creating 'better' solutions as a social construction as well. In methodological terms, we grasp this as a first-order construction (in the sense of Alfred Schütz). The researcher's task is to reconstruct first-order constructions and the judgments implied therein so as to develop second-order constructions, yet to do so without the researcher him- or herself adopting the judgments implicit in those first-order constructions.

Non-intentionality and intentionality: We take it that innovative practices or solutions can also emerge from modes of action that, from the actors' perspective, are geared toward 'better solutions' but not toward 'innovation.' Even so, third parties can still perceive such action to be 'innovative' and imitate it. Conversely, we can of course imagine practices that explicitly seek to produce innovation and in fact succeed in doing so. Yet it is also conceivable that what is pursued as an innovation and is semantically framed beforehand as being innovative ultimately fails to take hold as such.

Non-linearity and linearity: In principle, innovations must be considered unlikely events. Failure, setbacks, and changes in the course of development are not just a possibility but must actually be understood as fairly typical structural characteristics of innovation. Over the past few decades, this insight has led to fundamental criticism of linear models of innovation for being deterministic and not doing justice to the matter in question (Balconi et al. 2010). Circular models have increasingly replaced phase models to better reflect the iterative (Kline and Rosenberg 1986) and open-ended, ongoing nature ('permanently beta,' per Neff and Stark 2003) of innovation processes.

However, in our view, there are good reasons for retaining certain elements of linear thinking when conceptualizing the dynamics of innovation (Braun-Thürmann 2005: 45f.; Balconi et al. 2010). As innovations emerge, there are repeatedly critical moments in which facts are established that cannot be ignored in the further course of the process. For instance, if a pilot project has successfully demonstrated the benefit of a social innovation in principle, all subsequent initiatives must take this into account. In this case, it is no longer possible to act as if this established fact did not exist (Ibert and Müller 2015). The linearity of otherwise irregular and circular processes is a result of the existence of critical thresholds, the crossing of which has a crucial impact on the subsequent dynamics and path of development. What would be desirable is a phase model that identifies such thresholds in an ideal-typical manner and in this way takes into account that phases do not always proceed in a linear fashion but might also follow a spiral- or wavelike pattern until an innovation has been established. Such a phase model would resolve the tension inherent in the question of linearity versus non-linearity.

Implementation in practice, imitation, and spatial diffusion: A *conditio sine qua non* of any innovation, however, is that a new idea must not remain an idea but must be implemented in practice to qualify as an innovation—regardless of the phase of development in which this happens. This is largely consensual in the innovation literature. To the extent that this involves economic and technological innovations, 'market entry'—aside from the act of 'invention' as such—is seen as the crucial moment. The social innovation literature identifies the point of 'introduction into practice' accordingly (Neuloh 1977: 22; Gillwald 2000: 32). A social innovation can be introduced into practice by other actors imitating a novel practice, which is then spread spatially in this manner, thereby emancipating it from its ties to any specific place. In the absence of such diffusion, it represents merely a new practice; it is no more than a local project and not an innovation.

Institutionalization—the paradox of innovation: In his definition Zapf (1989: 177) rightly points out that novel practices must be institutionalized to qualify as social innovations. Other authors, too, agree that innovations must display some degree of longevity to distinguish them from temporary, more short-lived trends (Gillwald 2000: 41). A paradox lies in the fact that, as institutionalization progresses, innovative practices transform into an established order and, in the process, lose their aura of innovativeness (Häussling 2007: 370; Howaldt and Schwarz 2010: 66f.). In other words, when reconstructing the process of innovation over space and time, this act of reconstruction refers to an object that 'unfolds' only slowly (Knorr Cetina 2001). As it unfolds, it is not identical to itself at different points in time (ibid.).

Change: Whereas social change is always the unintended product of a chain of social processes, innovations can be intentional and developed in a highly strategic and coordinated fashion (cf. Howaldt and Schwarz 2010: 54f.). Of course, innovations can also be the result of non-intended processes (see above). Yet it must be emphasized that ever since modern societies were first described as knowledge societies, the reflexive pursuit of innovation has played a pivotal role (cf. Hutter et al., this volume). This does not mean that change can be sharply distinguished from innovation. Rather, both modes of social variation must be seen as an interacting relationship. A specific change in the social structure of a society, such as demographic change, for instance, can trigger innovation. At the same time, innovation can in turn—and this is part of Zapf's definition (1989: 177)—contribute to social change as well.

Innovation and conflict: As the pursuit of innovation is geared toward finding solutions that are different from the existing and established ones, innovation has an ambivalent impact on given structures (actor constellations, power relations, and so on). Schumpeter (1934) pinpointed the crux of the matter in coining the term 'creative destruction.' What he meant by this is that the emergence of new products and business models is invariably accompanied by the decline of previously dominant structures: the stagecoach became obsolete once the railroad entered the scene, as did the sailing ship once the steamship was introduced. The unfolding of an innovation hence always entails a redistribution of opportunities and risks (Lindhult 2008; Schwarz et al. 2010). While some of them might come as a surprise, they are in part also anticipated by the actors. For this reason, institutional friction and resistance motivated by vested interests are concomitants of innovation processes that must always be reckoned with (Ibert 2003). Negotiating new ideas can thus be expected to involve different levels of controversy in different local contexts. It is therefore likely that they will first take hold in places where resistance is weak and many of the actors involved expect to mostly benefit from the anticipated redistribution of opportunities and risks.

Conflict is hence not simply an unpleasant peripheral phenomenon that accompanies innovation processes; it is rather a fairly typical feature of innovation that different rationalities, patterns of interpretation, and rival approaches and interests will collide with one another. Conflict must in fact be perceived as an element that accounts for the productivity of innovation in the first place (cf. Martens 2010: 374) since it can disrupt routines and cause cracks in established patterns where the lever of change can be brought to bear. This has been emphasized by Neuloh (1977) and also by other conflict theorists who draw on Coser, Simmel, and Dahrendorf (cf., e.g., Dubiel 1999). And, lastly, the solutions that are arrived at through processes of innovation are themselves also far from perfect. That is to say, innovations do not only produce new solutions but inevitably new problems as well. Conflictuality must therefore be perceived as a dimension that pervades the entire innovation process, yet one that changes its nature in the course of the process (Christmann et al. 2016).

4   On Empirical Research on Innovations in Spatial Planning, Drawing on Examples from Four Fields of Planning

The processes involved in the emergence, implementation, and diffusion of innovations in spatial planning will be traced by drawing on four examples from the *InnoPlan* project in the fields of urban development, urban restructuring, neighborhood development, and regional development (see section 1). In all four fields of action, *InnoPlan* inquired into the *trajectories* (temporal dimension), *structural characteristics* (organizational dimension), and the *manifestations* (institutional dimension) of innovation processes.

1. *Trajectories* of innovation processes (temporal dimension): Which phases can we identify in the emergence, implementation, and diffusion of innovative approaches in spatial planning? What characterizes these phases and the transitions from one phase to the next?
2. *Structural characteristics* of innovation processes (organizational dimension): Which actors, arrangements, and entities affect innovations in spatial planning in which ways? What significance do they have for the various phases of the innovation process? How does collective action emerge around an innovative idea? How does a specific practice spread?
3. *Manifestations* of innovations that have become established (institutional dimension): What are the formal, legal, or symbolic manifestations of a newly established routine? What role do guiding visions play in pooling individual experiences in ways that give rise to collective reorientation?

4.1 Fields of Action

As mentioned above, we will use these three sets of questions to approach each of the four fields of spatial planning that have undergone reorientation in terms of content and procedures in recent years or over the past few decades. Each field can be addressed only briefly here. In choosing these areas of planning, it was important to us that they have great practical relevance and represent significant points of reference in planning discourse. Moreover, our intention was to include planning processes that range from the neighborhood to the regional level so as to capture the breadth of (innovative) planning action across various spatial scales. We were furthermore careful to make sure that these new modes of planning had evolved to the point that they could be considered successfully established and widespread models of planning and thus qualified as innovations in accordance with our definition (cf. section 3). Our sample nevertheless represents innovations at different points of maturity and includes quite well-established ('New Neighborhoods') as well as more recent innovations ('Temporary Use').

The field of neighborhood development: 'Neighborhood management'
The concept of neighborhood management (NM) represents a new, complex approach to urban renewal. Whereas the traditional toolbox was geared toward

an understanding of urban renewal as a technical process that revolved around construction and the technical instruments that this involved—the side effects of which were to be mitigated by social measures (prevention, compensation, participation)—the new approaches employing NM now render the social and organizational dimension as an integral part of the task of urban renewal. Not only the urban areas themselves but also the established way of dealing with them was to be subjected to renewal ('renewal of urban renewal'; 'institutional policy,' Walther and Güntner 2005; Güntner 2007). Within a period of two decades, neighborhood management has evolved from its first experimental stage (as an element in the programs of some German federal states) to a widely accepted and virtually standardized procedure. Evidence testifying to the relevance of this approach is the large number of NM measures that have been implemented and are ongoing, the legal framework, and the ongoing debate about the continuation of NM in other forms and within other organizational frameworks. To wit, a separate section titled 'Social City' was introduced into the German Building Code. Also, the debates over its long-term continuation, on mainstreaming its basic principles, and, ironically, the controversies on cutbacks reach far beyond the expert community and all testify to the increased relevance of NM in planning (e.g., Walther 2002, 2004; Deutsches Institut für Urbanistik 2003; Häußermann 2005).

The field of urban development: 'Designing new urban neighborhoods'
Planning new urban neighborhoods is among the classic tasks of municipal planning that local administrations have carried out time and again in recurrent cycles over the past 100 years. The cycle prior to the last one resulted in the large residential complexes of the 1960s and 1970s, which, in terms of urban development and as types of housing designs, are widely considered a failure. After a decade of stagnation, the dynamic growth in large West German cities in the early 1990s in the wake of German reunification triggered a new wave of building large-scale housing developments in many of these cities (Hafner et al. 1998; BBR 2007). All differences in detail notwithstanding, the new neighborhoods that emerged in Germany in the 1990s (and in other European countries as early as the 1980s) have a number of significant features in common that clearly distinguish them from the large residential complexes built during the '60s and '70s cycle and that have been interpreted as a paradigm shift—namely, from functionalist modernism to a compact city of mixed uses. Our project views this shift as an example of innovation. This innovation is manifest in the morphology of urban development (block construction), functional structure, types of housing designs, and its layout of transportation infrastructure, and conception of public space (Jessen 2004). It frequently also involved substantial changes in planning and implementation procedures.

The field of urban restructuring: 'Temporary uses by pioneers of urban space as a planning tool'

Temporary uses by pioneers of urban space first emerged as an issue in the field of urban restructuring in places where a multifaceted process of structural change confronted municipalities with vacated properties and buildings. In many cases, municipalities that were engaged in urban restructuring reached the limits of what classic urban development could accomplish; at least, they were not able to utilize urban wasteland as a resource for urban renewal. Unplanned uses by 'urban pioneers' (cf. Christmann and Büttner 2011)—i.e., citizens who creatively appropriate unused spaces and vacant buildings for new (temporary) uses—created opportunities that offered new prospects for development. Against this backdrop, temporary uses were soon deliberately utilized in the context of urban restructuring and developed into a planning tool. Temporary uses represent a sharp break with previous planning practice in that a kind of appropriation of space that was once perceived to be illegitimate and motivated attempts to stop it was now put to strategic use and later legitimized by building codes. This type of usage has gained increasing significance in municipal practice (cf., e.g., Senatsverwaltung für Stadtentwicklung Berlin 2007) and has drawn considerable attention from an expert public (BMVBS and BBR 2008; Haydn and Temel 2006; Kauzick 2007).

The field of regional development: 'Learning-region policies'

A key innovation in the field of regional development in recent decades has been a shift toward improving regional adaptability instead of attempting to make regions fit a particular model of development (Grabher 1994). This has led to municipal governments abandoning the focus on regional development as a 'catch-up' process along a predefined trajectory in favor of changing the development trajectory itself by means of a reflexive process of negotiating regional circumstances and future options of development. A prototypical example of this 'innovation-oriented regional policy' strategy (Ewers and Wettmann 1978)—designed to not only address the economy but also the dimensions of culture and social integration—was formulated and implemented for the first time in the context of the Internationale Bauausstellung (IBA) Emscher Park (Emscher Park International Building Exhibition, 1989-1999). The IBA pursued a multifaceted approach to regional development that sought to integrate several classic areas of planning, such as housing, landscape design, and commercial development (Häußermann and Siebel 1994a, 1994b). In the process, this tradition of German architectural and planning history has been turned into a regional policy instrument that has helped to initiate regional learning processes, at multiple levels and in various dimensions, that revolve around the exemplary transformation of an old industrial area in the Northern

Ruhr region. Since then, this model of a reflexive regional policy approach has clearly moved beyond its initial context of emergence and has evolved further (cf., e.g., Beierlorzer 2010). Internationally this shift has best been characterized by the notion of a 'learning region' (Morgan 1997).

4.2 Steps in the Research Process and Methodological Procedure

We have investigated these four fields of action in three steps by applying the same research questions and following roughly the same methodological procedure in all four areas. There are some minor variations in the details of the methodological tools to accommodate differences in the nature of the objects under study in the specific fields of action.

Step 1 was devoted to reconstructing ex post the major features of the process of innovation in the field in question and distinguishing its phases. The respective phases have been characterized in terms of crucial nodes and structural characteristics (places, projects, people, institutions, programs). We specified when, where, and under which circumstances the new ideas, concepts, modes of action, and pilot projects emerged in expert debate and became a topic among the wider public (and, in the event of international points of reference that are mentioned in the documents, whether they were or are being imported or exported), as well as when and how they were discussed, adopted, and modified (the 'trajectories' question set). We also inquired into the role of actor constellations and organizational arrangements (the 'structural characteristics' question set) and how the innovations under study formed into norms, guiding visions, and universalized concepts (the 'institutional manifestation' question set).

Data collection and analysis in step 1 involved several methods. The innovation process was reconstructed by subjecting documents collected nationwide and qualitative interviews with experts to quantitative and qualitative discourse analysis informed by a sociology of knowledge approach to discourse (Keller 2008). For each of the four fields of action, we used well-established methods (cf. Prior 2003; Wolff 2008) to analyze various types of documents from four fields of discourse: science, politics, planning practice, and public media. The types of documents were professional journals and books, reviews, conference programs, proceedings, and reports, documentations of competitions, official notices of state agencies and public institutions, brochures, and press releases. In analyzing these documents, we placed great importance on considering their chronology. They must not be reinterpreted ex post in light of later knowledge about the course of events. Only in this way can the dynamics, discontinuities, or setbacks in these processes of innovation be worked out. In addition, approximately ten expert interviews in each field of action were conducted with key individuals who had been involved in shaping, negotiating, or establishing the innovation in question at the national level either as participants or critical observers. These individuals are, for instance, federal government or state-level experts who reflect on these issues, decision-makers of organizations and associations, key actors prominently involved in planning, representatives of urban and regional research, and journalists. In conducting the expert interviews, we also drew on well-established methods (cf. Kvale 2007; Bogner et al. 2009; Gläser and Laudel 2010).

Step 2 served to reconstruct the innovation process in the four fields of action on the basis of two to three case studies at specific sites that are known to have or have had a special significance for the emergence, implementation, or establishment of an innovation process in its entirety. At this point, we thus investigated in detail the phases, actor constellations, crucial stimuli, organizational arrangements, influential factors, and institutional manifestations for specific local segments.

Here we applied the same methodological toolbox, which consists of document analyses and expert interviews as in step 1, yet with a stronger emphasis on interviews. The experts interviewed were responsible politicians and policy-makers in selected municipalities or regions, representatives of organizations involved in the issue (e.g., funding bodies or housing associations), and, not least, representatives of citizens' groups. Who actually qualifies as an expert depends on the specific issue and case study in question. Suitable individuals were identified and chosen by means of a snowball sampling procedure. The guided interviews (between six and ten per case study) revolved around questions such as, how did the idea at the heart of the new object of planning or planning procedure come into being, and how was it further developed, negotiated, and implemented locally? The document analyses served to compile additional information that the interviewees might have forgotten. For this purpose, we consulted plans, files, documentations, project outlines, and professional publications. Conversely, the expert interviews provided information that is not documented, not completely documented, or even misrepresented in other sources.

In *step 3* of the research process, the findings of the studies in the individual fields of action—from the nationwide studies of the fields as a whole (step 1) as well as the local and regional analyses (step 2)—were drawn together and subjected to a comparative analysis across all four fields. Comparing the commonalities and differences provided us with opportunities to draw conceptual conclusions on the typical course of innovation processes in spatial planning.

5 On Intentionality in the Innovation of Planning. Early Findings in Selected Fields of Action

This section presents early findings from step 1 of our research project devoted to reconstructing the innovation process (nationwide) for each of the four selected fields of action. We will focus on some of the findings for our research question that pertains to structural characteristics of innovations in planning (see our second research question, given in section 4). Aspects of this question are which actors were involved, to what extent the innovations in planning that they developed can be described as an intentional process, and how the reflexivity of this process can be characterized.

It became apparent—this much can be said in anticipation of the final results—that the key actors made a clearly intentional and reflexive effort to arrive at new and, above all, 'better' solutions or practices. That said, it also became clear that non-intentional factors—we might speak of 'incidental events' conducive to the process—were of great significance as well. In the following, we will outline this finding in more detail for the four selected fields of action.

In the field of neighborhood management, it was initially the practitioners of urban renewal planning, but also social workers, who from the mid-1970s on *intended* to find alternative (i.e., 'better') solutions, yet without deliberately seeking to produce 'innovations.' These actors were motivated to a high degree by the shortcomings in the existing set of planning tools that they experienced in their respective professional field, which were intended to achieve social objectives yet lacked the means to effectively address the mounting, spatially increasingly concentrated social problems in the neighborhoods. Another group of actors was social scientists who provided their expertise in the form of expert opinions, publications, and policy advice. Their scientific expertise furnished an explanatory framework on which other actors could draw when criticizing the status quo and searching for alternatives. The first steps in the emergence of neighborhood management were therefore intentional acts in that they can be described as professional, social scientifically mediated learning processes with a specific objective. It can be shown how the debates in the various disciplines began to converge: urban sociology turned to the study of planning issues (sociology of urban planning), the planning sciences directed their attention to social processes (community-oriented planning), and social work became increasingly aware of the spatial dimension of social problems (community-oriented social work, community organizing). In this first phase, individual actors sought to deliberately influence policy-making and, at least in some German states, were quite successful in terms of the practical implementation of their preferred policies. To this extent, neighborhood management can be viewed as the result of intentional efforts and professional learning.

Yet, at the same time, we also observed *non-intentional* conditions that had to be fulfilled to enable the breakthrough of the integrated neighborhood management approach. After the first pilot projects (IBA Berlin, 1984-1987), pertinent events occurred and discourses emerged in the 1980s and early 1990s that created extraordinarily favorable conditions for implementing neighborhood management. Even though some of the actors—for instance, the state of North Rhine-Westphalia (in 1993)—rightly stressed their contribution to the establishment of neighborhood management by having brought their political influence to bear at the EU level in Brussels, it was only to a very limited extent that these activities directly yielded any conclusive results. What they did do, however, is indirectly lay the groundwork for further progress in establishing this instrument. The process was facilitated, first and foremost, by the intense debates around issues of coping with structural change in Germany's old industrial regions and the increasing financial straits of the affected municipalities. These debates made it clear that simply perpetuating previous urban development policies was unlikely to yield satisfying results. Moreover, the gradual redefinition and reorganization of the European Structural Funds (from regional development to urban and district-level development) was also a key factor. Only thereafter was it possible to go beyond merely proposing an integrated approach, as the EU Commission did, and provide the criteria required and program funding earmarked for the respective pilot projects (URBAN) and exchanges of experience (URBACT) (cf. Koczy 2015).

The criticism of the functionalist modernist conception of urban development in the form of large-scale residential complexes that began to surface in the 1960s did not originate in the field of planning but rather in other disciplines (journalism, social sciences, and others) or came directly from the residents of those complexes. Among the important points of criticism were their monofunctionality ('dormitory towns', original: 'Schlafstädte'), the insufficient and belated provision of private and public infrastructure, and the lack of usable and attractive public spaces. Against this backdrop, planning practitioners at various levels and in different areas (spatial morphological, functional, etc.) soon began to engage in an active search for better solutions. However, since there was no longer a need for large-scale housing development in the years that followed, new concepts were initially developed only for certain segments, particularly in the context of urban renewal or as 'improvements' to the large housing complexes. This can nevertheless be interpreted as the profession of planning deliberately departing from established routines. In this context, the Internationale Bauausstellung Berlin (Berlin International Architecture Exhibition, 1979-1987) provided a prominent framework that was actively utilized to develop prototypes that drew on and modified the 19th-century repertoire of urban development (block construction, corridor streets, and so on). Although the semantics of innovation did not play a role here, the shift in terminology from *Siedlung* (settlement) to *Quartier* (neighborhood) nevertheless reflected this break. The fact that, in the course of establishing and disseminating the innovation, an actor network formed—largely mediated by a new generation taking a leadership role—that made a deliberate effort to overcome resistance and solidify the acceptance of the new practices can also be described in terms of an *intentionally motivated* process.

However, it was external circumstances and thus *non-intentional* factors that ultimately accounted for the concept's rapid breakthrough. The swift dissemination of the new guiding vision of the compact city of mixed uses only became possible once the emerging shortage of new housing in the early 1990s in the wake of German reunification caused large West German cities to once again plan an abundance of new neighborhoods. What could be demonstrated only in an exemplary, piecemeal fashion in the years prior could now be implemented in the building of these new neighborhoods—mostly by drawing on the results of urban development competitions—and became the new standard: perimeter blocks instead of *Zeilenbau* development (building in rows), creation of opportunities for local employment at a smaller scale, adherence to the principle of mixed development, and clear-cut separation of public and private open spaces (cf. Zupan 2015).

In the field of urban restructuring (temporary uses), new ways of appropriating spaces by members of the counterculture, artists, and other creative types formed the seedbed of innovation. Although these actors were primarily concerned with realizing their individual conceptions of life, their activities provided a living example of how the opportunity structures provided by vacant spaces and empty buildings could be utilized (temporarily) for various cultural projects. These projects that had evolved since the 1970s were neither perceived as 'temporary uses' nor as 'innovations' by the users at the time; yet, since the 1990s if not before, these so-called 'temporary-use projects' were increasingly labelled as innovative by journalists and social scientists. This lent these temporary uses an aura of innovativeness.

The IBA Emscher Park (from 1989 on) was the framework in which these temporary uses were *deliberately* utilized in the context of spatial development for the first time. The IBA actors *had the intention* of utilizing temporary cultural projects to plant the seed for later uses and initiate a spatial revitalization of the many vacant and unused spaces in those parts of the Ruhr region that were particularly hard hit by deindustrialization. Interestingly enough, the IBA Emscher

Park's effort to this end was never discussed in terms of representing an innovation in planning.

The systematic incorporation of procedures for temporary uses as a tool in spatial planning and the diffusion of this new type of planning practice occurred only by virtue of other developments that must be considered to be *non-intentional* factors in the innovation process. A crucial development in this context was the phenomenon of 'shrinking cities,' which was first perceived in the 1990s. In East Germany in particular, vast numbers of vacancies and tight public budgets called for creative planning tools in urban restructuring. Young planning scholars—inspired by temporary-use projects in Berlin—proposed employing temporary uses as a tool to address certain types of vacancies. These Berlin projects were framed as 'innovative.' However, it was not until the late 1990s, once the problem of urban shrinkage had come to a head, that the city of Leipzig began to deliberately experiment with temporary uses. To make this a manageable tool for planning, the city introduced a usage agreement—the so-called *Gestattungsvereinbarung*—in 1999. This agreement created a contractual basis for temporary uses of spaces and became a model for other cities. Other non-intentional factors were the European Union's URBAN programs (1994-1999), which were not developed specifically for the purpose of such temporary uses but could also be used for funding such projects. Another such factor was the amendment of the German Building Code in 2004, which involved the introduction of a temporary construction permit in art. 9, para. 2. The goal of this amendment was to shorten the cycles of commercial real estate usage and not primarily to support the employment of procedures for temporary uses in planning. Yet, in effect, this legal provision facilitated the use of these planning procedures. Not least, the discourse revolving around the concept of the 'creative city' was a significant factor in the diffusion of this planning innovation. In the wake of Richard Florida's theses on the significance of the creative class for urban development, temporary uses were increasingly framed as an expression of creativity. Henceforth, not just shrinking or poor cities but also growing or prosperous ones became interested in temporary use as a planning tool. These latter cities now hoped to enhance their attractiveness via creative experiments (cf. Honeck 2015).

The field of regional development (learning-region policies) was marked by a very deliberate, highly *intentional* search for better solutions in which professionals, particularly those from the fields of regional planning and economic development, pushed for strengthening cooperative forms of policy-making at the regional level. Their professionally motivated intent was directed against a parochial politics, which was considered to be geared to the short-term cycles of election periods and to be of limited effectiveness because of an approach to dealing with problems that ends at the city limits. In North Rhine-Westphalia, there were attempts to introduce new instruments to overcome these unsatisfactory limitations as early as in the second half of 1980s—for instance, the 'Regional Conferences' as part of the Zukunftsinitiative Montanregion (ZIM; Initiative for the Future of the Coal and Steel Region) or Zukunftsinitiative für die Regionen Nordrhein-Westfalens (ZIN; Initiative for the Future of the Regions of North Rhine-Westphalia). In Lower Saxony, there was some experimentation with regional development agencies, but this too yielded results that were still unsatisfactory. These approaches attracted criticism for their one-sided focus on economic development and their ineffectiveness in bringing about structural change, which owed to their emphasis on seeking consensus and their lack of a suitable funding model.

In addition to the first deliberate attempts to search for and experiment with alternatives, this field of action was, however, also marked by the presence of conducive events and processes that were not *pursued intentionally*. For instance, enormous pressing problems of deindustrialization in the Ruhr region in the late 1980s led to establishing the IBA Emscher Park, which would later turn out to be a window of opportunity for implementing reflexive regional policy strategies. The IBA Emscher Park had no intention of advancing regional policy approaches. The objective of the responsible ministry of urban development was instead to implement a program for the development of vacant properties in public ownership. This involved addressing two key problems that had already been an important issue in the first attempts to develop learning-region policies in North Rhine-Westphalia but could not be solved at the time. The first problem was securing the cooperation of municipal bodies when it came to policies transcending administrative boundaries, and the second one was finding solutions with an innovative edge. A unique approach of providing support and funding managed to overcome, in an exemplary manner, key weaknesses of the initial attempts toward a reflexive regional policy quasi in passing. An open call for project applications and the subsequent selection of projects according to quality criteria ensured that only projects with innovative potential were included in the IBA Emscher Park. The chosen projects received ongoing assistance by the IBA planning agency throughout the whole project development process to further enhance promising ideas. Furthermore, as the federal state government decided that all existing state programs should provide priority funding for IBA projects, there were strong incentives for municipalities to cooperate on IBA projects so that funding for innovative initiatives could be secured. Although IBA Emscher Park was not initiated with the primary intention of addressing problems of regional policy, such a connection was frequently made in later discourse (cf. Füg 2015).

As indicated above, all four fields of planning illustrate that the activities of the actors involved in each field displayed a clear intent to improve upon previous practices. In all four cases, this intent of improvement was motivated by public awareness of and discourse on the need to address pressing problems, partly supported by social scientific diagnoses and expertise, which altogether attests to a high level of reflexivity. At the same time, it is noticeable that the motive of developing an 'innovation' played only a secondary role, if at all, among the actors involved in planning.

In the case of temporary use, it was journalists and scholars from the social and planning sciences who, in the early stages of the innovation process, observing from the outside, attributed innovativeness to the changes in practices (whether on the part of the temporary users or the planning practitioners first to make use of them). It was only later that the planning practitioners themselves referred to the tool of temporary use in spatial planning as 'innovative'—at least in regard to individual projects such as Tempelhofer Freiheit in Berlin. However, this only happened once the tool as such had already become an established instrument of planning. It is nevertheless true for all of the planning fields under study that the intention to develop innovations was typically not at the forefront of action in the early stages of the innovation process. Rather, the primary objective was to find alternative ways of doing things to 'improve' a situation deemed problematic and/or an outdated practice. This does not hide the fact that the attempt to bring about improvement resulted in practices that clearly broke with established modes of action and thus can be characterized as innovations (see our description of novel practices in the four fields of action above; cf. section 4). In view of the planning innovations in our study, we can thus conclude in summary that they are characterized by high reflexivity in terms of changing established practices but low reflexivity in terms of developing an innovation.

It is also worth noting that action specifically geared to achieving a particular change or improvement is only one aspect of the innovation process. Another aspect is the manifold non-intentional events and processes that form the context of and can have a major influence on a specific innovation process. Our analyses of the selected fields of action indicate that the non-intended factors are at least as important for the implementation and diffusion of novel practices as the intended measures themselves. The example of IBA Emscher Park, which played a role in the fields of urban restructuring (temporary uses) and regional development (reflexive regional policy), showed that, oddly enough, it was ultimately not the initial experimentation with temporary uses by the highly reflective IBA planning agency that gave the decisive impulse for the establishment and diffusion of temporary use as an innovation in planning. Interestingly enough, this exhibition had a much greater impact on another innovation in planning—namely, reflexive regional policy—even though the measures developed in the IBA context were not even designed with this field in mind. The discourse on new practices in regional development, in which the significance of IBA Emscher Park was typically emphasized, attests to this. This example suggests that the dynamics of innovation processes in the field of planning are difficult to control.

This impression is supported by our empirical findings that innovation processes in the four fields of planning evolved over the course of decades and thus exhibit long timelines of development. It is also worth noting that these innovation processes involve complex actor constellations that can feature changing compositions at different points in time and can offer different opportunities for exerting influence accordingly (cf. Ibert et al. 2015).

6 Concluding Remarks

This contribution has aimed to show why and how concepts of innovation can be put to productive use in research in the field of spatial planning. For this purpose, we have presented conceptual considerations and the methodological design of a project funded by the German Research Foundation. The goal of the *InnoPlan* project is to employ practical examples to understand the emergence, implementation, and diffusion of innovations in spatial planning. To this end, we chose urban development, urban restructuring, neighborhood development, and regional development as fields of action for study. We have used a generic notion of (spatial) planning in the process and referred to the concept of social innovation. The project pursues questions about the trajectories (temporal dimension), structural characteristics (organizational dimension), and manifestations (institutional dimension) of innovation processes.

The initial results of the investigation attest to the fruitfulness of the approach presented here. New developments in spatial planning can be seen as social innovations: Even though any talk of innovation in the self-descriptions of those involved—and often even in the descriptions of others—was rarely a motive actually guiding action in the investigated cases, all the novel practices display elements of social innovation (in spite of all the differences between the four fields of action). Such elements of social innovation are present, for instance, in self-attributions of having engaged in a conflictual process of improving deficient planning tools or procedures, or in the paradox of institutionalization, and in many other practices. In short, it seems that we must assume that social innovations frequently unfold 'outside the limelight of attention' (Rammert 2010: 36, our translation).

References

Albrechts, Louis. 2004. "Strategic (Spatial) Planning Reexamined." *Environment and Planning B: Planning and Design* 31(5): 743-758.

Balconi, Margherita, Stefano Brusoni, and Luigi Orsenigo. 2010. "In Defence of the Linear Model: An Essay." *Research Policy* 39(1): 1-13.

Bayliss, Darrin. 2004. "Creative Planning in Ireland: The Role of Culture-led Development in Irish Planning." *European Planning Studies* 12(4): 497-515.

BBR (Bundesamt für Bauwesen und Raumordnung). 2007. *Neue Stadtquartiere. Bestand und städtebauliche Qualitäten. Vorgehen und Ergebnisse der laufenden Bestandserhebungen des BBR zu neuen Stadtquartieren* (BBR-Online-Publikation Nr. 01/2007). Bonn: BBR. Retrieved October, 15 2014 (http://www.bbsr.bund.de/BBSR/DE/Veroeffentlichungen/BBSROnline/2007/DL_NeueStadtquartiere.pdf?__blob=publicationFile&v=2).

Beierlorzer, Henry. 2010. "The Regionale. A Regional Approach to Stabilizing Structurally Weak Urban Peripheries Applied to the Southern Fringe of the Metropolitan Area Rhine-Ruhr." *disP—The Planning Review* 46: 80-88.

BMVBS and BBR. 2008. *Zwischennutzungen und Nischen im Städtebau als Beitrag für eine nachhaltige Stadtentwicklung* (Werkstatt Praxis, Heft 57). Berlin, Bonn: BMVBS, BBR.

Bogner, Alexander, Beate Littig, and Wolfgang Menz, eds. 2009. *Experteninterviews. Theorien, Methoden, Anwendungsfelder*. Wiesbaden: VS Verlag.

Braun-Thürmann, Holger. 2005. *Innovation*. Bielefeld: Transcript.

Christmann, Gabriela B. and Kerstin Büttner. 2011. "Raumpioniere, Raumwissen, Kommunikation—zum Konzept kommunikativer Raumkonstruktion." *Berichte zur deutschen Länderkunde* 85(4): 361-378.

Christmann, Gabriela B., Oliver Ibert, Johann Jessen, and Uwe-Jens Walther. 2016. *Innovation in Spatial Planning as a Social Process—Phases, Actors, Conflicts and Mobility*. Paper presented at the 5th Symposium on Culture, Creativity and Economy, Seville, Spain, October 6–8.

Deutsches Institut für Urbanistik. 2003. *Strategien für die Soziale Stadt. Erfahrungen und Perspektiven—Umsetzung des Bund-Länder-Programms "Stadtteile mit besonderem Entwicklungsbedarf—die soziale Stadt."* Berlin: DIFU.

Dubiel, Helmut. 1999. "Integration durch Konflikt?" Pp. 132-143 in *Soziale Integration. Sonderheft 39 der Kölner Zeitschrift für Soziologie und Sozialpsychologie*, edited by J. Friedrichs and W. Jagodzinski. Opladen: Westdeutscher Verlag.

Ewers, Hans-Jürgen and Reinhart W. Wettmann. 1978. "Innovationsorientierte Regionalpolitik. Überlegungen zu einem regionalstrukturellen Politik- und Forschungsprogramm." *Informationen zur Raumentwicklung* (7): 467-483.

Faludi, Andreas. 1985. "A Decision-Centred View of Environmental Planning." *Landscape Planning* 12(3): 239-256.

Füg, Franz. 2015. "Reflexive Regionalpolitik als soziale Innovation. Vom Blick in die Sackgasse zur kollektiven Neuerfindung." *Informationen zur Raumentwicklung* (3): 245-259.

Gillwald, Katrin. 2000. *Konzepte sozialer Innovation* (Working Papers P00-519). Berlin: Wissenschaftszentrum Berlin für Sozialforschung.

Gläser, Jochen and Grit Laudel. 2010. *Experteninterviews und qualitative Inhaltsanalyse als Instrumente rekonstruierender Untersuchungen*. Wiesbaden: VS Verlag.

Grabher, Gernot. 1994. *Lob der Verschwendung: Redundanz in der Regionalentwicklung*. Berlin: Edition Sigma.

Güntner, Simon. 2007. *Soziale Stadtpolitik. Institutionen, Netzwerke und Diskurse in der Politikgestaltung*. Bielefeld: transcript.

Hafner, Thomas, Barbara Wohn, and Karin Rebholz-Chaves. 1998. *Wohnsiedlungen. Entwürfe. Typen, Erfahrungen aus Deutschland, Österreich und der Schweiz*. Basel: Birkhäuser.

Häußermann, Hartmut. 2005. "Das Programm 'Stadtteile mit besonderem Entwicklungsbedarf—die soziale Stadt.' Gesamtbewertung und Empfehlungen der Zwischenevaluation 2003/2004." *Informationen zur Raumentwicklung* (2/3): 75-86.

Häußermann, Hartmut and Walter Siebel. 1994a. "Die Kulturalisierung der Regionalpolitik." *Geographische Rundschau* 45(4): 218-223.

Häußermann, Hartmut and Walter Siebel. 1994b. "Wie organisiert man Innovationen in nicht innovativen Milieus?" Pp. 52-62 in *Bauplatz Zukunft. Dispute über die Entwicklung von Industrieregionen* , edited by R. Kreibich et al. Essen: Klartext Verlag.

Häussling, Roger. 2007. "Sozialwissenschaftliche Innovationsforschung: Zum aktuellen Umgang der Gesellschaft mit dem Neuen." *Soziologische Revue* 30(4): 369-382.

Haydn, Florian and Robert Temel, eds. 2006. *Temporäre Räume. Konzepte zur Stadtnutzung*. Basel: Birkhäuser.

Healey, Patsy. 1997. "The Revival of Strategic Planning in Europe." Pp. 3-19 in *Making Strategic Plans: Innovation in Europe*, edited by P. Healey, A. Khakee, A. Motte, and B. Needha. London: Routledge.

Honeck, Thomas. 2015. "Zwischennutzung als soziale Innovation. Von alternativen Lebensentwürfen zu Verfahren der räumlichen Planung." *Informationen zur Raumentwicklung* (3): 219-231.

Howaldt, Jürgen and Michael Schwarz. 2010. *"Soziale Innovation" im Fokus. Skizze eines gesellschaftstheoretisch inspirierten Forschungskonzepts*. Bielefeld: transcript.

Hutter, Michael, Hubert Knoblauch, Werner Rammert, and Arnold Windeler. This volume. "Innovation Society Today. The Reflexive Creation of Novelty."

Ibert, Oliver. 2003. *Innovationsorientierte Planung. Verfahren und Strategien zur Organisation von Innovation*. Opladen: Leske und Budrich.

Ibert, Oliver and Felix C. Müller. 2015. Network Dynamics in Constellations of Cultural Differences. Relational Distance in Innovation Processes in Legal Services and Biotechnology. *Research Policy* 44(1): 181-194.

Ibert, Oliver, Gabriela Christmann, Johann Jessen, and Uwe-Jens Walther. 2015. "Innovationen in der räumlichen Planung." *Informationen zur Raumentwicklung* (3): 171-182.

Jessen, Johann. 2004. "Europäische Stadt als Bausteinkasten für die Städtebaupraxis—die neuen Stadtteile." Pp. 92-104 in *Die europäische Stadt*, edited by W. Siebel. Frankfurt a. M.: Suhrkamp.

Kauzick, Maren. 2007. *Zwischennutzung als Initiator einer neuen Berliner Identität?* (Grey Series nr. 7). Berlin: Institut für Stadt- und Regionalplanung. Retrieved October 16, 2014 (http://opus4.kobv.de/opus4-tuberlin/files/1702/Graue_Reihe_Heft_7_Zwischennutzung.pdf.).

Keller, Reiner. 2008. *Wissenssoziologische Diskursanalyse. Grundlegung eines Forschungsprogramms*. Wiesbaden: VS Verlag.

Kline, Stephen J. and Nathan Rosenberg. 1986. "An Overview of Innovation." Pp. 275-305 in *The Positive Sum Strategy: Harnessing Technology for Economic Growth*, edited by R. Landau and N. Rosenberg. Washington: National Academy Press.

Knorr Cetina, Karin. 2001. "Objectual Practice." Pp. 175-188 in *The Practice Turn in Contemporary Theory*, edited by T. R. Schatzki, K. Knorr Cetina, and E. von Savigny. London: Routledge.

Koczy, Oliver. 2015. "Neue Akteure im Stadtteil. Entstehungslinien des Quartiersmanagements." *Informationen zur Raumentwicklung* (3): 273-285.

Kunzmann, Klaus R. 2004. "Culture, Creativity and Spatial Planning." *Town Planning Review* 75(4): 383-404.

Kvale, Steinar. 2007. *Doing Interviews*. London: Sage.

Lindhult, Eric. 2008. "Are Partnerships Innovative?" Pp. 37-54 in *Partnership—As a Strategy for Social Innovation and Sustainable Change*, edited by L. Svensson & B. Nilsson. Stockholm: Satéruns Academic Press.

Luhmann, Niklas. 1971. *Politische Soziologie. Aufsätze zur Soziologie von Politik und Verwaltung*. Opladen: Westdeutscher Verlag.

Martens, Helmut. 2010. "Beteiligung als soziale Innovation." Pp. 371-390 in *Soziale Innovation. Auf dem Weg zu einem postindustriellen Innovationsparadigma*, edited by J. Howaldt & H. Jacobsen. Wiesbaden: VS Verlag.

Mayer, Sabine. 1999. *Relationale Raumplanung. Ein institutioneller Ansatz für flexible Regulierung*. Marburg: Metropolis-Verlag.

McCann, Eeugene and Kevin Ward. 2010. "Relationality/Territoriality: Toward a Conceptualization of Cities in the World." *Geoforum* 41(2): 175-184.

McFarlane, Colin. 2006. "Knowledge, Learning and Development: A Post-Rationalist Approach." *Progress in Development Studies* 6(4): 287-305.

Morgan, Kevin. 1997. "The Learning Region: Instititions, Innovation and Regional Renewal." *Regional Studies* 31(5): 491-503.

Moulaert, Frank, Bob Jessop, Lars Hulgard, and Abdelillah Hamdouch. 2013. "Social Innovation Research: A New Stage in Innovation Analysis?" Pp. 110-130 in *The International Handbook on Social Innovation: Collective Action, Social Learning and Transdisciplinary Research*, edited by F. Moulaert, D. MacCallum, A. Mehmood, & A. Hamdouch. Cheltenham: Edward Elgar.

Neff, Gina, and David Stark. 2003. "Permanently Beta: Responsive Organization in the Internet Era." Pp. 173-188 in *The Internet and American Life*, edited by P. N. Howard & S. Jones. Thousand Oaks: Sage.

Neuloh, Otto, ed. 1977. *Soziale Innovation und sozialer Konflikt*. Göttingen: Vandenhoeck & Ruprecht.

Ogburn, William F. 1937. "National Policy and Technology." Pp. 3-14 in *Technological Trends and National Policy, Including the Social Implications of New Inventions*, edited by National Resources Committee. Washington: United States Government Printing Office.

Peck, Jamie and Nik Theodore. 2010. "Recombinant Workfare, Across the Americas." *Geoforum* 41(2): 195-208.

Prior, Lindsay. 2003. *Using Documents in Social Research*. London: Sage.

Rammert, Werner. 2010. "Die Innovationen der Gesellschaft." Pp. 21-51 in *Soziale Innovationen. Auf dem Weg zu einem post-industriellen Innovationsparadigma*, edited by J. Howaldt and H. Jakobsen. Wiesbaden: Springer VS.

Schumpeter, Joseph A. 1934 [1912]. *The Theory of Economic Development*. Cambridge, MA: Harvard University Press.

Selle, Klaus. 2005. *Planen. Steuern. Entwickeln. Der Beitrag öffentlicher Akteure zur räumlichen Entwicklung von Stadt und Land*. Dortmund: Verlag Dorothea Rohn.

Senatsverwaltung für Stadtentwicklung Berlin, ed. 2007. *Urban Pioneers*. Berlin: Jovis.

Siebel, Walter. 2006. "Wandel, Rationalität und Dilemmata der Planung." *Planung neu denken* (4). Retrieved May 19, 2011(http://www.planung-neu-denken.de/content/view/40/41).

Suchman, Lucy. 1987. *Plans and Situated Action: The Problem of Human-Machine Interaction*. Cambridge: Cambridge University Press.

Walther, Uwe-Jens, ed. 2002. *Soziale Stadt—Zwischenbilanzen: Ein Programm auf dem Weg zur sozialen Stadt?* Opladen: Leske und Budrich.

Walther, Uwe-Jens. 2004. "Innovation durch Ambivalenz? Das Programm "Stadtteile mit besonderem Entwicklungsbedarf. Die soziale Stadt." Pp. 111-124 in *Praxis ohne Theorie? Wissenschaftliche Diskurse zum Bund-Länder-Programm Stadtteile mit besonderem Entwicklungsbedarf. Die soziale Stadt*, editey by S. Greiffenhagen and K. Neller. Opladen: Leske und Budrich.

Walther, Uwe-Jens and Simon Güntner. 2005. "Vom überforderten Fachprogramm zurück zur Stadtpolitik." *Informationen zur Raumentwicklung* (2/3): 183-192.

Wiechmann, Thorsten. 2008. *Planung und Adaption. Strategieentwicklung in Regionen, Organisationen und Netzwerken*. Dortmund: Verlag Dorothea Rohn.

Wiechmann, Thorsten. 2010. "Warum Pläne nicht ausreichen. Zur Übertragbarkeit von Managementansätzen auf regionale Governanceprozesse." Pp. 17-41 in *Strategische Planung. Zur Rolle der Planung in der Strategieentwicklung für Städte und Regionen* (Reihe Planungsrundschau Nr. 18), edited by G. Hutter and T. Wiechmann. Berlin: Altrock.

Wolff, Stephan. 2008. "Dokumenten und Aktenanalyse." Pp. 502-513 in *Qualitative Forschung*, edited by U. Flick, E. von Kardorff, and I. Steinke. Reinbek near Hamburg: Rowohlt.

Zapf, Wolfgang. 1989. "Über soziale Innovationen." *Soziale Welt* 40(1-2): 170-183.

Zupan, Daniela. 2015. Von der Großwohnsiedlung der Spätmoderne zum kompakten nutzungsgemischten Stadtquartier. Verlaufsformen eines städtebaulichen Erneuerungsprozesses. *Informationen zur Raumentwicklung* (3): 183-199.

Germany's *Energiewende*

Path Disruption or Reinforcement of the Established Path?

Johann Köppel

1 The Challenge

There are but few areas in innovation society that are currently subject to such profound renewal and in such a state of flux as the energy sector. A semantics of novelty—*Energiewende* (energy transition)—is the theme tune to a multifaceted process of fundamental change at the interface of innovation and environmental policy (Foxon and Pearson 2008). At the least, the *Energiewende* has also long become a European transition (Sühlsen and Hisschemöller 2014), and the iconic term as such even seems to have gained international currency. More than two-thirds of the EU member states have issued a national feed-in tariff system for renewable energy modeled predominantly on the German example (Sühlsen and Hisschemöller 2014). Even promotional schemes based on a more market-driven approach, such as those in France (Nadai 2007) or, similarly, in the UK (Bruns et al. 2008, 2011), have switched to the German course of action. In many cases, the forces driving this development are social constructs such as climate change or crisis-tainted perceptions of the predominant fossil and nuclear energy systems. Negotiating the transformation of an entire energy system (Strunz 2014) simultaneously changes the social perceptions of the resulting alternative paths of technological development; this pertains specifically to wind and solar power as well as expansion of the grid and the storage infrastructure.

This involves the respective actor constellations and their values and beliefs that are specific to the technologies and locations in question (Aas et al. 2014; Bidwell 2013) and that may be in line or in conflict with certain paths of development and influence these accordingly. Research on the social acceptance of the transformation of the energy system has demonstrated the need to distinguish between acceptance in principle and concrete acceptance of innovation and diffusion in the context of specific projects (ibid.). Whereas there is widespread general agreement that a large-scale transition at the global and national level is needed, people are often opposed to dynamic change that affects them locally (cf. Devine-Wright 2013). In this context, there are frequently surprising interrelations that are difficult to predict.

In their 'innovation biographies' of renewable energy sources, Bruns et al. (2008, 2011) depicted the ongoing transformation of the German energy system as a success story. One of the crucial factors was the innovative power of crises, initially the catastrophe of Chernobyl and later of Fukushima.[1] These events triggered social or, rather, political interventions, among which was the introduction of a long-term guaranteed feed-in tariff for renewable energy sources (ibid.). With this in mind, the renewable energy biography could also have been described in terms of a successful actor constellation disrupting an established path by way of deliberation—a line of reasoning that I will address in the next section. Strictly speaking, it involved technological and political innovations on the one hand and the diffusion of technologies on the other, which were in turn supported by other innovations, such as those in the system of spatial planning and in judicial rulings. For instance, the German Federal Administrative Court issued a groundbreaking decision that now requires municipal zoning plans to provide substantive opportunity for wind power, which is to say that municipalities may not ipso facto prevent wind-power facilities by means of token planning (cf. BVerwG 2008). The Renewable Energy Sources Act (*Erneuerbare Energien Gesetz—EEG*) was also successful in establishing incentives to accelerate learning curves in technology development (feed-in tariffs that are degressive over time; Bruns et al. 2011).

However, over the years, the growing reflexivity of the innovations underlying the transition has proven to be a challenge that is difficult to manage. General consent to a scenario based on an ever-increasing density of energy infrastructure (in terms of production, transmission, and storage) can no longer be assured. At the heart of this chapter is the emergence of obstacles and the reflexive mode of dealing with them in the field of innovations associated with the *Energiewende*.

---

1 In the same vein, hazards (e.g., local earthquakes) can slow down individual innovations in the field of renewable energy as well, which is what has happened to geothermal energy (Bruns et al. 2011). Notable earthquakes that affected (conventional) natural gas production near Groningen in the Netherlands have raised questions of whether similar events must also be expected when dealing with unconventional modes of natural gas production such as fracking (van der Voort and Vanclay 2014).

This involves a new type of competition with the established system of fossil energy sources. At this point, it is not yet clear whether these obstacles are transitional phenomena or, for example, the promotion of carbon storage and unconventional shale gas production will ultimately reinvigorate the fossil system. We thus face increasingly complex perspectives, which Bruns et al. (2011) have approached empirically using the method of constellation analysis (Schön et al. 2007).

Initially, this approach was not particularly theory driven since the main issue was to subject innovation phenomena to thorough analyses and gain an initial understanding. Since then, there have been a number of studies that have addressed the transformation of such energy systems from the theoretical perspective of path dependence and path disruption. This also applies to wind power, an area in which our studies on innovation and diffusion have made the most progress so far (Bruns et al. 2008; Gartman et al. 2014; Geißler, Köppel, and Gunther 2013). The significance of 'innovation society' for the *Energiewende* becomes manifest in the manifold actor constellations and practices involved. The article concludes by raising the question, yet to be answered, of whether the disruption of the established path and the transition to a low-carbon energy system will be successful or whether we will ultimately experience a revival of the established path and thus a 're-lock-in'[2] as a result of the ongoing competition with the fossil energy industry and its innovations (carbon capture and storage [CCS], fracking).

2   Path Disruption and Path Dependence in the Transformation of Energy Systems

Path dependence can be defined in negative terms as processes that fail in ridding themselves of their past and therefore making it difficult for the new to prevail (in line with the work of W.B. Arthur, e.g., 1994 and P.A. David, e.g., 1985; Meyer and Schubert 2007). It can, however, also be defined as a characteristic of stochastic processes that results in lock-in under conditions marked by contingency and self-reinforcement in the absence of exogenous shocks (Vergne and Durand 2010). A case in point is the German energy supply, which was long concentrated in the hands of a few large companies with a steadfast commitment to fossil

---

2   Foxon (2013: 123), for instance, defines 'lock-in' as: "The situation in which past increasing returns for a system creates barriers to changes in that system." Del Rio and Unruh (2007: 1512) use the following metaphor: "In the case of energy technology, fossil fuel-based systems can be considered 'locked in' the house, while renewable energy is 'locked out' of the house and excluded."

and nuclear power generation. Only in the wake of crises (the oil crisis in the 1970s) and catastrophes (Chernobyl 1986, Fukushima 2011) were determined actor constellations able to set a new course for energy policy. What was once a niche constellation around the pioneering developments of renewable energy sources in Germany was deliberately established as a path that moved the advancement of these renewables to the center stage. Although the fossil actor constellation was still present, it could barely make itself heard or attract much appreciation for a long period of time (Bruns et al. 2008, 2011). The fact that exogenous shocks do not necessarily immediately trigger the transformation of energy systems in innovation societies has been shown by Wakiyama, Zusman, and Monogan III (2014) for post-Fukushima Japan.

Today, there is an increasing number of studies that have addressed the course of energy policy from a path perspective (e.g., Garud, Kumaraswamy, and Karnøe 2010). Karnøe and Garud (2012) described the development path of wind power in Denmark. Among other things, they confirmed the role of windows of opportunity that Bruns et al. (2008, 2011) observed for Germany. For instance, Danish manufacturers were there at the right time, ready to equip the new 'Californian gold rush'—which is to say, the early blossoming of wind power in California. Their study also demonstrated the role of artifacts and environmental factors in the Danish innovation path, for instance, with Danish manufacturers learning from flawed rotor blade designs and utilizing lessons to be learned from storms in improving them. Simmie (2012) also drew on the concepts of path dependence and path development in describing the path created by Denmark as the pioneer of wind power in Europe. Similarly to Bruns et al. in their study of the innovation biographies for Germany (Bruns et al. 2008, 2011), Simmie directed attention to the incremental innovations of early pioneers, the specific situation in rural Denmark with its lack of a centralized energy supply system, its history of enterprises, emerging institutional and political support, and obstacles to path development.

Hellström et al. (2013) investigated the early stages of large-scale projects, in this case Finnish nuclear power plants. They acknowledged actors' anticipatory capacity and thus their ability to establish paths and avoid (re-)lock-in. Their empirical approach applied an exploratory single-case design based on document analysis, more than 30 interviews with individuals directly involved in the establishment of nuclear energy in Finland, and seminars with these interviewees for the purpose of validating and further refining the findings. In essence, we chose a similar design in our analysis and interpretation of the roughly 30-year innovation biography of renewable energy sources in Germany.

3 Innovation Biographies of Renewable Energy Sources

In two research projects (funded by the Volkswagen Foundation and the German Federal Ministry for the Environment, Nature Conservation and Nuclear Safety), we have begun to comprehensively analyze and interpret the innovation biographies of the advancement of renewable energy sources in Germany (Bruns et al. 2008, 2011). The liberalized energy markets are one of the factors that have benefited this development (Nesta, Vona, and Nicolli 2014). Moreover, domestic production capacities as well as high oil prices are additional factors that are well suited to predict these innovation activities worldwide (Bayer, Dolan, and Urpelainen 2013). Darmani et al. (2014) have developed a typology of drivers of renewable energy technologies and underpinned it empirically for eight European countries (they studied wind, solar, biomass, and tidal power). Yet the innovation biographies of renewable energy sources in Germany (Bruns et al. 2011) have already been influenced by the staying power of the established, hitherto dominant fossil and nuclear constellation (the 'incumbents'; Fuchs 2014). For a long time, it seemed as if renewables would simply break out of their niche and triumph in an uncontested manner (ibid.). Innovation society hence appeared to live up to its name in grand fashion.

And yet, as pragmatic action has found itself entangled in an increasingly complex field of innovation (including the expansion of the grid and storage capacity), the transformation process has turned out to be a challenge that has become ever more difficult to manage. The development of renewable energy sources has benefited from a variety of different lines of reasoning ('frames') that all draw on a semantics of novelty and complement one another (from climate policy to employment, innovation, and industrial policy; Bruns et al. 2011), which has resulted in renewables largely being viewed throughout society as an innovation with positive connotations; at the very least, they are perceived to enable the phasing out of nuclear energy.[3] All positive connotations notwithstanding, renewables, too, do not come without concomitant circumstances of a non-intended and inhibiting kind, such as environmental impacts (Köppel et al. 2014; Schuster, Bulling, and Köppel 2015), and therefore also raise acceptance issues (Groth and Vogt 2014). We have traced these innovation biographies for Germany (Bruns et al. 2011) and

---

3   For instance, breaking with nuclear energy was also the primary aspect mentioned (in addition to general support for wind power) by those taking a favorable stance in a survey on the acceptance of wind turbines in forests (conducted as part of a bachelor's thesis, completed in 2014, by David Weiß with the Environmental Assessment & Planning Research Group at TU Berlin).

in an internationally comparative perspective (cf. Bechberger, Lutz, and Sohre 2008; Portman et al. 2009); however, the period of investigation ended around 2009/2010.

To get a better grasp of these developments from the angle of innovation society, we have turned to constellation analysis (Bruns et al. 2011; Schön et al. 2007). Constellation analysis identifies and investigates innovation phenomena by analyzing and interpreting the relations between technical components, natural factors, actors, and symbol systems (regulatory elements). In the process, the heterogeneous complexity of the systems under study are deliberately reduced to four categories (and 'mapped' accordingly to assist the analysis; see Figure 1):

- Technical components: relevant artifacts (visualized in blue)
- Symbol systems: policies, strategies, laws, communication, and economic parameters such as prices or taxes (red)
- Natural factors: biotic and abiotic components in the environment (biodiversity, soil, water, climate) (green)
- Actors: individuals or groups and institutions (yellow)

The focus of constellation analysis is on identifying factors that drive or inhibit innovation (Bruns et al. 2011). Our experience so far shows that the advancement of renewable energy sources has involved the confluence of a number of factors: connections between the various political levels, a harmonization of the instruments and processes of governance, the motivation of relevant actors, the promotion of interconnectedness and optimization of technical infrastructure, as well as innovations in planning and the economy.

The methodology of constellation analysis has been influenced not only by policy analysis but also by actor-network theory, which is capable of taking social, technical, and natural objects into account in characterizing socio-technical constellations (Latour 2005; Weyer 2008). This design makes it possible to identify coalitions (Sabatier and Jenkins-Smith 1993) and address relevant solutions in policy making and planning. The visualization of the elements and their relationships aids the understanding and an iterative discussion of the constellations under study. This methodology also refers to (exploratory) case studies (Yin 2014).

Discourse on the energy transition has come a long way. Present-day debate revolves less around just producing 'green' energy (e.g., wind and solar) as the primary issue of concern but rather acknowledges that expansion of both the grid and storage capacity must be viewed in concert and advanced simultaneously. In the North Sea, for instance, offshore wind farms were initially not able to go online for lack of connections to the grid. By contrast, offshore grid expansion off the coast of the Mid-Atlantic states in the USA (and the involvement of interesting private investment activities by Google) was planned early on before permission to erect even the first wind farm was granted (Lüdeke, Geißler, and Köppel 2012). In this case, however, it has been the planning of and investments in the offshore wind farms as such that have stagnated.

4 Recent Heterogeneous Constellations

The widespread support for an ever-denser energy infrastructure is becoming more and more nuanced (different degrees of support for certain goals of the energy transition, debates on siting issues, technologies, risks and dangers, declining real-estate value in the vicinity of overhead power lines, and so forth). The rapid growth of wind and solar power in Germany stimulated by the EEG (Renewable Energy Sources Act) has resulted in a steady increase in the complexity of the governance task. This requires transparent synchronization and communication, as frequent instances of sharp controversy and strong local resistance (Bräuer 2012; Zimmer, Kloke, and Gaedtke 2012) call for changes in the established practices. At the same time, policymakers have been slow to take innovative steps toward more systematic planning and governing the process in accordance with clearly defined expansion targets (Steinbach 2013). So far, participation processes have rather served information and consultation purposes ('tokenism') and lacked genuine opportunities to influence decision making, for example, in matters of routing new transmission lines and the choice of technology for grid expansion (Koch, Odparlik, and Köppel 2014). In the last instance, a fair participation process would imply that rerouting or abandoning a project altogether would also have to be an option (Ciupuliga and Cuppen 2013).

The literature also describes rather refined patterns of reasoning along the lines of an emerging NIMBY (not in my back yard) effect and discusses more elaborate research designs, for instance, those that take into account that fears of being perceived as NIMBYists might lead respondents to modify their responses accordingly (van der Horst 2007). In some cases, we observe long-enduring, deeply entrenched disapproval (Groth and Vogt 2014); in other cases—for instance, controversial offshore wind farms in the USA (Firestone et al. 2012)—there have been reports of increasing support among local residents over time that is motivated by a growing desire for energy autonomy. In a comparative case study, Sovacool and Ratan (2012) identified nine crucial factors for the acceptance of wind (Denmark,

India) and solar power (Germany, USA).[4] Jolivet and Heiskanen (2010: 6753) drew on framing and overflow models as applied in actor-network theory and saw requirements that demand high levels of reflexivity on part of the actors involved in the field. They spoke of "an actor who is continuously reframing and adapting his or her project to channel and stabilize the process of wind farm creation, and gradually make it a shared material reality that fits its environment." A long-debated wind farm in the Hunsrück mountains is a case that displays such characteristics to some extent (Figure 1; Bauer 2015).

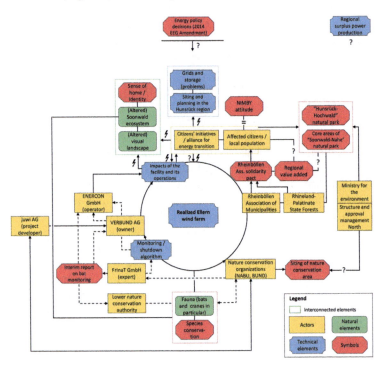

Figure 1 Constellation for Windpark Ellern, a wind farm in the Hunsrück region in Rhineland-Palatinate (source: Bauer 2015).

---

4 The nine criteria are strong institutional capacity, political commitment, favorable legal and regulatory frameworks, competitive installation/production costs, mechanisms for information and feedback, access to financing, prolific community/individual ownership and use, participatory project siting, and recognition of externalities or a positive public image (Sovacool and Ratan 2012).

The illustration depicts the constellation for the period 2013 to 2014. It focuses on local and regional conflicts. Positioned in the center of the figure are effects related to the facility proper and its operations that have a crucial impact on its environment and social acceptance. Also close to the center are technological and methodological aspects of a bat-monitoring program and the shutdown algorithm, both of which were agreed upon in negotiations between the project developer, a nature conservation organization, and the authorities in 2013. Although these aspects did not entail changes in the social perception of the facility, they have in fact involved institutional regulations and provisions for the protection of endangered species. The key factors that determine the constellation can be unraveled along the groups of actors involved—citizens' initiatives and the population affected, municipalities and authorities, nature conservation agencies, and businesses—and summarized clockwise as follows: The majority of the dynamics and conflicts are illustrated in the upper part of the graph. Although an intercommunal revenue-sharing scheme that the Rheinböllen association of municipalities had agreed upon as early as 2009 resulted in widespread local acceptance and positive feedback, higher-level decision making—such as a siting and planning process in the Hunsrück region that involved little coordination for years—gave rise to discontent. The all-encompassing question that remained here was whether—and if so, to what extent—the 2014 EEG amendment would change the innovation and diffusion dynamics of solar and wind power development in Germany.

Obvious shortcomings have continuously contributed to ever new and partially contradictory constellations. Among these shortcomings is a failure of governance and regulatory mechanisms. The EU's emissions trading system, for instance, has not proved to be an effective incentive. Aside from this, the guaranteed feed-in tariffs for renewable energy sources have also lost popularity and evolved into an issue at the center of much controversy; the latter is also true for the exemption of energy-intensive industries (and not just these) from the EEG surcharge (Nordensvärd and Urban 2015). Moreover, there is doubt and uncertainty about the actual requirements in regard to grid and storage capacity. Some studies (e.g., Swofford and Slattery 2010) show a frequent correlation between distance from the project and project acceptance among local residents. However, this is not always the case since people living in the immediate vicinity of projects that have been planned carefully and discussed locally have become supporters in some instances (Wüstenhagen, Wolsink, and Bürer 2007), not least if revenue is shared equitably (Bauer 2015). Reservations among local populations stand in contrast to the widespread approval of the *Energiewende* among the general population in Germany (Forsa 2013).

Hence, whereas the constellations at the outset of the energy transition was largely perceived favorably, recent discourses have partly called this general support into question. It now appears that 'no one' seems to want—technological—innovations such as the novel DC transmission lines any longer (at least not the diffusion of these innovations). This technology reduces transmission losses, whereas its health effects (such as the much-debated issue of higher leukemia rates in children living in the vicinity of overhead power lines) have been investigated far less than in the case of its conventional counterparts. The situation is similar for underground cables, which were heavily favored in the early debate on grid expansion (Menges and Beyer 2013). Even the recently revived display of engineering prowess in the form of pumped-storage plants faces stiff opposition. It is a long-established technology that is already being applied worldwide, yet is undergoing a semantic change and being reframed as providing a new contribution to the energy transition. For example, the pumped-storage plant in Atdorf in the Black Forest, which would be the largest such facility in Europe, is currently in planning. However, whether it can be built and operated profitably remains an open question. Juliana M. Müller has analyzed a constellation for such a storage project in her master's thesis (see text box below; cf. Müller 2013; Müller and Köppel 2014).

The Blautal pumped-storage plant is an example that demonstrates how an infrastructure project of this kind designed to contribute to the energy transition may not meet general disapproval among the local population, yet a flawed planning process can lead to protests, delays, and in this particular case ultimately to the choice of an economically less favorable location. Once the lot initially favored for the upper basin option could not be acquired, the project developer sought to realize an option that had previously been seen to have a detrimental impact. This decision was met with incomprehension, triggering resistance and leading to the formation of a citizens' initiative. The consequence was that the developer abandoned this option, making a new regional planning procedure necessary, which ultimately led to selecting the option that had initially not been considered for economic reasons. At the heart of the protests were environmental aspects, such as the potential impact on water resources, and landscape aesthetics. In addition to the issues raised by the opposition movement, doubts as to the liquidity of the main project developer also began to surface, which caused further concern among the municipalities, for instance, that the latter might have to shoulder restoration costs in the event of developer bankruptcy. The ensuing debates questioned the reasons initially given for the project, namely, to support the energy transition, as it could also not be guaranteed that only 'green' power would be stored.

Also, the main players of the energy transition were not aware early on of the feedback mechanisms, which can often respond promptly. An argument can be made that this also applies to the debates on pumped-storage plants in spite of the continued lack of large-scale technologically and economically viable storage alternatives (Steffen 2012; Trümper et al. 2014). The grid is unable to absorb surplus supply from renewable energy sources in periods of high power feed-in; this excess supply is then sold to neighboring countries at very low rates, temporarily stored in pumped-storage facilities (for instance, in Austria), and/or accommodated by temporarily suspending power feed-in. High midday solar power feed-in in combination with an increasing supply of wind power has already begun to undermine the business model of pumped storage plants, which is based on exploiting price differentials. The spread between purchase prices during periods of excess supply and off-peak periods is no longer sufficient to ensure profitable operations.

5 Carbon Storage and Unconventional Natural Gas Production: Is there a Threat of 'Re-lock-in'?

The processes of deliberation that have disrupted the established energy path and laid the groundwork for the energy transition are thus being increasingly dominated by the pragmatic demands for action. What is more, the outcome of the last election to the German Bundestag has partly changed how political players perceive the formerly dominant constellation in support of fossil energy use (although it is not quite certain whether this applies to society as a whole). It is not yet clear whether these are merely transitional phenomena accompanying change or whether the (worldwide) promotion of carbon capture and storage (CCS) will reinvigorate the old system (Hansson and Bryngelsson 2009; Stephens and Jiusto 2010). Similar questions arise with respect to unconventional shale gas production (fracking). It indeed seems justified to speak of a renaissance of coal to some degree, as the product of both political pressure (from the Social Democratic Party and the unions[5]) and the emission trading scheme's failed price mechanisms. Obvious path dependences have led parts of these advocacy coalitions to develop a pronounced aversion to innovation (e.g., in regard to lignite-based power production in Brandenburg and Saxony, which dates back to the GDR era) and, at least at the regional level, to pragmatically undermine, time and again, the supra-regional semantics of the energy transition.

CCS bears the promise of continued coal utilization while 'greenwashing' the respective constellation that supports the oligopoly of large power companies. In this case, a balanced strategy of promoting renewable energy on the one hand and continued interim use of fossil energy complemented by carbon sequestra-

---

5 Both of which claim that the simultaneous withdrawal from nuclear and fossil energy sources is not possible.

tion on the other ('transition management,' Meadowcroft 2009) would probably be doomed to failure, entailing socio-technological lock-in (ibid.). However, the situation worldwide is such that the promise of innovation represented by the prospect of developing the underground for carbon storage has yet to be realized on a large scale (upscaling). So far, mostly pilot projects have been conducted and a few large power plants designed to employ carbon capture technologies are either in planning or under construction; the Massachusetts Institute of Technology maintains a relevant CCS database.[6] Stephens and Jiusto (2010) quite aptly have called CCS at this stage 'embryonic, hybrid entities (part idea, part hardware, part people),' and it has yet to be proven whether these technologies can be upscaled at reasonable costs and acceptable risks.

In regard to CCS, a coalition with the epistemic community of the Intergovernmental Panel on Climate Change (IPCC[7]) seems to have emerged, which has also spoken out in favor of committing to the promise of CCS as a bridge technology for reducing global warming and, at the same time, as a condition for the coal power industry to carry on with business as usual: "As concerns CCS, we have lost years and harbored the illusion that renewables would automatically displace coal," said Ottmar Edenhofer of the IPCC (cited in Hecking 2014; my translation from German). In the Fifth IPCC Assessment Report of 2014, Working Group III makes multiple references to CCS (IPCC 2014)—fully aware that it will remain an end-of-pipe strategy for the foreseeable future (Stephens and Jiusto 2010; Unruh and Carrillo-Hermosilla 2006).

In the case of CCS specifically, reports testify to a sharply divided perception of its risks and benefits between industry, policymakers, and involved experts on the one hand and persistent general skepticism among the public on the other, despite the lack of experience with any large-scale implementation of this technology (van Alphen et al. 2007). In the same vein, the perspective adopted in assessing the general framework conditions suggests that CCS is both an urgent innovation required to mitigate the consequences of climate change (e.g., in Norway with its high rates of fossil energy production; Shackley et al. 2007; van Alphen et al. 2009) and a very risky and expensive path of innovation (Oltra et al. 2010). Laypeople often associate CCS with stigmatized technologies as applied in the chemical industry, coal production, or nuclear energy (ibid.). A reason for this might be the difficulty in demarcating CCS from the previously dominant constellation. For instance, high-voltage transmission lines also symbolize the transmission of power from nuclear and lignite, and carbon sequestration evokes fears similar to those associated

---

6   http://sequestration.mit.edu/tools/projects/index.html (Retrieved January 13, 2017).
7   http://www.ipcc.ch/ (Retrieved January 13, 2017).

with nuclear waste disposal. The general public tends to distrust overly optimistic experts directly involved with CCS and industry (Hansson and Bryngelsson 2009) and is more likely to place greater trust in NGOs (Huijts, Midden, and Meijnders 2007). A case in point is Vattenfall's exploration of carbon storage in Beeskow, Brandenburg, which provoked local resistance and ended in disaster. Vattenfall was in a problematic dual role of benefiting from carbon storage (by lending legitimacy to utilizing lignite in its *Schwarze Pumpe* power plant) and being the main, but not very credible, source of information (Dütschke 2011).

Another storyline is the reframing of fossil fuels through the introduction of fracking, particularly in the USA (Wang et al. 2014), which, at the semantic level, even revolves around the term 'natural gas.' Fracking's actual contribution to the overall carbon budget taken by itself is already unclear since, even though the fracking boom in the USA has led to reduced coal consumption there, it has also lowered the price of coal worldwide, triggering a gas-to-coal switch in Europe (Cotton, Rattle, and van Alstine 2014). Currently, this provides little incentive to substitute renewable for fossil energy sources (Rabe and Borick 2013). Yet, even in the USA, not all states have followed the lead of Pennsylvania (with its vast Marcellus shale gas deposits), which represents the epicenter of fracking and plays down its environmental impacts (Rabe and Borick 2013; Texas takes a similar and Colorado, for instance, a more differentiated approach; Davis 2012). In large parts of society, however, fracking is nevertheless seen as an environmental issue, as in most cases little information is disclosed to the public about what chemicals are used and the indirect costs involved (e.g., its detrimental impact on water quality) (Davis and Fisk 2014). New challenges also emerge from the perspective of institutional analysis: whereas the administrative jurisdictions that have traditionally applied to gas or oil production essentially fail to prove effective in the case of fracking because of its non-point-source effects, effective institutional responsibility has yet to be organized so as to internalize external environmental impacts (Holahan and Arnold 2013).

6   A Preliminary Conclusion

Whereas the overarching imperative of the energy transition still seems to be accepted, the perceptions of the innovations in question that arise in reflexive processes on the ground are frequently, and perhaps increasingly, being shaped by obstacles. I have given a brief overview of the reasons why not only the expansion of grid and storage capacity but also technological innovations such as carbon capture and storage are now viewed as inconclusive promises of innovation. Groups that might be perceived as otherwise homogenous actors can get caught up in the partly contradictory constellations that emerge here, as Yonk, Simmons, and Steed (2013) have demonstrated for environmental groups in the USA, which have adopted divergent views on renewable energy sources. At the same time, the advancement of renewable energy sources, which is still being pushed forward primarily by environmental policy, is seen to be a driver of employment and technological change (Corsatea 2014[8]). In the same vein, there are a multitude of different research perspectives on the energy transition in the light of innovation society. In Germany, there are signs of a new, politically induced process of path disruption in the development of renewable energy sources in that the 2014 EEG amendment has supplemented the previous promotion scheme based on fixed feed-in tariffs—which has proven to be highly effective so far—with a competitive tendering system that was previously seen to be inferior (Bruns et al. 2008, 2011).

Another question is which of the two visions of innovation associated with carbon storage will prove closer to reality: 'CCS as enhanced lock-in, or CCS as gateway to a green future' (Meadowcraft 2009: 331)? Underground carbon sequestration—which has yet to prove viable on a large scale and is largely an unknown in terms of the expected costs and risks—could at the same time inhibit the necessary investments in the advancement of renewable energy sources and could possibly turn out to be less a technology that bridges the transition, as so frequently claimed, and more one that paves the way for a resurrection of the initial fossil status quo (Unruh and Carrillo-Hermosilla 2006). In a positive vein, however, there is also the possibility of what Simmie (2012) has called 'layering,' that is to say, when a new line of technology (such as wind power technology in Denmark) supplements an existing (fossil and nuclear) constellation without automatically resulting in a re-lock-in, even though the established constellation continues to exist for the time being.[9]

---

8   In her comparative study of technological capacities and business activities in Europe (Germany, France, the UK, and Denmark), Corsatea (2014) also discovered regional differences; for instance, Germany's strong involvement in wind and solar power in contrast to France's greater commitment to bioenergy.

9   "It was started by the mindful deviation of knowledgeable actors in rural and publicly created niches. It was developed primarily through incremental innovations that added a new layer of electricity generation technology to the existing fossil fuel-based technologies. This layering process involved adding new rules in the form of legalizing grid connection of approved wind turbines; procedures in terms of government subsidies, tax relief and feed in tariffs; structures in the form of government regulations and technologies in the form of wind turbines and complementary technological systems to the existing electricity supply system in Denmark" (Simmie 2012: 768).

Thus, the central question, for Germany as well, of whether the deliberative disruption of the path away from a fossil and nuclear energy system in favor of one with a high share of renewables will ultimately prove successful is not very likely to be answered in the near future. This applies to pragmatic everyday action as well in that it is regularly torn between a clear commitment to the energy transition on the one hand and local resistance and concerns about energy security on the other. At the time this chapter was being completed, the German federal government had just adopted a bill on fracking that attracted much attention but avoided clear decisions in any direction. Along similar lines, the state of Bavaria, so successful economically, has been unsuccessful in grappling with a consistent energy strategy (cf. Nordensvärd and Urban 2015). It seems that the Federal Ministry of Economy has also not made major inroads thus far in establishing its current strategy to achieve the federal government's reduction goals for greenhouse emissions at the expense of large emitters such as lignite-fired power plants against the opposition of veto players in the respective states.

This is particularly troubling considering that, according to Jacobsson and Lauber (2006), the social costs of coal-based power generation are of the same magnitude as the funds devoted to promoting renewable energy sources in Germany. A major condition that Foxon et al. (2005) have identified for successful innovation systems in the field of renewable energy is that all relevant actors must work toward the same goal, each in its specific role, and government, industry, and research need to pursue a shared vision. The less this is the case, one is inclined to add, the less we can assume a shared perception of the transformation process in innovation society. At the moment, the situation looks more like what Meadowcraft (2009: 323) has characterized as the 'messy, conflictual, and highly disjointed' nature of the processes involved in the long-term transformation of energy systems. Currently, there is much evidence suggesting that, in the case of the energy transition, path dependence and path disruption/creation will empirically offset one another for the foreseeable future.

Acknowledgements

I would like to extend my gratitude to Juliane Bauer for her permission to use the case study of the Ellern wind farm from her bachelor's thesis and to Juliana Mercedes Müller, accordingly, for permission to use her study of the Blautal pumped-storage plant from her master's thesis. Arnold Windeler was so kind to review the manuscript and suggest discussing the findings in light of the concept of path dependence.

References

Aas, Øystein, Patrick Devine-Wright, Torvald Tangeland, Susana Batel, and Audun Ruud. 2014. "Public Believes about High-Voltage Powerlines in Norway, Sweden and the United Kingdom: A Comparative Survey." *Energy Research & Social Science* 2: 30-37.

Arthur, W. Brian. 1994. *Increasing Returns and Path Dependence in the Economy.* Ann Arbor: The University of Michigan Press.

Bauer, Juliane. 2015. *Windenergie im Wald – eine Konstellationsanalyse am Fallbeispiel des Windparks Ellern im Soonwald/ Hunsrück* (Unpublished bachelor's thesis). Technische Universität Berlin.

Bayer, Patrick, Lindsay Dolan, and Johannes Urpelainen. 2013. "Global Patterns of Renewable Energy Innovation, 1990-2009." *Energy for Sustainable Development* 17(3): 288-295.

Bechberger, Mischa, Lutz Mez, and Annika Sohre. 2008. *Windenergie im Ländervergleich: Steuerungsimpulse, Akteure und technische Entwicklungen in Deutschland, Dänemark, Spanien und Großbritannien.* Frankfurt a. M.: Lang.

Bidwell, David. 2013. "The Role of Values in Public Beliefs and Attitudes Towards Commercial Wind Energy. *Energy Policy* 58: 189-199.

Bräuer, Marco. 2012. "Regional Protests Against New Power Lines: How Citizen Action Groups Make Sense of Mass Media." *UVP-report* 26(5): 217-220.

Bruns, Elke, Johann Köppel, Dörte Ohlhorst, and Susanne Schön. 2008. *Die Innovationsbiographie der Windenergie unter besonderer Berücksichtigung der Absichten und Wirkungen von Steuerungsimpulsen.* Berlin: LIT Verlag.

Bruns, Elke, Dörte Ohlhorst, Bernd Wenzel, and Johann Köppel. 2011. *Renewable Energies in Germany's Electricity Market. A Biography of the Innovation Process.* Dordrecht, Heidelberg, London, New York: Springer.

Bundesverwaltungsgericht. Verdict from January 24, 2008. *4 CN 2.07.* ECLI:DE:BVerwG:2008:240108U4CN2.07.0.

Ciupuliga, Ana R. and Eefje Cuppen. 2013. "The Role of Dialogue in Fostering Acceptance of Transmission Lines: The Case of a France-Spain Interconnection Project." *Energy Policy* 60: 224-233.

Corsatea, Teodora D. 2014. "Technological Capabilities for Innovation Activities Across Europe: Evidence from Wind, Solar and Bioenergy Technologies." *Renewable and Sustainable Energy Reviews* 37: 469-479. doi:10.1016/j.rser.2014.04.067.

Cotton, Matthew, Imogen Rattle, James van Alstine. 2014. "Shale Gas Policy in the United Kingdom: An Argumentative Discourse Analysis." *Energy Policy* 73: 427-438.

Darmani, Anna, Niklas Arvidsson, Antonio Hidalgo, and Jose Albors. 2014. "What Drives the Development of Renewable Energy Technologies? Toward a Typology for the Systemic Drivers." *Renewable and Sustainable Energy Reviews* (38): 834-847.

David, Paul A. 1985. "Clio and the Economics of QWERTY." *American Economic Review* 75(2), 332-337.

Davis, Charles. 2012. "The Politics of 'Fracking': Regulating Natural Gas Drilling Practices in Colorado and Texas." *Review of Policy Research* 29(2): 177-191. doi:10.1111/j.1541-1338.2011.00547.x.

Davis, Charles and Jonathan M. Fisk. 2014. "Energy Abundance or Environmental Worries? Analyzing Public Support for Fracking in the United States." *Review of Policy Research* 31(1): 1-16. doi:10.1111/ropr.12048.

Del Rio, Pablo and Gregory Unruh. 2007. "Overcoming the Lock-Out of Renewable Energy Technologies in Spain: The Cases of Wind and Solar Electricity." *Renewable and Sustainable Energy Reviews* 11(7): 1498-1513.

Devine-Wright, Patrick. 2013. "Think Global, Act Local? The Relevance of Place Attachments and Place Identities in a Climate Changed World. *Global Environmental Change* 23(1): 61-69.

Dütschke, Elisabeth. 2011. "What Drives Local Public Acceptance – Comparing Two Cases from Germany." *Energy Procedia* 4: 6234-6240.

Firestone, Jeremy, Willett Kempton, Meretidh B. Lilley, Kateryna Samoteskul. 2012. "Public Acceptance of Offshore Wind Power Across Regions and Through Time." *Journal of Environmental Planning and Management* 55(10): 1369-1386. doi:10.1080/09640568.2 012.682782.

Forsa. 2013. *Verbraucherinteressen in der Energiewende. Ergebnisse einer repräsentativen Befragung.* vzbv: Berlin. Retrieved January 13, 2017 (http://www.vzbv.de/sites/default/files/downloads/Energiewende_Studie_lang_vzbv_2013.pdf).

Foxon, Tim J. 2013. "Technological Lock-In." Pp. 123-127 in *Encyclopedia of Energy, Natural Resource and Environmental Economics*, edited by J. Shogren. doi:10.1016/B978-0-12-375067-9.00067-X.

Foxon, Tim. J., Robert Gross, Adam Chase, Jo Howes, Alex Arnal, and Dennis Anderson. 2005. "UK Innovation Systems for New and Renewable Energy Technologies: Drivers, Barriers and Systems Failures." *Energy Policy* 33: 2123-2137.

Foxon, Tim and Peter Pearson. 2008. "Overcoming Barriers to Innovation and Diffusion of Cleaner Technologies: Some Features of a Sustainable Innovation Policy Regime." *Journal of Cleaner Production* 16(1): 148-161.

Fuchs, Gerhard. 2014. "The Governance of Innovations in the Energy Sector: Between Adaptation and Exploration." *Science & Technology Studies* 27 (1), 34-53.

Garud, Raghu, Arun Kumaraswamy, Peter Karnøe. 2010. "Path Dependence or Path Creation?" *Journal of Management Studies* 47(4): 760-774.

Gartman, Victoria, Kathrin Wichmann, Lea Bulling, Maria E. Huesca-Pérez, and Johann Köppel. 2014. "Wind of Change or Wind of Challenges: Implementation Factors Regarding Wind Energy Development, an International Perspective." *AIMS Energy* 2(4): 485-504.

Geißler, Gesa, Johann Köppel, and Pamela Gunther. 2013. "Wind Energy and Environmental Assessments: A Hard Look at Two Forerunners' Approaches: Germany and the United States." *Renewable Energy* 51: 71-78.

Groth, Theresa M. and Christine Vogt. 2014. "Residents' Perceptions of Wind Turbines: An Analysis of Two Townships in Michigan." *Energy Policy* 65: 251-260.

Hansson, Anders and Mårten Bryngelsson. 2009. "Expert Opinions on Carbon Dioxide Capture and Storage: A Framing of Uncertainties and Possibilities." *Energy Policy* 37(6): 2273-2282.

Hecking, Claus. 2014. "Weltweiter Energieboom: Comeback der Kohle. Im Westen gilt Kohle als Relikt der industriellen Frühzeit, doch der Rohstoff wird zum wichtigsten Energieträger der Welt. Kein Brennstoff ist so billig wie der Klimakiller Nummer eins."

Spiegel January 29. Retrieved January 13, 2017 (http://www.spiegel.de/wissenschaft/natur/kohle-wird-wichtigster-energietraeger-der-welt-noch-vor-oel-a-946168.html).

Hellström, Magnus, Inkeri Ruuska, Kim Wikström, and Daniel Jåfs. 2013. "Project Governance and Path Creation in Early Stages of Finnish Nuclear Power Projects." *International Journal of Project Management* 31(5): 712-723.

Holahan, Robert and Gwen Arnold. 2013. "An Institutional Theory of Hydraulic Fracturing Policy." *Ecological Economics* 94: 127-134.

Huijts, Nicole M. A., Cees J.H. Midden, and Anneloes Meijnders. 2007. "Social Acceptance of Carbon Dioxide Storage." *Energy Policy* 35(5): 2780-2789.

IPCC. 2014. *Climate Change 2014: Mitigation of Climate Change. Contribution of Working Group III to the Fifth Assessment Report of the Intergovernmental Panel on Climate Change* [O. Edenhofer, R. Pichs-Madruga, Y. Sokona, E. Farahani, S. Kadner, K. Seyboth, A. Adler, I. Baum, S. Brunner, P. Eickemeier, J. Savolainen, S. Schlömer, C. Von Stechow, T. Zwickel & J. C. Minx (eds.)]. Cambridge and New York: Cambridge University Press.

Jacobsson, Staffan and Volkmar Lauber. 2006. "The Politics and Policy of Energy System Transformation—Explaining the German Diffusion of Renewable Energy Technology." *Energy Policy* 34(3): 256-276.

Jolivet, Eric and Eva Heiskanen. 2010. "Blowing Against the Wind: An Explanatory Application of Actor Network Theory to the Analysis of Local Controversies and Participation Processes in Wind Energy." *Energy Policy* 38: 6746-6754.

Karnøe, Peter and Raghu Garud. 2012. "Path Creation: Co-creation of Heterogeneous Resources in the Emergence of the Danish Wind Turbine Cluster." *European Planning Studies* 20(5): 733-752.

Koch, Sabine, Lisa Odparlik, and Johann Köppel. 2014. "Wo steht die Partizipation beim Netzausbau? Eine Analyse der Beteiligungsverfahren zu ausgewählten Projekten aus dem Bedarfsplan des Energieleitungsausbaus." *Naturschutz und Landschaftsplanung* 46(4): 116-123.

Köppel, Johann, Marie Dahmen, Jennifer Helfrich, Eva Schuster, and Lea Bulling. 2014. "Cautious but Committed: Moving Toward Adaptive Planning and Operation Strategies for Renewable Energy's Wildlife Implications." *Environmental Management* 54(4): 744-755. doi: 10.1007/s00267-014-0333-8.

Latour, Bruno. 2005. *Reassembling the Social. An Introduction to Actor-Network-Theory*. Oxford: Oxford University Press.

Lüdeke, Jens, Gesa Geißler, and Johann Köppel. 2012. "Der neue Offshore-Netzplan zur Regelung der Anbindung von Offshore Windparks. Analyse und Diskussion der Prüfung seiner Umweltauswirkungen." *UVP-report* 26(3+4): 183-190.

Meadowcraft, James. 2009. "What about the Politics? Sustainable Development, Transition Management, and Long Term Energy Transitions." *Policy Sciences* 42(4): 323-340. doi: 10.1007/s11077-009-9097-z.

Menges, Roland and Gregor Beyer. 2013. "Energiewende und Übertragungsnetzausbau: Sind Erdkabel ein Instrument zur Steigerung der gesellschaftlichen Akzeptanz des Leitungsbaus? Eine empirische Untersuchung auf Basis der Kontingenten Bewertungsmethode." *Zeitschrift für Energiewirtschaft*. 37(4): 277-295. doi: 10.1007/s12398-013-0118-4.

Meyer, Uli and Cornelius Schubert. 2007. "Integrating Path Dependency and Path Creation in a General Understanding of Path Constitution. The Role of Agency and Institutions in the Stabilisation of Technological Innovations." *Science, Technology & Innovation Studies* 3(1): 23-44.

Müller, Juliana M. 2013. *Managing the Energiewende – A Constellation Analysis of the Pumped Hydro Energy Power Plant Blautal* (Unpublished master's thesis). Technische Universität Berlin.

Müller, Juliana M. and Johann Köppel. 2014. *Managing the Energiewende – A Constellation Analysis of the Pumped Hydro Energy Power Plant Blautal*. ISSRM (20st International Symposium on Society and Resource Management), conference paper, June 13, 2014, Hanover.

Nadai, Alain. 2007. "'Planning,' 'Siting' and the Local Acceptance of Wind Power: Some Lessons from the French Case." *Energy Policy* 35(5): 2715-2726.

Nesta, Lionel, Francesco Vona, and Francesco Nicolli. 2014. "Environmental Policies, Competition and Innovation in Renewable Energy." *Journal of Environmental Economics and Management* 67(3): 396-411.

Nordensvärd, Johann and Frauke Urban. 2015. "The Stuttering Energy Transition in Germany: Wind Energy Policy and Feed-In Tariff Lock-In." *Energy Policy* 82: 156-165.

Oltra, Christian, Roser Sala, Rosario Solà, Marina Di Masso, and Gene Rowe. 2010. "Lay Perceptions of Carbon Capture and Storage Technology." *International Journal of Greenhouse Gas Control* 4(4): 698-706.

Portman, Michelle E., John A. Duff, Johann Köppel, Jessica Reisert, and Megan E. Higgins. 2009. "Offshore Wind Energy Development in the Exclusive Economic Zone: Legal and Policy Supports and Impediments in Germany and the US." *Energy Policy* 37(9): 3596-3607.

Rabe, Barry G. and Christopher Borick. 2013. "Conventional Politics for Unconventional Drilling? Lessons from Pennsylvania's Early Move into Fracking Policy Development." *Review of Policy Research* 30(3): 321-340. doi: 10.1111/ropr.12018.

Sabatier, Paul A. and Hank C. Jenkins-Smith. 1993. *Policy Change and Learning. An Advocacy Coalition Approach* (Theoretical Lenses on Public Policy). Boulder Colorado: Westview Press.

Shackley, Simon, Holly Waterman, Per Godfroij, David Reiner, Jason Anderson, Kathy Draxlbauer, and Todd Flach. 2007. "Stakeholder Perceptions of CO_2 Capture and Storage in Europe: Results from a Survey." *Energy Policy* 35(10): 5091-5108.

Schön, Susanne, Sylvia Kruse, Martin Meister, Benjamin Nölting, and Dörte Ohlhorst. 2007. *Handbuch Konstellationsanalyse. Ein interdisziplinäres Brückenkonzept für die Nachhaltigkeits-, Technik- und Innovationsforschung*. Munich: oekom.

Schuster, Eva, Lea Bulling, and Johann Köppel. 2015. "Consolidating the State of Knowledge: A Synoptical Review of Wind Energy's Wildlife Effects." *Environmental Management* 56(2): 300-331. doi: 10.1007/s00267-015-0501-5.

Simmie, James. 2012. "Path Dependence and New Technological Path Creation in the Danish Wind Power Industry." *European Planning Studies* 20(5): 753-752.

Sovacool, Benjamin K. and Pushkala Lakshmi Ratan. 2012. "Conceptualizing the Acceptance of Wind and Solar Electricity." *Renewable and Sustainable Energy Reviews* 16(7): 5268-5279.

Steffen, Bjarne. 2012. "Prospects for Pumped-Hydro Storage in Germany." *Energy Policy* 45: 420-429. doi: 10.1016/j.enpol.2012.02.052.

Steinbach, Armin. 2013. "Barriers and Solutions for Expansion of Electricity Grids—the German Experience." *Energy Policy* 63: 224-229. doi: 10.1016/j.enpol.2013.08.073.

Stephens, Jennie C. and Scott Jiusto. 2010. "Assessing Innovation in Emerging Energy Technologies: Socio-Technical Dynamics of Carbon Capture and Storage (CCS) and Enhanced Geothermal Systems (EGS) in the USA." *Energy Policy* 38(4): 2020-2031. doi: 10.1016/j.enpol.2009.12.003.

Sühlsen, Kathrin and Matthijs Hisschemöller. 2014. "Lobbying the 'Energiewende.' Assessing the Effectiveness of Strategies to Promote the Renewable Energy Business in Germany." *Energy Policy* 69. doi: 10.1016/j.enpol.2014.02.018.

Strunz, Sebastian. 2014. "The German Energy Transition as a Regime Shift." *Ecological Economics* 100: 150-158. doi: 10.1016/j.ecolecon.2014.01.019.

Swofford, Jeffry and Michael Slattery. 2010. "Public Attitudes of Wind Energy in Texas: Local Communities in Close Proximity to Wind Farms and Their Effect on Decision-Making." *Energy Policy* 38(5): 2508-2519.

Trümper, Sören C., Sebastian Gerhard, Stefan Saatmann, and Oliver Weinmann. 2014. „Qualitative Analysis of Strategies for the Integration of Renewable Energies in the Electricity Grid." *Energy Procedia* 46: 161-170. doi: 10.1016/j.egypro.2014.01.169.

Unruh, Gregory C. and Javier Carrillo-Hermosilla. 2006. "Globalizing Carbon Lock-In." *Energy Policy* 34(10): 1185-1197.

van Alphen, Klaas, Quirine van Voorst tot Voorst, Marko P. Hekkert, and Ruud E.H.M. Smits. 2007. "Societal Acceptance of Carbon Capture and Storage Technologies." *Energy Policy* 35(8): 4368-4380.

van Alphen, Klaas, J. van Ruijven, Sjur Kasa, Marko Hekkert, and Wim Turkenburg. 2009. "The Performance of the Norwegian Carbon Dioxide, Capture and Storage Innovation System." *Energy Policy* 37(1): 43-55.

van der Horst, Dan. 2007. "NIMBY or Not? Exploring the Relevance of Location and the Policies of Voiced Opinions in Renewable Energy Siting Controversies." *Energy Policy* 35(5): 2705-2714.

Vergne, Jean-Philippe and Rodolphe Durand. 2010. "The Missing Link Between the Theory and Empirics of Path Dependence: Conceptual Clarification, Testability Issue, and Methodological Implications. *Journal of Management Studies* 47(4): 736-759.

van der Voort, Nick and Frank Vanclay. 2014. "Social Impacts of Earthquakes Caused by Gas Extraction in the Province of Groningen, The Netherlands." *Environmental Impact Assessment Review* 50: 1-15.

Wakiyama, Takako, Eric Zusman, and James E. Monogan III. 2014. "Can a Low-Carbon-Energy Transition be Sustained in Post-Fukushima Japan? Assessing the Varying Impacts of Exogenous Shocks." *Energy Policy* 73: 654-666.

Wang, Qiang, Xi Chen, Awadhesh N. Jha, and Howard Rogers. 2014. "Natural Gas from Shale Formation – The Evolution, Evidences and Challenges of Shale Gas Revolution in United States." *Renewable and Sustainable Energy Reviews* 30: 1-28.

Weiß, David. 2014. *Windkraft im Wald – Befragung zu Einstellungen, Wahrnehmungen und Akzeptanz* (Unpublished bachelor's thesis). Technische Universität Berlin.

Weyer, Johannes. 2008. *Techniksoziologie: Genese, Gestaltung und Steuerung soziotechnischer Systeme. Grundlagentexte Soziologie*. Weinheim, Munich: Beltz Juventa.

Wüstenhagen, Rolf, Maarten Wolsink, and Mary Jean Bürer. 2007. "Social Acceptance of Renewable Energy Innovation: An Introduction to the Concept." *Energy Policy* 35(5): 2683-2691. doi: 10.1016/j.enpol.2006.12.001.

Yin, Robert K. 2014. *Case Study Research. Design and Methods*. Thousand Oaks: Sage.

Yonk, Ryan M., Randy T. Simmons, and Brian C. Steed. 2013. *Green vs. Green. The Political, Legal and Administrative Pitfalls Facing Green Energy Production*. New York: Routledge.

Zimmer, René, Sarah Kloke, and Max Gaedtke. 2012. *Der Streit um die Uckermarkleitung – Eine Diskursanalyse. Studie im Rahmen des UfU-Schwerpunktes "Erneuerbare Energien im Konflikt"* (UfU-Paper 3/2012). Berlin: Unabhängiges Institut für Umweltfragen. Retrieved January 13, 2017 (http://opus.kobv.de/zlb/volltexte/2013/20508/pdf/ Streit_um_die_Uckermarkleitung.pdf).

Innovating Governance

Epistemic and Political Reflexivities in the Remaking of Democracy

Jan-Peter Voß

1 Introduction

Reflexivity is tricky. It leads to endless regression. Once one commits to a process of not just doing things without thinking—not submitting to interactions and their dynamics and conforming with outcomes—but instead makes this conduct itself the subject of observation, communication, and new action then there is no escape. This observing, communicating, and doing itself occurs according to its own dynamics and gives rise to new patterns. These provide a vantage point for a new cycle of reflexivity, thereby turning the process of reflection itself into an object of observation, reflexive action, and communication. It can easily be seen where this leads. A spiral of reflection is set into motion that winds into infinity, like a reflection tunnel created by two mirrors placed opposite each other. But unlike the mirrors, the tunnel does not remain the same. This is because subjects change in the process of reflexive interaction (Joas 1985; Giddens 1986; Hacking 2002). In endless perpetuation, reflexivity erodes Archimedean points: fixed standpoints of perception, knowledge, judgment, and action. Any act of enlightenment might itself be subject to a new act of enlightenment that exposes it as a specific obscuration.

This process along with the resulting dissolutions, reconfigurations, and reproductions can be seen as a characteristic of modern Western society (Giddens 1990: 38-43; Beck, Giddens, and Lash 1994). We can speak of a liquefaction of reality at the level of individual identity and subject structure as well as at the level of societal organization and praxis (Bauman 2000). And even the articulation of the diagnosis of liquefaction can be questioned in relation to its societal embedding and effects and thus be engaged with reflexively (Selgas 2011).

Determining an ultimate reality therefore becomes impossible. At best, partial ordering can be created as part of an ongoing process of reflection (Strathern 2005). Consequently, such partial ordering may also apply to the patterns of reflexive entanglement themselves. This is the attempt I wish to undertake here— even if only for the attempt itself to become an object of reflective observation in just a moment. So much for the entanglements. Now things will get a little simpler.

Let me begin by defining a few terms. They relate to the reflexivity of governance innovations as well as to the specific case of citizen panels by which I develop my argument. I use the term *governance* to refer to processes of shaping collective orders. *Governance innovations* are processes of designing and developing new and alternative patterns in the shaping of collective orders.

The concrete case that I draw on to discuss the reflexivity of governance innovations is the development of *citizen panels*. This term refers to a particular model of public participation that initially developed in the 1970s in various country and problem contexts and under various monikers, such as *citizens' jury, planning cell,* and *consensus conference*. Such models spread translocally and witnessed a global boom in the 1990s and have since been further developed in transnational expert discourses and in the practical work of professional service providers under the umbrella term of 'citizen panels' or 'mini-publics' (Hörning 1999; Hendriks 2005; Brown 2006; Grönlund, Bächtiger, and Setälä 2014). Their shared format entails deliberating 'public views' on a given topic in professionally assembled and moderated groups of 10-25 citizens. In a broader perspective, citizen panels are to supplement (and relativize) liberal representative nation-state democracy with a new mobile and flexible format for legitimating decisions of collective order.

I understand the term *reflexivity* to refer to the phenomenon in which social conduct recursively becomes an object of observation and analysis in relation to its own determinants and consequences (for a compilation of the various conceptions and an extensive discussion, see Lynch 2000). This precipitates action that addresses such determinants and hence 'denaturalizes' social conduct.[1] My aim

---

1 On a societal level, this applies to the observation, analysis, and shaping of societal interaction such as, for example, politics, jurisdiction, engaged art, and social science. On a personal level, reflexivity relates to the observation, analysis, and shaping of one's own conduct. To give an example, a couple's relationship can be deemed reflexive insofar as its interaction patterns themselves become a subject of communication, are analyzed in terms of their determinants, and are thus influenced in their (re-)production.

in this chapter is to show that innovation processes are reflexive in multiple and intertwining ways. This leads to a differentiated concept of reflexivity as connected with the diagnosis of an 'innovation society,' at the center of which is "[...] the purportedly new *reflexive quality* of actions, orientations, and institutions, *both as an overarching and cross-cutting social phenomenon [...]*" (Hutter et al. 2015: 31, emphasis in the original).

In the following I want to show, for one, that reflexivity plays out *to various degrees*, that is to say, it affects numerous interlocking strata of meaning that intermingle in innovation processes (on reflexivity in innovation processes, see also the essay by Arnold Windeler in this volume). Each individual act of reflexive observation and shaping can itself become subject to reflexivity. The 'new reflexive quality' of innovations thus cannot, as standard, be understood as a one-stage relationship between a primary innovative act and its reflexive consideration and shaping, for example, in explicit communications of its meaning (Knoblauch 2013, and in this volume) or its instrumental use (Schubert 2014, and in this volume). I would rather like to argue that the challenge lies in investigating the dynamics of innovation processes with respect to *specific types of reflexivity* and more complex *reflexivity loops*.

In a nutshell, my thesis on 'citizen panels' is this: I seek to show that governance innovations are invariably processes of societal (re-)ordering that involve several degrees of reflexivity: first, the reflexive shaping of ongoing collective ordering and, second, the problematization and redesign of patterns emerging in the process of doing the shaping. Then, as also this problematization and redesign is observed and shaped, this leads to a third degree of reflexivity. Finally, by considering specific activities such as impact assessment or activities that pursue alternative courses for the future development of citizen panels—an issue that we will address later in this paper—we are already looking at the sixth degree of reflexivity. Activities that explicitly contest the methods that are used in this process of impact assessment open the seventh degree (see Figure 1). So rather than a simple relation between primary innovative action and a process of observation that adds reflexivity, we have a cascade of manifold observations of observations and numerous acts of shaping the acts of shaping, which results in reflexivity of seven degrees.

A second point that I want to contribute is the differentiation of various framings of reflexivity. As is generally the case for any observation, analysis, or other engagement with reality, reflections on innovation processes also do not 'come out of nowhere.' They take place within particular perspectives, make reference to particular horizons of meaning, and are embedded in specific contexts of social interaction. As a result, *reflexivities* (in the plural) possess a particular selectivity.

I wish to make this clear by differentiating different 'framings.'[2] In the following, I concentrate on political and scientific framings of reflexivity.

Here, too, I shall begin by stating my central thesis: What I intend to show is that specific dynamics of the innovation process result from a somewhat dialectical interaction of political and scientific reflexivity. In an open-ended variation of politicization and scientization, the innovation of governance essentially unfurls in an endless spiral of reflexivity.

This article is organized as follows: I begin with further remarks on the concept of governance and governance innovations as well as on the degrees and framings of reflexivity. Then I describe the case referred to here by providing a short reconstruction of the historical innovation process of citizen panels. As part of this description, I discuss an exercise in constructive impact assessment, which I pursued with colleagues. Finally, I conclude this article by discussing the implications and consequences of a differentiated consideration of the reflexive quality of innovation.

2 Governance: The Reflexivity of Collective Ordering Processes

With the term governance, I refer to the shaping of collective orders. I use the term heuristically in order to identify the various forms in which collective orders are shaped. In so doing, I am following an understanding that is formed in distinction to a notion of 'government' that assumes that collective orders are primarily shaped through hierarchical regulation, the monopoly of violence of the state, and institutionalized politics.[3] However, the conceptual extension of 'governing'

---

2 This does not imply a decision in favor of any particular concept of framing (or any more specific framing of the social process of framing, one could say). My argument can be specified by reference to Goffman's concept of framing (Goffman 1974) but also by drawing on other concepts such as social worlds (Clarke and Star 2008), social fields (Bourdieu 1993), value spheres (Weber 1920), provinces of meaning (Schütz 1945), communications systems (Luhmann 1975), orders of discourse (Foucault 1972), pragmatic regimes of worth (Boltanski and Thévenot 2006), or institutional logics (Thornton, Ocasio, and Lounsbury 2012).

3 As variously as 'governance' is used in the literature, there is one shared point of reference: the departure from a notion of 'government' according to which society is centrally governed and constituted through the collective ordering activities of nation states. This is often based on observations of a transformation of collective ordering patterns over the last half century. Among other things, contemporary observers have witnessed an expansion of neo-corporatist negotiations, the rise of new social move-

pursued here goes beyond what is commonly associated with the term in political science in that I explicitly include techno-scientific processes of ordering as a mode of shaping collective order, that is, as a dimension of governance (Callon and Latour 1981; cf. Irwin 2008).

That said, what does it mean to investigate innovation in governance with respect to its reflexive quality? By definition, the suggested term *governance* already implies the reflexivity of societal ordering processes because it describes the observation, problematization, and shaping of emergent and ongoing processes of social ordering. Governance is *per se* already a reflexive (re-)ordering of social relations. I wish to underline this by conceptually delineating governance from purely emergent ordering processes: Even if processes of institutionalization, lifestyle formation, language development, and so on can be claimed to shape social relations as well (Berger and Luckmann 1966; Bourdieu 1987; Foucault 2005), I reserve the notion of governance for activities in which the ordering effects of institutions, lifestyles, and language are deliberately addressed and shaped.

If we now turn to innovation, then the question is how forms of governance are renewed. This comes down to asking how new actors, interaction patterns, and institutions are configured that play a part in the observation, problematization, and shaping of collective orders. Attending to innovation in governance thus adds a further level of reflexivity. While governance *per se* already entails active societal self-referentiality, governance innovations add reflexivity to that self-referentiality. They actively articulate and shape the ways in which governance is performed.

The question about *reflexive innovation* in governance takes the issue even a step further. Here, the focus is on the *activities that create* new forms of govern-

---

ments and civil society organizations, and the development of transnational expert regulation. According to this diagnosis, the governing of society has been decentralized.

This move towards governance has both an analytical and a political-programmatic dimension. Analytically, it points to a *de facto* existing plurality of intertwining forms of collective that are to be empirically investigated with an expanded conceptual arsenal (Colebatch 2009), also looking at deeper cultural and material dimensions of social order (Shore and Wright 1997; Antoniades 2003; Djelic and Sahlin-Andersson 2006; Braun, Whatmore, and Stengers 2010; Feldman 2011). In a political-programmatic sense, the notion of governance serves to promote a pushing back of the state as a functional requirement of complexity. This also promotes a draining of governing power from institutions of democratic control (Papadopoulos 2004; Heinelt 2008). Correspondingly, there are heated discussions about whether the shift in terminology from *government* to *governance* reflects a given change in reality or brings about this so-described change in the first place (Offe 2008; Bevir 2010; Bevir and Krupicka 2011; Peters 2011a, 2011b).

ance, that is, on the ways in which the process of innovating governance is reflexively problematized.[4]

By focusing on the reflexive quality of governance innovations, we have already arrived at a third degree of reflexivity: Reflexivity of the first degree addresses governance as an active, formative reference to collective order. Reflexivity of the second degree addresses innovations in governance as an active, formative reference to existing patterns of governance (i.e. to reflexivity of the first degree). And reflexivity of the third degree addresses innovation in governance as an active, formative reference to the process of renewing patterns of governance (i.e. to reflexivity of the second degree).

It is important to note that these degrees of reflexivity are only analytically separate. The activities that they involve blend into each other; in concrete situations, different degrees of reflexivity are active at the same time. This may, for example, manifest itself in a process of citizen participation on the 'utilization of nature.' The interactions observed here might refer to existing patterns of shaping the collective utilization of nature, e.g. through rules for nature conservation (this would be governance). At the same time, they may refer to ongoing attempts at enhancing participation in the process of devising rules for nature conservation (this would be an innovation in governance), or they might refer to difficulties encountered in articulating and introducing more participatory modes of rule-making for nature conservation (this would be a reflexive innovation in governance). All this is not a matter of separate forums, committees, or agenda items but is part of one single ongoing discussion.

I now return to the point that there are also different framings of reflexivity, not just different degrees. What is at issue here are specific qualitative orientations and selectivities in observing, problematizing, and shaping collective ordering processes.

---

4   I reserve the term innovation to describe novelty resulting from (distributed) acts of shaping this novelty. Actual results may not mirror the intentions of those seeking to shape them. Yet, I would not use the term innovation for emergent novelties which do not bear the imprint of any intended shaping. Hence, as is true for governance, innovation is also *per se* reflexive. It presupposes the problematization of existing orders.

3 The Co-Production of Order: Political and Epistemic Reflexivity

The term 'politics' is often used to describe collective ordering and governing in its entirety, that is, to describe what I call governance here. However, I consider it analytically more useful to reserve the term 'politics' for a particular dimension of governance. I use it to refer to a specific mode of shaping collective orders. This specific political mode works via the construction of collective subjects and the representation of their will and interests. This is based on a constructionist understanding of political representation, which acknowledges that collective subjectivities do not exist prior to but come into existence only through their representation. Representation is thus performative.[5] The practical challenge of politics is to experimentally create acceptance for representational claims and to wield the authority thus generated to mobilize and regulate collective agency (Bourdieu 1985; Hitzler 2002; Rosanvallon 2002; Soeffner and Tänzler 2002; Latour 2003; Saward 2006; Disch 2009, 2011). This is how politics engages in the shaping of collective orders by symbolically and materially constructing groups, collective identities, common will and interests, and public goods.

This means that not every order and not even every system of rule or every form of power or domination is political. Orders may be justified in the name of tradition or in the name of nature and practical necessity. Ruling may utilize violence and not care much about justification and authority at all. What holds for upholding a collective order applies similarly to attempts at subverting it. Not every instance of contestation, problematization, or resistance is political (in contrast, for example, to Rancière 2015; Barry 2001; Li 2007). Such acts are political only when claims that an existing order represents the collective will and interest are contested or when alternative identities and collective subjects voice demands for recognition. Only in cases of this kind do I speak of politics as a specific form of governing via the generation of *political authority*.

Against the background of a broad notion of governance, we can investigate science as a further mode in the shaping of collective orders that works alongside and in combination with politics. Employing science in the process of ordering does not take place via the representation of collective subjects but via the representation of objective realities. The role of science here is to establish representations of objects and factual conditions by way of generating *epistemic* authority. To the extent that science succeeds in securing acceptance for its representative claims,

---

5 For the difference between constructivist (phenomenological) and constructionist (pragmatist) conceptions of reality-making see, for example, Knorr Cetina (1995).

it can resolve matters of fact and provide a shared reality. Here, too, I make reference to constructionist studies that have investigated the practical work that goes into establishing representations (Knorr-Cetina 1995). These studies acknowledge that the objective realities of science, in order to match a theoretical description, must be experimentally constructed in the protected spaces of research, as a local reduction of complexity. The challenge is to first reduce broader public interference in the process of constructing some selectively reduced order and then to muster acceptance for ready-made results among a broader collective to adopt them for a shared perception of objective reality (Hacking 1983; Shapin 1984; Knorr-Cetina 1995; Latour 1999; Callon, Lascoumes, and Barthe 2009). To the extent that this is successfully accomplished, for example by claiming that research results are neutral representations of nature, science can generate epistemic authority to orient collective action and mobilize support for the installation of technology that 'applies' the 'discovered' functional mechanisms. This epistemic mode of ordering can be termed 'technoscience' (Bachelard 1984; Rheinberger 2007). Alluding to a broader notion of politics as the taking of collectively binding decisions, the decision-making about collective realities implied in technoscience has been termed 'politics by other means' (Latour 1983), 'ontological politics' (Mol 1998), or 'cosmopolitics' (Stengers 2010).

By bringing together politics and science as two modes of collective ordering, we gain a broader view of governance as a 'co-production' of political and epistemic authority in the interaction of politics and science (see Jasanoff 2004; Voß 2014, 2016b; Pfister 2016). In both modes, authority is generated via the representation of a unity that transcends individual subject positions—either normatively, by representing the will and interest of a collective subject, or factually, by representing objective reality as given independently of any subjective engagements. In both modes, practices of representation are *performative*: they constitute their referents (collective subjectivity and objective reality) in the process of representing them.

If we now return to the topic of innovation in governance, we can take account of the entanglement of politics and science.[6] In the contexts of real-world experiments that simultaneously entail political reform and the production of scientific

---

6   This conception has been developed from empirical research on the historical emergence and spread of new forms of governance, such as environmental markets (emissions trading, biodiversity certificates, Voß 2007b; Mann and Simons 2014; Simons and Voß 2014; Voß and Simons 2014), public participation methods (consensus conferences, citizen juries, planning cells, Voß and Amelung 2013; Voß 2016a), the regulation of infrastructure sectors (Voß 2007a; Voß and Bauknecht 2007), and experimental sustainability strategies (transition management, Voß, Smith, and Grin 2009; Voß 2014).

evidence, political and scientific work contribute to the realization of new models of governance (Voß 2014, 2016b). Likewise, governance innovations can 'hit a wall' in either the political or the epistemic dimension. Furthermore, political and epistemic authority can also deliberately be pitted against each other: the political anchorage of governance patterns may be disrupted via problematizing the dysfunctionality of apparently just and equal orders, or the epistemic anchorage may be unhinged via problematizing exclusionary and discriminatory effects of apparently efficient orders.

This conceptual repertoire allows us to probe the reflexivity of innovation processes not only in terms of different degrees of reflexivity but also in terms of the framings that orient the ways in which collective ordering processes are observed, problematized, and shaped. A *political* framing is concerned with the relations between diverse identities, values and interests and how innovations affect the 'common good.' An *epistemic* framing revolves around factual conditions, functionality, and potentials to optimize effectiveness and efficiency. Let us now turn to the case study of citizen panels, which I will use to show how political and epistemic reflexivity are interwoven and how they feed a particular dynamic of innovation.[7]

4 Reflexivity in the Innovation of Citizen Panels

As an innovation in governance, citizen panels addresses the process of constructing a collective will and interest and the generation of political authority. It thus concerns a particular dimension of governance: the production and contestation of legitimacy.[8] Citizen panels propose a new way of practicing politics (in the aforementioned sense of working towards accepted representations of collective will and interest). More specifically, we might say that they are an innovation in democracy because the collective that is to be represented is the general public of equal citizens. Citizen panels come with the claim that they provide a procedure to elicit public reason as a collective property of the lifeworld. The verdict of citizen panels on specific issues is thus claimed to represent a common will.

---

7 In addition, there are other framings, for instance, of an aesthetic or spiritual nature, that can inspire reflexivity. Here, I restrict myself to the interaction of politics and science.

8 Other innovations in governance address problems of effective steering and implementation. Examples include what is usually discussed as 'policy instruments,' such as the installation of independent regulatory agencies or the introduction of emissions-trading schemes for climate protection.

There is ample room for debate as to whether these new forms of democracy perform better than established procedures of political party competition, parliamentarianism, or referendums (Wakeford et al. 2007; Smith 2009; Geissel and Newton 2011; Grönlund et al. 2014). But this shall not concern us here. I do not want to focus on the 'what' of this innovation but on the 'how': How have citizen panels become established as a new form of governance? In what way can the process of innovating citizen panels be said to be 'reflexive'? For this purpose, I will briefly sketch the innovation process.[9] This description will show how during the innovation process seven degrees of reflexivity have unfolded. Each of them has emerged from the confrontation of political and epistemic problematizations of the innovation process. As a point of departure for the process that led to the innovation of citizen panels, we can refer to an initial problematization of infrastructure and technological developments as issues of public concern (cf. Dewey 2012). As it became politically problematized with regard to its serving of collective interests, it successively became a task of the (emerging welfare) state. What we see here is a first degree of reflexivity in ongoing processes of collective ordering: the uncoordinated development of science and technological infrastructures as the result of distributed social interactions was politically problematized and established as an object of governance to be addressed by the state.

A further degree of reflexivity can be identified in what followed the initial political problematization and public regulation of infrastructures and technology development through the state. The ways in which the political institutions of state planning went about the task of shaping technology and infrastructure was problematized for a lack of functional effectiveness and efficiency. For 'rationalizing' the planning process it was removed from the arena of contentious party politics and handed over to experts for decision-making based on objective analysis. The public management of technology and infrastructure was instrumentally optimized

---

9 This is based on our work in the Innovation in Governance Research Group. The group was funded from 2009 to 2014 by the Federal Ministry of Education and Research (grant number 01UU0906). We reconstructed transnational innovation processes in governance by looking at formative events (for example, experimental implementations of particular models, the establishment of research facilities and network organizations, key publications and conferences). We used materials such as academic literature, practitioner guidelines and handbooks, project reports, personal archives, websites, as well as transcripts from 30 interviews and a group discussion with 25 actors involved in innovation processes (Amelung 2012; Amelung, Voß, and Grabner 2012; Amelung and Grabner 2013a, 2013b; Voß and Amelung 2013; Mann et al. 2014). Starting from a set of conceptual propositions, we developed an interpretation of the patterns and dynamics of these innovation processes by means of testing and abduction (Van de Ven et al. 1999; Yin 2003; Van de Ven 2007: chapter 7).

by applying scientific tools of assessment (like system modeling and cost-benefit analysis). This new 'technocratic' way of governing (Saretzki 1994) accompanied the development of the modern welfare state well into the 1960s. It sought to put the shaping of collective order on a factual basis in order to effectively realize an objectively defined common good (for example, Lerner and Lasswell 1951).

Around the late 1960s, however, a further reflexivity loop set in when technocratic state planning became subject to political contestation for how it defined the collective interest. New social movements and intellectuals effectively called into question the neutrality of functional analysis and collective legitimacy of expertocratic planning (Habermas 1971; Marcuse 1991). Critique shed light on the value decisions implicit in factual and functional analyses and illustrated the fusion of technocratic policy analysis with societal power relations. Technocratic governance was hence once again politically problematized, raising demands for a democratization of state planning and science policy (Fischer 1990). Emergent forms of participation took shape in the form of public protests, resistance to infrastructural and technical projects, as well as initiatives for developing alternative, and more 'appropriate' science, technology and expertise (Saretzki 2001).

These 'wild' forms of participation marked the beginning of the development of citizen panels as a specific procedure: the direct involvement of citizens and spontaneously emerging publics in controversial topics triggered efforts to develop specific procedures that would ensure constructive and legitimate citizen participation. They aimed at facilitating the articulation of public opinion as a considered rational consensus. 'Wild' participation was problematized on functional grounds. In the 1970s, various kinds of citizen panels developed in different regional and issue contexts. The 'planning cell' evolved in the context of municipal politics and infrastructure planning in the German state of North Rhine-Westphalia (Dienel 1970, 1971, 1978; Vergne 2009), the 'citizens' jury' emerged in the U.S. state of Minnesota (Crosby 1974, 1975, 1995; Crosby, Kelly, and Schaefer 1986; Crosby and Nethercut 2005), and the 'consensus conference' was developed for parliamentary technology impact assessments in Denmark (Joss and Durant 1995; Andersen and Jæger 1999). In the 1990s, these methods of citizen involvement spread rapidly beyond the contexts in which they were originally developed (Stewart, Kendall, and Coote 1994; Coote and Lenaghan 1997). Since then, they have been used in professional public participation work, particularly in connection with contested technoscientific development projects (genetic engineering, nuclear technology, neuroscience, nanotechnology, etc.) and applied in thousands of cases in various regions and at different levels ranging from municipal administrations to the United Nations (Amelung 2012; Voß and Amelung 2016).

Towards the end of the 1990s epistemic work was further intensified for 'hardening' the functional claims which supported particular procedures of citizen participation. This was a reaction to the proliferation beyond local contexts and the entry of new actors from commercial public relations and market research onto the scene (Parkinson 2004, 2006; Hendriks 2006; Hendriks and Carson 2008). This began to erode the trust in citizen panels that had earlier been cultivated within personal relationships within local networks. While, in the early 1970s, the development and implementation of participation procedures were embedded in specific political situations and only loosely connected with theoretical considerations, the erosion of local networks required more abstract forms of legitimation in form of explicit theories and scientific evidence of the functioning of particular designs. This prompted a technoscientific approach for establishing evidence-based design standards (Chilvers 2008; Bogner 2010; Laurent 2011b). First efforts were made to systematically compare and evaluate forms of organized citizen participation (Renn, Webler, and Wiedemann 1995; Hörning 1999; Rowe and Frewer 2000; OECD 2001). Dedicated research centers, networks, and professional associations were established. The European Commission played a prominent role in this respect by supporting research and development projects to establish standards. As part of the effort to build an epistemic authority in support of, methods were explicitly linked to the theory of deliberative democracy (Sulkin and Simon 2001; Smith and Wales 2002). Evidence on the functioning of particular designs was produced in laboratory experiments and monitored field trials so as to allow for the disciplining of practitioners within an emerging profession and to secure legitimacy for the procedure and its results with target groups and the wider public. In the 2000s, processes such as the 'citizen jury,' 'planning cell,' and 'consensus conference' were united under umbrella terms like 'citizen panels,' 'deliberative forums,' or 'mini-publics' (Hendriks 2005; Brown 2006; Goodin and Dryzek 2006). This was for developing a shared methodological basis, also for being used in transnational regulation processes (Rask and Worthington 2012). Academic discourse discussed citizen panels as a new instrument of participatory governance (Elliott et al. 2005) or a democratic innovation (Smith 2009; Geissel and Newton 2011). A transnational knowledge network for the development and application of citizen panels took shape at the intersection of a new academic research field (with specialist journals, web portals, regular conferences, etc.) and a new service industry (with its own associations and ongoing efforts at professionalization) (Chilvers 2008, 2012; Hendriks and Carson 2008; Saretzki 2008; Voß and Amelung 2016). Participation has become an epistemic issue and a matter of functional design.

Yet, during the 2000s, this renewed technoscientization of governance was again reflected upon from a political perspective. At this point, it was not a technocracy in terms of substantial political decisions that was problematized but a technocracy of political process, a technocracy of participation that prescribed the ways in which citizens could legitimately engage in public issues and produce collective views. From a political point of view, the emerging technoscience of participation was challenged for assuming a particular ontology of social life, public communication, politics, and democracy, and for ignoring a diversity of political values, rationalities, and situational conditions with the claim to represent a universalistic approach. Dedicated studies demonstrated the artificiality of organized deliberation as well as exclusionary practices and built-in biases even if procedures were carried out by the book, which they indeed seldom were (Irwin 2001; Gomart and Hajer 2003; Lezaun and Soneryd 2007; Bogner 2010; Braun and Schultz 2010; Felt and Fochler 2010). In addition to discursive problematization, organized participation procedures were soon accompanied by protest actions that demonstrated how technoscientifically configured participation processes reproduced dominant discourses and power structures (Laurent 2011a; Pallett and Chilvers 2013). In addition, alternative forms of 'open designs' were proposed that left procedural settings to be defined by the participating citizens themselves (Wakeford 2003; Wakeford and Singh 2008; Chilvers 2013). All these activities revolve around the ways by which we engage in innovation processes as something that needs to be reflected on in terms of political implications (Laurent 2011b; Law, Ruppert, and Savage 2011; Law 2012).

But the story does not end there. In a further turn, at around 2010, the outburst of controversy over technoscientifically devised procedures of participation became subject to epistemic analysis. The confrontation of well-intended participation work with fundamental critique and radical protest was described in terms of underlying social dynamics (Chilvers 2013; Pallett and Chilvers 2013). And it became subject to a practical experiment to apply 'constructive technology assessment (CTA)' for systematically articulating and feeding back political issues in the development of citizen panels. In April 2013, we organized a workshop with 25 actors who were practically involved in the development of citizen panels to explicate various concerns and ontological assumptions implicit in the controversies over their design. The report has made these issues accessible to political evaluation and public debate (Mann et al. 2014). In this case, CTA procedures had been devised to redress the political debate in scientific terms, that is with regard to functional considerations on the organization of political debate about methods of participation (Voß 2016a).

A final step in the reflexivization of collective ordering can be seen in the criticism launched by one of the participants against the procedure applied for the assessment process. This participant invoked a collective interest to work towards consensus. He thus problematized our design of an assessment procedure geared towards the explication of conflicts. Thus, we had the spiral turn further, with another degree of political reflexivity added to our epistemic approach at ordering political controversy over the development of participation methods. This opened up a seventh degree of reflexivity in the process of collective ordering.

The innovation process as a whole can thus be described as a reflexivity spiral, which, in a dialectic interplay of political and epistemic problematization, leads to further degrees of reflexivity. In so doing, the innovation of a new form of governance comprises several political and scientific innovations. Politically, there is the constitution of new 'public issues' and corresponding political interest groups, first, in relation to uncoordinated infrastructural and technological development, then, in relation to technocratic state planning, later, in relation to an emerging technocracy of participatory process, and, finally, also in relation to the procedure for the constructive assessment of citizen panel designs. Such political innovations are constitutively interlocked with a series of scientific innovations: New objects of study and scientific research fields have been established, first, in relation to the public management of infrastructural and technological development, then, in relation to the design and organization of participation processes, and, finally, in relation to the social dynamics of controversies over the design of participatory procedures. The dynamics of innovation of governance arise from the interaction of these political and scientific innovations. The result is a cascade of politicization and scientization (see Figure 1).

This portrayal of the process makes it clear that, in each case, the reflexivity of innovation processes has a form and direction that is connected with a specific framing for observing and shaping ongoing processes of collective ordering. Various reflexivities are possible in a given situation, each of which is selective in specific ways. The reflexivities articulated in the historical process are not necessarily forgotten as the innovation process continues. Instead, they can become institutionalized so that the perspectives accumulate and work in parallel. From this it follows that, in the long term, the reflexivity of innovation becomes a phenomenon with multiple aspects. Depending on which framing asserts itself. Reflexivity can give rise to different dynamics of innovation.

Innovating Governance

Politicization 1: Problematization of infrastructural and technological development as an issue of public concern, state planning	
	Scientization 1: Epistemic rationalization of public action, scientific policy analysis, and technocratic administration
Politicization 2: Critique of state planning technocracy, spontaneous emergence of new forms of citizen participation	
	Scientization 2: Functional assessment of spontaneous participation and problematization of the unprofessional management of the participation process, technoscientific development of participation methods
Politicization 3: Critique of transnational technocracy of political procedure, protest against organized participation, development of alternative approaches	
	Scientization 3: Scientific analysis of political controversy over participation methods, designs, and the implementation of constructive assessment of participation methods
Politicization 4: Critique of the assessment procedure in relation to the implied diagnosis and goals	

Figure 1 Reflexivity spiral in the innovation of citizen panels, a cascade of politicization and scientization of collective ordering (source: own illustration).

In specific reflexivities, particular aspects of the collective ordering process are called into question. In combination, they are then stripped of their self-evident quality. They hence become accessible and amenable to discussion and negotiation. Depending on the orientation according to which reflexivity is practiced, this results in various disturbances with the potential to affect any particular approach to engaging in collective ordering and the positions and authority of actors involved therein. The question as to which reflexive mode of framing should be applied is thus a question that is immediately connected with the interests of the actors involved. Conflicting reflexivities may prompt controversies over the basic question whether the ongoing process of collective ordering shall be considered, politically, in relation to the various representations of collective values and interests or, scientifically, in relation to various representations of objective conditions and functionality. The question as to which reflexive mode of framing should be applied is thus a question that is immediately connected with the interests of the actors involved. The articulation of competing reflexivities may thus itself become an area of struggle. And the competitive assertion of reflexive perspectives on innovation may itself turn reflexive, in which case the establishment of specific meanings of reflexivity becomes a strategic challenge for realizing certain preferred courses in the innovation process. Practically speaking, this means that actors might seek to avoid a technical-functional analysis of political value-oriented discussion because of their fear of repercussions that might impair their ability to pursue a certain line of development. The struggle over reflexivities may hence become an arena for the meta-governance of the innovation process.

5 Conclusion

I wish to claim that real innovation processes play out at this level of complexity. What can we learn from the conceptual differentiation of reflexivities and the illustration of their interplay in the case of citizen panels as an instance of innovation in governance? I divide my conclusions into three parts: First, I present general conclusions on the reflexivity of governance innovations, then I specifically discuss the differentiation of degrees and framings, and, finally, I discuss the effects of continuous reflexivity in the creation of collective orders.

Responding to the research program of the 'innovation society,' we can determine that the innovation of governance considered here is reflexive: The creation of new patterns of shaping collective order is accompanied by communication about the conditions and strategies for articulating, introducing, stabilizing, and spreading citizen participation. It is not just the performance of citizen panels that is heatedly debated but also the ways in which performance is conceived and how it is materially configured. The dynamics of innovation cannot be described appropriately without considering this reflexivity.[10]

---

10 Yet the approach pursued here cannot be used to determine the extent to which that observed reflexivity constitutes a special type of innovation. Conceptual considerations give us reason to suspect that reflexivity is by no means a recent phenomenon. However, the accumulation of further degrees of reflexivity suggests that a gradual increase in the intensity and complexity of the reflexivity of innovation is likely to occur over the history of modern societies. The semantics of innovation gained currency in the field of politics and governance as early as in the 1960s (in German and in English, and with noteworthy variance in their conceptual approaches, for example, Lowi 1963; Senghaas 1965; Thompson 1965; Klages 1968; Walker 1969). Nevertheless, the public debate on the renewal of governance continued to be dominated by the

There are two central findings on the reflexive creation of novelty that I wish to highlight. First, it is important to note that the reflexivity of innovations unfolds to various degrees. It thus seems appropriate to specify the diagnosis of an innovation society in relation to specific qualities of reflexivity in innovation. The challenge is to analytically differentiate between various forms of problematization and formative influences, even if they blend into each other in practical terms. In the case of our constructive assessment exercise for citizen panels, for example, efforts at scientifically developing and standardizing the procedure (the fourth degree of reflexivity) were directly interwoven with efforts at problematizing the assessment procedure in political terms (the seventh degree of reflexivity). An interesting question in this context might be whether such a differentiation of degrees of reflexivity would also be a fruitful endeavor in regard to other innovation processes.

As a second finding, I wish to expose the multiplicity of reflexivity, not just in degrees but also in terms of frames that might be applied in observing processes of collective ordering. The case of citizen panels shows how the multifaceted problematization involved in this reflexivity equips this innovation with a particular dynamic. On some occasions, the consideration of a diversity of worldviews, values, and interests, which are served by particular orders, moves to the foreground, whereas on other occasions, it is the rational consistency and empirical functionality of those orders that take center stage.

It is of interest to note that governance innovations actually figure as hybrid innovations. Their development has comprised different political and scientific innovations. These innovations have involved politicizing new issues and mobilizing new collective interests as well as identifying new research problems and producing new scientific facts. In the case of citizen panels, the creation of collective order must thus be understood as a political and scientific co-production. Accordingly, the resulting innovation in governance spans a political and an epistemic dimension.[11] This multiplicity and the infinite nature of reflexivity lends the innovation

---

    semantics of 'reform.' A hypothesis for future discourse-oriented analyses could be that the term 'innovation' came into play with further degrees of reflexivity. Whereas 'reform' relates to processes of renewal that are embedded in particular state orders or political systems, 'innovation' relates to the development and spread of new political and governance forms across specific contexts of implementation. A decontextualized understanding of new forms of governance renders their scientific articulation more important—and, with it, the notion of innovation. In the case of citizen panels, this was the case in the mid-1990s (See Figure 1: Scientization 2).

11 In this account of the innovation process, I have focused on the entanglement of political and scientific innovations. However, with respect to the market for professional public participation services that has established itself in connection with the devel-

process its dynamics. Heterogeneous framings and the specific activities that they trigger accordingly keep fueling innovation. Is the co-production and constitutive entanglement of innovations in various fields and the resulting dynamic of 'hyper-reflexivity' a general characteristic of the innovation society?

Finally, I wish to discuss the effects of continuous reflexivity in the creation of collective orders. I will address two aspects: the potential of intertwining reflexivities for integrating multiple societal rationalities and the practical challenges that arise from the irony that efforts at reflexively improving collective orders tend to contradict one another.

The potential of reflexivity may be seen in the fact that it represents a practical way of dealing with side effects, which are seen as an inherent problem of modern society. What this case of innovating citizen participation reveals is not a progressive decoupling of differentiated rationalities but rather their mutual enveloping and increasing entanglement. What we see is not a drifting apart but rather a closer intertwining of institutionalized rationalities (cf. Rammert 1997, 2010). Politics and science appear to be part of a fundamental division of power in the shaping of collective orders (cf. Shapin and Schaffer 1985; Rip 1986; Latour 1993). The reflexivity spiral thus exhibits a practical way of integrating multiple rationalities and evaluative approaches into collective ordering processes.

However, there are also specific practical challenges. One is that all certainty is lost that could provide an Archimedean point in the practical pursuit of problematizing and shaping collective orders. Once one recognizes that no one reflexive approach is more than only a partial rationalization, any attempt at being consistently reflexive will eventually dissolve in an endless regression. This entails a threat of paralysis. When multiple ways of reflexively problematizing and shaping are sought to be synthesized, rather than keeping them separate, institutionally or by sequentially learning and forgetting them, then this may result in subverting the very dynamics described above. The endlessness of mutually transgressing reflections does not serve as a point of departure for actively engaging in collective ordering. If the process of shaping collective order would consequently seek to anticipate the excluded other, it would open a bottomless pit of dialectical self-ref-

---

opment of citizen panels, we can recognize that this participatory innovation is also constitutively intertwined with innovations in the commercial field. There have been a number of specific technological artifacts that have been developed in association with participation procedures (e.g., Metaplan equipment and other facilitator's toolkit, software for online deliberation). And we can further observe the emergence of a new aesthetic genre that is closely linked with this innovation in governance: Artists are often hired to assist participative deliberation processes by providing graphic or visual contributions.

utation, so that any ability to act seriously would be undermined (Brodocz 2003; Reckwitz 2003). As certainties liquefy, the act of thinking about, talking about, and creating social order of any kind becomes an ironic endeavor (Rorty 1989). Without their orienting illusion of progress considered engagement with collective ordering would turn into play. This would, however, lead to the dialectic division of epistemic and political powers collapsing and the reflexivity spiral losing its momentum. Conjectures could be made on how such a postmodern process of playful engagements with collective ordering would unfold.

What could also be done is to cultivate an orientation for action that neither requires certainty nor unambiguity about purpose for seriously engaging with collective orders, but that would understand itself as a local and temporally restricted engagement in practices that are partially rational: their actual worth was not in their immediate purpose but in their interplay with other practices and their contribution to a balancing of diverse partialities. The practical challenge of reflexive innovation would then lie in cultivating immanent rationalities (e.g. of politics and science) at certain moments of engagement in order to become an agent in collective ordering, even though one might know that they are partial and that other positions are required to balance them (Brodocz 2003; Rip 2006). Only in this way can a diversity of various approaches to ordering, the resulting tensions, mutual balancing, and the dialectical dynamics of innovation be preserved. The conclusion that we might draw from all this is that reflexivity demands that the modern task of ordering be performed, even in light of a postmodern liquefaction of realities.

References

Amelung, Nina. 2012. "The Emergence of Citizen Panels as a De Facto Standard." *Quaderni* (79): 13-28.
Amelung, Nina and Louisa Grabner. 2013a. *Report on Constituency Formation and Dynamics in the Innovation of Citizen Panels* (Unpublished Working Papers of Innovation in Governance Research Group). Berlin: Technische Universität Berlin.
Amelung, Nina and Louisa Grabner. 2013b. *Report on Design Controversies in the Innovation of Citizen Panels* (Unpublished Working Paper of Innovation in Governance Research Group). Berlin: Technische Universität Berlin.
Amelung, Nina, Jan-Peter Voß, and Louisa Grabner. 2012. *Report on the Innovation Journey of Citizen Panels* (Unpublished Working Paper of Innovation in Governance Research Group). Berlin: Technische Universität Berlin.
Andersen, Ida-Elisabeth and Birgit Jæger. 1999. "Scenario Workshops and Consensus Conferences: Towards More Democratic Decision-Making." *Science and Public Policy* 26(5): 331-340.
Antoniades, Andreas. 2003. "Epistemic Communities, Epistemes and the Construction of (World) Politics." *Global Society* 17(1): 21-38.
Bachelard, Gaston. 1984 [1934]. *The New Scientific Spirit*. Boston: Beacon Press.
Barry, Andrew. 2001. *Political Machines: Governing a Technological Society*. London: Athlone Press.
Bauman, Zygmunt. 2000. *Liquid Modernity*. Cambridge: Polity Press.
Beck, Ulrich, Anthony Giddens, and Scott Lash, eds. 1994. *Reflexive Modernization: Politics, Tradition and Aesthetics in the Modern Social Order*. Stanford: Stanford University Press.
Berger, Peter. L. and Thomas Luckmann. 1966. *The Social Construction of Reality*. New York: Free Press.
Bevir, Mark. 2010. *Democratic Governance*. Princeton: Princeton University Press.
Bevir, Mark and Benjamin Krupicka. 2011. "On Two Types of Governance Theory. A Response to B. Guy Peters." *Critical Policy Studies* 5(4): 450-453.
Bogner, Alexander. 2010. "Partizipation als Laborexperiment. Paradoxien der Laiendeliberation in Technikfragen." *Zeitschrift für Soziologie* 39(2): 87-105.
Boltanski, Luc and Laurent Thévenot. 2006. *On Justification: Economies of Worth*. Princeton: Princeton University Press.
Bourdieu, Pierre. 1985. "Delegation and Political Fetishism." *Thesis Eleven* 10-11(1): 56-70.
Bourdieu, Pierre. 1987. *Distinction. A Social Critique of the Judgement of Taste*. Cambridge: Harvard University Press.
Bourdieu, Pierre. 1993. *Sociology in Question*. London: SAGE.
Braun, Bruce, Sarah J. Whatmore, and Isabelle Stengers. 2010. *Political Matter: Technoscience, Democracy, and Public Life*. Minneapolis: University of Minnesota Press.
Braun, Kathrin and Susanne Schultz. 2010. "'... A Certain Amount of Engineering Involved': Constructing the Public in Participatory Governance Arrangements." *Public Understanding of Science* 19(4): 403-419.
Brodocz, André. 2003. "Das Ende der politischen Theorie? Über die Rechtfertigung der Demokratie und die Ironie ihrer Unmöglichkeit." Pp. 52-64 in *Die Ironie der Politik*.

Über die Konstruktion politischer Wirklichkeiten, edited by T. Bonacker, A. Brdocz, and T. Noetzel. Frankfurt a. M.: Campus.
Brown, Mark. 2006. "Survey Article: Citizen Panels and the Concept of Representation." *Journal of Political Philosophy* 14(2): 203-225.
Callon, Michel, Pierre Lascoumes, Yannick Barthe. 2009. *Acting in an Uncertain World: An Essay on Technical Democracy.* Cambridge: MIT Press.
Callon, Michel and Bruno Latour. 1981. "Unscrewing the Big Leviathan: How Actors Macro-Structure Reality and How Sociologists Help Them to do so." Pp. 277-303 in *Advances in Social Theory and Methodology*, edited by K. Knorr-Cetina and A. V. Cicourel. London: Routledge and Kegan Paul.
Chilvers, Jason. 2008. "Environmental Risk, Uncertainty, and Participation: Mapping an Emergent Epistemic Community." *Environment and Planning A* 40(12): 2990-3008.
Chilvers, Jason. 2012. *Expertise, Technologies and Ecologies of Participation* (Working Papers 3S WP 2012-17). Norwich: Science, Society and Sustainability Research Group, University of East Anglia.
Chilvers, Jason. 2013. "Reflexive Engagement? Actors, Learning, and Reflexivity in Public Dialogue on Science and Technology." *Science Communication* 35(3): 283-310.
Clarke, Adele E. and Susan Leigh Star. 2008. "The Social Worlds Framework: A Theory/Methods Package." Pp 113-137 in *The Handbook of Science & Technology Studies*, edited by E. J. Hackett, O. Amsterdamska, M. Lynch, and J. Wajcman. Cambridge: MIT Press.
Colebatch, Hal K. 2009. "Governance as a Conceptual Development in the Analysis of Policy." *Critical Policy Studies* 3(1): 58-67.
Coote, Anna and Jo Lenaghan. 1997. *Citizens' Jury. Theory into Practice.* London: Institute for Public Policy Research.
Crosby, Ned. 1974. *The Educated Random Sample. A Pilot Study on a New Way to Get Citizen Input into the Policy*□*Making Process.* Minnesota: The Center for New Democratic Processes.
Crosby, Ned. 1975. *In Search of the Competent Citizen.* Minneapolis: Jefferson Center.
Crosby, Ned. 1995. "Citizens Juries: One Solution for Difficult Environmental Questions." Pp. 157-174 in *Fairness and Competence in Citizen Participation*, edited by O. Renn, T. Webler, and P. Wiedemann. Dordrecht: Springer.
Crosby, Ned, Janet M. Kelly, and Paul Schaefer. 1986. "Citizens Panels: A New Approach to Citizen Participation." *Public Administration Review* 46(2): 170-178.
Crosby, Ned and Doug Nethercut. 2005. "Citizens Juries: Creating a Trustworthy Voice of the People." Pp. 111-119 in *The Deliberative Democracy Handbook. Strategies for Effective Civic Engagement in the 21st Century*, edited by J. Gastil and P. Levine. San Francisco: Jossey-Bass.
Dewey, John. 2012 [1954]. *The Public and its Problems: An Essay in Political Inquiry.* University Park: Penn State Press.
Dienel, Peter. 1970. "Techniken bürgerschaftlicher Beteiligung an Planungsprozessen." Pp. 144-156 in *Partizipation. Aspekte politischer Kultur*, edited by H. Boss-Stenner, U. von Pufendorf, and K. F. Schade. Wiesbaden: Westdeutscher Verlag.
Dienel, Peter. 1971. "Wie können die Bürger an Planungsprozessen beteiligt werden? Planwahl und Planungszelle als Beteiligungsverfahren." *Der Bürger im Staat* 21(3): 151-156.

Dienel, Peter. 1978. *Die Planungszelle. Eine Alternative zur Establishment-Demokratie*. Opladen: Westdeutscher Verlag.
Disch, Lisa. 2009. *'Faitiche'-izing the People: What Representative Democracy Might Learn from Science Studies* (APSA 2009 Toronto Meeting Paper). Ann Arbor: University of Michigan.
Disch, Lisa. 2011. "Toward a Mobilization Conception of Democratic Representation." *American Political Science Review* 105(1): 100-114.
Djelic, Marie-Laure and Kerstin Sahlin-Andersson. 2006. *Transnational Governance, Institutional Dynamics of Regulation*. Cambridge: Cambridge University Press.
Elliott, Janice, Sara Heesterbeek, Carolyn J. Lukensmeyer, Nikki Slocum. 2005. *Participatory Methods Toolkit. A Practitioner's Manual*. Brussels: King Baudoin Foundation, Flemish Institute for Science and Technology Assessment.
Feldman, Greg. 2011. "Illuminating the Apparatus: Steps Toward a Nonlocal Ethnography of Global Governance." Pp. 32-49 in *Policy Worlds: Anthropology and the Analysis of Contemporary Power*, edited by C. Shore, S. Wright, and D. Peró. New York: Berghahn.
Felt, Ulrike and Maximilian Fochler. 2010. "Machineries for Making Publics: Inscribing and De-scribing Publics in Public Engagement." *Minerva* 48(3): 319-338.
Fischer, Frank. 1990. *Technocracy and the Politics of Expertise*. Newbury Park: SAGE.
Foucault, Michel. 1972. "The Discourse on Language." Pp. 215-237 in *Archaeology of Knowledge and the Discourse on Language*. New York: Pantheon Books.
Foucault, Michel. 2005. *Analytik der Macht*. Frankfurt a. M.: Suhrkamp.
Geissel, Brigitte and Kenneth Newton. 2011. *Evaluating Democratic Innovations: Curing the Democratic Malaise?* London: Routledge.
Giddens, Anthony. 1986. *The Constitution of Society*. Berkeley: University of California Press.
Giddens, Anthony. 1990. *The Consequences of Modernity*. Cambridge: Polity Press.
Goffman, Erving. 1974. *Frame Analysis: An Essay on the Organization of Experience*. Cambridge: Harvard University Press.
Gomart, Emilie and Maarten Hajer. 2003. "Is That Politics? For an Inquiry Into Forms in Contemporary Politics." Pp. 33-61 in *Social Studies of Science and Technology: Looking Back, Ahead*, edited by B. Joerges and H. Nowotny. Dordrecht: Kluwer.
Goodin, Robert E. and John S. Dryzek. 2006. "Deliberative Impacts: The Macro-Political Uptake of Mini-Publics." *Politics & Society* 34(2): 219-243.
Grönlund, Kimmo, André Bächtiger, and Maija Setälä, eds. 2014. *Deliberative Mini-Publics: Involving Citizens in the Democratic Process*. Colchester: ECPR Press.
Habermas, Jürgen. 1971. "Technology and Science as 'Ideology'." Pp. 81-122 in *Toward a Rational Society*, edited by J. Habermas. Boston: Beacon Press.
Hacking, Ian. 1983. *Representing and Intervening: Introductory Topics in the Philosophy of Natural Science*. Cambridge: Cambridge University Press.
Hacking, Ian. 2002. *Historical Ontology*. Cambridge: Harvard University Press.
Heinelt, Hubert. 2008. *Demokratie jenseits des Staates: Partizipatives Regieren und Governance*. Baden-Baden: Nomos.
Hendriks, Carolyn M. 2005. "Participatory Storylines and Their Influence on Deliberative Forums." *Policy Sciences* 38(1): 1-20.
Hendriks, Carolyn M. 2006. "When the Forum Meets Interest Politics: Strategic Uses of Public Deliberation." *Politics & Society* 34(4): 571-602.

Hendriks, Carolyn M. and Lyn Carson. 2008. "Can the Market Help the Forum? Negotiating the Commercialization of Deliberative Democracy." *Policy Sciences* 41(4): 293-313.
Hitzler, Ronald. 2002. "Inszenierung und Repräsentation. Bemerkungen zur Politikdarstellung in der Gegenwart." Pp. 35-49 in *Figurative Politik. Zur Performanz der Macht in der modernen Gesellschaft*, edited by H.-G. Soeffner and D. Tänzler. Wiesbaden: VS Verlag.
Hörning, Georg. 1999. "Citizens' Panels as a Form of Deliberative Technology Assessment." *Science and Public Policy* 26(5): 351-359.
Hutter, Michael, Hubert Knoblauch, Werner Rammert, and Arnold Windeler. 2015. "Innovation Society Today. The Reflexive Creation of Novelty." *Historical Social Research* 40(3): 30-47.
Irwin, Alan. 2001. "Constructing the Scientific Citizen: Science and Democracy in the Biosciences." *Public Understanding of Science* 10(1): 1-18.
Irwin, Alan. 2008. "STS Perspectives on Scientific Governance." Pp. 583-608 in *The Handbook of Science and Technology Studies*, edited by E. J. Hackett, O. Amsterdamska, M. Lynch, and J. Wajcman. Cambridge: MIT Press.
Jasanoff, Sheila, ed. 2004. *States of Knowledge: The Co-Production of Science and Social Order*. London: Routledge.
Joas, Hans. 1985. *G. H. Mead: A Contemporary Re-examination of His Thought*. Cambridge: Polity Press.
Joss, Simon and John Durant. 1995. *Public Participation in Science: The Role of Consensus Conferences in Europe*. Peterborough: Science Museum.
Klages, Helmut. 1968. *Soziologie zwischen Wirklichkeit und Möglichkeit*. Wiesbaden: Springer.
Knoblauch, Hubert. 2013. *Communicative Action, Reflexivity, and Innovation Society (Working Papers TUTS-WP 3-2014)*. Berlin: Technische Universität Berlin.
Knorr-Cetina, Karin. 1995. "Laboratory Studies: The Cultural Approach to the Study of Science." Pp. 140-166 in *Handbook of Science and Technology Studies*, edited by S. Jasanoff, G. E. Markle, J. C. Petersen, and T. Pinch. Thousand Oaks: SAGE.
Latour, Bruno. 1983. "Give Me a Laboratory and I Will Raise the World." Pp. 142-169 in *Science Observed. Perspectives on the Social Studies of Science*, edited by K. Knorr-Cetina and M. Mulkay. London: SAGE.
Latour, Bruno. 1993. *We Have Never Been Modern*. Cambridge: Harvard University Press.
Latour, Bruno. 1999. *Pandora's Hope. Essays on the Reality of Science Studies*. Cambridge: Harvard University Press.
Latour, Bruno. 2003. "What If We Talked Politics a Little?" *Contemporary Political Theory* 2(2): 143-164.
Laurent, Bice. 2011a. *Democracies on Trial. Assembling Nanotechnology and Its Problems*. Paris: Mines Paris Tech, Centre de Sociologie de l'Innovation.
Laurent, Brice. 2011b. "Technologies of Democracy: Experiments and Demonstrations." *Science and Engineering Ethics* 17(4): 649-666.
Law, John. 2012. "Collateral Realities." Pp. 156-178 in *The Politics of Knowledge*, edited by F. D. Rubio and P. Baert. London: Routledge.
Law, John, Evelyn Ruppert, and Mike Savage. 2011. *The Double Social Life of Method (CRESC Working Papers No. 95)*. Milton Keynes: Centre for Research on Socio-Cultural Change, Open University.

Lerner, Daniel and Harold D Lasswell. 1951. *The Policy Sciences: Recent Developments in Scope and Method*. Stanford: Stanford University Press.
Lezaun, Javier and Linda Soneryd. 2007. "Consulting Citizens: Technologies of Elicitation and the Mobility of Publics." *Public Understanding of Science* 16(3): 279-297.
Li, Tania M. 2007. *The Will to Improve. Governmentality, Development and the Practice of Politics*. Chapel Hill: Duke University Press.
Lowi, Theodore. 1963. "Toward Functionalism in Political Science: The Case of Innovation in Party Systems." *American Political Science Review* 57(3): 570-583.
Luhmann, Niklas. 1975. "Interaktion, Organisation, Gesellschaft. Anwendungen der Systemtheorie." Pp. 9-20 in *Soziologische Aufklärung 2. Aufsätze zur Theorie der Gesellschaft*, edited by N. Luhmann. Opladen: Westdeutscher Verlag.
Lynch, Michael. 2000. "Against Reflexivity as an Academic Virtue and Source of Privileged Knowledge." *Theory, Culture & Society* 17(3): 26-54.
Mann, Carsten and Arno Simons. 2014. "Local Emergence and International Developments of Conservation Trading Systems: Innovation Dynamics and Related Problems." *Journal of Environmental Conservation* 42(4): 325-334.
Mann, Carsten., Jan-Peter Voß, Nina Amelung, Arno Simons, Till Runge, and Louisa Grabner. 2014. *Challenging Futures of Citizen Panels. Critical Issues for Robust Forms of Public Participation. A Report Based on Interactive, Anticipatory Assessment of the Dynamics of Governance Instruments, April 26, 2013*. Berlin: Technische Universität Berlin.
Marcuse, Herbert. 1991. *One-Dimensional Man: Studies in Ideology of Advanced Industrial Society*. London: Routledge.
Mol, Annemarie. 1998. "Ontological Politics. A Word and Some Questions." *The Sociological Review* 46(S1): 74-89.
OECD. 2001. *Citizens as Partners. OECD Handbook on Information, Consultation and Public Participation in Policy-Making*. Paris: OECD.
Offe, Claus. 2008. "Governance—'Empty signifier' oder sozialwissenschaftliches Forschungsprogramm?" Pp. 61-76 in *Governance in einer sich wandelnden Welt*, edited by G. F. Schuppert and M. Zürn. Wiesbaden: VS Verlag.
Pallett, Helen and Jason Chilvers. 2013. "A Decade of Learning About Publics, Participation, and Climate Change: Institutionalising Reflexivity?" *Environment and Planning A* 45(5): 1162-1183.
Papadopoulos, Yannis. 2004. "Governance und Demokratie." Pp. 215-237 in *Governance— Regieren in komplexen Regelsystemen*, edited by A. Benz and N. Dose. Wiesbaden: Springer.
Parkinson, John. 2004. "Why Deliberate? The Encounter Between Deliberation and New Public Managers." *Public Administration* 82(2): 377-395.
Parkinson, John. 2006. *Deliberating in the Real World: Problems of Legitimacy in Deliberative Democracy*. Oxford: Oxford University Press.
Peters, B. Guy. 2011a. "Governance as Political Theory." *Critical Policy Studies* 5(1): 63-72.
Peters, B. Guy. 2011b. "Response to Mark Bevir and Benjamin Krupicka, Hubert Heinelt and Birgit Sauer." *Critical Policy Studies* 5(4): 467-470.
Pfister, Thomas. 2016. "European Integration Research as Agent of European Integration." Pp. 63-85 in *Knowing Governance. The Epistemic Construction of Political Order*, edited by J.-P. Voß and R. Freeman. Basingstoke: Palgrave Macmillan.

Rammert, Werner. 1997. "Innovation im Netz. Neue Zeiten für technische Innovationen: Heterogen verteilt und interaktiv." *Soziale Welt* 48(4): 396-415.

Rammert, Werner. 2010. "Die Innovationen der Gesellschaft." Pp. 21-51 in *Soziale Innovation*, edited by J. Howaldt and H. Jacobsen. Wiesbaden: Springer VS.

Rancière, Jaques. 2015 [2000]. *Dissensus: On Politics and Aesthetics*. London: Bloomsbury.

Rask, Mikko and Richard K. Worthington. 2012. "Prospects of Deliberative Global Governance." *Journal of Environmental Science and Engineering* 1(1): 556-565.

Reckwitz, Andreas. 2003. "Die Krise der Repräsentation und das reflexive Kontingenzbewusstsein. Zu den Konsequenzen der post-empiristischen Wissenschaftstheorien für die Identität der Sozialwissenschaften." Pp. 85-103 in *Die Ironie der Politik. Über die Konstruktion politischer Wirklichkeiten*, edited by T. Bonacker, A. Bordocz, and T. Noetzel. Frankfurt a. M.: Campus.

Renn, Ortwin, Thomas Webler, and Peter Wiedemann. 1995. *Fairness and Competence in Citizen Participation: Evaluating Models for Environmental Discourse*. Dordrecht: Kluwer.

Rheinberger, Hans-Jörg. 2007. *Historische Epistemologie*. Hamburg: Junius.

Rip, Arie. 1986. "Controversies as Informal Technology Assessment." *Knowledge: Creation, Diffusion, Utilization* 8(2): 349-371.

Rip, Arie. 2006. "A Co-Evolutionary Approach to Reflexive Governance and Its Ironies." Pp. 82-100 in *Reflexive Governance for Sustainable Development*, edited by J.-P. Voß, D. Bauknecht, and R. Kemp. Cheltenham: Edward Elgar.

Rorty, Richard. 1989. *Contingency, Irony, and Solidarity*. Cambridge: Cambridge University Press.

Rosanvallon, Pierre. 2002. *Le peuple introuvable: Histoire de la représentation démocratique en France*. Paris: Gallimard.

Rowe, Gene and Lynn J. Frewer. 2000. "Public Participation Methods: A Framework for Evaluation." *Science, Technology & Human Values* 25(1): 3-29.

Saretzki, Thomas. 1994. "Technokratie, Technokratiekritik und das Verschwinden der Gesellschaft. Zur Diskussion um das andere politische Projekt der Moderne." Pp. 353-386 in *Politikwissenschaft als Kritische Theorie. Festschrift für Kurt Lenk*, edited by M. T. Greven. Baden-Baden: Nomos.

Saretzki, Thomas. 2001. "Entstehung, Verlauf und Wirkung von Technisierungskonflikten: Die Rolle von Bürgerinitiativen, sozialen Bewegungen und politischen Parteien." Pp. 185-212 in *Politik und Technik. Analysen zum Verhältnis von Technologischem, politischem und staatlichen Wandel am Anfang des 21. Jahrhunderts*, edited by G. Simonis, R. Martinsen and T. Saretzki. Wiesbaden: Westdeutscher Verlag.

Saretzki, Thomas. 2008. "Policy-Analyse, Demokratie und Deliberation: Theorieentwicklung und Forschungsperspektiven der 'Policy Sciences of Democracy'." Pp. 34-54 in *Die Zukunft der Policy Forschung. Theorien, Methoden, Anwendungen*, edited by F. Janning and K. Toens. Wiesbaden: VS Verlag.

Saward, Michael. 2006. "The Representative Claim." *Contemporary Political Theory* 5(3): 297-318.

Schubert, Cornelius. 2014. *Social Innovations. Highly Reflexive and Multi-Referential Phenomena of Today's Innovation Society? (TUTS-Working Papers 2-2014)*. Berlin: Technische Universität Berlin.

Schütz, Alfred. 1945. "On Multiple Realities." *Philosophy and Phenomenological Research* 5(4): 533-576.
Selgas, Fernando J. García. 2011. "Social Fluidity: The Politics of a Theoretical Model." Pp. 135-155 in *The Politics of Knowledge*, edited by F. D. Rubio and P. Baert. London: Routledge.
Senghaas, Dieter. 1965. "Politische Innovation. Versuch über den Panafrikanismus." *Zeitschrift für Politik* 12(4): 333-355.
Shapin, Steven. 1984. "Pump and Circumstance: Robert Boyle's Literary Technology." *Social Studies of Science* 14(4): 481-520.
Shapin, Steven and Simon Schaffer. 1985. *Leviathan and the Air-pump: Hobbes, Boyle, and the Experimental life*. New Jersey: Princeton University Press.
Shore, Cris and Susan Wright. 1997. *Anthropology of Policy. Critical Perspectives on Governance and Power*. London: Routledge.
Simons, Arno and Jan-Peter Voß. 2014. "Politics by Other Means. The Making of the Emissions Trading Instrument as a 'Pre-History' of Carbon Trading." Pp. 51-68 in *The Politics of Carbon Markets*, edited by B. Stephan and R. Lane. London: Earthscan/Routledge.
Smith, Graham. 2009. *Democratic Innovations. Designing Institutions for Citizen Participation*. Cambridge: Cambridge University Press.
Smith, Graham and Corinne Wales. 2002. "Citizens' Juries and Deliberative Democracy." *Political Studies* 48(1): 51-65.
Soeffner, Hans-Georg and Dirk Tänzler. 2002. "Figurative Politik. Prolegomena zu einer Kultursoziologie politischen Handelns." Pp. 17-33 in *Figurative Politik. Zur Performanz der Macht in der modernen Gesellschaft*, edited by H.-G. Soeffner and D. Tänzler. Wiesbaden: VS Verlag.
Stengers, Isabelle. 2010. *Cosmopolitics I*. Minneapolis: University of Minnesota Press.
Stewart, John, Elizabeth Kendall, and Anna Coote. 1994. *Citizens' Juries*. London: Institute for Public Policy Research.
Strathern, Marilyn. 2005. *Partial Connections*. Lanham: Rowman & Littlefield Publishers.
Sulkin, Tracy and Adam F. Simon. 2001. "Habermas in the Lab: A Study of Deliberation in an Experimental Setting." *Political Psychology* 22(4): 809-826.
Thompson, Victor. A. 1965. "Bureaucracy and Innovation." *Administrative Science Quarterly* 5(6): 1-20.
Thornton, Patricia H., William Ocasio, and Michael Lounsbury. 2012. *The Institutional Logics Perspective: A New Approach to Culture, Structure, and Process*. Oxford: Oxford University Press.
Van de Ven, Andrew H. 2007. *Engaged Scholarship: A Guide for Organizational and Social Research: A Guide for Organizational and Social Research*. Oxford: Oxford University Press.
Van de Ven, Andrew H., Douglas Polley, Raghu Garud, and Sankaran Venkataraman. 1999. *The Innovation Journey*. Oxford: Oxford University Press.
Vergne, Antoine. 2009. *Die Diffusion der Planungszelle: Eine Langzeitperspektive*. Unpublished manuscript.
Voß, Jan-Peter. 2007a. *Designs on Governance. Development of Policy Instruments and Dynamics in Governance*. PhD thesis. Enschede: University of Twente.
Voß, Jan-Peter. 2007b. "Innovation Processes in Governance: The Development of 'Emissions Trading' as a New Policy Instrument." *Science and Public Policy* 34(5): 329-343.

Voß, Jan-Peter. 2014. "Performative Policy Studies: Realizing 'Transition Management'." *Innovation: The European Journal of Social Science Research* 27(4): 317-343.
Voß, Jan-Peter. 2016a. "Reflexively Engaging With Technologies of Participation. Constructive Assessment for Public Participation Methods." Pp. 238-260 in *Remaking Participation: Science, Environment and Emergent Publics*, edited by J. Chilvers and M. B. Kearnes. London: Routledge.
Voß, Jan-Peter. 2016b. "Realizing Instruments: Performativity in Emissions Trading and Citizen Panels." Pp. 127-154 in *Knowing Governance. The Epistemic Construction of Political Order*, edited by J.-P. Voß and R. Freeman. Basingstoke: Palgrave Macmillan.
Voß, Jan-Peter and Nina Amelung. 2016. "Innovating Public Participation Methods: Technoscientization and Reflexive Engagement." *Social Studies of Science* 26(5): 749-772.
Voß, Jan-Peter and Dierk Bauknecht. 2007. "Der Einfluss von Technik auf Governance-Innovationen: Regulierung zur gemeinsamen Netznutzung in Infrastruktursystemen." Pp. 109-131 in *Gesellschaft und die Macht der Technik. Sozioökonomischer und institutioneller Wandel durch Technisierung*, edited by U. Dolata and R. Werle. Frankfurt, New York: Campus.
Voß, Jan-Peter and Arno Simons. 2014. "Instrument Constituencies and the Supply-Side of Policy innovation: The Social Life of Emissions Trading." *Environmental Politics* 23(5): 735-754.
Voß, Jan-Peter, Adrian Smith, and John Grin. 2009. "Designing Long-Term Policy: Rethinking Transition Management." *Policy Sciences* 42(4): 275-302.
Wakeford, Tom. 2003. *Teach Yourself Citizen Juries. A Handbook*. Retrieved March 13, 2017 (https://www.researchgate.net/publication/275218861_Teach_Yourself_Citizens_Juries_2nd_Edition).
Wakeford, Tom and Jasber Singh. 2008. "Towards Empowered Participation: Stories and Reflections." *Participatory Learning and Action* (58): 6-10.
Wakeford, Tom; Jasber Singh, Bano Murtuja, Peter Bryant, and Pimbert, Michel. 2007. "The Jury is Out: How Far Can Participatory Projects Go Towards Reclaiming Democracy?" Pp. 333-349 in *The SAGE Handbook of Action Research: Participative Inquiry and Practice*, edited by P. Reason and H. Bradbury. London: SAGE.
Walker, Jack L. 1969. "The Diffusion of Innovation Among the American States." *American Political Science Review* 63(3): 880-899.
Weber, Max. 1920. *Gesammelte Aufsätze zur Religionssoziologie, Vol. 1*. Tübingen: Mohr Siebeck.
Yin, Robert K. 2003. *Case Study Research. Design and Methods*. Thousand Oaks: SAGE.

Part IV
Between Science and Public Policy

Epistemic Innovation

How Novelty Comes About in Science

Martina Merz

1   Introduction[1]

Recent scholarship in the social sciences subsumes the entire range of social innovations under the concept of innovation (e.g., Hutter et al., this volume; Rammert 2010, 2014; Passoth and Rammert, this volume). In this literature a concept of innovation oriented towards scientific and technical progress and its economic dimension serves as a counterfoil for such an expanded understanding of innovation. In so doing, technical innovations in particular but also scientific innovations are presumed to be adequately understood and rarely considered explicitly. The present text addresses innovation in the sciences against this backdrop. It focuses on the question of what concepts of epistemic innovation predominate in science studies. The term *epistemic innovation* is intended to express the focus on the generating of scientific knowledge. Accordingly, neither the social dynamics of the development and establishment of new fields of research[2] nor the institutional innovations that originate in science will be addressed.[3] The focus will instead be on constructivist and practice-oriented science studies with an emphasis on a selection of central concepts and debates.

---

1   For stimulating and wide-ranging discussions, I would like to thank Werner Rammert, Barbara Grimpe, and Thomas Völker.
2   On this see, e.g., the chapters in Merz and Sormani (2016a, 2016b).
3   Examples include technological platforms, new practices of computer-supported cooperation, and the Internet and its forms of use.

It should first be noted that the concept of innovation is not prevalent in science studies; or rather, when it occurs, it refers to technical innovations (artifacts, processes, and systems) and/or the interaction between science and the economy. In this respect, this text will be less about a semantic analysis of the debates on innovation of whatever kind in science studies; it concerns instead the question of how the production and establishment of novelty in science (with regard to its conditions, modalities, etc.) is dealt with conceptually.[4] I speak here of science studies rather than, more comprehensively, of science and technology studies (STS) only to emphasize that technology-oriented innovation research will be disregarded.

Starting with a short reflection on Thomas Kuhn's seminal works on scientific revolutions (2), I will take a selective look at (early) laboratory studies with their micro perspective on knowledge generation (3). On this basis, two prominent object-centered perspectives of epistemic innovation are presented (4). A related perspective, the argument goes, is also fruitful for the analysis of computer simulation as a new innovation practice: accordingly, simulation is examined both as a practiced and as a productive entity with a view to the computer models on which simulation is based (5). The text concludes with a comparison of the concepts of epistemic innovation presented, particularly as regards the ideas associated with them on how scientific innovations are established and stabilized (6).

2 Essential Tension Between Tradition and Innovation

Kuhn's concept of scientific revolutions and his criticism of the idea that science develops only by accumulating new insights are among the most prevalent and well-known positions in more recent science studies (Kuhn 1970). Nonetheless, it is worth taking a fresh look at his observations on how novelty comes about in science. In so doing, I would like to start with an assessment by Kuhn on the significance of scientific revolutions that may at first be surprising. He writes:

> Novelty for its own sake is not a desideratum in the sciences as it is in so many other creative fields. (ibid.: 169)

This statement is to be interpreted in the context of the central and ambivalent significance that Kuhn attributes to 'normal science' for creating the new. On the one

---

4   The basis is a concept of innovation that is not associated with new developments per se but rather implies the establishment, stabilization, and institutionalization of novelties (see, e.g., Rammert 2010; Passoth and Rammert, this volume).

hand, Kuhn writes, normal science "often suppresses fundamental novelties because they are necessarily subversive of its basic commitments" (ibid.: 5). On the other hand, "the very nature of normal research ensures that novelty shall not be suppressed for very long" (ibid.). How can this apparent contradiction be resolved? The starting point is the assertion that an 'anomaly' must first be recognized as such before a crisis manifests itself; as a consequence, new theories can arise. In Kuhn's words this context is as follows:

> Anomaly appears only against the background provided by the paradigm. The more precise and far-reaching that paradigm is, the more sensitive an indicator it provides of anomaly and hence of an occasion for paradigm change. (ibid.: 65)

The cumulative concentration of the knowledge base in the normal science mode consequently creates an increasingly secure reference system, as well as reliable expectations by which an anomaly can distinguish itself. Of great significance for this process of manifesting itself is the 'elaborate equipment' that develops within a paradigm through the progress of research, for example, terminology appropriate to the paradigm, an interaction between theory and data that is specific to each case, and special skills. Normal science therefore promotes the creation of the new through, among other things, its routines and the advancement of the practices and instruments upon which they are based. In the process, Kuhn situates the creation of the new in science in the interplay between 'convergent' and 'divergent' modes of scientific research—an interplay that is fraught with tension (Kuhn 1977: 226). What is significant here for the understanding of scientific innovation but has until now rarely been accorded attention in the literature seems to me Kuhn's idea of, and emphasis on, *normal science* as one "of two complementary aspects of scientific advance" (ibid.: 227).[5]

Outside of science studies, Kuhn's name is primarily associated with the idea of scientific revolutions and mutually incommensurable paradigms. However, scholars of more recent science studies who see Kuhn as being one of their founding fathers have not placed these two concepts at the heart of their work.[6] Instead, in the dispute with the dominant positions of a rationalist philosophy of science, they mobilized Kuhn primarily as someone who focused his attention on "the cultures

---

5   Kuhn writes that "revolutions are but one of two complementary aspects of scientific advance" (Kuhn 1977: 227). I have made normal science—the implicitly mentioned second aspect in the quotation—the subject of the sentence.
6   See on this Edge et al. (1997), Pinch (1997), and Sismondo (2012).

and activities of scientific research" rather than "formalist accounts" (Sismondo 2012: 415).[7]

3 Micro Perspective on Epistemic Innovation

The early 'laboratory studies', the authors of which refer positively to Kuhn, have changed our view of science, at first methodologically.[8] In contrast to Kuhn's historical approach and the analytically reconstructing methodology of the philosophy of science, an ethnographic and often ethnomethodological approach has come to the fore that goes hand in hand with the program of analyzing science in terms of its practices *in situ*. In the early works, this perspective was primarily applied to the observation of scientific practices in laboratories. It is associated with a specific concept of how novel insights come into being that has (at least) three key characteristics.

First, the view that laboratory studies takes of science is *dynamic*: science is not identified with its facts and/or final products, as is found, for instance, in publications or textbooks, but rather analyzed as an activity and a practical accomplishment. As a consequence, a process is at the heart of the analysis: the process of manufacturing (or 'fabricating' or 'constructing') scientific facts.[9]

Second, this process is dismantled from a *micro perspective*. That means in particular that the scientific production process is "broken down" in laboratory studies "through multiplication" (Knorr Cetina 1995: 109, my translation), which reveals a great number and variety of incremental decisions, interactions, and interventions (see also Latour and Woolgar 1986). In early laboratory studies, such a micro perspective served less to characterize the innovations arising in that way or the possibilities of their increase; the interest was aimed instead at the social constitution of the process and its individual elements. Thus, for example, Karin Knorr Cetina identifies "contextual contingency as a principle of change" (Knorr Cetina 1981: 10), thereby referring to the fact that the contextuality of any decision (in terms of its dependency on place and time etc.) is not at odds with a success-

---

7   See on this critically Jasanoff (2012).
8   I will not go further into other precursors of the laboratory studies, particularly the sociology of scientific knowledge. For an overview of laboratory studies, see, e.g., Merz (2005).
9   See on the metaphor of fabrication Knorr Cetina (1981) and on the equivocal concept of 'construction,' inter alia, Sismondo (1993), Hacking (1999), and Merz (2006).

ful scientific innovation.[10] In this respect, 'constructiveness' can be understood in a dual sense: on the one hand, as already noted, as an explication of the social construction mechanisms; on the other hand, as an indication that the "products of fabrication" are "purposefully 'new' products" (ibid.: 12). Here it should not be overlooked that the expression 'constructiveness' exhibits an interesting tension that is likely to be typical of constructivist approaches. The idea that something new is produced in a targeted construction process is promptly counteracted by the author's distancing emphasis (the quotation marks). The new is thus characterized as an attribution, an emic construction, towards which the analyst acts agnostically in a conscious and demonstrative manner.[11]

Third, Knorr Cetina's micro perspective on scientific innovation is closely associated with the *scientific laboratory*, whereby the contextuality of scientific activity is first articulated in terms of its socio-material and spatially specific embedding. But the concept of the laboratory goes beyond the idea that it is the place from which experiments obtain the necessary resources. Instead, the laboratory has been turned into a theoretical concept and is considered "an important agent of scientific development" (Knorr Cetina 1992: 116). The focus here is the idea that the laboratory constitutes an "enhanced environment which improves upon the natural order in relation to the social order" (ibid.). The key process is the transformation of natural objects into scientific objects in the laboratory: these are miniaturized, enlarged, accelerated, slowed down, or the like to such an extent that they become more manageable, which thus promotes or enables the creation of new insights in the first place (ibid.; also Latour 1983). This approach moves beyond the micro perspective outlined above in that the local production of research objects and their relationship to research subjects shifts into focus. Typically, it is not explicitly discussed by means of what *specific* transformation and adaptation processes insights from the laboratory can become effective beyond this local context.[12] In this regard, these are primarily innovations *within* the laboratory.

In conclusion, the micro perspective of knowledge production of laboratory studies shows only little interest in an explicit notion of innovation. Instead, it is directed toward the unfolding of the various social processes and practices of

---

10 On the different concepts of the relationship between contingency and innovation in Knorr Cetina, Collins, and Pickering, see also Pickering (1987) and Zammito (2004: 160f.).
11 Presumably, one is less likely to come across such a distancing from claims of novelty in the innovation literature.
12 Latour (1983) gives a general answer to this question: scientific facts are only valid outside of the laboratory where the conditions and practices of the laboratory are applied (i.e., where 'society' is transformed into a laboratory). See also Merz (2006).

knowledge production and the constitution and nature of the research objects in the context of the laboratory.

4 Object-Centered Perspectives of Epistemic Innovation

In the following, two approaches are presented that explicitly address the dynamics of epistemic innovation from an object-centered perspective. The first concerns Rheinberger's concept of experimental systems (4.1); the second is Knorr Cetina's concept of epistemic objects in the context of an object-centered sociality (4.2).

4.1 Experimental Systems and Their Innovation Dynamics

Like the authors of the early laboratory studies, Hans-Jörg Rheinberger also starts with a critical examination of the concept of experiments long predominant in the philosophy of science. He criticizes a theory-dominated understanding of science, as a result of which experiments are understood as "singular, well-defined empirical instances" (Rheinberger 1997: 27). One example of this is Popper's idea that the experiment serves to test theoretical hypotheses. In a study on the history of molecular biology, Rheinberger develops as an alternative the concept of the *experimental system*, inspired by work by Fleck and Bachelard as well as by ideas and metaphors he comes across in his specific area of investigation, namely, biology.

An experimental system, as Rheinberger writes about the case of molecular biology, is a system "designed to give unknown answers to questions that the experimenters themselves are not yet able clearly to ask" (ibid.: 28). It is constitutive for innovation in science: as a 'surprise generator' and a space of emergence. This characteristic of an experimental system is based on the dynamic interweaving of its two components, which are functionally separated from each other: the epistemic things and the technical (or technological) objects. *Epistemic things* are thus material research objects that "embody what one does not yet know" (ibid.). In their indeterminacy they are 'question-generating machines.' By contrast, the experimental conditions that are designated as *technical objects* are 'answering machines.' They 'embed' the epistemic things, 'restrict and constrain' them (ibid.: 29).

The concept of the experimental system contains a model of the dynamics of epistemic innovation. These dynamics are set in motion by the interplay between its two components: epistemic things and technical objects. First, it is significant for this that the research objects that materialize in the scope of an experimental system require an instrumental setting so that the constantly newly raised questions are answered. Second, a dynamics of innovation is driven forwards through a transformation movement. Epistemic things can transform into technical objects and thus become a component of that set of instruments with the help of which new research questions in turn can be dealt with. Thus an analytical separation of the two functions is necessary

> because otherwise we are not able to name and to denote the game of innovation, the occurrence of *events* within the epistemic field. [Footnote discarded] Scientific activity is scientific only and just in that it aims at producing future. (Rheinberger 1992: 311)

Rheinberger (1992, 1997) traces such a dynamics of innovation exemplarily based on the history of the protein biosynthesis system. In his next step (Rheinberger 2007), he expands the concept of the experimental system to that of experimental cultures that he understands as ensembles of experimental systems associated with each other. In accordance with Bachelard's concept of culture (1949), he ultimately understands scientific cultures as "milieus in which the new can be revealed, in which things occur which cannot be anticipated"—i.e., as "contexts of innovation" (Rheinberger 2007: 138, my translation).

4.2 Epistemic Objects in the Context of an Object-centered Sociality

Epistemic innovation in Rheinberger's conception is achieved through the interplay and the reciprocal effect between epistemic things and technical objects *within* an experimental system. In contrast, Knorr Cetina (1997, 2001) stresses the particular significance and the special character of today's objects of knowledge or 'epistemic objects,' as she also calls them. In the process, she does not start, as Rheinberger does, from the interaction of different types of objects but rather expands the concept of epistemic objects itself. She upgrades this object category in accordance with the justification that present-day technologies (e.g., in computer hardware and software) are not pure answering machines in terms of instruments functioning in an unproblematic way but are also in the category of epistemic objects. Starting from Rheinberger's concept of epistemic things and strongly rooted in Heidegger, the author characterizes objects of knowledge through their "lack in completeness of being" (Knorr Cetina 2001: 181). The objects are continuously becoming; they have the "capacity to unfold indefinitely" (ibid.) and change their characteristics in the process. It is this indisputable incompleteness and the 'unfolding ontology' of epistemic objects that supplies the dynamics of epistemic innovation:

> Only incomplete objects pose further questions, and only in considering objects as incomplete do scientists move forward with their work (ibid.: 176).

The author combines the notion of epistemic object with the conception of a new social form: a 'sociality with objects' (Knorr Cetina 1997). Condensing a complex argument, the idea behind this is that, for the case of science, the objects' lack of completeness has an equivalent in the object relations of the researchers:

> The idea of a structure of wanting implies a continually renewed interest in knowing that appears never to be fulfilled by final knowledge. (Knorr Cetina 2001: 186)

In this respect, epistemic innovation would presuppose an "object-oriented sociality" that is expressed in an "orientation towards objects as sources of the self, of relational intimacy, of shared subjectivity, and social integration" (Knorr Cetina 1997: 23).

5 Computer Simulation as a New Practice of Epistemic Innovation

An object-centered perspective as associated with the approaches referred to above is, as I would like to show, fruitful for understanding computer simulation as a new epistemic practice with its own dynamics of innovation. Computer simulation has in recent decades attained extraordinary significance in the most varied science and technology fields. A few examples would include climate research, astronomy, particle physics, ecology, molecular biology, and industrial development and production. Against the backdrop of its widespread use, the question arises of the innovation potential of computer simulation—that is, of its ability to raise new questions and answer existing ones.

The epistemic significance of simulation, as well as of modeling in general, is explained and positioned in varied ways in science studies (cf. Knuuttila, Merz, and Mattila 2006; Merz and Hinterwaldner 2012). One central position in the philosophy of science, for instance, attributes the effectiveness of models to their ability to 'represent' a research subject more or less precisely. *Practice-oriented* approaches, which have gained ground since the 1990s in the sociological, historical, and philosophical debates waged over models in science studies, draw attention more strongly to the location, role, and use of (computer) models in specific scientific contexts. Such a focus is also fruitful for discussing the specific contribution that computer simulation can make to epistemic innovation, and thus forms the starting point for the following arguments.

It is beneficial to the analysis to take an object-centered perspective here as well. Simulation is accordingly to be considered at the same time in its practical use and with a view to the objects on which it is based, that is, the computer models. Thus, our main argument is that computer models are *productive entities* that create explicit as well as implicit knowledge (for a detailed account, see Knuuttila and Merz 2009). That means that models are not only effective in a depictive role—as 'models of'—but just as much in a performative, instrumental role—as 'models for'—as Evelyn Fox Keller (2000) so succinctly described the crux of the matter.

The productivity of computer models—and thus their innovation potential—is associated with their characteristic as autonomous and materially embodied artifacts. The *autonomy* of models was first addressed as regards their relative independence from both theories and data. This partial independence makes them mediators between the two poles and enables models to be deployed as instruments in order to investigate these two areas (Morgan and Morrison 1999). Correspondingly, computer simulation is considered an independent and qualitatively new scientific practice that constitutes a third aspect between (and also to a certain extent beside) theory and experiment. As an *applied theory*, it processes abstract entities and mathematical procedures. In *virtual experiments*, it enables the exploration of natural phenomena and instrumental settings through the deliberate variation of parameters, followed by observation of the effects produced in this way. Models are not only autonomous; they are also in their own specific way *materially embodied*, concrete, and resistant (Merz 2002). The computer models on which the simulation is based are embodied in the form of software and require a hardware environment to become productive.

On the basis of these characteristics, researchers can interact with computer models in different ways. Models activate learning effects and generate knowledge of a theoretical, implicit, or practical nature in a great number of possible interaction situations that are geared toward developing and improving the models as well as applying them for instrumental or exploratory purposes. This observation refers to two additional characteristics of particularly complex simulations or computer models that additionally increase their innovation potential.

Especially complex computer models are characterized by constant unfolding and a '*multiplex*' character (Merz 1999). This means that the same simulation model can fulfill distinct functions for different actors and in different contexts of use. In one context it might raise new questions as an object of research; in a second context, it might at the same time generate answers as an instrument; and in a third context, it might be applied in yet other ways. It should be stressed that this *co-occurring multifunctionality* of constantly unfolding objects can be of lasting duration without, as described by Rheinberger, resulting in a transformation into (purely) technical objects.

Lastly, computer simulation may make a contribution to epistemic innovation through its potential to generate and present *alternative futures*, whereupon it is possible to explore these future options, evaluate them, and compare them with each other. An initial example is climate change research with its scenario calculations of future global warming, which have attracted much public debate. A second example are the accelerator experiments of elementary particle physics, which would not be possible today without computer simulation. Simulation is here both a future and a surprise generator (for details see Merz 1999). Just a few indications will be given below about their efficacy in this field of research.

As a future generator, computer simulation enables *on the one hand* generation of knowledge about the functioning of material structures (e.g., accelerators, detectors, and their components) that have not been realized so far. Physicists explore various design options and optimize them in terms of often conflicting scientific, technical, political, or economic priorities. In the preparatory phases of an experiment, simulation has great significance for mediating and negotiating among very different fields of practice and actors.[13]

The generation of the future refers *on the other hand* to the research objectives, which target specific physical processes and phenomena (e.g., the search for supersymmetry). Various *theoretical scenarios* are encoded into simulation programs, the consequences of which are tested by means of simulation and can be extrapolated with a view to the planned experiments. For example, it can thus be seen whether certain theoretical assumptions can be explored at all in the planned experiment.

As a consequence, simulation is a generator for (possible) future equipment as well as for (conceivable) alternative theories. At the same time, it is a generator for the knowledge associated with the individual scenarios. Thus, from the interplay between the two complementary poles—experimental setting versus theoretical framework—results the particular efficacy of simulation, which lies in the fact that

---

13 With 'collaborations' involving 3,000 people working together on a single experiment, elementary particle physics also constantly needs important institutional innovations, for example, as regards issues of authorship in publications or the organization of a peer review system within the collaboration.

simulation can mediate between the paradoxical requirements of an experiment to be open-ended and at the same time to adjust the equipment in accordance with previously defined scientific assumptions. As a future generator, computer simulation is therefore effective in particle physics both as a thinking tool and as a tool for material intervention, as a generator of new questions as well as a generator of reliable answers.

6 Conclusion

To conclude, I would like to juxtapose the analytical perspectives of epistemic innovation presented in this chapter. In accordance with an innovation concept that implies not only the *generation of* innovations but their *implementation, stabilization, and institutionalization* as well (cf. Rammert 2010; Passoth and Rammert, this volume), particular attention shall be paid to the tension between these two poles.

According to Kuhn, epistemic innovation is rooted in the interrelationship between a 'normal' and a deviating mode of research. The occurrence of anomalies is an initial indication of possible innovations. However, anomalies are not sufficient to help an epistemic innovation to be established. There need to be veritable crises that are capable of destabilizing the prevailing paradigm and can trigger the negotiation of a new one. A scientific revolution, substituting one paradigm for another, is accompanied by a reconstruction of the entire field, one that involves its key characteristics, its objectives, methods, and theoretical generalizations (Kuhn 1970).

Kuhn's *macro perspective* on epistemic innovation provides an interesting comparative foil for a new look at laboratory studies, with their interest in constructing scientific facts from a *micro perspective*.[14] First of all, a surprising analogy between the two perspectives stands out. The routine processes, procedures, and interactions observed in laboratory studies seem for the most part to originate from the sector of 'normal science' (Kuhn). Extraordinary events such as crises were not of much interest, at least for the early laboratory studies, because the authors were interested in reconstructing the day-to-day processes of knowledge generation. The associated innovations are, one could say, *epistemic micro innovations*. Their stabilization does not take place at a subsequent point in time—in contrast

---

14 On the difference between micro and macro perspectives of innovation, see, e.g., Braun-Thürmann (2005).

to Kuhn's macro conception—but rather as a central component of the generation process.[15]

Object-centered perspectives of knowledge generation that are at the same time practice-oriented in turn yield new aspects of the dynamics of epistemic innovation, whereby the approaches considered differ in their focus. The playing field of epistemic innovation envisaged by Rheinberger is neither the scientific community (Kuhn) nor the laboratory (laboratory studies) but rather the *experimental system*, which is also the key concept for this approach. Of significance for the discussion of epistemic innovation here is on the one hand that the conditions for generating new questions are also explicitly considered. "What is genuinely new must come to pass, and one has to create favorable conditions for it to be able to do so" (Rheinberger 2006: 3, my translation). Precisely these conditions are given by an experimental system. What is of interest on the other hand is the positioning of the stabilizing of innovations within an experimental system. Specifically, it is about the shift of transforming epistemic things into technical objects. One could also say it is about the sedimentation of epistemic innovation in the form of technical equipment and as a component of an infrastructure that blazes the trail for further innovations.

Also alternative object-centered approaches such as Knorr Cetina's or the approach we developed in the case of computer simulation (Merz 1999; Knuuttila and Merz 2009) emphasize that epistemic innovations have a *material (or medial) dimension* and that they are at the same time *technical* innovations. The approaches differ, however, in their idea of how scientific innovations become established. Whereas Rheinberger assumes a stabilization through transformation, Knorr Cetina stresses the ongoing openness, mutability, and unfolding of epistemic objects, as I analogously claim for the case of computer simulation. These object characteristics have as a consequence that the production process of innovations is spread over time and concurrently distributed across different actors and contexts. This being the case, a stabilizing of innovations remains essentially partial and temporary.

In an interesting way, such a concept of scientific objects and the associated object-centered perspective of epistemic innovation shift the time references. In this case, one is dealing with a dynamics of innovation predominantly aligned towards *future and potentiality* rather than towards the "relationship between old and new" (Rammert 2010: 29, my translation). Here computer simulation offers an instructive example, as I have endeavored to show.

---

15 The existence of more advanced processes of stabilizing and institutionalizing epistemic innovations, for example, by means of specific forms of representation when disseminated beyond the context of origin, is only mentioned here (on this, see Latour and Woolgar 1986; Lynch and Woolgar 1990).

References

Bachelard, Gaston. 1949. *Le rationalisme appliqué*. Paris: P.U.F.
Braun-Thürmann, Holger. 2005. *Innovation*. Bielefeld: transcript.
Edge, David, Rom Harré, Andrew Brown, Barry Barnes, Michael Mulkay, Steve Fuller, Martin Rudwick, Ronald N. Giere, and David Bloor. 1997. "Obituary: Thomas S. Kuhn (18 July 1922 – 17 June 1996)." *Social Studies of Science* 27(3): 483-502.
Hacking, Ian. 1999. *The Social Construction of What?* Cambridge: Harvard University Press.
Hutter, Michael, Hubert Knoblauch, Werner Rammert, and Arnold Windeler. This volume. "Innovation Society Today. The Reflexive Creation of Novelty."
Jasanoff, Sheila. 2012. "Genealogies of STS." *Social Studies of Science* 42(3): 435-441.
Keller, Evelyn Fox. 2000. "Models Of and Models For: Theory and Practice in Contemporary Biology." *Philosophy of Science* 67(3): 72-86.
Knorr Cetina, Karin. 1981. *The Manufacture of Knowledge: An Essay on the Constructivist and Contextual Nature of Science*. Oxford et al.: Pergamon Press.
Knorr Cetina, Karin. 1992. "The Couch, the Cathedral, and the Laboratory: On the Relationship between Experiment and Laboratory in Science." Pp. 113-138 in *Science as Practice and Culture*, edited by A. Pickering. Chicago: University of Chicago Press.
Knorr Cetina, Karin. 1995. "Laborstudien: Der kulturalistische Ansatz in der Wissenschaftsforschung." Pp. 101-135 in *Das Auge der Wissenschaft: Zur Emergenz von Realität*, edited by R. Martinsen. Baden-Baden: Nomos.
Knorr Cetina, Karin. 1997. "Sociality with Objects: Social Relations in Postsocial Knowledge Societies." *Theory, Culture & Society* 14(4): 1-30.
Knorr Cetina, Karin. 2001. "Objectual Practice." Pp. 175-188 in *The Practice Turn in Contemporary Theory*, edited by T. Schatzki, K. Knorr Cetina, and E. von Savigny. London, New York: Routledge.
Knuuttila, Tarja and Martina Merz. 2009. "Understanding by Modeling: An Objectual Approach." Pp. 146-168 in *Scientific Understanding: Philosophical Perspectives*, edited by H. W. de Regt, S. Leonelli, and K. Eigner. Pittsburgh: University of Pittsburgh Press.
Knuuttila, Tarja, Martina Merz, and Erika Mattila. 2006. "Editorial: Computer Models and Simulations in Scientific Practice." *Science Studies* 19(1): 3-11.
Kuhn, Thomas S. 1970 [1962]. *The Structure of Scientific Revolutions*. 2nd ed. Chicago: University of Chicago Press.
Kuhn, Thomas S. 1977 [1959]. "The Essential Tension: Tradition and Innovation in Scientific Research." Pp. 225-239 in *The Essential Tension: Selected Studies in Scientific Tradition and Change*. Chicago: University of Chicago Press.
Latour, Bruno. 1983. "Give Me a Laboratory and I will Raise the World." Pp. 141-170 in *Science Observed: Perspectives on the Social Study of Science*, edited by K. Knorr Cetina and M. Mulkay. London: SAGE.
Latour, Bruno and Steve Woolgar. 1986 [1979]. *Laboratory Life: The Construction of Scientific Facts*. 2nd ed. Princeton: Princeton University Press.
Lynch, Michael and Steve Woolgar, eds. 1990. *Representation in Scientific Practice*. Cambridge MA: MIT Press.
Merz, Martina. 1999. "Multiplex and Unfolding: Computer Simulation in Particle Physics." *Science in Context* 12(2): 293-316.

Merz, Martina. 2002. "Kontrolle—Widerstand—Ermächtigung: Wie Simulationssoftware Physiker konfiguriert." Pp. 267-290 in *Können Maschinen handeln? Soziologische Beiträge zum Verhältnis von Mensch und Technik*, edited by W. Rammert and I. Schulz-Schaeffer. Frankfurt a. M.: Campus.

Merz, Martina. 2005. "Knowledge Construction." Pp. 249-255 in *Science, Technology, and Society: An Encyclopedia*, edited by S. Restivo. Oxford: Oxford University Press.

Merz, Martina. 2006. "The Topicality of the Difference Thesis—Revisiting Constructivism and the Laboratory." *Science, Technology & Innovation Studies* (Special Issue 1): 11-24.

Merz, Martina and Inge Hinterwaldner. 2012. "Neue Bilder, Modelle und Simulationen: Zwischen Repräsentativität und Produktivität." Pp. 303-316 in *Handbuch Wissenschaftssoziologie*, edited by S. Maasen, M. Kaiser, M. Reinhart, and B. Sutter. Wiesbaden: Springer VS.

Merz, Martina and Philippe Sormani, eds. 2016a. *The Local Configuration of New Research Fields: On Regional and National Diversity*. Cham et al.: Springer.

Merz, Martina and Philippe Sormani. 2016b. "Configuring New Research Fields: How Policy, Place, and Organization Are Made to Matter." Pp. 1-22 in *The Local Configuration of New Research Fields: On Regional and National Diversity*, edited by M. Merz and P. Sormani. Cham et al.: Springer.

Morgan, Mary S. and Margaret Morrison, eds. 1999. *Models as Mediators: Perspectives on Natural and Social Science*. Cambridge UK: Cambridge University Press.

Passoth Jan-Hendrik and Werner Rammert. This volume. "Fragmental Differentiation and the Practice of Innovation. Why Is There an Ever-Increasing Number of Fields of Innovation?"

Pickering, Andrew. 1987. "Forms of Life: Science, Contingency and Harry Collins." *British Journal for the History of Science* 20(2): 213-221.

Pinch, Trevor J. 1997. "Kuhn—The Conservative and Radical Interpretations: Are Some Mertonians 'Kuhnians' and Some Kuhnians 'Mertonians'?" *Social Studies of Science* 27(3): 465-482.

Rammert, Werner. 2010. "Die Innovationen der Gesellschaft." Pp. 21-51 in *Soziale Innovationen. Auf dem Weg zu einem post-industriellen Innovationsparadigma*, edited by J. Howaldt and H. Jakobsen. Wiesbaden: Springer VS.

Rammert, Werner. 2014. "Vielfalt der Innovation und gesellschaftlicher Zusammenhalt." Pp. 619-639 in *Vielfalt und Zusammenhalt. Verhandlungen des 36. Kongresses der Deutschen Gesellschaft für Soziologie in Bochum und Dortmund 2012*, edited by M. Löw. Frankfurt a. M.: Campus.

Rheinberger, Hans-Jörg. 1992. "Experiment, Difference, and Writing: I. Tracing Protein Synthesis." *Studies in History and Philosophy of Science* 23(2): 305-331.

Rheinberger, Hans-Jörg. 1997. *Toward a History of Epistemic Things: Synthesizing Proteins in the Test Tube*. Stanford: Stanford University Press.

Rheinberger, Hans-Jörg. 2006. *"Über die Kunst, das Unbekannte zu erforschen."* The Cogito Foundation. Retrieved December 15, 2015 (http://www.cogitofoundation.ch/pdf/2006/061025DieKunst_dasUnbekannte.pdf).

Rheinberger, Hans-Jörg. 2007. "Kulturen des Experiments." *Berichte zur Wissenschaftsgeschichte* 30(2): 135-144.

Sismondo, Sergio. 1993. "Some Social Constructions." *Social Studies of Science* 23(3): 515-553.

Sismondo, Sergio. 2012. "Fifty Years of The Structure of Scientific Revolutions, Twenty-five of Science in Action." *Social Studies of Science* 42(3): 415-419.
Zammito, John H. 2004. *A Nice Derangement of Epistemes: Post-positivism in the Study of Science from Quine to Latour.* Chicago, London: University of Chicago Press.

Projectification of Science as an Organizational Innovation

A Figurational Sociological Perspective on Emergence, Diffusion, and Impact

Nina Baur, Cristina Besio and Maria Norkus

1   Figuration, Innovation, and Science

A central question of innovation research is how innovation processes occur at the macro, meso, and micro levels (Hutter et al., this volume). In this contribution, we use figurational sociology to make sense of this dynamic interaction (Elias 1978, 2009) and illustrate the usefulness of figurational sociology for innovation research. We focus on one sphere of action (Baur 2008): science. Science is oriented towards the constant production of the new and, at the same time, has itself been affected by innovations over the past hundred years. More specifically, we focus on one innovation in the field of science, namely, the projectification of science.

We argue that figurational sociology is particularly well suited to grasp simultaneous processes at different levels of action, as figurational sociological analysis typically consists of a triad that systematically associates different levels of social interaction with each other (Baur and Ernst 2011):

1. *the reconstruction of a figuration's rules, structure, and power relations*—in our case, the figuration is the organization of German-speaking science (meso or macro processes);
2. *the reconstruction of the social and spatial placement of people*—in our case of scientists—and the individuals' knowledge and potential for action associated with their specific placement in the figuration (micro processes); and

3. *an analysis of the figuration's sociogenesis* via intentional and unintentional consequences of individual actions (linking micro, meso, and macro processes in time).

When applying this approach to innovation research, there are some specific theoretical and methodological problems. First, figurational sociology is a process-oriented theory, that is, it assumes that social change is normal. In comparison to other approaches to innovation, this reverses the way innovations are approached since it is not novelties that have to be explained but rather routines, structures, and regularities. This raises the question of *how 'normal' social change can be distinguished from innovation*. A minimum condition is that an innovation must involve a rupture (i.e., a turning point or radical change) of an existing social pattern. Methodologically, this implies that the time frame that is subject to empirical observation must be long enough to allow for observing a 'before' and an 'after' the radical change (Baur 2005: 142-147). However, not every rupture is automatically an innovation. Rather, an additional condition is required: a turning point only becomes an innovation if actors (in addition to their actual behavior) also discursively construct this change as an innovation on the semantic level (in the sense suggested by Hutter et al., this volume), as Besio and Schmidt (2012) have argued from a systems theory perspective and Knoblauch (2014a) from the perspective of communicative constructivism. Consequently, to analyze how projectification has influenced the figuration of science, a fourth level has to be taken into account in addition to the three analytical levels mentioned above: (4) *the reconstruction of the discourse*.

Second, the concept of figuration emphasizes that interdependent actors are integrated into complex networks of relationships and that therefore various *action levels* always manifest themselves simultaneously when people act. Yet Norbert Elias (1995) does not systematically differentiate between micro, meso, and macro processes but analytically distinguishes only two levels of action (meso/macro = figuration; micro = individual). In the case of science, however, at least one further level of action is relevant: the meso level (Baur et al. 2016). In science, the macro level is constituted by the (national and global) science system and its disciplines. To ensure long-term continuity and reproduction, the science system is constituted by organizational units—for example, universities (Meier 2016), non-university research institutes (Heinze 2016), and new organizational forms such as collaborative research centers ('Sonderforschungsbereiche' or SFBs) and clusters of excellence. These are in turn divided into individual working units (e.g., research groups, research projects), which organize concrete, everyday research at a practical level (meso level). At the individual level, personal career planning is required

(Norkus, Besio, and Baur 2016), which in turn is both socially structured and inscribed into the person's CV. Specific social interactions can likewise be identified at this lowest level of action at which research is undertaken (micro level).

Applying Elias' framework in analyzing the case of modern science brings a third problem to light: In his empirical analyses, Elias primarily dealt with societies as a whole, for which the nation state was the dominant organizing principle at the time. All social spheres (e.g., the system of social stratification, politics, the economy) coincided with the nation state's territory, mutually stabilized each other, and were conceived as part of the very same figuration to which an individual belonged. Elias did not address conflicts between fields. However, in the case of modern science, there seem to be several and increasing numbers of different figurations to which the individual scientist belongs and the logics of which partially contradict each other. Each scientist has to simultaneously pay respect to all these figurations' demands. For example, academic disciplines usually place different demands on scientists than the university (Meier 2016)—but neither one can be ignored because the university is a scientist's current employer, while the discipline is more relevant to a scientist's long-term career.

To deal with these problems theoretically, we refer concepts from systems theory (Besio 2009; Besio and Schmidt 2012). In particular, we reconstruct innovation processes as a specific form of social evolution at the structural level that is accompanied by a specific semantics, and we stress that these kinds of processes can also take place at the organizational level—with consequences that primarily concern organizations but also extend beyond their boundaries to change broader figurations.

We apply this heuristic frame to analyze projectification in science. Projects are an innovation at the structural level—'grammar' in Hutter et al.'s (this volume) terminology— that also affects scientists' everyday research practices ('pragmatics'). Both aspects are considered by our analysis of projects' sociogenesis. Additionally, we show how they were discursively constructed as an innovation ('semantics').

Methodologically, in line with the recommendations of Baur and Ernst (2011), we mixed methods because different data are suitable to different degrees for capturing the specific time layers. We re-analyzed historians' and social scientists' academic writings in order to reconstruct the sociogenesis of the figuration of 'science' before and after projectification as well as the semantic construction of 'projects' as an innovation (for a discussion of the methodological problems of this approach, see Hergesell 2015).

In our analysis of projectification's consequences, we limit ourselves to two levels due to a lack of space: the meso level of the university as an organization and the micro level of the individual career. This analysis is based on several qualitative case studies (Baur and Lamnek 2005) of both natural science (chemistry, physics) and social science (sociology) research projects in Germany and Switzerland. For each case study, we triangulated semi-structured interviews with scientists (Helfferich 2014), ethnographies (Knoblauch 2014b), and process-generated data (Baur 2011; Salheiser 2014) such as websites, project proposals, project reports, minutes of project meetings, and so on. The data were purposefully selected (Akremi 2014) and analyzed by using qualitative content analysis (Ametowobla, Baur, and Norkus forthcoming).

More specifically, we collected process-produced data and conducted 14 qualitative interviews between 2000 and 2004, which provided information on ten research projects at Swiss universities and other research institutions (for more details, see Besio 2009). Most of these projects were funded by third parties for a period of two to three years. As a rule, they were only poorly or not at all embedded in permanent organizational structures or long-term research programs, meaning that the larger research context provided little guidance for research practice in individual projects.

Additionally, we undertook ethnographic research and conducted more than 80 interviews with scientists (mainly chemists and physicists) in Germany. A special focus were the new forms of research organization—that is, collaborative research centers (SFBs) and clusters of excellence in Berlin and Munich (Petschick 2015).

2 Grammar and Pragmatics of the 'Science Figuration' before Projectification: The Classical German University System

To understand how the innovation 'projectification' changed the figuration of 'science,' it is necessary to know both the grammar and the pragmatics of the classical German university system. The German university evolved in the second half of the 19th century, and one of its central ideas was that government-funded research should ensure the *independence of research* from outside influence. Researchers should conduct *fundamental research* with no direct application in mind, concentrating primarily on 'sound' and 'innovative' results (according to scientific criteria). From the outset, German universities were thus intended as places of research. To ensure this, universities offered their researchers a basic (government-funded) infrastructure. In this vein, German universities since the 20th century have supplied things such as equipment in physics and a laboratory, including laboratory assistants, in chemistry (Schimank 1976: 393).

Furthermore, German universities are not organized hierarchically like most 19th-century companies were but instead consist of departments ('Institute' or

'Fachbereiche') that are independent insofar as the regional public administration directly funds them for specific research purposes, without having to go via the university or faculty ('Fakultät'). The departments in turn are divided into chairs ('Lehrstühle') or research groups ('Fachgebiete'). Each professor also chairs his research group, which consists of associated laboratories and staff, for instance, a secretary, student assistants, doctoral and post-doctoral researchers, and—if necessary—lab assistants. The professor is supposed to lead and define research in his group and enjoys a large degree of autonomy (Nipperdey 1998: 571).

Another important feature of German universities is the Humboldtian ideal of the unity of research and teaching. This means that every scientist has the duty to do research *and* teach. The institutionalization of this ideal has resulted in the departments being organized along the lines of scientific disciplines, which in turn further differentiate and specialize into sub-disciplines via the chairs, and the specializations themselves being organized along the needs of teaching. For each chair this implies that it has to ensure that it contributes to the progress of research in its specific sub-discipline and that it must guarantee the teaching in this sub-discipline as well. The equipment (laboratories, materials, personnel, and financial resources) corresponds with the teaching and research needs of the respective sub-discipline (Teichler 1990). The result of this arrangement is that research within a *specialization* is highly efficient. This organizational structure has been extremely persistent because the specific research program is not bound to a specific person (the chair holder) but to a particular teaching program, and the specific organizational structure endures even if the chair holder retires or changes jobs. To illustrate this, imagine that a professor leaves a department and the department would like to change the research program. In engineering and the natural sciences, for instance, this would require dismantling laboratories worth between several hundreds of thousands up to several million euros and installing equally expensive new laboratories. Because of the costs involved, the chair's denomination customarily remains unchanged and a newly appointed professor takes over his predecessor's laboratories and staff.

For research, this means that, although research is highly efficient within established fields, it is difficult to almost impossible to conduct research outside the established (sub-)disciplinary boundaries or to pursue new lines of research that are distinct from established paths.

University education is divided into several distinct but consecutive phases (undergraduate, graduate, doctoral study, post-doctoral research, tenured professorship), which offer both to the organization and to junior researchers a clear framework for orientation as to what stages have to be mastered by acquiring which degrees (Magister-Zwischenprüfung/Vordiplom/Bachelor, Magister/Diplom/Master, Ph.D. thesis/Promotion, Habilitation, appointment to a tenured professorship) and in which order to pursue an academic career (Heinz, Briedis, and Jongmanns 2016). In addition, to prevent social and intellectual closure, universities not only traditionally exchange personnel, but tenure tracks within a single university are explicitly forbidden. That is to say, scientists are not allowed to become a professor at the same university where they completed their post-doctoral phase and achieved their 'Habilitation' (this is called 'Hausberufungsverbot'). For young scientists, this implies that, if they want to stay in academia, they have to change institutions during their career. Historically, there were also implicit requirements on which institutions young scientists had to pass through during their career, as there was an implicit ranking of the universities: From the 19th century until World War II, Berlin was the center of intellectual thought, whereas the Anglo-Saxon scientific network was not only largely separated from but also mostly inconsequential to the Continental European scientific network. The consequence for German academia was that almost all exchanges of personnel (and therefore academic career paths) went via Berlin (Taylor, Hoyler, and Evans 2008). In contrast to the Anglo-Saxon scientific network, this German system of academic labor migration prevented a hierarchy between sites insofar as academic *career opportunities* were almost the same no matter where a career began (Baier and Münch 2013).

Hence, the German university system has traditionally strongly encouraged not only the university as an organization but also individual researchers to conduct research along already established paths. Thus, still today, career paths tend to follow the established (sub-)disciplinary lines. In the natural and engineering sciences, the chair holders also provide access to expensive laboratories (without which research is impossible) and facilitate joint publications in major journals (Petschick 2016).

Once scientists are appointed as a professorial chair, they typically are tenured and receive a lifetime contract (typically as a civil servant, which, among other things, means that they cannot be dismissed unless they severely violate their obligations as a civil servant or commit a capital crime). In contrast to many other countries, in Germany, holding a university chair has always been one of the most prestigious jobs, one that has been considered equivalent in status to (and thus equally well paid as), for instance, judges or middle management in large companies, but much better regarded. Today, according to a survey, professors are the seventh most respected profession in the German public (following doctors, nurses, police officers, teachers, craftpersons, and priests) (IfD Allensbach 2013). The job and income security of a professorship stands in contrast to the path of getting there: all contracts for earlier career stages are fixed term-contracts, and pay is typically much lower than other jobs at the same career level (Norkus et al. 2016).

This has consequences for the *power relationships within the figuration*: At the organizational level, there is hardly any kind of hierarchy between chairs and chair holders. Within the chairs as organizational units, by contrast, the organizational structure can be, and typically is, extremely hierarchical. Chair holders are the senior managers of all personnel in the research groups. They are therefore not only crucial but have the final say in all decisions within their research group. At the same time, they supervise and examine younger scholars' current academic work (including that of post-doctoral researchers). In the natural sciences, professors thus decide how resources are allocated, what content will be taught, and even who is allowed to publish with whom (Petschick 2016). Consequently, professors can either strongly support and promote junior researchers' careers or actively inhibit the advancement of unpopular or unruly 'progeny' and severely limit their career options. What is more, the density of scientific networks enables professors to still exert influence even if their 'offspring' has long been working in a different research group at a different university for a long time. Scientists therefore only truly become independent once they themselves are appointed professors.

This figuration has reproduced itself in a relatively stable manner at the level of pragmatics and grammar, yet like all figurations it has not been static but subject to constant change. Since the 19th century, *underfunding of research* has been a permanent problem and has accelerated figurational change. This underfunding at first only affected individual scientists. For instance, if a post-doctoral researcher was not appointed to a chair, the academic's only option to remain in science was to become a so-called private lecturer ('Privatdozent', who is typically meagerly paid or not paid at all) or an extraordinary professor ('Extraordinarius' or 'Außerordentlicher Professor'). However, underfunding quickly became a structural problem: As progressive internal specialization increased the need for laboratories and equipment, research soon could no longer be financed by the money intended for teaching. The problem of research funding was exacerbated by the strong growth of German universities in the closing decades of the 19th century. During this period, the number of professors as well as of lecturers and extraordinary professors grew considerably (Nipperdey 1998: 568-572).

Since the 19th century, a second development may have caused this figuration to waver, namely, the changing nature of research. To examine certain research questions, research units needed to be larger than the traditional chairs. Furthermore, certain questions could only be addressed if researchers engaged in interdisciplinary collaboration across the specializations and disciplines. Thus, the question arose of how to finance and coordinate such *interdisciplinary issues* and *big science*.

3 Semantics of Projectification: Constructing Projects as an Innovation

In order to solve both the problem of underfunding and of coordinating heterogeneous research teams, a form for coordinating and funding research that originated in industry also came to prominence in science: the project. Compared with other organizational forms, a project's specific feature is that it organizes endeavors that are both substantially and temporally limited (Besio 2009: 27-33). A research project defines its goals and the suitable means of achieving them in advance and does not redefine or change them during the research process. Each project is thus characterized by limited and short-term planning, which bundles objectives, resources, responsibilities, deadlines, and (where appropriate) people (Besio, Norkus, and Baur 2016). In contrast to long-term structures (such as academic disciplines, universities, departments, or chairs), projects are not intended to manage activities continuously or permanently. Rather, they are created to carry out a one-time task within a designated time period (Levene 1996: 4164). Today, externally funded projects in science can take diverse forms: one can find both small project teams and large-scale collaborative projects; both interdisciplinary and purely disciplinary projects; projects committed both to fundamental research and to applied research. While these distinctions may be relevant in other contexts, in this paper we focus on projects' general characteristics as a structure—that is, the features common to all these forms.

Since the 1920s and 1930s at the latest, projects have been a central form of organizing academic research both in Germany and the U.S.A. The process of projectification was first encouraged by American philanthropy and German foundations; the latter had been created by German industrialists to support scientific progress. Semantically, the project was defined as 'new' in two ways, or, one could say, two innovative moments were attributed to it. It was designed to be a particularly efficient and productive form of (1) coordinating and (2) funding research, and these two functions were discursively interrelated:

1. With regard to *coordinating research*, projects were first introduced at a time when science was no longer conceived as the work of an individual ingenious scholar who conducted research independently in his office or private library. Instead, it seemed necessary to do research in a (larger and possibly interdisciplinary) group that worked together as a team. This change in the nature of academic work motivated the introduction of projects (Krauch 1970: 100-105) that were designed to successfully organize teamwork. The idea was that projects contribute to good research management and can thus guarantee efficien-

cy. This idea is particularly relevant because research is not a routine activity that can be easily planned and controlled. In fact, research is open in terms of results and duration and thus characterized by a high degree of uncertainty. As a consequence, the project was explicitly intended as an organizational tool that could manage creative and innovative activities.
2. From the outset, projects were additionally intended for *financing research* in a targeted way. Even the first funding agencies that introduced projects as a way of funding research already believed that projects would increase research productivity (in comparison to classical institutional funding of scientific organizations such as universities; Forman 1974: 52-53). According to this line of reasoning, projects were more efficient because the competitive grant system directly supported high-quality research endeavors. In addition, there was an element of self-interest involved, as the funding agencies' agendas, needs, and requirements could be incorporated into the process of allocating research funds. In this vein, American foundations defined the subject areas they intended to support from the very beginning. This moved criteria measuring how research contributed to societal welfare into the foreground (Geiger 1986: 149-160).

This constellation of problems (underfunding and coordination of research groups) and the discursive construction of the project as an appropriate solution led to the project being first introduced as a 'new' form of organizing and financing science in the 1920s, and, by the mid-1980s at the latest, it became a standard form of organizing scientific research. In the next two sections, we reconstruct the project's sociogenesis (i.e., the grammar and pragmatics of innovation). We will discuss the two entwined sub-processes of projectification separately—namely, changes in the typical forms of coordinating and financing research—by reconstructing three sequences of these processes (variation, selection, and restabilization). To do so, we consider developments not only in Germany but also in the U.S.A. since after World War II the balance of power in the global science system shifted from Germany to the United States as the power center of global science. Since that time, not Germany but the U.S.A. has been the major driver of innovation in the science system itself.

4 The Project's Sociogenesis: Changing Grammar and Pragmatics in Science

4.1 Projects as a New Form of Coordinating Research

Variation: Searching a New Method of Invention
Innovation research has termed the first phase of innovation processes as the *phase of variation*, *phase of discovery*, or *phase of invention*. In this phase, something is observed as being different from current standard practices. This can, for instance, be a technique, instrument, or, in our case, an organizational form.

The project's sociogenesis as a new form for coordinating research began with the first industrial laboratories in the late 19th century. The key prerequisite was that industry (particularly the chemical and electrical industries) identified scientific knowledge as a key factor in competition between companies. A case in point is the German paint industry, which was one of the first industries to acknowledge the economic importance of science in light of an emerging steady market demand for new colors (Beer 1975: 106).

However, what was decisive for the invention of the organizational form of the 'project' was that the industrial laboratories, which were originally developed around certain gifted individuals, began appointing research teams (Hack and Hack 1985: 123-142). The managers of these laboratories were convinced that— in contrast to the self-reliant individual scholar—organized groups of researchers would not produce knowledge on the basis of creative, unique, and therefore less controllable ideas but that certain ways of organizing research would ensure the generation of a controllable stream of knowledge and technical discoveries. These managers also believed that one could control this so-called new 'method of inventing' (Kreibich 1986: 335) and thus do without the ingenuity of individuals.

As a first step towards improving the coordination of research work, the offices and laboratories of those involved in research were spatially pooled into one 'research unit' to enable better management and monitoring of the research activities (Carlson 1997: 211). Companies added to this by developing assessment systems. In the early decades of the 20th century, Bell's lab managers started allocating specific tasks to each employee and asked them to keep track of their activities in a laboratory notebook and also record what results were actually achieved in the end (Noble 1977: 120).

While these developments laid the groundwork for introducing the project, the first genuine moment of projectification only occurred once research was conducted to achieve a fixed goal from the outset. Such objectives were very important for industrial companies, which had to ensure market profits by introducing promising new technologies and thus depended on being able to direct research efforts towards solving the problems arising while these technologies were still immature. An early example is the 'Nylon' project developed in DuPont's laboratories in the 1930s. The organizational technique used there included the following characteristics: a plan, deadlines, definition of milestones, and monitoring (Hounshell 1992: 243-245). This method of organizing research made it possible to set targets for a specific period of time and focus on them without being distracted by other possible research paths. The project leader or client defines only *one* application, *one* material, and a limited range of products, and the whole project team is bound to these decisions for a specified period. As a result, this structure shifts power relations within the project team: now it is the project manager—and not the individual inventor—who controls the research process.

It should be noted that in contrast to Elias's (1978) concept of sociogenesis, these first experiments in changing the standard method of coordinating research show that the project did not emerge silently as an unintended side effect of action but was deliberately introduced as a new management method to achieve specific targets. These first experiences then set a process in motion that ultimately resulted in a fundamental change in how research activities were carried out.

Selection: Coordinating Big Science
In the phase of variation, there are always many different discoveries and inventions that imply different futures. Thus, the next phase of innovation processes is *selection*, in which out of the whole set of possibilities, one single variation is selected and pursued. A variation has been selected when it is applied as a structure in practice, that is, when it is *used, confirmed,* and *condensed*. For example, after the first positive experiences in business, the 'project' as a new organizational form soon became the preferred method of organizing research in big science. Since then, the project has been considered a good way of organizing research if

1. this (university or non-university) research requires and processes large amounts of data;
2. there is a need for combining phases of fundamental research, applied research, and development; and
3. the research has to be interdisciplinary in character.

Projects promised to solve the problems of coordination in the circumstances described above. As an organizational form, the project was also in line with the values, interests, and needs in the specific context of big science. This led to the *positive selection* of the project as an organizational instrument and structure for coordinating science and was decisive in bringing about the use of the project as an organizational innovation.

After some initial experiences with organized scientific research in the laboratories of large American companies in the electrical and chemical industries (Noble 1977: 121), from the 1950s onwards, the organizational form of the 'project' was rapidly transferred to the military and government-funded research and became the dominant form of research organization in aeronautical and aerospace technology as well as in nuclear research. A prototype of organizational success via project work in a team was the Manhattan Engineering District Project (Kreibich 1986: 336), which is also a striking example of how the problem of coordinating research can be successfully solved even in cases in which staff members work in separate departments or research groups in the same organization or even in different organizations.

Restabilization: Projectification of Science I
In the footsteps of the Manhattan Project, the military and industry carried out a host of research projects in subsequent years. In the 1960s, a wide range of company R&D departments used projects to solve temporally limited and interdisciplinary problems that involved high degrees of complexity and innovation (Riedl 1990: 2), thus introducing the third phase of innovation processes: *restabilization*.

Projects *diffused* so quickly because project management methods were formalized early on. A professional understanding regarding planning and organizing science and technology development emerged as early as the 1940s. In the late 1950s, PERT (program evacuation and review technique) was developed. This management technique, supported by the U.S. Department of Defense, was so well established by the 1960s that it was used as a synonym for project management (Blomquist and Söderholm 2002: 27-28). PERT—and other techniques of project management that had been developed later—were introduced into companies mainly by consultants. The emergence of professional organizations for project management experts further strengthened this process of projectification (Blomquist and Söderholm 2002: 28-34).

Another diffusion mechanism was cooperation between scientists from different fields. The project as an organizational form spread particularly in research involving industry and large, publicly funded research centers. Examples include the collaborations of the Massachusetts Institute of Technology in the fields of electrical, communications, energy, and process engineering as well as with the military (particularly with the U.S. Air Force). Other examples are the collaborations of the University of Pennsylvania and the Institute of Advanced Study in Princeton, NJ, in the field of IT development or the collaboration of Harvard University with IBM

(Kreibich 1986: 335-339). Projects were introduced to universities as a result of precisely this kind of cooperation with companies and non-university government institutions. The process of projectification was further stabilized by new forms of research funding (see below).

At the same time, reflection continued on how projects could be best organized and managed and how research processes could be optimized. In the phase of restabilization, the project as a management method was continuously changed and adapted to different contexts. Various specialized manuals for project management were compiled, and the methods that were applied in companies differed from those used in other areas, for example, in small teams in the humanities. One can also view the phase of diffusion as a phase of *incremental innovation*, in which an innovative product is adapted to specific circumstances, meaning that the new structure is not only introduced but permanently incorporated within the established routines and proven processes.

In the end, a new grammar of the organization of research emerged. Projectification introduced new rules of scientific coordination: research in project form means producing new knowledge on the basis of a plan (which is a type of organization that had previously not existed in this form in the classical German university system).

4.2 Projects as a New Form of Funding Research

Variation: Financing Science in Times of Crisis
As mentioned above, the process of projectification consisted of two entwined sub-processes: projects were conceived as a new form of both coordinating and funding research. They were first introduced as a form of research funding by the big American philanthropic foundations such as the Rockefeller Foundation and the Carnegie Foundation. In the early 20th century, these foundations did not attach research funding to concrete objectives because they were convinced that the growth of knowledge would automatically lead to social progress. The situation was similar in Germany in the second half of the 19th century. At the time, foundations sustained by industrialists' private wealth were established (Stichweh 1988: 72-78). Examples include the Carl-Zeiss-Stiftung (1889), the Göttingen Association for the Advancement of Applied Physics (1898), the Jubilee Foundation of German Industry for the Promotion of Technical Sciences (1899), or even, a bit later, the Helmholtz Society for the Advancement of Physical-Technical Research (1920) (Richter 1979: 27-39). What these various foundations had in common is that the wealthy benefactors upon whom they relied did *not* seek to fund a pre-

cisely defined research endeavor corresponding to their specific business interests. Rather, the power relations in these foundations were balanced in such a way that no one individual could directly assert his personal interests. The fact that this group of donors needed to find a common goal uniting everyone despite personal differences made it possible to finance research for its own sake.

However, the research foundations' desire to finance *research* does not necessarily imply that they had to finance *projects*. On the contrary, in the second half of the 19th century, the ways in which German research foundations funded research ranged from awarding scholarships, financing specific infrastructures, and supporting a local university up to founding new technical universities (Richter 1979). In the 1920s, important foundations such as the Rockefeller Foundation still promoted science primarily by structurally strengthening universities (Kohler 1978: 488-489).

It was only later that the foundations changed course and started financing specific research proposals. This type of funding was introduced in Germany in the 1920s, and in the United States in the 1930s by American philanthropists (especially the Rockefeller Foundation) (Geiger 1986: 164-167).

There are strong indications that these transition phases are accelerated when economic crises concur with expansion phases of academic research. This constellation could be observed in Germany in the 1920s. World War I destroyed the German economy, and Germans had to pay severe reparations to the Allies, resulting in a scarcity of available funds for research. This forced scientists to seek out new ways of funding and efficiently distributing these funds. The traditional German foundations mentioned above had less capital for funding research (also as a result of World War I) while research was becoming increasingly expensive owing to a growing need for laboratories and larger research teams. The foundations' resources did not suffice to finance all necessary buildings, personnel, and infrastructure. To make the best possible use of scarce resources and maintain an influence on academic research, the foundations began to switch to supporting promising research projects (Forman 1974: 52-53).

The most explicit example of the relationship between economic crisis and targeted funding is the 'Notgemeinschaft der Deutschen Wissenschaft' (NDW) (German Science Emergency Association), which was founded in 1920 to support science and later became the 'Deutsche Forschungsgemeinschaft' (DFG) (German Research Foundation)—an organization that has always been largely government-funded and up until today is Germany's foremost funding organization for academic research, comparable, for instance, to the U.S. 'National Science Foundation' (NSF). The NDW's mission statement reveals that it was explicitly established in 1920 to (among other things) promote science during the economic crisis (Zierold 1968: 12; Nipperdey and Schmugge 1970: 14). According to a foundational document, the NDW's goal was to inspire the confidence that individual scientific contributions would not disappear in the maelstrom of the general emergency and be severely limited in their impact but rather that good scientific contributions would be sustained and become a firm emergency support structure (Fritz Haber's application to the Rector of the University of Berlin for establishing the NDW, March 29, 1920, as cited in Zierold 1968: 12).

In summary, severe underfunding increasingly changed the figuration of 'science.' Private foundations and the NDW aimed to close these funding gaps and make research more efficient. This also implied changes in science's structure, working methods, and practices.

Selection: The Project Grant System

The transition from a system of funding long-term structures of research (such as universities and long-term positions) to a system of project-oriented funding (*project grant system*) can be regarded as a substantial reorientation in the system of research funding. However, this new system of funding could be widely applied only if an appropriate procedure of selecting projects eligible for funding was found. For such a procedure to be considered appropriate, it had to correspond with the norms of the figuration of 'science.'

The procedure that was introduced for the first time in the 1920s by German foundations, among them the NDW and the Helmholtz Association (Forman 1974: 51), is the *peer review*, that is, the evaluation of project ideas by fellow researchers. To date, peer review remains firmly in place, as it is considered the most suitable way of evaluating academic research, despite all criticism, disadvantages, and shortcomings. From the beginning, the NDW distributed funds on the basis of a peer review system of project proposals (Hohn and Schimank 1990: 45).

The project grant system was of great interest to scientists from the outset, as it amplified their power within the figuration by lending primary importance to expert opinions when choosing projects to be funded (Price 1978: 78-79). In addition, the project grant system has the advantage of appearing to be fair. It seemingly reduces privileges in the figuration of 'science,' because it replaces the practice of allocating funds to heads of departments, who then further distribute these funds at their own discretion, with a system of distributing money according to the quality of individual researchers' work.

Consequently, projectification and the ensuing changes in the figuration of 'science' were perceived as advancing the *inclusion of scientists* at the phase of selection via the project grant system. These perceived advantages provided an impetus to further pursue and consolidate projectification, marking the beginning of the next phase of the innovation process: restabilization.

Restabilization: Projectification of Science II

The practice of using projects for funding research has become increasingly widespread (Kreckel and Pasternack 2008; Besio 2009). In the course of this diffusion process, projects themselves have been transformed from an exceptional form of financing research in times of crisis into a standard form of funding research. This was only possible because the project corresponded perfectly with central structures, values, and interests both within the figuration of science and its environment.

Projects organize science in a way that was intended to weaken privileges by basing funding on the quality of research. For this reason, the project grant system has always been semantically conceived as being strongly connected to and securing the autonomy of science. After 1968, not only but especially in Germany, the need for a long-term democratization of universities arose as well as the desire for greater equal opportunity, fairness, and a reduction of hierarchies and professorial privileges (Korte 1987).

In this context, projects changed the power balances in science: Unlike institutional financing, projects made it possible for funding agencies to target research toward desired areas. To meet this objective, the project as an organizational form was incrementally innovated, resulting in more advanced forms such as the 'research program' ('Forschungsprogramm'). From the outset, some institutions (especially American foundations) identified specific subjects or research areas that they intended to support (Geiger 1986: 149-160).

Projects also matched the classic characteristics of the German university system very well with its solid infrastructural base, as discussed above. By providing a model for financing short-term research endeavors, projects simultaneously strongly depend on this infrastructural base, put it to use, and hence legitimize it and, in so doing, strengthen the institutional embedding of projects in the figuration. Project-oriented financing is further legitimized by the fact that academic research at universities is increasingly not a matter of individual scholars but of research groups.

Another factor that provided a favorable climate for the proliferation of project work was the poor financial situation of the individual researcher. Initially, project-based financing was an additional source of income for researchers precisely because it was not institutional funding. This meant, for instance, that the many private lecturers and extraordinary professors could gain access to a steady salary and income for the duration of the project. Even for research staff such as professors who had a steady income, projects were attractive as they provided opportunities to acquire additional special equipment.

As a result of the interaction of these factors, projectification has been accelerating since the mid-1980s at the latest. This acceleration process is reflected in the fact that 'only' about 15% of German university budgets, with minor fluctuations, were funded via third parties between 1980 and 2000 (WR 2000, 2002: 59) and still only roughly 19% were externally funded in 2006, whereas, by 2012, the figure for third-party funding was already nearly 25%. At the same time, there are strong regional variations in the degree of universities' dependence on external funding, which ranged from 17% in the state of Hesse in 2012 to an average of 25% in Bavaria and up to 33% in Berlin and Saxony (Destatis 2012). Projects have thus become a standard form of coordinating and financing research and have hence also changed individual researchers' options for (strategically) operating inside the figuration.

5 Grammar and Pragmatics of the 'Science Figuration' after Projectification

To sum up the discussion so far, the sociogenesis of the project consisted of two parallel processes: searching for efficient forms of coordinating scientific work conducted by several researchers as well as searching for a form of funding research in times of economic austerity. As a result of these processes, projects have prevailed as a form of organizing scientific research, and (mainly externally funded) projects have long been shaping everyday research practices (Besio 2009; Torka 2009). The project as organizational innovation has diffused and restabilized only gradually and over a long period of time. During these phases of transition, the 'project' as an organizational form changed both its own nature and the contexts in which it was applied. We call this specific innovation process 'projectification.'

Projectification has had serious consequences at all levels of the figuration of 'science,' that is, it has affected both the scientific system (macro level), the organizational level (meso level), and academic careers as well as everyday research practices (micro level). Projectification has been affecting science in manifold ways and has changed, among other things, the ways of generating scientific knowledge itself. In order to illustrate this point, the following section focuses on the consequences of projectification at two levels—the university as an organizational form (meso level) and academic careers (micro level)—by drawing on our interviews with scientists and our ethnographic observations.

5.1 Projectification's Impact on the University as an Organization (Meso Level)

At the organizational level, our data show first of all that projects still fulfil the tasks for which they were originally intended: they are a useful form of coordinating research to address specific topics within a defined time period. Furthermore, projects regulate research processes in a particular way. A central aspect of this innovation's grammar and pragmatics is that projects function as clearly definable units that structure decisions and thereby reduce uncertainty. More specifically, any activity in the context of a project is expected to be related to the project-specific task: during the project, the project team can neglect time- and energy-consuming decision-making procedures as well as other topics and research activities in favor of the project objective (Baecker 1999; Besio 2009: 206-207, Besio et al. 2016). In this vein, one of the researchers we interviewed underlined that projects exempt researchers from other tasks:

> "The greatest benefit of working in projects is that you're no longer obligated to give countless courses nor do you need to attend obligatory university meetings" (Interview S_I13).

This makes it easier to successfully address the specific research questions defined by the project objectives. In our interviews, many scientists felt that a clearly defined research design was helpful for focusing on one's research:

> "With projects, you have to think in realistic limits [...]. The project provides a framework for reflecting on possible problems" (Interview S_I3).

> "[A] schedule [...] facilitates coming to an end and moving on to something else" (Interview S_I7).

After completing a project, researchers can turn to new research questions. From the organization's perspective, this means that project work has to be treated as a series or a network of separate research endeavors. In this way, scientific organizations are not bound to specific issues in the long term and can instead plan various research questions for the foreseeable future. This promotes *flexibility* in terms of resources and seemingly also leads to greater innovativeness: As the organization is not tied to a particular line of research, riskier topics can be dealt with more easily (Besio 2009). Given the limited time span of projects, researchers also build new collaborations in a flexible way. This flexibility opens up the opportunity to develop new ideas in cooperation with new partners (Schwab and Miner 2011). When projects become the actual sites of research, the traditional figuration of the German universities changes in that the connection between research and teaching weakens.

While projects have the advantage of building specific spaces for research, there are almost always unwanted side effects of social action (Elias 1978), and this is also true for projectification. One of the biggest problems is time pressure (Besio et al. 2016). A projects' tight time frame makes it *difficult to pursue unexpected results* during a project, which threatens the heart of academic research because identifying and pursuing unexpected results is a core trait of scientific work (Merton and Barber 2004). Instead, research becomes more output-oriented. The researchers we interviewed repeatedly complained that exploring unexpected results in more depth is almost impossible and that this also inhibits innovation. In this spirit, one interviewee complained that

> "[…] it is very difficult [, for instance,] to reflect on and handle methodological difficulties that emerge during the project. That would mean that projects could change their course—which may lead to complications. […] You can only reflect on the project up to a certain point, otherwise you lose your footing" (Interview S_I11).

These negative side effects are especially strong in the social sciences. Natural science institutions have enduring scientific structures, lines of research, and machine infrastructures (Heinze 2016), making it possible to bundle and link projects and incorporate the surprising results of one project into a new one within the context of the same research program (Hallonsten and Heinze 2013). In the natural sciences, these enduring structures in fact combine with projects (Heinze 2016), which results in projects' pragmatics being very different from those of the social sciences.

However, projectification's biggest problem is *ensuring the continuity and reproduction* at both the organizational and—as we will illustrate below—the individual level (Besio et al. 2016). This problem is already implicitly addressed in the difficulties of pursuing *long-term lines of research* owing to time constraints and short project duration. Further, the problem of reproduction points to the well-known problem of organizational learning (e.g., Hobday 2000; Prencipe and Tell 2001; Sydow, Lindkvist, and De Filippi 2004; Schwab and Miner 2011). Along these lines, the researchers we interviewed emphasized the problem of securing knowledge and skills. For the organization, the *knowledge about project management* (planning, organization, coordination of partners, communication with funding sources) also includes knowledge about scientific practices, for example, on properly documenting and archiving data and research results (Barlösius 2016). An important part of this knowledge is *tacit knowledge* (such as knowledge about sampling or field contacts including, e.g., addresses). This kind of knowledge in particular is difficult to pass on from project to project.

The problem of organizational learning is exacerbated by the *decoupling of research and teaching* mentioned above. Individual researchers often perceive this as an advantage since not having to teach strongly reduces their workload even if they actually like to teach. However, this has also the consequence that they no longer rely on teaching to give their research findings continuity.

Although German universities as well as the DFG currently attempt to mitigate these consequences, these are side effects of the project that are difficult to control. Again, the natural sciences are in a better position to counter these negative side effects than the social sciences because their long-term lines of research (Heinze 2016) and infrastructure (Barlösius 2016) outlast individual projects and provide research continuity. It is therefore not surprising that our data show that organizational learning not only remains difficult, especially in the social sciences (Buchhofer 1979: 27), but is increasingly endangered. In the absence of strong structures, the only solution for long-term continuity are individual researchers' memories:

"People give continuity to the research" (Interview S_I13).

However, from the point of view of the whole figuration as well from a organizational perspective, this is far from being a good solution. The problem owes itself to a characteristic of the classical figuration of the German academic system. As discussed above, only professors are tenured and have permanent positions. All other researchers have fixed-term contracts with potential gaps between contracts, that is, the system is deliberately based on staff turnover and not on a continuity of personnel. This structural problem is even amplified by projectification because now the typical contractual periods no longer correspond to the typical phases of education (4-6 years). While research associates with teaching duties, who are traditionally institutionally funded, have 4-6 year work contracts (depending on location), most projects (and hence third-party-funded work contracts and scholarships) usually last only 2-3 years. To ensure organizational continuity, the scientific staff members are forced to take on additional and very time-consuming administrative tasks that are not stipulated in their employment contracts (and that in turn prevent them from doing research and teaching). Ironically, these time-consuming administrative tasks that are not funded include writing proposals for new projects and—once a project is funded—project management. Consequently, more and more time is invested in applying for projects. In particular, professors spend less and less time on doing research themselves and supervising younger researchers and spend more and more time on project management, which further complicates organizational reproduction. In 2009, university teachers in the social sciences invested only 20% of their working time (instead of the 33% intended by their work contracts) in doing research and 12% in applying for projects. Professors from the natural sciences were even able to invest only 17% of their time in research while 16% of their time was spent on project applications (EFI 2012: 48).

The problem of pursuing unexpected findings and ensuring the continuity of research shows that projects work best if they are combined with other, more permanent structures (Besio et al. 2016). However, these structures require additional funding. It thus becomes clear that projects cannot solve the problem of *underfunding* at the organizational level: research institutions (such as universities) either have the resources to pay for an expensive scientific infrastructure or they have to constantly acquire additional external resources to pursue the new findings and research questions to create some degree of continuity.

This points another problem. Projectification implicitly has resulted in a *shift from fundamental to applied research*. There are three reasons for this:

1. Projectification entails the requirement to constantly raise additional external resources to ensure the continuity of research.
2. Research funding today is not only a matter of the DFG and EU but also of ministries and privately funded foundations.
3. The latter strongly and openly influence research topics and designs (which is precisely what projects were supposed to accomplish).

This shift from fundamental to applied research is accelerated because, currently, the classical figuration of the German university, which ensured researchers' (relative) independence from third-party interests (in the past), is changing, and it is feared that expanding projectification will result in research being increasingly aligned with the interests of donors.

5.2 Projectification's Impact on Academic Careers (Micro Level)

In addition to its consequences for universities, projectification has also had consequences for the scientists who belong to the figuration. To individual researchers in both the social and natural sciences, projects are a double-edged sword that involves career opportunities and risks. Although one reason for furthering projects was because they were believed to structurally improve the position of junior researchers in the figuration, younger scholars' situation today is as severe as ever (Norkus et al. 2016). Projects provide only a limited solution to the *underfunding* of universities and the *precariousness* of scientific careers because, although they fund researchers for the time of the project, the problem of transitions between work contracts has not only gone unresolved but has even become worse owing to the typically short project durations of 2-3 years. To successfully complete an educational phase (doctorate or habilitation), an individual usually needs at least two projects that thematically build on each other to pursue a personal line of research. However, it is almost impossible to guarantee that an appropriate project will be funded at the right time. More frequently than was the case before projectification's effects on the figuration unfolded, this results in job insecurity and repeated periods of unemployment (Norkus et al. 2016), which exacerbates the already insecure employment situation in academia (Kreckel and Pasternack 2008). In this way, the problem of the *reproduction* of the academic field at the organizational level is mirrored at the individual level.

Projectification also has ambivalent effects with regard to the predictability of a scientific career and the *development of an individual research profile*: At the beginning of an academic career, projects have the advantage that young scientists have more time (because they do not have to teach) and social space for developing their own research profile. However, this is only true if the personal research interests happen to coincide with the project aims since it is ultimately not the individual scientist but the project that defines what kind of research is done. By comparison, researchers in classical government-funded university positions have much less time for exchange within a team, but—at least in the social sciences—they are almost completely free in their choice of research topic.

Furthermore, projects can help scientists at a more advanced career level to improve their own research profile by focusing on a specific topic during the project. In addition, project results can usually be used for a researcher's own publications. The knowledge gained during this time acts as a form of knowledge capital that can be applied to new projects or other employment fields outside of science (Arthur, De Fillippi, and Candace 2001). Nevertheless, advanced researchers, too, are not entirely free in shaping their research profiles. In order to secure follow-up funding, they have to keep their research profiles flexible enough to adapt to the (sometimes very rapidly changing) *interests of donors.*

This hopping from one topic to the next may hinder researchers in developing their own scientific profile and result in a curriculum vitae that seems fragmented. Moreover, potential conflicts between the *demands of the project and the demands of the discipline* may arise, as the former provides work contracts while the latter is still decisive for a researcher's chances of being appointed a professor: the research lines established by funding bodies do not necessarily conform with the requirements of a specific discipline or scientific community, and certain key competencies can only be acquired with difficulty in projects, for example, experience in teaching and educational administration.

At the same time, scientific careers are harder to plan today because the *binding orientation framework* that the classical university system once provided has been lost: First, projectification has added a second career path ('the project career') to the classical career path that still is in place for those who work in government-funded university positions. Second, younger scholars today need to acquire more and more diverse competences in order to have the chance for tenure because it no longer suffices to have (1) a good track record in research and (2) experience in teaching and educational administration; rather younger scholars must now additionally be able to (3) raise external funding and manage projects. Whereas the first skill set can be acquired both in project and classical university positions, the second skill set is typically acquired only in university positions and the third skill set in projects. A benefit of university positions over projects is that they provide better individual work contracts; projects, however, provide more time and funding (e.g., of equipment) necessary for building a research profile (which is crucial for the next career steps). As both senior university and project positions require some knowledge of the respective skills, it is difficult to switch between university and project positions. This being the case, projectification has complicated academic careers. One of our interviewees puts it as follows:

> "There are no permanent positions in research. The situation is difficult because academic careers are in the meantime defined by the most recent research programs. A researcher's publications can be too narrow, thematically speaking, or they are basically a dead end [...] Or the researcher grows older and doesn't have enough time to commit to a completely new topic. Scientific trends can lose out to political trends" (Interview S_I9).

At first glance, projects seem to satisfy the desire for the democratization of higher education; they appear to decrease professorial privileges and reduce hierarchies within universities. Projects can give scientists more autonomy in their own research because, to some extent, project objectives can shield them from their supervisor's objectives. Social scientists in particular perceive projects as a space for conducting research without external intervention. However, this is only true for certain forms of projects. Favorable examples are the 'Temporary Positions for Principal Investigators' ('Eigene Stelle') or 'Junior Research Groups' ('Nach-

'Wuchsgruppe') funded by the DFG. However, it is apparent that, in many other cases, the universities' hierarchical structure remains firmly in place because almost every project must be embedded in a permanent structure, for instance, a research group with labs and long-term personnel (Besio et al. 2016). Therefore, especially doctoral students are strongly pressured to be on good terms with university professors. In order to secure their next contract, younger scholars in particular have to offer professors incentives to invest time in applying for new projects and—once funded—offer this new position to them.

Ironically, hierarchies have actually decreased in another way. Instead of improving the situation of younger researchers, the overall situation of the whole profession seems to have declined by downgrading professorships. Since the 1990s, chairs' occupational prestige has been slowly but continuously declining (IfD Allensbach 2013). Simultaneously, their workloads have increased while their pay has decreased. On top of this, there have been several (albeit so far unsuccessful) attempts to abolish chairs' status as civil servants with lifetime tenure. In a way, this can be interpreted as an attempt by public administrators to transfer the volatile nature of early academic careers (due to a succession of short-term contracts in projects) to the later career phases. So instead of shifting the figuration's power balance from chairs to junior researchers, projectification has helped to shift the power balance from chairs to public administrators.

6 Conclusion and Outlook

In this contribution, we have used the example of projectification to analyze the dynamic interrelationship between an innovation ('the project') and other levels of action from a figurational theoretical perspective. We have shown that 'the project' as innovation solves problems specific to the figuration of 'science': Projects have proven quite suitable for coordinating both big science and interdisciplinary research. However, projects provide a solution neither for the question of how to deal with the unexpected nor for the problem of the underfunding of German universities. Their effect on scientific careers is double-edged since, for untenured, younger researchers, projects have both advantages and disadvantages. Moreover, projectification also has unintended side effects (Elias 1978) at the organizational level (i.e., universities): projects threaten the independence of research, discriminate against fundamental research (which plays an essential role in innovation) in favor of applied research, and they above all endanger organizational reproduction and continuity in research and teaching.

This results in a number of unanswered questions for future research, both for figurational sociology and for STS studies:

We have indicated that figurational sociology can only be fruitfully applied to innovation processes in science when it is linked to other theoretical approaches, such as systems theory, as illustrated above. As the focus of this article was the substantial discussion of a specific innovation process (projectification), we have deliberately refrained from providing a discussion of the difficulties of this theoretical integration—but it is still important that this discussion takes place in the future. Furthermore, a number of methodological issues still need to be addressed in future research, including the question of how to fruitfully analyze the interaction of processes at different levels of action and over time, that is, how to conduct a process-oriented macro and micro analysis in the longue durée.

In this paper, we have further focused on two levels of analysis: the university as an organization and the individual career. At both levels of action, the question of how continuity and reproduction can be ensured requires closer analysis. At the level of the organization, it would be desirable to conduct an analysis of how projects are interwoven with other organizational contexts (such as with different disciplines or with other forms of organization). These interconnections should be of interest because one of our empirical findings is that especially the (seemingly) distinct organizational forms of universities (Meier 2016), non-university research institutes (Heinze 2016), and new forms of organization (SFBs, clusters of excellence) cannot be separated in practice because researchers may often be funded by different organizational forms (e.g., project A as part of a cluster of excellence and a classical university position) but, in terms of their actual everyday research, consider themselves as part of the same research group. Moreover, in research practice, researchers frequently have a work contract with one form of organization (for example, project A as part of a cluster of excellence) but actually work in the context of a different organizational form (for example, project B at a university)— or even work for both at the same time. These complex funding/working networks remain to be untangled. Further, it needs to be clarified how projectification is refracted or reshaped by these various contexts and how specific combinations of projects and contexts affect other levels of action (e.g., individual careers).

At the level of individual careers, a detailed analysis of social inequality within science would be desirable: Are all researchers affected by projectification in the same way, or do the effects differ depending on factors such as researchers' gender, social class, ethnicity, age, or disability? When, where, and how is intersectionality (Baur and Wagner 2014) operative?

We have limited ourselves to analyzing two levels of action. In a next step, an analysis of projectification's synchronic and diachronic effects over several levels of action would be desirable, which would mean systematically including the levels of the (national and global) science system, the individual working units (e.g., working groups, research projects), and the interaction situations in everyday research.

A particular challenge is the relationship between science, innovation, and locality. We found in our data (as an unexpected result, as we were not looking for it) that locality and space are central to innovation processes in science at all levels of action. Our original research design intended to systematically compare different organizational forms (SFBs, clusters of excellence, universities) in Berlin and Munich. An early result was that the type of research organization at one location (regardless of the formal organizational form) differed little but that greater differences were evident between various locations (even for the same organizational form). This confirms results from economic sociology that different regions not only exhibit different potentials for innovation but that, after every (economic) crisis since the 16th century, regional disparities have been reproduced according to basically the same pattern that existed prior to the crisis (e.g., formerly successful sites wound up in the same relatively powerful position as before). Approaches such as 'international business studies' and 'regional innovation systems' argue that this stability is caused by a historically evolved combination of institutions, research facilities (including universities), economic structures, and infrastructures that is specific to the locality in question and significantly affects a region's overall performance (Heidenreich and Mattes 2012; Heidenreich and Baur 2015). 'Economics of conventions' argues that local culture also plays an important role: local suppliers and buyers develop conventions (i.e., common beliefs) about how things (including innovations) are done best and by which means (Baur et al. 2014). Furthermore, lifestyle research has shown that people with modern lifestyles who like to try new things prefer to settle in certain regions and big cities (Otte and Baur 2008). These factors seem to mutually stabilize each other and to solidify the boundaries of regions—but how lifestyles, science, and business practices interact locally and what similarities and differences exist between local conventions is a question for future research.

References

Akremi, Leila. 2014. "Stichprobenziehung in der qualitativen Sozialforschung." Pp. 265-282 in *Handbuch Methoden der empirischen Sozialforschung*, edited by N. Baur and J. Blasius. Wiesbaden: Springer Fachmedien.
Ametowobla, Dzifa, Nina Baur, and Maria Norkus. Forthcoming. "Analyseverfahren in der empirischen Organisationsforschung." In: *Handbuch Empirische Organisationsforschung*, edited by S. Liebig, W. Matiaske, and S. Rosenbohm. Wiesbaden: Springer.
Arthur, Michael B., Robert J. De Fillippi, and Candace Jones. 2001. "Project-Based Learning as the Interplay of Career and Company Non-Financial Capital." *Management Learning* 32(1): 99-117.
Baecker, Dirk. 1999. "Einfache Komplexität." Pp. 169-197 in *Organisation als System - Aufsätze*, edited by D. Baecker. Frankfurt a. M.: Suhrkamp.
Baier, Christian and Richard Münch. 2013. "Institutioneller Wettbewerb und Karrierechancen von Nachwuchswissenschaftlern in der Chemie." *Kölner Zeitschrift für Soziologie (KZFSS)* 65(1): 129-155.
Barlösius, Eva. 2016. "Wissenschaftliche Infrastrukturen." Pp. 206-236 in *Wissen – Organisation – Forschungspraxis*, edited by N. Baur, C. Besio, M. Norkus, and G. Petschick. Weinheim: Juventa.
Baur, Nina. 2005. *Verlaufsmusteranalyse*. Wiesbaden: VS-Verlag.
Baur, Nina. 2008. "Taking Perspectivity Seriously. A Suggestion of a Conceptual Framework for Linking Theory and Methods in Longitudinal and Comparative Research." *Historical Social Research* 33(4): 191-213.
Baur, Nina. 2011. "Mixing Process-Generated Data in Market Sociology." *Quality & Quantity* 45(6): 1233-1251. doi:10.1007/s11135-009-9288-x.
Baur, Nina and Siegfried Lamnek. 2005. "Einzelfallanalyse." Pp. 241-252 in *Qualitative Medienforschung*, edited by L. Mikos and C. Wegener. Constance: UVK.
Baur, Nina and Stefanie Ernst. 2011. "Towards a Process-Oriented Methodology. Modern Social Science Research Methods and Norbert Elias' Figurational Sociology." *The Sociological Review* 59(s1): 117-139.
Baur, Nina and Pia Wagner. 2013. "Die moderne Sozialstrukturanalyse und das Problem der Operationalisierung von Intersektionalität." *Erwägen Wissen Ethik (EWE)* 24(3): 357-359.
Baur, Nina, Martina Löw, Linda Hering, Anna Laura Raschke, and Florian Stoll. 2014. "Die Rationalität lokaler Wirtschaftspraktiken im Friseurwesen." Pp. 299-327 in *Soziologie des Wirtschaftlichen*, edited by D. Bögenhold. Wiesbaden: Springer.
Baur, Nina, Cristina Besio, Maria Norkus, and Grit Petschick. 2016 "Wissenschaft als Mehrebenen-Phänomen." Pp. 13-46 in *Wissen – Organisation – Forschungspraxis*, edited by N. Baur, C. Besio, M. Norkus, and G. Petschick. Weinheim: Juventa.
Beer, John J. 1975. "Die Teerfarbenindustrie und die Anfänge des industriellen Forschungslaboratoriums." Pp. 106-118 in *Moderne Technikgeschichte*, edited by K. Hausen and R. Rürup. Cologne: Kiepenheuer & Witsch.
Besio, Cristina. 2009. *Forschungsprojekte*. Bielefeld: transcript.
Besio, Cristina and Robert J. Schmidt. 2012. *Innovation als spezifische Form sozialer Evolution* (Working Papers TUTS-WP-3-2012). Berlin: Technische Universität Berlin.

Besio, Cristina, Maria Norkus, and Nina Baur. 2016. "Projekte und Wissenschaft." Pp. 343-372 in *Wissen – Organisation – Forschungspraxis*, edited by N. Baur, C. Besio, M. Norkus and G. Petschick. Weinheim: Juventa.

Blomquist, Tomas and Anders J. Söderholm. 2002. "How Project Management Got Carried Away." Pp. 25-38 in *Beyond Project Management*, edited by K. Sahlin-Andersson and A. Söderholm. Kopenhagen: Liber.

Buchhofer, Bernd. 1979. *Projekt und Interview*. Weinheim, Basel: Beltz Verlag.

Carlson, W. Bernard. 1997. "Innovation and the Modern Corporation." Pp. 203-226 in *Science in the Twentieth Century*, edited by J. Krige and D. Pestre. Amsterdam: Harwood Academic Publishers.

DeStatis (Statistisches Bundesamt). 2012. *Monetäre hochschulstatistische Kennzahlen* (Fachserie 11 Reihe 4.3.2-2012). Wiesbaden: Statistisches Bundesamt.

EFI (Expertenkommission Forschung und Innovation), ed. 2012. *Zur Situation der Forschung an Deutschlands Hochschulen* (Studien zum deutschen Innovationssystem 16-2012). Shared paper of ISI (Frauenhofer Instituts für System- und Innovationsforschung), JR (Joanneum Research), Stifterverband für die deutsche Wissenschaft/Wissenschaftsstatistik GmbH, WZB (Wissenschaftszentrum Berlin), and ZEW (Zentrum für Europäische Wirtschaftsforschung GmbH). Berlin, Vienna: EFI. Retrieved March 25, 2015 (http://www.e-fi.de/fileadmin/Innovationsstudien_2012/StuDIS_16_ZEW_WZB_Joanneum_ISI.pdf).

Elias, Norbert. 1978. *What is Sociology?* New York: Columbia University Press.

Elias, Norbert. 1995. "Figuration." Pp. 75-78 in *Grundbegriffe der Soziologie*, edited by B. Schäfers. 4th ed. Opladen: Leske + Budrich.

Elias, Norbert. 2009. "Sociology in Danger: the Case for the Reorientation of a Discipline." Pp. 93-98 in *Essays III: On Sociology and the Humanities* (Collected Works, vol. 16), edited by R. Kilminster and S. Mennel. Dublin: UCD Press.

Forman, Paul. 1974. "The Financial Support and Political Alignment of Physicists in Weimar Germany." *Minerva* 12(1): 39-66.

Geiger, Roger L. 1986. "Organized Research Units—Their Role in the Development of University Research". *Journal of Higher Education* 61(1): 1-19.

Hack, Lothar and Irmgard Hack. 1985. *Die Wirklichkeit, die Wissen schafft*. Frankfurt a. M.: Campus.

Hallonsten, Olof and Thomas Heinze. 2013. "From Particle Physics to Photon Science: Multi-Dimensional and Multi-Level Renewal at DESY and SLAC." *Science and Public Policy* 40(5): 591-603.

Heidenreich, Martin and Nina Baur. 2015. "Locations of Corporate Headquarters in Europe." Pp. 177-207 in *Transnational Corporations and Transnational Governance*, edited by S. Lundan. Basingstoke: Palgrave.

Heidenreich, Martin and Jannika Mattes. 2012. "Regional Embeddedness of Multinational Companies and their Limits. A Typology." Pp. 29-58 in *Institutional Embeddedness of Multinational Companies*, edited by M. Heidenreich. Cheltenham: Edward Elgar.

Heinz, Walter R., Kolja Briedis, and Georg Jongmanns. 2016. "Alter(n) und Wissenschaftskarrieren." Pp. 552-579 in *Wissen – Organisation – Forschungspraxis*, edited by N. Baur, C. Besio, M. Norkus, and G. Petschick. Weinheim: Juventa.

Heinze, Thomas. 2016. "Außeruniversitäre Forschung." Pp. 259-307 in *Wissen – Organisation – Forschungspraxis*, edited by N. Baur, C. Besio, M. Norkus, and G. Petschick. Weinheim: Juventa.

Helfferich, Cornelia. 2014. "Leitfaden- und Experteninterviews." Pp. 559-574 in *Handbuch Methoden der empirischen Sozialforschung*, edited by N. Baur and J. Blasius. Wiesbaden: Springer Fachmedien.
Hergesell, Jannis. 2015. *Soziogenetische Dispositive der Pflegefiguration – zur soziohistorischen Entwicklung der beruflichen Krankenpflege in Deutschland* (Unpublished master's thesis). Technische Universität Berlin.
Hobday, Mike. 2000. "The Project-Based Organization: An Ideal Form for Managing Complex Products and Systems?" *Research Policy* 29(7-8): 871-893.
Hohn, Hans-Willy and Uwe Schimank. 1990. *Konflikte und Gleichgewichte im Forschungssystem*. Frankfurt a. M.: Campus.
Hounshell, David A. 1992. "Du Pont and the Management of Large-Scale Research and Development." Pp. 236-264 in *Big Science*, edited by P. Galison and B. Hevly. Stanford: Stanford University Press.
Hutter, Michael, Hubert Knoblauch, Werner Rammert, and Arnold Windeler. This volume. "Innovation Society Today. The Reflexive Creation of Novelty."
IfD Allensbach. 2013. "Allensbacher Berufsprestige-Skala 2013. Hohes Ansehen für Ärzte und Lehrer – Reputation von Hochschulprofessoren und Rechtsanwälten rückläufig." *Allensbacher Kurzbericht*, August 20, 2013. Retrieved December 30, 2015 (http://www.ifd-allensbach.de/uploads/tx_reportsndocs/PD_2013_05.pdf).
Knoblauch, Hubert. 2014a. *Communicative Action, Reflexivity, and Innovation Society* (Working Papers TUTS-WP-3-2014). Technische Universität Berlin.
Knoblauch, Hubert. 2014b. "Ethnographie." Pp. 521-528 in *Handbuch Methoden der empirischen Sozialforschung*, edited by N. Baur and J. Blasius. Wiesbaden: Springer Fachmedien.
Kohler, Robert E. 1978. "A Policy for the Advancement of Science." *Minerva* 16(4): 480-515.
Korte, Hermann. 1987. *Eine Gesellschaft im Aufbruch*. Frankfurt a. M.: Suhrkamp.
Krauch, Helmut. 1970. *Die organisierte Forschung*. Berlin and Neuwied: Luchterhand.
Kreckel, Reinhard and Peer Pasternack. 2008. "Prämissen des Ländervergleichs." Pp. 1-79 in *Zwischen Promotion und Professur*, edited by R. Kreckel. Leipzig: AVA.
Kreckel, Reinhard. 2011. "Universitäre Karrierestruktur als deutscher Sonderweg." Pp. 7-60 in *Traumjob Wissenschaft? Karrierewege in Hochschule und Forschung*, edited by K. Himpele, A. Keller, and A. Ortmann. Bonn: Friedrich-Ebert-Stiftung.
Kreibich, Rolf. 1986. *Die Wissenschaftsgesellschaft*. Frankfurt a. M.: Suhrkamp.
Levene, Ralph J. 1996. "Project Management." Pp. 4162-4181 in *International Encyclopedia of Business & Management, No. 4*, edited by M. Warner. London: Routledge.
Meier, Frank. 2016. "Universitäten." Pp. 237-258 in *Wissen – Organisation – Forschungspraxis*, edited by N. Baur, C. Besio, M. Norkus, and G. Petschick. Weinheim: Juventa.
Merton, Robert K. and Barber Elinor. 2004. *The Travels and Adventures of Serendipity*. Princeton: Princeton University Press.
Nipperdey, Thomas. 1998. *Deutsche Geschichte, 1866-1918, Bd. 1: Arbeitswelt und Bürgergeist*. Munich: Beck Verlag.
Nipperdey, Thomas and Ludwig Schmugge. 1970. *50 Jahre Forschungsförderung in Deutschland*. Bonn: Deutsche Forschungsgemeinschaft.
Noble, David F. 1977. *America by Design*. New York: Knopf.
Norkus, Maria, Cristina Besio, and Nina Baur. 2016. "Effects of Project-Based Research Work on the Career Paths of Young Academics. " *Work Organisation, Labour & Globalisation* 10(2): 9-26.

Otte, Gunnar and Nina Baur. 2008. "Urbanism as a Way of Life?" *Zeitschrift für Soziologie* 37(2): 93-116.
Petschick, Grit. 2015. "Ethnographic Panels for Analyzing Innovation Processes." *Historical Social Research* 40(3): 210-232.
Petschick, Grit. 2016. "Publikationspraktiken." Pp. 480-509 in *Wissen – Organisation – Forschungspraxis*, edited by N. Baur, C. Besio, M. Norkus, and G. Petschick. Weinheim: Juventa.
Prencipe, Andrea and Fredrik Tell. 2001. "Inter-Project Learning: Processes and Outcomes of Knowledge Codification in Project-Based Firms." *Research Policy* 30(9): 1373-1394.
Price, Don K. 1978. "Endless Frontier or Bureaucratic Morass?" *Daedalus* 107(2): 75-92.
Richter, Steffen. 1979. "Wirtschaft und Forschung." *Technikgeschichte* 46(1): 20-44.
Riedl, Josef E. 1990. *Projekt-Controlling in Forschung und Entwicklung*. Berlin: Springer.
Salheiser, Axel. 2014. "Natürliche Daten: Dokumente." Pp. 813-828 in *Handbuch Methoden der empirischen Sozialforschung*, edited by N. Baur and J. Blasius. Wiesbaden: Springer Fachmedien.
Schimank, Hans. 1976. "Physik und Chemie im 19. Jahrhundert. Ihre Abkunft, ihre Hilfsmittel und ihre Wandlungen." Pp. 371-397 in *Naturwissenschaft, Technik und Wirtschaft im 19. Jahrhundert, Bd. 2*, edited by W. Treue and K. Mauel. Göttingen: Vandenhoeck & Ruprecht.
Schwab, Andreas and Anne S. Miner. 2011. "Organizational Learning Implications of Partnering Flexibility in Project-Venture Settings." Pp. 115-145 in *Project-Based Organizing and Strategic Management (Advances in Strategic Management 28)*, edited by G. Cattani, S. Ferriani, L. Frederiksen, and F. Täube. Bringley: Emerald Group Publishing Limited.
Stichweh, Rudolf. 1988. "Differenzierung des Wissenschaftssystems." Pp. 45-115 in *Differenzierung und Verselbständigung*, edited by R. Mayntz, B. Rosewitz, U. Schimank, and R. Stichweh. Frankfurt, New York: Campus.
Sydow, Jörg, Lars Lindkvist, and Robert De Fillippi. 2004. "Project-Based Organizations, Embeddedness and Repositories of Knowledge: Editorial." *Organization Studies* 25(9): 1475-1489.
Taylor, Peter J., Michael Hoyler, and David M. Evans. 2008. "A Geohistorical Study of 'The Rise of Modern Science': Mapping Scientific Practice Trough Urban Networks, 1500-1900." *Minerva* 46(4): 809-846.
Teichler, Ulrich. 1990. *Das Hochschulwesen in der Bundesrepublik Deutschland*. Weinheim: Deutsche Studien Verlag.
Torka, Marc. 2009. *Die Projektförmigkeit der Forschung*. Baden-Baden: Nomos.
WR (Wissenschaftsrat). 2000. *Drittmittel und Grundmittel der Hochschulen 1993 bis 1998*. Cologne: Wissenschaftsrat. Retrieved March 26, 2015 (http://www.wissenschaftsrat.de/download/archiv/4717-00.pdf).
WR (Wissenschaftsrat). 2002. *Eckdaten und Kennzahlen zur Lage der Hochschulen von 1980 bis 2000*. Cologne: Wissenschaftsrat. Retrieved March 25, 2015 (http://www.wissenschaftsrat.de/download/archiv/5125-02.pdf).
Zierold, Kurt. 1968. *Forschungsförderung in drei Epochen*. Wiesbaden: Steiner.

Social Innovation

A New Instrument for Social Change?

Cornelius Schubert

1 Introduction

Rampant, unbridled change appears as a ubiquitous phenomenon that holds broad segments of contemporary society in its grasp. Industrialization, individualization, rationalization—they are all seemingly fateful processes that dismantle and reconstruct society in a never-ending parade of novel forms. The more differentiation occurs within societal fields, the more interdependent they are and the more complex and dynamic the exchanges that constitute social order between them inevitably become. No matter its outcome, change is virtually the only constant.

These observations reflect essential insights of modern theories of society. As such, they continue to present challenges both on the ground in various societal fields and from a bird's-eye view, that is, from the perspective of sociological theory, for the refinement thereof. On a general level, sociologists have long since reflected on how modern societies cope with the competing challenges of differentiation and integration (Durkheim 2014) and how specific fields such as politics keep up with an endless stream of transformation. At issue is what defines a 'good' balance between renewal and the status quo, so that change can happen without fully discrediting established structures. Sociologists are also called on to analyze social change as an immanent process and reflect on its implications.

What I want to argue in the present context is that societal change itself is currently undergoing a structural shift in the context of an increasingly reflexive and multi-referential 'innovation society' (Hutter et al., this volume): institutions of political governance, which are tasked with the job of guiding societal change, have registered the increasing ineffectiveness of top-down interventions and now look to new bottom-up approaches for solutions. As one example of this shift, I will look at so-called *social innovations*, which have become a popular topic in many societal and political fields as well as academic discourses. Social innovation, as others have argued, has become a dominant mode of social transformation in modern industrialized society and has consequently developed into a reflexive tool to control this change (cf. Beck and Kropp 2012). In the political sphere, this tool meshes well with postmodern conditions: instead of top-down bureaucratic or market-based interventions, it is held to promote community-based grassroots inventions (cf. Grimm et al. 2013). This view of social innovation takes the widespread pessimism, both general and theoretical, regarding the governability of complex societies (à la Luhmann), observable since the 1970s, and bolsters it with new data while also pairing it with a solution. As I will show, in this perspective, social innovations are often conceived as *immaterial, grassroots initiatives that are conducive to civil society*. Regardless of its specific intentions, this restrictive take on social innovation promotes an instrumental (i.e., active and directed), entrepreneurial view of social change.

To explain the above claims and the transformation processes they entail, I will start by outlining a brief overview of social innovation as a mode of social change from a sociological perspective before moving to a more specific examination of social innovation as a policy instrument for social change. Then I will critically analyze the two primary connotations of social innovation as both immaterial and bottom-up processes with presumably positive outcomes for civil society. My analysis of the heightened interest in social innovations at the European Union level should serve as a case in point of the difficulties inherent in this dually restrictive interpretation.

2   Transformation of (Post-)Modern Societies

To explore the link between social innovation and social change, I will start with an overview of how the former concept has developed. Discussions of social innovation have gained momentum in recent decades, but its underlying ideas and definitions date back much further. Going back in time, innovation itself reveals a story of twists and turns, along with close links to more recent discussions of social innovation.

Canadian historian Benoît Godin (2015) has noted the changing connotations of 'innovation' over the centuries. In the late 1400s, it was a derogatory term applied to religious or political subversives who aimed to derail existing social or religious structures. This connotation remained throughout the 19th century, when innovation was increasingly joined with the adjective 'social' to denote and devalue—mainly communist—ideas and ideals concerning social change. Such negative connotations of social innovation stand in stark contrast to more recent attributes that are actively expressed in current discourses, namely, social innovation as a positive force for local, sustainable social change (cf. Howaldt and Jacobsen 2010; Rückert-John 2013). According to Godin, social innovation only acquired a positive connotation after taking a detour through technology and market discourses in the early 20th century, around which time its meaning started to shift away from a problematic subversion of social order to instead become a desirable generator of growth and value in capitalist economies. Once applied to socio-political processes, innovation suddenly acquired a clear techno-economic connotation. Joseph Schumpeter, regarded as the originator and primary advocate of this turn, coined the phrase 'creative destruction' (1942) to emphasize the inherent dynamics of capitalist production and the crucial role of innovation for economic growth. Even today, the positive connotation of techno-economic innovation remains largely unscathed and present in numerous economic and political initiatives that aim to secure Germany's or Europe's competitiveness in the global marketplace of the future (see, e.g., the 2014 Federal Report on Research and Innovation of the German Federal Ministry for Education and Research (BMBF 2014)).

In the course of the 20th century, social change was mainly attributed to technological and economic impulses (Schumpeter's references to Marx are no coincidence). Some theorists did, however, manage to look beyond these sources. William F. Ogburn in particular developed a more encompassing sociological theory of innovation not limited to a solely economic perspective (Ogburn 1922; see also Godin 2010). Like Schumpeter, Ogburn assumed that technical and economic factors were the primary drivers of change in modern societies. He bundled these factors under the term 'material culture,' citing examples such as new production equipment and means of transportation that relied on steam, electricity, or gas. The term also included new techniques in housing construction as well as various consumer products (Ogburn 1922: 268ff.). 'Non-material culture,' on the other hand, consisting primarily of social values, norms, habits, and customs, was forced to adapt to the steady stream of changes in material culture. Ogburn coined the term 'cultural lag' (ibid.: 200ff.) to describe the maladjustment between a non-material culture that was always one step behind its material counterpart. Ogburn noted that this observation mainly referred to a specific form of change in modern societies and that change could just as well emanate from non-material culture—for example, as a product of changing religious or political ideas—with material culture lagging behind.[1] These formative arguments aside, what matters in the present context is the underlying view of society they entail: 'cultural lag' is more likely to occur in complex and functionally interdependent societies. Differentiation and functional interdependencies in modern society supply, first, the basic conditions for different societal segments to operate independently and 'do their own thing.' Second, they come with a clear mandate for governance mechanisms to ensure the ongoing functioning of society as a viable 'whole.' For Ogburn, modern societies existed in a fundamental state of disequilibrium that required constant work to coordinate between various interdependent segments. From this perspective, many social innovations would appear to be a means of repair or *innovative fixes* meant to re-insert some degree of adjustment into a perpetually disjointed social order.

Drawing on Ogburn and Schumpeter's concepts, we can distill some fundamental characteristics of social change and innovation in modern society:

- First, processes of differentiation subject established patterns of social order to a *continuous pressure to change*. Modern society is essentially permeated by change.
- Second, this state of society demands *ongoing, active adjustments*. In Schumpeter's writings, this aspect of society is represented by entrepreneurial creativity and its constant focus on renewal. For Ogburn, adjustments could be ascribed to other sources, especially politics, as with occupational safety legislation introduced to combat the growing number of workplace accidents with the rise of industrialized society.

No longer an incidental product or an inevitability, social change thus becomes a central governance issue for modern societies—depending on the lens that theorists apply in diagnosing the political governability of modern societies (Mayntz and Scharpf 1995). If governance is viewed with some modicum of optimism, societal change becomes a large-scale endeavor that can reach even relatively stable social institutions. Everett C. Hughes already addressed the need for entrepreneurial action (understandable in a broad sense as coordination and decision-making activities in the face of uncertainty) in the 1930s to stabilize institutions. Entrepreneurial action as a corrective agent was to be a "crucial feature of institutions in a society where the mores, whatever else they may do, do not foreordain that

---

1 Ogburn did not introduce material lag as a direct counterpart to cultural lag. He used cultural lag to refer to varying rates of change and 'adjustment problems' in complex modern societies, no matter where the change originally emerged.

the individual shall stay put and remain within the framework of given corporate units throughout his life" (Hughes 1936: 183). Similar to the perspectives offered by Schumpeter and Ogburn, Hughes' thoughts on social change reveal an inherent tug of war between change and stability.

The concepts of creative destruction, cultural lag, or institutional entrepreneurialism present various ideas that mediate between these two ends of the rope. Novelty is both engendered from and replaces what has gone before. Furthermore, whatever counts as 'old' is constantly called on to adapt in modern societies. This basic conflict can already be found in the 'problem of society' as described by George H. Mead (1936: 361): "That is the problem of society, is it not? How can you present order and structure in society and yet bring about the changes that need to take place, are taking place? How can you bring those changes about in orderly fashion and yet preserve order?"

In the face of sweeping societal change, innovations or the actions that produce them, regardless of whether novel developments are classified as techno-economic or social innovations, appear to be an increasingly dominant *mode of social change*. Although use of the actual term 'social innovation' was seldom to non-existent well into the mid-20th century, we can find evidence for a specific perspective of a *social order defined by permanent change*. With his ideas of 'piecemeal social experiments' or 'piecemeal social engineering' (Popper 1945: 138ff.) applied to denote incremental changes in circumscribed action contexts, Karl Popper provided the closest approximation of an early concept of social innovation. Change in society, he held, does not stem from grand utopian agendas but from countless minor innovations: "The introduction of a new kind of life-insurance, of a new kind of taxation, of a new penal reform, are all social experiments which have their repercussions through the whole of society without remodelling society as a whole" (ibid.: 143). Social change in modern society thus becomes a positive force, something that can be shaped and formed—fully unlike the negative connotations of social innovation in the 19th century and before.

Yet even Popper expressed a clear skepticism toward large-scale political interventions and their efficacy. Change comes from all corners of society, sometimes with unforeseen and unintended consequences. Social innovations in Popper's view are more like tenuous experiments rather than predictable instruments. In this sense, modern societies are inevitably innovation societies in which the activity of novelty production no longer remains the exclusive domain of the market or politics (Hutter et al., this volume).

In light of the increasingly reflexive use of social innovations as 'fixes' for current societal problems, in the next section I consider the growing importance of social innovation as a specific form of political governance; in other words, my objective is to analyze the active use, labelling, and discussion of social innovations as intruments for social change.

3 Social Innovations

As explained in the previous section, social innovations are hardly new. Ever since the emergence of modernity—at the latest—they have been integral to various processes, at times circulating under different names, designed to shape and transform society. In her overview of different concepts of social innovation, Katrin Gillwald (2000) includes Bismarck's social welfare legislation among its ranks, and Wolfgang Zapf acknowledges in general terms, with a nod to Robert K. Merton, that "social innovations employ new means to achieve recognized objectives more effectively" (1989: 177, my translation). Gillwald and Zapf list an impressive range of social innovations (both top-down and bottom-up) in civil society, the market, and the state, such as new lifestyles and social movements, new services and ways of organizing work, political transformations and territorial reforms. More recent studies on social innovation as well cover a broad range of topics, for instance, sustainability (Rückert-John 2013), services and management practices (Howaldt and Jacobsen 2010), and protest movements or software development (Aderhold and John 2005). In short, no part of society seems to have been spared from social innovations. This would appear to hold true for Germany, frequently referred to by itself and others as an 'innovation nation,' even internationally (Franz, Hochgerner, and Howaldt 2012; Nicholls and Murdock 2012; Ruiz Viñals and Parra Rodríguez 2013).

Academic treatment of the subject confirms that social innovation is no longer just a general mode of social change. Social innovations and their associated dynamics have become an established topic in scholarly circles, one that is eyed with increasing interest from the political sphere (Grimm et al. 2013). To a growing extent, social innovations are—or promise to be—tools for actively shaping society with the capacity to counteract the tensions in highly differentiated industrialized contexts. They are also portrayed as creative policy instruments. Stakeholders and scholars alike analyze and evaluate the potential of social innovations; they produce and revise systematic knowledge about how social innovations can be used reflexively to leverage social change. Scientific and political discussions at the EU level in particular, presented in further detail in the empirical section of this paper, appear to confirm this shift in social innovation from a general mode to a reflexive instrument of social change.

Presenting a broad discussion of social innovation here would be amiss—the empirical material and theoretical approaches are far too varied. Instead, I am interested in how the now popular concept of bottom-up social innovation is juxtaposed with a purported loss of top-down control in national and international policy and what consequences this portrayal has for an understanding of social innovation. This shift in the concept of social innovation from a general mode to a reflexive tool for social change carries with it certain restrictive connotations related to social change and social innovation. Two of these readings and their implications for an analysis of social innovation will be presented below. The first sets up an antithetical relationship between social innovation and technical innovation (cf. Howaldt and Schwarz 2010). The second portrays social innovations as politically convenient social technologies at the EU policy level or, in other words, as promising grassroots solutions to combat a growing ineffectiveness in traditional top-down governance structures (cf. Young Foundation 2012).

3.1 Innovation: Technical or Social?

One important aspect and at once the first problematic connotation of social innovation in current discussions is how to distinguish it from technical innovation. As they are generally perceived, social innovations do not produce tangible new technologies such as new means of production, transportation, or communication. What they do create are new forms of social organization in terms of "the intentional, effective *reconfiguration of social practices*" (Howaldt and Schwarz 2010: 89). Although a line is drawn here between tangible technical innovations and intangible social innovations, the latter still profit from the positive connotation of their technical—or techno-economic, as Schumpeter would have it—counterparts. Talking about social innovation then implies that creative problem-solving potential can be found in non-market contexts and that whatever novelty is brought forth has to do with social organization instead of technical artifacts. This take on social innovation versus technical innovation primarily aims to steer academic and political discourse away from dominant interpretations of techno-economic innovation and towards a broader social science perspective. It is of little value, however, when trying to create an analytic or empirical distinction between social and technical innovation.

Social innovations are in fact usually socio-technical developments; in the same vein, technical innovations rarely happen without some amount of social change (Bijker, Hughes, and Pinch 1987). The indivisibility of socio-technical dynamics has been a mainstay in sociological research, whether for social practices in general (Reckwitz 2003) or for social and technical innovations in particular. The utility of this divide can clearly be questioned altogether. Tracing the use of the term 'social innovation' in sociology over the past 50 years reveals its use as a foil for a number of concepts; technical innovation is rarely among them.

Wilbert Moore (1960) characterizes social innovations as patterns of social change that contradicted then prevalent functionalist ideas about continuity. Moore's interest lies in the dynamics of societal change, which he attributes to the increasing delegation of social problems to science and technology, an approach that, in turn, required the re-calibration (like Ogburn's 'cultural lag') of other areas of society. According to Moore, social innovations are central to societal transformation, a force that cannot be kept at bay, and technical innovation is almost always the impulse for this change. Social innovation is therefore, more or less, an adaptive response to technical change, that is, a part of the same process, the two cannot be considered separately. Social innovation in Moore's reading closely approximates Ogburn's description of innovations as a means of adjustment that are undertaken to preserve or restore social order in processes of socio-technical change.

James Taylor (1970) pursues a similar argument but identifies the difference between social and technical innovation in that technical innovations (he uses the example of new mouse-traps) are typically adopted at a faster rate than social innovations, for example, school reforms or rehabilitative programs for offenders. Social innovations, Taylor argues, supplant established forms of social order and threaten existing sets of values, roles, and skills. This is why social innovations are much harder to implement than technical innovations, which can do little, at best minor, damage to the social fabric. Unlike Moore, in Taylor's conceptualization, social innovations are not always playing catch-up; instead, the need for major social changes can stand in the way of technical innovations. Whether Moore or Taylor presents the more convincing argument is ultimately secondary. In considering how society changes, both thinkers focus on socio-technical dynamics, thus providing a strong basis for the explanatory potential of sociological analysis.

Harvey Brooks (1982) also assumes that technical and social innovation go hand in hand. While he does distinguish between social, socio-technical, and technical innovations, Brooks was quick to add that this distinction is not always clear cut (ibid.: 9). Even 'pure' social innovations like those found in healthcare or the introduction of the supermarket rely on technical artifacts to some extent, for example, telescopic or 'nesting' shopping carts or machine-readable barcodes on products. In these examples, technical innovation follows social or organizational innovation. Socio-technical innovations such as passenger car traffic or television, on the other hand, require several different social and technical innovations, even legislative changes, all of which need to happen in a relatively short time period. Brooks' third category of 'pure' technical innovation mainly pertains to innovations in materials engineering or in chemical processes. Brooks describes these innovations as almost purely technical, since social or organizational changes can always be found in their midst. Furthermore, technical innovations always have a strong potential to become socio-technical innovations, as Brooks explains, citing developments such as the transistor or the laser.

From this perspective, the merit in postulating a fundamental distinction between social and technical innovation seems questionable. When applied as a heuristic prism to capture current societal dynamics, however, focusing on the social and the technical aspects of innovation, as well as their interactions, could prove to be a fruitful distinction. Speaking of 'social innovation,' then, would circumvent an overly restrictive interpretation of 'innovation,' specifically, innovation defined solely by processes of technology development, without neglecting the technical or material aspects of social innovation. The distinction between technical and social innovations can only be made in analytic terms, with different reference points in mind or when talking about specific patterns of stability or change. Once innovation is conceptualized more generally as a social practice or observed in different empirical cases, its socio-technical or material-semiotic constitution becomes apparent (Bijker and Law 1992).

In summary, an interpretation of social innovation that focuses solely on its social character falls too short in three respects:

- First, it implies that innovation is solely technical, an idea that has long been laid to rest in sociological innovation research. Technical innovations are always produced socially, from their development through to their execution.
- Second, it relies on a dematerialized model of sociality that maintains a clear divide between technical and social orders. Yet the search for a 'purebred' social innovation, free of any essential technical or material aspects, will also ultimately turn out to be too limited.
- Third, creating a fundamental difference between social and technical innovation obscures the constitutive interactions between the technical and social aspects of societal transformation. Positing an analytic distinction, in contrast, makes it possible to paint a more precise picture of the various facets of change in modern societies. Then, drawing on the ideas of Ogburn or Moore, we can discover which technical developments demand adaptive responses or innovative repairs to the social fabric and vice versa. With Taylor we can investigate how well social structures and practices hold up in the face of technical innovations, and Brooks helps us see socio-technical entanglements in modern infrastructure.

In addition to these concrete questions, sociological inquiry into the topic of social innovation clearly indicates a more far-reaching pattern of social change. There is widespread agreement that in increasingly differentiated modern societies, established patterns of social order are in transformation. Researchers in this area see social innovation happening precisely where different sectors in society struggle to become aligned. Social innovation therefore not only possesses disruptive qualities, similar to Schumpeter's characterization, but it also stabilizes society in two ways: first, as a solution to perceived problems (innovation as a fix) and, second, as Zapf describes it (1989: 177, my translation), as a "new means to achieve recognized objectives more effectively" (innovation as an improvement).

Social innovation differs from general processes of social change in that relevant stakeholders must stand behind it, actively asserting and implementing its novel qualities, without any guarantee of its success (cf. Rogers 2003 for a wealth of empirical evidence). Social innovations can thus be grasped as specific coordination and decision-making activities under the condition of uncertainty, as postulated by Hughes (1936), for example. Seen in this light, it becomes clear that social innovation primarily denotes the means to a specific end—or the creation of a new means entirely. This entrepreneurial approach to social change is not the exclusive domain of society's 'movers and shakers.' Starting in the 1960s, sociologists began to reflect on innovation as a template for social change and to employ it to diagnose current social macro dynamics.

In recent years, alongside this practice and observation, social innovation has been increasingly infused with positive normative connotations. These new qualities can be attributed in part to infectiously positive interpretations from science spilling over into the field of policy. However, NGO leaders are also increasingly pushing their own 'pro-innovation' agendas. I have presented my critique of a fundamental divide between social and technical innovation above; now I will address the second problematic reading of social innovation owing to a doubly positive normative connotation of the concept.

3.2 Innovation: Top-down or Bottom-up?

Taken at face value, a purely analytic separation between technical and social innovation requires no additional qualifiers. All innovations, tangible or not, must be recognized as novel and establish themselves over other alternatives (Braun-Thürmann 2005). Staying for a moment with this basic premise, we can note that it makes no mention of dominant actors, the specific thrust of innovative activities, or their means of implementation. Once again, analytically speaking, no innovation, whether social or technical, is good or bad per se, and innovations can range in scope from local solutions to global interventions.

In contrast to a purely analytic perspective, social innovations—especially at the EU policy level—have increasingly been introduced and discussed as a normative model for a specific form of social change.[2] This normative interpretation results in several provisos to an analytic understanding of the concept. I want to explain these stipulations based on the central criteria contained therein:

- First, and most importantly, social innovations are understood as *bottom-up* processes initiated and advanced by local actors. These efforts contrast with a *top-down* logic of governance. This rather simplistic contrast, top-down versus bottom-up, appears in the political discourse to underline the potential of social innovations as novel instruments for shaping society. In the sociological discourse as well, the grassroots level is a recognized source of innovative change. William F. Whyte (1982), for example, portrayed social innovations as a series of local social *inventions* in contrast to more far-reaching political *interventions*. Social inventions, Whyte argued, are developed and applied within a group, while interventions are an exogenous force that impacts on the group. In other words, social innovations sprout up at the base of society but are rarely able to grow beyond their source niches—a perspective also highlighted by more recent authors (Mulgan et al. 2007: 37).
- Second, social innovations, in line with Ogburn, are seen as *responses to societal problems* and therefore as innovative 'fixes.' In the EU policy context, these social 'repairs' are not limited to local problems. Policy-makers instead see social innovations as having the potential to solve major macro-level challenges such as achieving carbon-neutral objectives, providing universal healthcare, or fighting poverty (Murray, Caulier-Grice, and Mulgan 2010: 2).
- Third, building on the previous dimensions, social innovations are conceived as stopgaps for *market and policy failures* (ibid.: 3). Neither market mechanisms nor political regulations are thus conceived to be able to furnish satisfactory solutions to the complex problems of modern societies. The failure of top-down models is countered with the promise of social innovation as a form of bottom-up governance.

---

2 The definitions and framings of social innovation found in the *Open Book of Social Innovation* (Murray et al. 2010) constitute my main reference point for the following discussion.

- Fourth, although social innovations are presented as a promising solution in the above three points, there is *still not a strong connection between creative, locally organized, but often financially ill-equipped actors and powerful EU institutions* (ibid.: 4). This means social innovation cannot make good on its promise since there is still no viable link between top-down and bottom-up in terms of the selection, financing, and scaling of local social innovations (i.e., there is a governance deficit at the macro level).
- Fifth, this deficit continues to be promoted by an *inadequate scholarly understanding of social innovation*. While innovation and its dynamics are well researched for various engineering or medical fields, comparable expertise for social innovation is still lacking (Mulgan et al. 2007: 5). Faced with this relative lack of knowledge, the fundamentally reflexive character of social innovation as a means of political governance becomes all the more apparent. Without a specific understanding of its dynamics, however, social innovation can hardly be applied as a tool for social engineering. In other words, the aforementioned governance deficit is compounded by a knowledge gap. Necessary expertise must therefore be generated through scientific research and made available to policy-makers.

Given this situation, Geoff Mulgan, one of the most prominent advocates of social innovation in the EU political discourse, defines social innovation as follows:

> Social innovation refers to innovative activities and services that are motivated by the goal of meeting a social need and that are predominantly diffused through organizations whose primary purposes are social (Mulgan 2006: 146).

Unlike techno-economic innovation, which aims for economic profit, social innovation endeavors to bring about social progress. The 'social' in social innovation is not about creating a strict boundary between the social and the technical. 'Social' in this context consists of (a) a positive assessment, (b) the fulfillment of a societal need, and (c) a contrast between the social and economic. In this sense, social innovation can be conceived more specifically as *innovations driven by civil society* and *social welfare*.[3] Thus, 'social' carries a distinctly positive and normative connotation; so does the second part of the social innovation equation, 'innovation.' It comes with its own positive and normative qualities, derived more or less directly from a growth-oriented perspective on techno-economic innovation (Mulgan et

---

3 I am indebted to Miira Hill's phrasing of 'social welfare innovation' in a comment on this paper.

al. 2007: 5). Technical and economic innovations, with a nod to Schumpeter, are widely believed to fuel economic success in the competition between companies and countries. From this vantage point, 'innovation' promotes both prosperity and progress, and 'social innovation' can be seamlessly appended to these positive semantics.

With this doubly positive normative interpretation, social innovation starts to develop an increasingly ambiguous relationship to techno-economic innovation. On the one hand, the difference between the two is clearly postulated: social innovation is geared toward civil society and public welfare; techno-economic innovation produces technical artifacts and maximizes profits. On the other hand, social innovation resembles Popper's 'piecemeal social engineering' (Popper 1945: 138) or, in other words, incremental improvements designed to fix specific problems and *not* to achieve utopian ideals by means of revolutionary change (i.e., 'utopian social engineering'). Social innovation is thus assigned an optimistic and instrumental connotation as a social technology (already apparent in Small 1898: 131) by enabling the efficient improvement of social relations based on new social scientific findings. The latter interpretation borders on the growth-oriented understanding of techno-economic innovation. In this case, the proximity of social innovation to social technology as a form of social change bent more on the idea of an instrumental fabrication of social change. Even if social innovation does not produce technical artifacts, social and technical innovations still exhibit similarities through the shared assumption that progress can be engineered or planned—or so they promise.

Despite the asserted differences from economically motivated innovation, such a characterization of social innovation clearly borrows from some of its ideas. One of the most obvious indicators is the prominence of entrepreneurs, viewed as indispensable for the invention and accomplishment of social innovations (see, e.g., the *Open Book of Social Innovation* or Murray et al. 2010). Entrepreneurial agency is not necessarily pared down to economically rational action but consists, as discussed by Hughes (1936), more broadly of deliberate coordination and decision-making activities in an uncertain environment. The entrepreneurs behind social innovations form a complement of sorts to economic entrepreneurs, or perhaps even a 'new breed' of actors who are likewise bold and creative in their pursuit of novelty. The difference between social and economic entrepreneurs is primarily one of orientation: the latter seek to maximize profits while the former focus on the greater good—even when they achieve it through new forms of economic activity (Nicholls and Murdock 2012).

Yet social entrepreneurialism is not a satisfying common denominator since, just like other forms of innovation, social innovation can rarely be guided and controlled by individual actors (cf. Phills Jr., Deiglmeier, and Miller 2008). Its purported potential in terms of social engineering can also turn out to be a fictitious control narrative. Where top-down political interventions fail, social innovations are portrayed optimistically as grassroots alternatives that give policy-makers and society access to local creative potential—once certain gaps in knowledge and governance are overcome. Optimism in this case is dubious; as emergent phenomena in modern societies, social innovations can rarely be planned, much less controlled by the political sphere (Beck, Giddens, and Lash 1994).

This dual notion of social innovation, as a feat of engineering and entrepreneurialism, enables its metamorphosis from a general mode of social change to a reflexive tool in the political discourse. Social innovations are politically framed as change instruments, wielded and stylized as problem-solution packages for current and future challenges (like aging, chronic illnesses, criminality, and climate change, to name a few; see Mulgan 2006: 147). Social innovations also become reflexive because, without an *a priori* guarantee of their success, they cannot get by without ongoing scientific support and evaluation (Preskill and Beer 2012): first, like any business or technical endeavor, they can also fail; second, uncalculated and unintended consequences can emerge, which then fuel subsequent innovation activities.

When social innovation becomes a reflexive tool for political intervention, it is transformed in part from a simple means to an end in its own right. More succinctly, ends often reflect their chosen means (Dewey 1939). And as a means, the positive normative concept of social innovation also conveys the instrumental and entrepreneurial undertones of techno-economic innovation. This interpretation of social innovation quietly harbors a specific concept of social change and the potential for macro-level governance: the focus on bottom-up processes can also be understood as an emphasis of state withdrawal paired with the increasing importance of entrepreneurial activity. The problems addressed by social innovations simultaneously undergo a dramatic upscaling from local needs to global challenges, climate change being an apt example. The failure of large-scale political and market-oriented approaches in solving these conflicts is enacted on a stage where the innovative potential of local, creative actors in civil society forms the immediate backdrop.

Discussions of social innovation at the EU policy level ultimately appear as an attempt by certain stakeholders—in a sense social entrepreneurs such as the UK-based Young Foundation[4] (Young Foundation 2012)—to establish a new political

---

4   The Young Foundation is a London-based think tank named after the British sociologist Michael Young. Its mission is to eliminate social inequality through social

problem-solution package. In other words, what we are witnessing can itself be taken as a social innovation in the EU policy field. This social innovating of social innovation will constitute the focus of the next and last section before I conclude by summing up my arguments. The goal will be to describe the shift in social innovation from a general mode to a reflexive instrument of social change.

4 Reflexive Social Innovation in the EU: New Hopes of Governance

Compared to social innovation's long empirical and conceptual history, its career in the international political discourse is still young. In the USA and Australia, for example, the White House Office of Social Innovation and Civic Participation and the Australian Centre for Social Innovation were both founded in 2009. The Bureau of European Policy Advisers published a report on the state of social innovations in the EU around this same time (BEPA 2010).

Political initiatives to establish various social innovations as tools for change in society can be understood as social innovations in their own right: first, they are relatively new, and second, they offer alternative solutions to existing problems. These initiatives are part of an increasingly reflexive, that is, continuously mindful and active, approach to social innovation driven by civil society stakeholders such as the Young Foundation and are observable at the national and international policy levels.

Once innovation becomes reflexive (Hutter et al., this volume), the countless social innovations that had previously been adopted as largely experimental forms of social change, outside of politics and throughout society, are made available to researchers and policy-makers. This includes a systematic reflection of the sources, dynamics, and consequences of social innovation. Consequently, scholars can identify a multitude of local social innovations on the one hand and a lack of knowledge and governance on the part of science and politics on the other (Mulgan et al. 2007). Innovations in technology or the economy have been subject to intense study; comparable findings for social innovation, however, are few and far between. Scholars have also identified new sites of innovative activity in most, if not all, parts of society. In the report *Empowering People, Driving Change. Social*

innovation. The foundation was created in 2005 through a fusion of the Institute for Community Studies, founded by Michael Young, and the Mutual Aid Centre (http://youngfoundation.org, retrieved November 19, 2016).

Innovation in the European Union from the Bureau of European Policy Advisers, this problem-solution bundle is summarized as follows:

> Firstly, solutions must be found, in a time of major budgetary constraints, to deliver better services making more effective use of available resources. Second, the traditional ways in which the market, the public and the civil sector have provided answers to social demands are no longer sufficient. In this context, social innovation represents an important option to be enhanced at different levels (local, regional, national, European) and sectors (public, private, civil) as its purpose is to innovate in a different way (through the active engagement of society itself) and to generate primarily social value (BEPA 2010: 30).

From BEPA's standpoint, to tap into the governance potential of social innovation for EU policy, the first step would be to eliminate existing deficits in expertise and governance. This would involve closing gaps in financing and scaling up solutions from the local to the EU level and developing a better grasp of social innovation dynamics. Indeed, there are already several reports and initiatives that are working to map and systematically explore the field of social innovation in Europe.

In 2012, for example, a European research consortium on social innovation started to receive funding as part of the Seventh EU Framework Programme for Research and Technological Development (FP7) under the project title *Theoretical, Empirical and Policy Foundations for Social Innovation in Europe* (TEPSIE[5]). This consortium is tasked with providing preliminary research to develop the field of social innovation. The results are meant to enable actors such as the Young Foundation to assume central positions in the future field of social innovation in Europe—in other words, precisely where gaps in expertise and governance are identified between local social innovation initiatives and the European framework programs. Together with the non-profit organization NESTA[6], for example, the Young Foundation launched the Internet platform *Social Innovation eXchange* (SIX[7]), and the two organizations co-published the *Open Book on Social Innovation* (OBSI, Murray et al. 2010). In conjunction with SIX, the Young Foundation authored the 2010 *Study on Social Innovation* (SSI[8]). Largely similar to the OBSI, the study was created as an overview for the European Commission's Bureau of

---

5 www.tepsie.eu, retrieved November 19, 2016.
6 www.nesta.org.uk, retrieved November 19, 2016.
7 www.socialinnovationexchange.org, retrieved November 19, 2016.
8 http://youngfoundation.org/wp-content/uploads/2012/10/Study-on-Social-Innovation-for-the-Bureau-of-European-Policy-Advisors-March-2010.pdf, retrieved November 19, 2016.

European Policy Advisors. Furthermore, the Young Foundation participated in the EU-sponsored initiative *Social Innovation Europe* (SIE[9]). In February 2013, the European Commission, led by the Directorate-General for Regional and Urban Policy published the *Guide to Social Innovation* (GSI[10]). The Directorate-General for Enterprise and Industry[11] supported several activities related to social innovation, some of which include the SIE Initiative and a competition entitled *European Social Innovation Competition*. In *Horizon 2020*, the current EU Framework Programme for Research and Innovation, social innovation is, tellingly, part of the sixth so-called 'Societal Challenge' entitled *Europe in a changing world—Inclusive, innovative and reflective societies*,[12] which also clearly expresses the reflexive nature of social change in society today.

The European Commission's GSI identifies social innovation in the context of a whole series of challenges facing society, from the current financial crisis with its severe consequences for employment to demographic change, competition in the global marketplace, climate change, and long-term solutions for healthcare and social welfare systems. Social innovation is characterized as a process that can be applied to scale up local social innovation to the EU level: "This process is composed of four main elements:

- Identification of new/unmet/inadequately met social needs;
- Development of new solutions in response to these social needs;
- Evaluation of the effectiveness of new solutions in meeting social needs;
- Scaling up of effective social innovations" (GSI: 6).

This model reveals an underlying concept of social innovation borrowed from managerial research or the engineering sciences. Strictly speaking, the EU is less interested in an analysis of social innovation than in finding and proposing ways to scale up effective local solutions to the national or international levels. The metamorphosis of social innovation, from a general mode to a reflexive means of social change, thus indicates a shift towards a more widespread application of local social innovations in civil society as well as in political and even economic

---

9 https://webgate.ec.europa.eu/socialinnovationeurope/; retrieved November 19, 2016.
10 http://s3platform.jrc.ec.europa.eu/documents/20182/84453/Guide_to_Social_Innovation.pdf/88aac14c-bb15-4232-88f1-24b844900a66; retrieved November 19, 2016.
11 http://ec.europa.eu/enterprise/policies/innovation/policy/social-innovation/index_en.htm; retrieved November 19, 2016.
12 http://ec.europa.eu/programmes/horizon2020/en/h2020-section/europe-changing-world-inclusive-innovative-and-reflective-societies; retrieved November 19, 2016.

spheres. As mentioned above, not only the problematic aspect of governance but also inadequate expertise in science and policy-making are cited as barriers to the broad diffusion of social innovations. Both obstacles, however, can hardly be overcome when 'social innovation' embodies competing normative claims or a narrow focus on purely social grassroots innovation. These two interpretations muddy the analysis of positive and negative socio-technical processes of change at different levels of society.

5 Conclusion

In the last section, I advocated understanding the growing political discussion and support for social innovation by the EU as an innovation process in itself that is driven by relevant stakeholders. With the explicit installation of social innovation in the European funding framework, it is also safe to assume an increasingly reflexive approach to social innovation as an instrument for social change. The indisputably positive objectives, such as strengthening civil social actors at the local level or combating social inequality, still remain bound to a highly instrumental concept of social innovation, which conveys a clear slant towards entrepreneurial agency. As a means of change in society, from this standpoint, social innovation is hardly a neutral device. Instead it conveys a specific image of transformation processes as well as its own diagnosis of social problems.

In this conceptualization, social innovation is an innovative fix that recalibrates poorly attuned segments of society. It is also a response to more general transformations, such as the global economic crisis or the aging populations of many industrial nations. These problems are generally perceived as too complex for any top-down intervention at the national or international policy level. Instead, local actors in civil society are thought to supply an apparently endless reserve of creative solutions that should become accessible for use at higher political levels.

In observing these local processes, it quickly becomes clear that a normative distinction between social innovation and techno-economic innovation cannot hold water. It might even result in an overly restrictive perspective since it obscures the constitutive socio-material interrelatedness of innovation in the making while also blurring the structural similarities between 'technical' and 'social' innovations when they are perceived solely as such. Moreover, with this perspective, the entrepreneurial undertones associated with 'innovation' tend to go unnoticed, and social innovations introduced in business organizations fall under the radar. While drawing a clear line between social innovation and technical or economic innovation does draw attention to gaps in expertise and governance, it does little service to the analysis of social innovation itself. A far more interesting approach would be to explore technical and economic aspects in EU-funded social innovation projects or how these projects respond to technical and economic changes as reflexive means of political design.

References

Aderhold, Jens and Rene John, eds. 2005. *Innovation. Sozialwissenschaftliche Perspektiven*. Constance: UVK.
Beck, Ulrich, Anthony Giddens, and Scott Lash, eds. 1994. *Reflexive Modernization: Politics, Tradition and Aesthetics in the Modern Social Order*. Stanford: University Press.
Beck, Gerald and Cordula Kropp, eds. 2012. *Gesellschaft innovativ. Wer sind die Akteure?* Wiesbaden: VS Verlag.
BEPA. 2010. *Empowering People, Driving Change Social Innovation in the European Union*. Bureau of European Policy Advisers. Retrieved January 6, 2017 (http://ec.europa.eu/DocsRoom/documents/13402/attachments/1/translations/en/renditions/native).
Bijker, Wiebe E., Thomas P. Hughes, and Trevor J. Pinch, eds. 1987. *The Social Construction of Technological Systems*. Cambridge: MIT Press.
Bijker, Wiebe E. and John Law, eds. 1992. *Shaping Technology / Building Society. Studies in Sociotechnical Change*. Cambridge: MIT Press.
BMBF. 2014. *Bundesbericht Forschung und Innovation*. Berlin: Referat Grundsatzfragen der Innovationspolitik des Bundesministeriums für Bildung und Forschung. Retrieved January 6, 2017 (http://www.bundesbericht-forschung-innovation.de/files/BUFI_2014_Kurzfassung_bf.pdf).
Braun-Thürmann, Holger. 2005. *Innovation*. Bielefeld: transcript.
Brooks, Harvey. 1982. "Social and Technological Innovation." Pp. 1-30 in *Managing Innovation. The Social Dimensions of Creativity, Invention and Technology*, edited by S. B. Lundstedt and E. W. Colglazier. New York: Pergamon Press.
Dewey, John. 1939. "Theory of Valuation." *International Encyclopedia of Unified Science* 2(4): 1-67.
Durkheim, Emile. 2014 [1893]. *The Division of Labor in Society*. New York: Free Press.
Franz, Hans-Werner, Josef Hochgerner, and Jürgen Howaldt, eds. 2012. *Challenge Social Innovation. Potentials for Business, Social Entrepreneurship, Welfare and Civil Society*. Heidelberg: Springer.
Gillwald, Katrin. 2000. *Konzepte sozialer Innovation* (Working Papers P00-519). Berlin: Wissenschaftszentrum Berlin für Sozialforschung.
Godin, Benoît. 2010. "Innovation Without the Word: William F. Ogburn's Contribution to the Study of Technological Innovation." *Minerva* 48(3): 277-307.
Godin, Benoît. 2015. *Innovation Contested. The Idea of Innovation Over the Centuries*. London: Routledge.
Grimm, Robert, Christopher Fox, Susan Baines, and Kevin Albertson. 2013. "Social Innovation, an Answer to Contemporary Societal Challenges? Locating the Concept in Theory and Practice." *Innovation: The European Journal of Social Science Research* 26(4): 436-455.
Howaldt, Jürgen and Heike Jakobsen, eds. 2010. *Soziale Innovation. Auf dem Weg zu einem postindustriellen Innovationsparadigma*. Wiesbaden: Springer VS.
Howaldt, Jürgen and Michael Schwarz. 2010. "Soziale Innovation – Konzepte, Forschungsfelder und -perspektiven." Pp. 87-108 in *Soziale Innovation. Auf dem Weg zu einem postindustriellen Innovationsparadigma*, edited by J. Howaldt and H. Jacobsen. Wiesbaden, Springer VS.

Hughes, Everett C. 1936. "The Ecological Aspect of Institutions." *American Sociological Review* 1(2): 180-189.
Hutter, Michael, Hubert Knoblauch, Werner Rammert, and Arnold Windeler. This volume. "Innovation Society Today. The Reflexive Creation of Novelty."
Mayntz, Renate and Fritz W. Scharpf, eds. 1995. *Gesellschaftliche Selbstregulierung und politische Steuerung*. Frankfurt a. M.: Campus.
Mead, George H. 1936. *Movements of Thought in the Nineteenth Century*. Chicago: University of Chicago Press.
Moore, Wilbert E. 1960. "A Reconsideration of Theories of Social Change." *American Sociological Review* 25(6): 810-818.
Mulgan, Geoff. 2006. "The Process of Social Innovation." *Innovations: Technology, Governance, Globalization* 1(2): 145:162.
Mulgan, Geoff, Simon Tucker, Rushanara Ali, and Ben Sanders. 2007. *Social Innovation. What It Is, Why it Matters and How It Can Be Accelerated* (Working Paper, Skoll Centre for Social Entrepreneurship). Oxford: Saïd Business School.
Murray, Robin, Julie Caulier-Grice, and Geoff Mulgan. 2010. *The Open Book on Social Innovation*. London: The Young Foundation / NETSA.
Nicholls, Alex and Alex Murdock, eds. 2012. *Social Innovation: Blurring Boundaries to Reconfigure Markets*. London: Palgrave Macmillan.
Ogburn, William Fielding. 1922. *Social Change*. New York: H. W. Huebsch.
Phills Jr., James A., Kriss Deiglmeier, and Dale T. Miller. 2008. "Rediscovering Social Innovation." *Stanford Social Innovation Review* 6(4): 34-43.
Popper, Karl. 1945. *The Open Society and Its Enemies. Volume I: The Age of Plato*. London: Routledge.
Preskill, Hallie and Tanya Beer. 2012. *Evaluating Social Innovation*. Washington DC: FSG & Center for Evaluation Innovation.
Reckwitz, Andreas. 2003. "Grundelemente einer Theorie sozialer Praktiken. Eine sozialtheoretische Perspektive." *Zeitschrift für Soziologie* 32(4): 282-301.
Rogers, Everett M. 2003. *Diffusion of Innovations*. 5th ed. New York: Free Press.
Rückert-John, Jana, ed. 2013. *Soziale Innovation und Nachhaltigkeit. Perspektiven sozialen Wandels*. Wiesbaden: Springer VS.
Ruiz Viñals, Carmen and Carmen Parra Rodríguez, eds. 2013. *Social Innovation: New Forms of Organisation in Knowledge-Based Societies*. London: Routledge.
Schumpeter, Joseph. 1942. *Capitalism, Socialism, and Democracy*. New York: Harper & Row.
Small, Albion W. 1898. "Seminar Notes: The Methodology of the Social Problem. Division I. The Sources and Uses of Material." *American Journal of Sociology* 4(1): 113-144.
Taylor, James B. 1970. "Introducing Social Innovation." *The Journal of Applied Behavioral Science* 6(1): 69-77.
Whyte, William F. 1982. "Social Inventions for Solving Human Problems." *American Sociological Review* 47(1): 1-13.
Young Foundation. 2012. *Social Innovation Overview. A Deliverable of the Project "The Theoretical, Empirical and Policy Foundations for Building Social Innovation in Europe" (TEPSIE), European Commission – 7th Framework Programme*. Brussels: European Commission, DG Research.
Zapf, Wolfgang. 1989. "Über soziale Innovationen." *Soziale Welt* 40(1-2): 170-183.

Contributors

Nina Baur, Prof. Dr., is Professor for Methods of Social Research at the Department of Sociology at Technische Universität Berlin.

Cristina Besio, Prof. Dr., is Professor for Sociology, especially Sociology of Organizations at the Department of Social Sciences at Helmut-Schmidt-Universität Hamburg.

Knut Blind, Prof. Dr. rer. pol., is Professor for Innovation Economics at the School of Economics and Management at Technische Universität Berlin and Fraunhofer Institute for Open Communication Systems FOKUS.

Gabriela Christmann, extraordinary Prof. (apl.) Dr., is Head of Department and Deputy Director at Leibniz-Institute for Research on Society and Space (IRS) Erkner. She is also Adjunct Professor for Sociology of Space, Knowledge and Communication at the Department of Sociology at Technische Universität Berlin.

Paul Gebelein, Dr. phil, works with the Multimedia Communications Lab at Technische Universität Darmstadt.

Stefan Hopf, Dr. oec. publ, MBR, is Research Assistant at the Research Center for Information, Organization, and Management at Ludwig-Maximilians-Universität München.

Michael Hutter, Prof. (em.) Dr., was Director of the Research Unit "Cultural Sources of Newness" at WZB Berlin Social Science Center until 2014. In addition, he was Professor at the Department of Sociology at Technische Universität Berlin.

Oliver Ibert, Prof. Dr., is Head of Department at Leibniz-Institute for Research on Society and Space (IRS) Erkner. He is also Professor for Economic Geography at the Institute of Geographical Sciences at Freie Universität Berlin.

Johann Jessen, Prof. (em.) Dr., was Professor for Urban and Regional Planning at the Institute of Urban Design and Urban Planning of the Department of Architecture and Urban Planning at Universität Stuttgart.

Hubert Knoblauch, Prof. Dr., is Professor for General Sociology and Theories of Modern Societies at the Department of Sociology at Technische Universität Berlin.

Johann Köppel, Prof. Dr., is Professor for Environmental Assessment and Planning at the Department of Landscape Architecture and Environmental Planning at Technische Universität Berlin.

Franz Liebl, Prof. Dr., is Professor of Strategic Marketing at Universität der Künste Berlin.

Martina Löw, Prof. Dr., is Professor for Sociology of Planning and Architecture at the Department of Sociology at Technische Universität Berlin.

Martina Merz, Prof. Dr., is Professor of Science Studies and Head of Department at the Department of Science Communication and Higher Education Research at Alpen-Adria-Universität Klagenfurt, Wien.

Maria Norkus, Dipl., is PhD Student at the Department of Sociology at Technical University Berlin.

Jan-Hendrik Passoth, Dr. phil., is Research Group Leader of the Post/Doc Lab "Digital Media" at the Munich Center for Technology and Society at Technische Universität München.

Thomas Paul, Dr. Ing., is Research Assistant at the Department of Computer Science at Technische Universität Darmstadt.

Contributors

Arnold Picot, Prof. Dr. Dres. h.c., was Director of the Research Center for Information, Organization, and Management at Ludwig-Maximilians-Universität München.

Werner Rammert, Prof. (em.) Dr., was Professor for Sociology and Social Studies of Technology at the Department of Sociology at Technische Universität Berlin.

Andreas Reckwitz, Prof. Dr., is Professor for Cultural Sociology at Europa-Universität Viadrina Frankfurt (Oder).

Cornelius Schubert, PD Dr. phil., is Akademischer Rat at the Department of Social Sciences at University of Siegen.

Jan-Peter Voß, Prof. Dr., is Juniorprofessor for Sociology of Politics at the Department of Sociology at Technische Universität Berlin.

Uwe-Jens Walther, Prof. (em.) Dr., was Professor for Urban and Regional Sociology at the Department of Sociology at Technische Universität Berlin.

Arnold Windeler, Prof. Dr., is Professor for Sociology of Organizations at the Department of Sociology at Technische Universität Berlin.

Printed by Printforce, the Netherlands